Horsemastership

Horsemastership

METHODS OF TRAINING
THE HORSE AND THE RIDER

By

Margaret Cabell Self

With Illustrations by

SARAH MASON

ARCO PUBLISHING COMPANY, INC.
New York

Published by ARCO PUBLISHING COMPANY, Inc.
219 Park Avenue South, New York, N. Y. 10003

Fifteenth Printing, 1974

Library of Congress Catalog Card Number 73-76549
ISBN 0-668-02778-9

Printed in the United States of America

To Verl Sturgis Crew, Director of the Silvermine School of Horsemastership, who loves horses as I do, and at whose suggestion this book was written.

Foreword

In early times, the mark of a gentleman—and virtually his only requisite—was his ability to use a sword and to ride. Hence terms such as *caballero* and *chevalier*, which originally meant *horseman*, came to mean *gentleman*. The term *horseman* also came to signify *soldier*. The earliest known school of horsemanship which had a standardized seat was the *Estradiota*, which prevailed in all the countries bordering the Mediterranean and into Europe. The term came from the Greek word στρατιώζηα, meaning soldier. In Spain, this school was succeeded by the *Jineta* (or *Gineta*), probably deriving from the Arabic word (*ajamada*), meaning to recruit troops.

As early as 1400 B. C., it was recognized by the Hittites that a horse should undergo a systematic method of training. The Arabs devised methods of dressage training. The bas-reliefs on the Parthenon show that the Greeks were excellent horsemen as well as horsemasters, since they taught their horses to do such movements as the levade, the corbette, and the ballotade, on demand.

The horse himself, as an animal with certain characteristics, has remained the same, although man's treatment of him has varied with the times in which he lived. During epochs when the civilized world was interested in careful and scientific study, the art of horsemanship and horsemastership flourished. In periods when emphasis was put on brutality and force, the arts of riding and training horses deteriorated.

No one who wishes to develop as far as possible as a horseman and a horsemaster should shut his mind to constructive methods of working with horses and of teaching others to work with them. There are certain well-established rules governing the training of the horse, laid down by Xenophon in 400 B. C., and based on the fundamental principle that the horse should be trained by developing his confidence in his master, rather than by subduing him through artificial means. This same principle is important in training the rider, who should be taught to have confidence in himself, in his instructor, and in his horse.

The position in which one sits on a horse has been altered,

through the ages, according to the type of riding that was being done and to the type of armour or other clothes that were worn. If one accepts the fundamental principles—that to ride a horse one must first be relaxed, in order to feel what the horse is doing; next, be experienced, in order to interpret what one feels; and last, be in balance, so that, without depending on strength, which would immediately nullify the first principle of relaxation, one can influence the horse—then many faddish ideas about how one should sit upon a horse are automatically eliminated. To ride without abuse to the horse and with the least effort on the part of the rider should be the goal. One must be careful to analyze exactly what constitutes abuse. Putting weight on the horse's kidneys is abuse. Being behind the motion of the horse so that one cannot post without undue effort and without using the reins to balance is both abuse of the horse and a waste of effort for the rider.

Keeping these things in mind, I have tried, in this book, to describe many different techniques and methods which can be used by the trainer in training the horse, or by the teacher in teaching the child or adult. Every trainer or instructor should make a point of questioning and observing, of reading and studying every method so that he can either learn more of what he wants to do, or more of what he does not want to do. In the last analysis, the horse himself is the best teacher, for each horse is different. In his response, he shows the horseman or the trainer how he has succeeded; in his failure to respond, he shows the trainer where his weakness has been.

I would like to thank Mr. Marius de Zayas for his kindness in lending me many interesting volumes from his library, including a copy of *The Czechoslovakian Journal,* containing the French translation of the Hittite treatise by Kikkulis; and photostatic copies of the Spanish book *The Gineta,* by Luis de Bañuelos; *L'École de Cavalerie,* by La Gueriniere; *L'Instruction du Roi* by Pluvinel; *Ordini de Cavalcare,* by Grisone; and the Berenger translation of the Xenophon treatise. Mr. de Zayas also provided many of the photographs of early horsemen shown in the beginning of this book.

Mr. Fritz Stecken, who wrote the Introduction and chapter on training horses for advanced dressage and *haute école,* is a very fine rider with many years of successful training of Olympic horses and riders to his credit. This chapter is the first complete treatment of this subject to be published originally in English in America.

New Canaan, Connecticut
1951

TABLE OF CONTENTS

LIST OF PLATES

These photographs appear between page
136 and page 137 of the text.

LIST OF ILLUSTRATIONS

PART I

Training the Horse

Chapter 1

HISTORY AND EVOLUTION
OF THE TRAINING OF HORSES

*T*he earliest treatise now in existence on the training of horses is that written by Kikkulis, of the country of Mitanni, in 1400 B.C. Kikkulis was evidently a man of great importance, regarded with esteem by his compatriots, and considered the prime authority on his subject. The five tablets on which his instructions are engraved in cuneiform were found in the archives of the kings of the Hittites in the Hittite capitol Hattusas. The Treatise has been assembled and translated into French by Bedřuch Hrozný and was published in Prague in the *Archiv Orientalni*, the Journal of the Czechoslovak Oriental Institute.

This treatise is extremely interesting to the horseman from several points of view. In the first place, in reading it, one is continually reminded of the fact that though civilizations and cultures have come into being, grown and flourished, then declined and disappeared, the horse, as an animal and as a servant, has remained the same, presenting certain problems in his temperamental and physical characteristics which must be met if he is to be most useful to man. Furthermore, even in the time of Kikkulis, certain important fundamentals in connection with the care and training of the horse had come to be recognized and accepted. Since the methods recommended by Kikkulis were obviously based on experience, one must suppose that the Hittites and the Indo-Europeans had been training their horses systematically for many centuries, and that the methods described by Kikkulis really go back many hundreds of years before his time.

3

Kikkulis started with the assumption that he must have only the hardiest and strongest horses in the royal stable, to be used for chariot racing and for battle. He did not want to waste time on weaklings, so he began, on the day the horse was brought in from winter pasturage, by putting him through a very severe test. The animal was hitched to a war chariot and taken 30 kilometers at the amble and 1860 meters at the gallop. For the next four days, these distances were gradually increased while the amount of feed was diminished, obviously for the purpose of getting rid of the "hay belly" engendered by the horse's winter on grass. He was then sweated out with heavy covers and given a purgative. The best horses were then chosen and put on a very strict schedule. Kikkulis prescribed from day to day for the next seven months every step, every feed, each amount of water, and each bath that the horse must have, in the most detailed and methodical manner. At periodic intervals, the ordinary routine was interrupted, and the horse, after long hours of work without feed to harden him and accustom him to battle conditions, was turned out at pasture for several days. Kikkulis well understood the value of grain, chopped straw and hay, and fresh grass as feed, as well as the importance of careful grooming and bathing. One must conclude from this treatise that the stable of this king of the Hittites was well organized and run, and that these people had a somewhat better idea of how to preserve and condition their horses than do many men who earn their living today as trainers.

The next and best-known early treatise on the training of the horse is that of Xenophon, written in approximately 400 B.C. A number of translations of this work exist, among them that of Richard Berenger, Esq., Gentleman of the Horse to His Majesty, whose *History and Art of Horsemanship* was published in London in 1771.

Xenophon was indeed a master of his subject. With one or two very slight exceptions, everything he recommended and every comment he made is as pertinent today as anything that has been written since. Furthermore, he gave the reasons behind his advice and his conclusions. He gave very careful instructions as to how to select a good horse, going into each point and explaining what are "beauties" and what are "blemishes" and why.

Xenophon recognized and drew attention to all of the important physical and temperamental features of the horse which make it possible for man to train him. He emphasized particularly the importance of developing the horse's confidence in his master. Nowhere did he recommend violence or the use of fear to subdue the animal. One could wish that those who use brutality in breaking and schooling a horse—the method of throwing a horse, tying him up, wearing him out, or flogging him over jumps—that these products of modern civilization who take pride in the strength which has enabled them to "break" and subdue their mounts could have the understanding of the ancients.

When the Roman civilization succeeded the Greek, the art of horsemanship, along with the other arts and sciences, declined. It was almost two thousand years—in 1569—before the next important work on horses and riding was written by Federico Grisone. Unfortunately, Grisone, although he understood the basic technical principles of horsemanship, did not follow Xenophon's principles of using gentleness, and his book is full of recommendations for using brutality to subdue the horse. These include such methods as pushing the horse's head under water and nearly drowning him if he shows fear of crossing streams, to say nothing of the various instruments of torture which he designed for use as bits.

Among the pupils of Grisone was Pignatelli, who conducted a school of horsemanship. One of his most famous students was La Broue, who studied with Pignatelli for five years, and wrote a book in 1612 which is the epitome of brutality. One learns from his text that his horses were constantly becoming lame, or so vicious that they could not be handled. Another famous pupil of Pignatelli, Antoine de Pluvinel, drew quite different conclusions as to how horses should be trained, although he had had the same instruction as La Broue. To him, each horse was an individual, and he saw as the trainer's first duty the need to inspire in the horse confidence in the trainer. Pluvinel adjured the trainer never to use a whip on an excitable young horse but to train him with calmness. The illustrations for this book (see Plates XI and XII) are among the finest examples of copperplate engraving and are really responsible for the fact that the book was accepted for publication, since the world had taken for granted at that time that La Broue's methods were the correct ones, and looked down upon Pluvinel, who advocated kindness. Pluvinel's book *L'Instruction du Roi,* published after his death in 1666, is in the form of a dialogue between Pluvinel and King Louis XIII. Pluvinel was not only Master of Horse to the king, but also State Counsellor and Lord Chamberlain. His book is delightfully and clearly written, and the engravings show the horse doing such movements as the levade and the capriole with the rider mounted but with the reins dropped. Pluvinel is noted as being the first to use the "pillars" (sometimes one and sometimes two) for dressage and *haute école* training, and the illustrations show all of the movements being executed between pillars. This method of training has been retained by the Spanish Riding School of Vienna, and the famous Lipizzan stallions are so trained.

At about the same time that La Broue and Pluvinel were writing their books, the Duke of Newcastle, then exiled from England, established a riding school at Antwerp. Like La Broue, Newcastle got his results by using brutality and artificial aids such as the "sliding rein," whereby the animal was greatly overflexed. He published a book in 1657 called *The Art of Horsemanship*, which advocated these harsh methods.

In Spain at this time the arts of horsemanship and training horses were influenced by the Arabian conquest of Spain. The Arabs have always been noted for the intelligence of their horses, which is due to the fact that to the Arab a horse is a valued member of the household, to be treated more like a pet than like a beast of burden. In Spain, the horse was used not only in cavalry but also in games and in bull fighting. The influence of the Arabic methods of horsemanship on the Spanish schools is confirmed by the fact that the art of riding in Spain is known as the Jineta, which word probably derives from the Arabic *ajamada*, meaning to recruit troops, and *jundi*, soldier.

A most interesting book written around this time (1605) by Luis de Bañuelos on the Guzmanes (Andalusian) horses, their care, training, and the training of the rider, further shows the influence of Arabian methods in Spain. The book deals with the origin of the Andalusian horse, his superiority in looks, stamina, and intelligence over all other breeds, and discusses in detail his training for games with the lance and for bull fighting.

Perhaps the most important early work on horsemanship was the book *École de Cavalerie*, by M. de la Guérinière, published in France in 1733. The sub-title of the book, "The Understanding, Instruction, and Care of the Horse," tells the reader at once that here is a man, like Xenophon and Pluvinel, who put the horse and his well-being first. This book is considered one of the most fundamentally correct and practical of any work on the subject. De la Guérinière admonished his readers to study the disposition, aptitudes, and weaknesses of every horse they rode or trained, and to use this knowledge to get the most out of the animal and to bring him to the highest possible stage of training. It is Guérinière that set the goal of quiet, calm obedience, realizing, as did Xenophon, that unwilling or forced movements in horses, as in dancers, are not harmonious or beautiful. He stated definitely that all horses—whether they are to be used for war, for games, for racing, or for *haute école*—should receive the same early training in obedience and flexibility. It was during de la Guérinière's time that the art of horsemastership reached its peak.

Unfortunately, in France and in England, the French Revolution had its effect upon riding, and the high standards for the training of horses set by this early master gradually died out, to be supplanted by the less exacting training of the war horse. Horsemanship did not reach its former heights again until Max von Weyrother came to the fore in Austria, first as a civilian teacher in 1810 to 1813, then as junior trainer, and in 1819, as manager of the Spanish Riding School of Vienna. Von Weyrother did not write extensively, but his methods have been transmitted by word of mouth in the school of which he was head.

The French writer and horseman Baucher, who produced a book in 1841, returned somewhat to the school of thought of the Duke of Newcastle, advocating the use of force and overbending his horses, especially laterally. He trained horses for Emperor Wilhelm II, who had to have horses that were easily controlled with one hand, and many of Baucher's pupils contended that this accounted for the extreme overbending of his horses.

James Fillis, a pupil of Baucher, first appeared as a circus rider. He was undoubtedly a fine horseman, but differed from the classical school in that he included many of the circus steps—i.e., those not based on natural movements of the horse—in his *haute école* work. Fillis, although not as brutal in his methods as Baucher, still aimed for the submission of the horse to the determination of the rider rather than for de la Guérinière's goal, a study of the horse by the rider with the idea of bringing out the best in the animal through willing obedience. A new edition of Fillis' book has recently been published by Hurst and Blackett of London, with comments by Major General Geoffrey Brooke. His methods are thus brought up to date.

The twentieth century has seen the publication of a great number of valuable books on horsemanship. Edward L. Anderson and Price Collier wrote a book called *Riding and Driving*, published early in 1900 by the Macmillan Company. Although the book is not widely known, and the authors do not give the sources of their studies or the names of their teachers, they have a very clear idea of how to train and ride a horse, and present their material in a highly readable manner. At a time when no one in America was interested in anything more than very elementary equitation, when horses were being schooled by the "Rarey System" of casting a horse in order to

7

confuse and subdue him, Anderson and Collier came out with theories closely approximating those expressed by the great masters. The book contains many photographs and very detailed steps of training, beginning with the young horse. It emphasizes the importance of flexions, of longeing, and of how the work on such movements as the half-halt and "traveling on two paths" (the travers or two-track) improves the balance and obedience of the horse. In regard to the rider, it emphasizes relaxation and suppleness. For many years, this was the only book published in America which was based on fundamentally correct principles.

Americans have always run to fads. It is not surprising, therefore, that as each new light appeared on the horizon, as each horseman of foreign training arrived to impress his method on the public, he was received with fanfares and kudos and his method was, for a few years, considered the only right one. Count de Souza was among the first of the modern Europeans to receive public acclamation in this country. De Souza was of the classical school and advocated all of the methods used by that group. His methods of teaching were new to Americans, who were not used to being shouted at and paying well for such treatment. They accepted these methods as ideal, and came thirstily back for more. De Souza did much to awaken in America a desire for higher standards in equitation, and his two books, *Elementary Equitation* and *Advanced Equitation*, are still valuable aids.

De Souza was followed by a rider of completely opposite opinions, Piero Santini. Santini's book *The Forward Impulse,* published in 1936, brought to the attention of the public the method of riding known as *il systema* in Italy, which was first devised by Federico Caprilli. Caprilli spent many years studying the natural movements of the horse, and came to the conclusion that the horse could move best and most freely if the rider allowed him to extend his head and neck and placed all his weight forward on the horse's withers. Santini, in advocating this system of training horses, forgot one or two important factors. He states, for example, that one should never ask a horse to go slower than its natural gait, overlooking the fact that in the hunt field, in polo, in cross-country riding, and in riding in company, the rider very often must ask his horse to limit the extent of its stride, either because of the terrain, or because of other factors such as the natural gait of his companions. In throwing out all forms of collection and flexion as contrary to nature and therefore undesirable, Santini showed that he had not really observed horses in freedom. A stallion, or even a mare or gelding, when excited by the sight

8

of another horse, will often collect himself with neck and poll flexed and hindquarters brought under, and will execute a beautiful piaffe or passage. Just as a dancer or boxer improves by a series of gymnastic exercises, so too does a horse, since the dressage training supples and exercises every muscle of his body, putting the horse at the command of the rider. The complete abandonment of all forms of collection and of dressage training has not improved the accomplishments of the Italian jumping and field horses, according to the results of the Olympic trials, since these horses have not won or even placed very high in either the jumping or field categories since 1924. But, as is pointed out in Part II, Chapter I: History and Evolution of the Seat, Caprilli's method has greatly influenced the position of the rider on the horse, expecially in jumping and racing.

An excellent book on training horses and riders is the one prepared by the Fort Riley Cavalry School, *Horsemanship and Horsemastership*. "H and H", as the book is generally known, is the result of a very careful study by officers of the American Cavalry School of all of the European methods of riding and training horses. From these studies, they developed what has become known as the "balanced" seat. This book is universally accepted as being sound and modern without being faddish. "H and H" is strictly a textbook, designed for the use of army instructors, and consequently it is somewhat difficult reading for the layman.

The two books by General Harry D. Chamberlin, *Training Hunters, Jumpers and Hacks* and *Riding and Schooling Horses*, are without question the finest books on riding and training horses published in this country for the average horseman. We see in these books that the wheel has completed its cycle, and that the trainer has returned to the principles of Xenophon, Pluvinel, and de la Guérinière. The horse is made the willing servant of the man, not the slave subdued by force. The man studies the horse as an individual, striving to develop his aptitudes as far as possible and to help him overcome his weaknesses.

There have been many books on advanced equitation published abroad and also some designed for the average horseman. One of these, recently translated into English, is *Riding Logic* by Wilhelm Müseler. This book, which presents the academic method of riding, is very well worth reading. It is profusely illustrated and easily understood. In the present volume, the three writers, Müseler, Chamberlin, and Santini, are used as representatives of the three systems of riding, the Academic, the balanced and the forward. There is much to be learned from all three, and the rider who believes in one method only and closes his mind to the good points of the others is limiting himself.

One of the finest books on the training of horse and rider is the one written by Colonel Alois Podhajsky, leader of the famous Spanish Riding School of Vienna. It is called *The Spanish Riding School.* The photographs are very beautiful and the text clear and most interesting. The book was published in Vienna in 1948 by Verlaf Rudolph Hans Hammer, and was later translated into French and English. It is one of the most sought-after books for a horseman's library.

Eight of the riders from this school and twelve horses recently came to the United States and Canada to give the people of this hemisphere their first glimpse of the art of horsemanship as carried to its highest degree. It is unfortunate that only relatively few of those people interested in the finer points of horsemastership could be present at the demonstration, for if all horse lovers could have seen the stallions at Kenilworth, where they were stabled; if they could have watched while these horses were left in their stalls, the doors open, or left standing in the aisle unattended; if they could have seen the careful progression of exercises given each day, beginning with work on the long rein and continuing through to the difficult figures; they would have realized that the performance of these riders was as far superior to what has been shown in this country before as is a ballet performed by a Nijinsky to a jitterbug exhibition by a teen-ager.

An important factor in the development of the art of riding and of training horses which should be mentioned is the influence that war has had upon it. Sometimes this influence has been good, sometimes the reverse. We learn trom the Hittite treatise that the chariot horse was an important weapon. Had this not been so, it is doubtful that horses would have been conserved and trained as they were. In early times the horse was taught the capriole and the pirouette so that the soldier could escape and defend himself from his enemies. In hand-to-hand encounters, the man on the best-trained horse had a tremendous advantage over the man on the poorly trained horse.

When the knights in armour took over, the necessity for agility in the horse lessened somewhat. This was because a knight heavily encased in armour was pretty helpless. He could ride straight at his adversary with a lance, but he could not use *haute école* movements to help him defeat his enemies. The weight and rigidity of his armour prevented him even from mounting without assistance, and the horses that he used had to be heavy-weight animals. Only in Arabia, where horsemen did not wear heavy armour, did the development of the agile horse and rider continue.

The invention of the cross-bow, with its ability to penetrate armour, changed the method of warfare once more, and again a gentleman's charger was taught to be flexible and quick and his rider learned the higher forms of equitation. After the invention of gunpowder for warfare, the cavalry horse was used for three main purposes: for reconnoitering, for formation fighting, and for transportation. Today the new weapons have taken away the cavalry horse's usefulness in fighting. He is still used sometimes for transportation of guns in terrain which cannot be negotiated easily by jeep or tank. In World War II the Army purchased horses in Italy to carry field guns up and down the mountains, and both the Poles and the Germans used cavalry to get through the mud

Every lover of horses is pleased that the horse is no longer required to go through the ordeal of battle, but every horseman also feels that in doing away with cavalry training, the United States Army has lost an invaluable tool for training its men in quick thinking, athletic prowess, and the ability to assume responsibility.

The history of the training of horses is a far-from-static process. Yet one can learn the true fundamentals by reading the treatise of Xenophon, written more than two thousand three hundred years ago. The horse's character and physical attributes are as they have been since he developed from the prehistoric little animal Eohippus, and these characteristics were catalogued and thoroughly understood by our masters, the ancients.

Chapter 2

THE TRAINER AND HIS GOAL

*N*ot everyone is qualified to become a successful trainer of horses. Experience, knowledge, and ability as a horseman are important—in fact, without these one cannot go very far; but love of the horse is the first qualification in a good trainer, and there is no substitute for it. If you are a trainer just for the purpose of making money, or for personal prestige, and care nothing about the horses with which you work, you may succeed in "taming" some of them, but you will never succeed in obtaining willing obedience.

That the trainer must have patience, and an inexhaustible fund of it, goes without saying, but beyond that he must have the ability to analyze the character of his pupil and find out the method best suited to overcome his difficulties.

The trainer must have a quiet, carrying voice, one which inspires confidence without being threatening. He must be willing to make haste slowly, never advancing more than a short step at a time, always ready to go back to the lesson before if the pupil seems confused. The attention span of individual horses varies as much as it does among children. The trainer must recognize immediately when his pupil has had enough and is becoming bored or tired. He must never go beyond this point, never ask for one more jump or one more well-executed movement.

The trainer needs the lightest and most educated of hands, for it is the hands that, by ceasing to act, give the horse its most immediate reward. His legs must be able to squeeze slightly, tap, push, or hold, as the case may be, each leg able to work independently or in conjunction with the other. The trainer's back must be flexible and under complete control; he must be able to use it "unilaterally" or "bilaterally" at will. Through his back and his base of support, the trainer must be able to sense what his mount is doing under him. A pilot is said to "fly by the seat of his pants" and the rider must have the same instinctive control of the horse.

The trainer must have an open and inquiring mind, always on the lookout for new ideas, always willing to listen to other people's opinions and to learn from their experience, as well as from his own. But despite this open-mindedness, he should not be gullible. He should not believe that something is so just because someone tells him that it is or because he sees it written in a book. He should examine the fundamental principles behind each new method or technique.

But the trainer's best teacher is, in the long run, the horse itself. The trainer must take advantage of his contact with the horse and must study each animal's reactions, applying what he learns from one pupil to his methods of handling another.

If you are a trainer of horses, occasionally you will run across an animal for which you have an antipathy. When this occurs, don't waste your time or the horse's; turn him over to someone else. You cannot conceal your dislike. The horse will realize it, and he will not do well for you, no matter how you try.

Physically, the trainer who is lightly built will have a great advantage over the one who tips the scales at 160 plus. One seldom sees a really fat trainer or riding instructor. (Perhaps there is too much mental tension in their callings to allow instructors and trainers to put on much extra weight!) The lightly built man can ride younger and lighter mounts than can the six-footer. Women, for this reason and also because of their patience and their willingness to pay attention to details, to depend on sensitivity rather than strength, and because they can usually arrange a schedule which doesn't interfere with other duties, make excellent trainers. They must be bold, however, and self-confident, and must have enough muscular strength for the work on foot. The colt being taught his first lesson on the longe is certain to play a bit, and the trainer must be able to hang on.

The final qualification necessary in a trainer is that he must have a clear picture in his own mind as to what constitutes a perfectly trained horse. He may never actually succeed in attaining perfection, for this state is as rare in the equine as in the human race, but unless he can at least build toward it, he is not and can never be a good trainer.

By this I do not mean that the trainer must say to himself, "Here is a colt of Thoroughbred ancestry—he should make a good hunter;

I shall make him into a champion lady's hunter-hack," or "This colt is purest saddle-bred. He is fine, with good action, an excellent show prospect; I shall make him a champion in the fine harness classes." Rather the trainer must work first towards the fundamental characteristics which mark the perfectly trained animal, regardless of the specialized field for which he is being or has been trained—those characteristics that set him apart from the badly or partly trained animal.

In this country there are a number of so-called "light breeds"— the Thoroughbred, with his grace, fleetness, jumping ability, heart, and his "look of eagles"; the two types of saddlers—the five- and the three-gaited—known for their fineness, showiness, good disposition, and high action; the Tennessee Walker, a comparatively new breed which is taking its place in the show ring and on the bridle trail; the Morgan, for years a road horse only, now being bred for use as a show horse (saddle type), a parade horse, or a stock horse; the Quarter horse, a sprinter noted for his speed on the race paths of Virginia in the early 1800's, now being crossed with the Thoroughbred and with ranch stock for use as a polo pony and a cow pony. The Standard-bred remains a harness racer, for which purpose he has been bred for many years. The stock horse earns his keep on the ranches through his intelligence and his stamina. The grandfather of them all, the Arabian, whose blood is to be found in all of the light breeds, is becoming more and more popular. Classes are given over to him in the shows and he is trained for many different purposes. His blood is still deemed valuable for crossing with all light breeds for the purpose of improving them. In addition to the above-mentioned types of pure-breds, there are a great variety of cross-breds in this country used for many kinds of work. There are also a few so-called breeds which are not really breeds but colors, among them the albinos, the palominos, and the appaloosas.

Since all of these breeds and types have been assigned a specific role in the horse world of today, one might think that the fundamental training of each would be different, but this is not so. There are certain basic traits which every well-trained horse must possess, regardless of the type of work he is to do. When he has learned these fundamentals, and not before, it is time to decide whether or not he is to become a specialist.

One speaks of hunters, jumpers, hacks, trail horses, and so forth. The term "field horse" as employed in international competition can be used to denote any or all of these types. The good field horse is a flexible and obedient animal. He can carry his rider across country over natural obstacles as well as artificial obstacles. The field horse must be responsive and able to execute the elementary and intermediate dressage figures. The purpose of the Three-day Event in the Olympic Trials is to test the horse as a field horse. On the first day of the event the horse must execute a dressage course in order to demonstrate his obedience, flexibility, and calmness. The second day is a gruelling cross-country ride at a fast rate of speed over high fences and spread obstacles of every type. The third day is a jumping competition to prove the fitness of the horse after the hard ride of the day before.

It is evident from these requirements that the field horse is not trained for one specific purpose; he is a useful, well-trained animal, strong and muscular, obedient and willing, both in the ring and across country. It is for these goals that the trainer should work, making each of his horses into a competent field horse before he thinks of any specialization.

The basic qualities of the well-trained horse which the trainer must work to develop are as follows:

The horse must be obedient. He must be willing to sublimate his own desires and inclinations to those of his master.

The horse must be attentive. He must listen and wait to be told what is expected of him. Other horses, people, noises, or unusual sights should not take his attention away from the messages that the rider is conveying to him through his reins, weight, legs and voice.

The horse must be calm. No matter what gait he is put to, what type of jump he is asked to negotiate, or what type of terrain he is required to cross, the horse must perform in a relaxed manner.

The horse must have confidence in his master. He must trust him, lean on him, and ask for his support and help. Thus, in a crisis, he will accept the judgment of the master and will not become hysterical.

The horse must be an athlete. He must be perfectly flexible and supple in every muscle and sinew. He must be balanced like a boxer or a ballet dancer, and must have his body under such perfect control that the rider need only think to obtain the desired change of direction, gait, or movement.

Each of these attributes, four mental and one physical, is completely dependent on the others. No one of them can be developed by itself. The horse cannot be obedient unless he is attentive, calm, confident, and fit, physically, to do what is asked of him. He cannot become calm before he has established habits of confidence, obedience, and attentiveness, nor until he has control of his own body.

15

He cannot have confidence in his master until the other four traits are established, nor can he become supple, flexible, and well developed in every muscle without the training which will depend on his obedience, calmness, confidence, and attentiveness. One cannot say, "I will first make my horse obedient, then I will teach him to be calm and ttentive." All these traits must be kept in mind from the first esson; the development of each must augment and help the development of the others.

When all trainers, in looking over a new prospect, learn to say to themselves, not, "I will make this horse into a jumper, or a hunter, or a show horse," as the case may be, but rather will say, "I will so train this colt that he will be obedient, calm, attentive, confident, and perfectly developed physically; willing and able to do everything I ask of him to the very best of his ability," then and only then will we no longer see the appalling examples of ruined horses and bad horsemanship that now confront us at almost every big show.

Chapter 3

THE COLT

The horse has certain physical, mental, and moral characteristics which must be taken into consideration in handling him. His fundamental characteristic is perhaps his "excitability to motion." This is readily understood when one considers that for the little prehistoric horse, the only defense was flight. Animals equipped with natural protective weapons do not flee in the presence of danger. Those with horns and antlers charge, those with tearing fangs attack, as do those with poison sacs. Those with camouflaged exteriors hide.

Coupled with this reaction of flight is the innate timidity (or susceptibility to fear) of the horse. But, fortunately, to counterbalance this, the horse can and will develop confidence in his master. Without this ability he would be unreliable and invariably hysterical in emergencies.

The horse has a phenomenal memory—much better than the memory of the average child. This quality can work both for and against the trainer, for the horse remembers bad habits and unpleasant situations as readily as he does good and pleasant ones. From the beginning, the trainer should utilize the horse's memory to his advantage, making sure that the experiences which he gives him are those which the horse should remember.

The horse, through conditioning, can "associate" ideas. He can associate the idea of reward with good actions, of punishment with bad. However, the reward or the punishment must follow immediately after the action; ten seconds later is too late. The trainer uses rewards continuously. The reward may be a pat, an encouraging word, or a tidbit. Physical punishment should be used rarely, and

17

only when the horse is disobeying through stubbornness or is behaving in an anti-social manner. A sharp word is all that is needed in many cases of minor disobedience, though a sharp, well-timed slap with the whip is necessary in cases of kicking or biting at another horse or backing up and refusing to leave the stable. The better the trainer, and the more thorough the early training of the horse, the less often will physical punishment be necessary. But there is a more subtle way to use punishment in training the horse. The fixing of the rider's hands has the effect of pressure on the bars of the horse, which to him is punishment; when the horse stops, the relaxing of the hands constitutes his reward. The pressure of the rider's legs on the horse's sides to cause him to move forward is, in the language of the horseman, punishment; the relaxing of the pressure is the reward.

Horses also associate objects with environments and situations. The trainer must keep this characteristic in mind. Because the horse is familiar with a wheelbarrow in the stable does not mean that he will not shy at one, should he meet it unexpectedly on the roadside. A rake in the hands of the stableman or standing alongside a building is an innocuous tool. If it is carried slung over a man's shoulder it may, in the eyes of the horse, transform a normal human being into a monstrosity. The trainer must take into consideration this tendency of the horse to associate objects with their surroundings rather than to reason about them, and must develop a sort of anticipatory sense which will cause him to notice immediately anything in the distance which might frighten the young horse, and so be prepared for the horse's reaction.

The horse is willing by nature. Some horses are more willing than others, and most will be stubborn occasionally, but the careful trainer never puts his pupil in such a situation that the horse is tempted to disobey willfully. Willful disobedience is almost always the result of too-hurried training. The horse is being asked to do more than he is able, physically or mentally. Disobedience may also be the result of brutal handling. The horse is afraid and wants to attack first. Many a stallion has become vicious because the groom thinks that he must be handled roughly.

Horses are not born mean. I have yet to see the colt that was handled with firmness and kindness from birth show any inclination to attack his trainer. Foals are often playful and will nip and kick when at liberty. This is their nature, and they are not being deliberately mean. It is by playing such games that they learn to move quickly in times of danger. Two foals brought up together will usually use up their surplus energy on each other and will be much more tractable toward man than will the foal that has no companion with which he may rough-house. Meanness in horses, and even more in ponies, may also be the result of overindulgence or of timidity on the part of the trainer. If a foal, meaning to be playful, runs up to the trainer, and the trainer, through fear, retreats, the foal will presently develop the habit of charging as a vice. If a pony is continually fed sugar while loose in the field, he will come to expect it, and should the trainer approach without the sugar, the spoiled pony will bite in vengeance. Rewards during work periods should be given for obedience and good behavior, not handed out indiscriminately as tidbits.

One must also consider the horse's temperamental characteristics as they affect his manner with other horses. Horses have very definite likes and dislikes. A new animal brought into the stable spends his first week being chased around by the others. He is like the new boy who comes to school after the beginning of the term and after the other boys have made friends. Usually, at the end of a week, the new horse picks out another animal to be his companion and these two, from then on, pair off together. More often than not, the new horse chooses the animal that has become a member of the herd just prior to himself, or he will "buddy up" with the horse whose stall is next to his. Since for pair and team riding, as well as for exhibition drills and formation riding, one usually places horses that match in color and size together, I have found that it pays to stable these horses next to each other. It goes without saying, however, that the perfectly disciplined horse performs correctly no matter how much he may dislike his companions, and that the experienced rider seldom has any trouble with his horse, even though the animal may not be well disciplined. One should never put an inexperienced rider up on a young horse known to have a dislike for a certain animal and then ask these two to ride in close formation. This is only inviting the establishing of vice in the young horse, who will soon find that he can do what he likes with his rider. Nor should one ride a young horse, especially a timid young horse, that has never shown any disposition to bite or kick a neighbor, beside a badly disciplined horse in the hands of a bad rider. Methods of teaching good manners in company will be discussed in a later chapter.

The horse can develop confidence in his rider as stated before, and in so doing, he will develop calmness and obedience. Teaching him to respond to the trainer's voice will do much to establish this confidence. The horse depends largely on his hearing to warn him of impending danger. He can be conditioned to ignore loud and sudden noises, but this takes time and too much should not be expected from a young animal. However, the colt quickly learns to respond to the trainer's tone of voice and eventually comes to know the exact meaning of many words. Horses have methods of communicating with each other which are not intelligible to human beings. I have seen many little dramas enacted among the horses when loose in the field which prove to me their ability to communicate very complicated ideas. The trainer learns to utilize some of his knowledge of equine methods of communication and so to circumvent trouble.

The horse has certain physical attributes and points of conformation which must be taken into consideration when handling and training him. The well-bred horse is very sensitive physically, with a highly developed nervous system. One often uses the term "thin-skinned" to describe an over-sensitive person. This expression was derived from the discovery that Thoroughbreds and Arabians, having a thinner skin, with the nerves nearer to the surface than cold-blooded horses, were therefore more sensitive. I often feel sorry for the poor horses that one sees on the bridle trails. How they must be suffering, with the pounding and bouncing that goes on on top of them! And in many a case the rider has no idea that he is causing discomfort.

The sensitivity of the horse's bars to rough hands often accounts for his misbehavior in company. This is proved by the fact that many a horse with impeccable manners under light hands will start biting and kicking his companions when under a heavy-handed rider. Unable to voice his complaints or to take revenge on his rider for the pain he is suffering, he takes it out on the nearest horse. Using a hackamore on the horse being ridden by beginners or taken over jumps by the not-so-experienced rider will save both the animal's mouth and his disposition.

The horse's eyes, their construction and their position, should be carefully studied, as they vitally affect his behavior. Because his eyes are placed at the sides of his head, the horse is able to see equally well in all directions, a fact frequently overlooked by both experienced and inexperienced horsemen. The position of the eye also has a very definite effect on the horse's field of vision. Everyone has three fields of vision—that of the right eye, that of the left eye, and the field of vision in which the two eyes unite. In animals such as horses, whose eyes are set on the sides of their heads, the third field of vision disappears when the object is very close. The chicken cocks his head and looks at the worm with one eye, then strikes at it blindly. The horse has a more unified field of vision than the chick because his eyes protrude more, but it differs from that of the human being in that the fields of the right and left eyes are more widely separated. Hold one finger up at arm's length, close one eye, and focus on your finger with the other eye; then close that eye and open the other. Repeat this in rapid succession while still focusing on the finger. Your finger will appear to jump from side to side. This is because you are using your right and left fields of vision alternately. As your eyes are spaced only an inch apart, your finger appears to jump only a short distance. But suppose we look at it from the horse's standpoint. He is trotting down the road, and with his left eye, he catches sight of a piece of paper on the right side of the road. All well and good, but suddenly, as he moves toward it, it gets out of the field of vision of his left eye into the field of vision of his right. To the horse, the scrap of paper appears to jump suddenly, just as your finger seemed to jump, but the jump is greater, since his eyes are set further apart. Add to this the fact that the horse sees things at a distance rather fuzzily, then suddenly larger and sharper as he nears them. No wonder horses shy at small things more readily than at big ones.

The hearing of horses is acute. Their reactions to sounds vary. Some will jump at the sound of a match being struck, others pay little attention even to firecrackers. Most horses can be conditioned to ignore sudden noises. All cavalry horses are trained to ignore gun-fire, for example. The rider must know each individual horse and in the case of the sensitive horse, prevent trouble by being prepared for his sudden reactions.

To sum up, we find that the mental, moral, and physical characteristics of the horse which must be taken into consideration by the trainer are:

> his excitability to motion,
> his susceptibility to fear,
> his ability to develop confidence in his trainer,
> his ability to associate ideas,
> his tendency to associate objects with specific environments,
> his willingness,
> his propensity toward liking or disliking his companions,
> his ability to interpret the meaning of the tones of the trainer's voice and to understand many words,
> his tender skin,
> his peculiar vision, resulting from the position and construction of his eyes,
> his acute hearing.

Chapter 4

THE FIRST STAGE OF TRAINING

$\mathscr{T}$he foal should be handled from the day it is born so that, from the beginning, it will not fear its trainer but will have confidence in him. By the time it is a week old it should have a little halter fitted loosely, but this must be carefully watched since the baby skin is tender and the hair at the cheekbones rubs off very easily. Should this happen, take off the halter for a few days and apply vaseline, lanolin, or leaf lard to the chafed skin.

TEACHING THE FOAL TO STAND

Teach the foal to stand quietly while you pass your hand all over it (Figure 1). This is best done by standing about opposite the barrel, one hand resting on the halter and restraining the foal from forward movement. Begin stroking forward at the rump, as this discourages backward movement, and the stroking hand is ever ready to apply pressure at the buttock point. All movements should be gentle. Work on both sides. Keep up a continuous monologue in a soothing tone of voice—what you actually say doesn't matter; it is the tone that counts. When the foal is thoroughly accustomed to the hand rubbing, a cloth may be introduced.

Next, with the help of an assistant, who stands on the opposite side and steadies the colt, you can teach the baby to pick up its feet, one after the other. Work slowly, hold the foot up only a second at first, then put it down and pat the little fellow's shoulder by way of reward. Pick up the same foot and hold it a little longer, then go on to the next foot. Before many days you will be able to keep the foot up while you clean it out. This training will save a great deal of trouble when the time comes for the first visit to the blacksmith.

Foals differ in the time it takes them to make adjustments. None are afraid of humans during the first twenty-four hours after birth since their eyes do not focus clearly enough for them to see anything very distinctly. Usually they will show fear the second day, even though they may have been handled on the first. Some foals, however, never go through this period of fear. Even though the foal may ap-

FIG. 1.   Teaching the foal to stand quietly.

pear very timid—trying to hide behind its mother, jumping forward or back at the touch of the hand—avoidance of sudden movements, patience, and persistence will soon have their effect, and certainly by the end of the first week the new baby should be willing to accept the stroking and to nuzzle its trainer without fear or excitement.

The technique for teaching the horse to stand where placed is the same as that used for teaching him to stand for grooming. A switch pointed at him will help him to understand (Figure 2). Cowboys teach their horses to stand when the reins are pulled over their heads by tying the reins to a heavy log or stump. The horse is encouraged to pull back and keep on pulling until he finds out for himself that he cannot get away. From then on the dangling rope is his signal to stand.

S.Mason

FIG. 2.   Later the colt can be trained to stand where placed.

HALTER-BREAKING

These lessons begin soon after birth—as soon, in fact, as the foal has conquered his initial fear of the trainer. The goal is to train him so that he will stand when tied, follow on a slack lead rope no matter where the trainer chooses to go, stop at a word with only a slight tension on the lead strap, stand while the mare is led away from him, and leave his mother without a struggle. All of this takes about a month and is accomplished in a series of lessons, one leading into another. A lesson, incidentally, does not mean one period of training. It refers rather to the objective of the particular step in the training, and it may take several lesson periods to teach a "lesson" successfully. This should be remembered throughout the training of both the horse and the rider.

When the foal has become accustomed to the feel of the halter and to the presence and voice of the trainer, have an assistant lead the mare from the stall to the paddock in which she has been regularly turned while the trainer leads the foal. At this period of his education, the foal is allowed to follow more or less at will beside his mother, the trainer walking beside him with a short halter shank attached to the halter. In the paddock the mare may be led in circles with the foal following. If he attempts to fight the halter shank, he should not be checked too suddenly; rather he should be given time to find out what is expected of him. Above all else, should the foal rear or plunge, the trainer must place himself so that any pull on the shank is in a direct line with the foal's neck and spine, (Figure 3) since a sideways pull may result in a permanent injury.

Fig. 3.   When the colt plays, the lead line should be kept on a direct line with his neck and spine to avoid injury.

Once the foal has learned to follow without fighting, the next lesson is to teach him to remain in one place while the mare is led a few steps away and halted, then to catch up to his mother at a walk. When this has been accomplished successfully, the hardest lesson is then begun: asking the foal to leave his mother. An assistant is helpful for this lesson. Bracing his body against the rump of the foal, the assistant gently pushes while the trainer urges his pupil with gentle pulls on the halter shank. Demand only a few steps at first, then lead the mare forward to her baby and reward the colt with pats and compliments. If there is no one to help and you have to work entirely alone, the lesson is harder, but it may be accomplished in the following manner: Tie the mare to the corner of the paddock. Then take a rein long enough to go around the foal from front to rear and back again, the strap resting just below the buttock points. Walking in front of the foal and facing him, carry the lead shank in one hand and both ends of this strap in the other. By pulling on the strap, urge the foal on from behind, and with the other hand, check the forward movement if it is too fast (Figure 4). The foal should at first be led in this way in little circles near the mare, the circles being gradually enlarged until he is willing to go quite far from her without struggling. This lesson in halter-breaking is the only one in the entire education of the colt during which excitement or refusal to obey is to

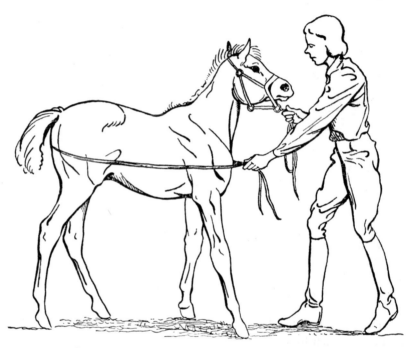

FIG. 4.   Teaching the foal to leave the mare.

be expected. From now on, each new lesson is based on something previously learned, and so does not come as a shock to the colt. Any evidence of excitement or resistance indicates bad preparation for that lesson. In such cases the colt must be taken back a few steps in his training and more thorough preparation given.

The work described above is usually accomplished by the end of the first month. At feeding time the foal may be tied beside his mother. The mare is also tied, and mother and colt each has its own feeding box. Some mares fight their foals when the babies try to steal from the mares' grain boxes. Others will eat all their baby's as well as their own rations. As soon as he has learned to chew and follow on the halter, the foal should have his own grain in addition to his

26

mother's milk, and, for the reason cited before, it is best that both be tied so that neither can dip into the other's manger.

In the paddock, when the foal is loose, make a practice of walking up to him frequently and patting him. As soon as he is a few months old and thoroughly obedient to the halter, he should be taken for little walks without his mother over rough ground, over low rails, and especially in and out of a trailer or van. If there is no trailer on the place which is used for training, it might be well to build a little chute to simulate a loading ramp. Lessons given in loading now will save countless hours and probably injuries later on.

WEANING

Weaning time is always a time of wailings and sadness for both the mare and foal. There is a variety of opinion on the best time to wean a foal. Racing stables, desiring to get size quickly on their yearlings, sometimes take the foals away at the early age of six weeks and keep them on milk, plus sixteen quarts of crushed oats, given in four feedings. That this does get size on the foals is undisputable, but whether it is best in the long run for their health and stamina is questionable. Most breeders like to leave the foals with the mares until they are at least six months old. Then, if the mare has been bred again, they usually wean the foal so that the mare is not supporting three creatures. With a mare that has not been bred again, the foal may be allowed to continue nursing for several months more, although again it is questionable whether this is advisable. In the wild state, mares wean their own foals just before the new one comes.

If possible, when first separating the foal from his mother, let him have another foal also being weaned in the box stall with him, for misery dearly loves company. Some authorities believe in having the mare in an adjoining stall. Others feel that a clean break is best, and get the two out of earshot of one another. Whatever method is used, remember that at least six weeks must pass before they can be permitted to run together again. Some mares refuse to wean their foals unless they have a newer one at heel, and I know of a case in which a mare who had been separated from her first-born for a year, and who had meanwhile had another foal, took the older one back as a two-year-old and had him nursing along with his younger brother.

When the mare is first separated from her foal, her grain ration should be drastically reduced and her water limited for several days. Do not attempt to relieve the fullness of the bag by milking it as this will stimulate the flow of milk. If the bag becomes hard, distended, and hot, rub it gently with camphorated oil and milk only a few drops.

When the foal has stopped fretting for his mother, he may be kept in a stall by himself. A box stall is preferable since, even though he is well halter-broken, a youngster can get badly tied up in his tie rope at night.

STABLE MANNERS

The foal should be taught good stable manners from the beginning. The well-trained horse, stabled in a straight stall, moves from side to side at a word. He does not crowd the trainer when the trainer enters the stall. He stands quietly for blanketing or grooming, picks up his feet on command, backs out of the stall willingly, but without rushing. He is not afraid to have a broom used behind him, nor does he shy at a wheelbarrow. He does not kick at horses passing behind him or at people.

Horses stabled in box stalls should be taught to come to the door when the trainer comes up to it. They should not push past when it is opened. The well-trained horse will stay in his stall even though the door is open, and no one is nearby. When he is being returned to his stall, the well-trained horse enters quietly, never rushing in. Some trainers teach their horses to turn and back into the box stall. This is a useful habit, as the horse moves more carefully when going backward and is in such a position that the trainer may remove the halter without having to enter the stall.

Unfortunately, not all horses are carefully educated in regard to stable manners, and it is often necessary for the trainer to reschool new animals coming into his stable.

Kicking at the Side of the Stall at Feeding Time

One of the most common bad habits of poorly trained horses is kicking. This vice sometimes proves incurable, but it may often be corrected by tying a little rubber ball to a short length of elastic and attaching this to the horse's fetlock joint (Figure 5). When the horse kicks, the ball bounces back and hits him on the ankle, thus punishing him immediately and automatically.

Some horses kick the sides of their stalls simply out of boredom or because they dislike their neighbor. In this case, change the animal's stall, if possible. I broke one mare of this habit by putting her in a stall where she could look out of the window. If you cannot change the stall, wrap straw or carpeting around the post so that the horse does not injure himself. A greedy horse will often start kicking at feeding time when he hears the others getting their oats. You have the choice of putting up with the kicking or of feeding him first.

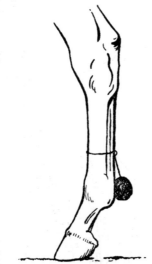

FIG. 5.   A cure for kicking.

Backing Suddenly Out of a Straight Stall

This is another bad habit, but one which is readily cured. The technique is as follows: Equip the stall with a heel chain running across the back a little above the height of the point of the hock (Figure 6). Enter the stall, fastening the heel chain behind you, and detach the tie rope. If the horse has been in the habit of dashing out backwards, he will probably try to do so as soon as he is untied. Finding himself checked abruptly by the heel chain, he will stop. Lead him forward, retie the halter shank, and go out of the stall. Repeat this until the horse no longer starts backward when the tie rope is removed. Now go into the stall again, but instead of fastening up the heel chain, have an assistant hold it. If the horse again starts out too suddenly when he finds that the heel chain is no longer fastened, the assistant should close in on him quickly with a chain. A few such lessons, making the horse go all the way back into his stall each time he rushes until he is willing to come out quietly, will soon teach him better manners. Some horses will back out more quietly if the trainer avoids standing directly in front of them.

Refusal to Back Out of the Stall

The horse that refuses to back out of his stall can also be a problem. When the usual method of right hand on the shoulder point, left

29

hand on the halter shank, has been tried and has failed, try tapping the cannon bones with your foot, at the same time pushing the horse backwards. If this does not work, turn the animal's head around to

FIG. 6.   A stall fitted with a heel chain.

throw him a little off balance and make him think he is going to be made to turn in the stall. Continue tapping on the cannons and pushing on the shoulder point.

Slipping the Halter or Shank

Heel chains are useful in the case of a horse that slips his halter or has learned to untie his shank. Sometimes, with heel chains, it will not be necessary to use a halter at all. Heel chains also serve the purpose of teaching the horse to become used to the feeling of ropes coming behind and across his hindquarters. However, there is always the chance that a restive horse, kicking at another, may get his leg over the heel chain. For this reason, heel chains must not be made of rope, which would cause a severe burn, or of uncovered chain, which can gouge and cut. Instead they should be made of a length of chain run through a length of rubber hose. This, being smooth, cannot possibly injure the animal should he become entangled in it.

Crowding In the Stall

Young colts never develop this habit unless something is done to frighten or hurt them when the trainer is in the stall with them. Old offenders sometimes develop the habit until it becomes a dangerous vice. Overly heavy-handed grooming on sensitive portions of the anatomy such as the hocks or belly can cause crowding. Quiet handling and patience will prevent or cure the habit in young horses. The trainer takes a board slightly longer than the width of his body, sharpened to a rounded point on each end (Figure 7a). He carries it as shown in Figure 7b whenever he enters the stall, holding it and

FIGS. 7a and 7b.   Methods used for curing a horse of crowding in the stall.

his body at right angles to the horse and the side of the stall. If the horse attempts to crowd, one end of the board will push into him and the other end can be braced against the stall; meanwhile the trainer is protected from being squeezed.

Occasionally one finds a horse that is really vicious in a box stall, that will not permit the trainer to go up to his head but always turns his heels toward the trainer with the idea of pinning him in a corner and kicking him. Horses are never born with these habits, and no foal that is gently handled will ever develop them. Unfortunately, however, not all foals are so handled, and every now and again a trainer is faced with such a renegade. Such horses should not be

FIG. 8.   One method of catching a vicious horse in a stall.

stabled in loose boxes but should be fastened so that the trainer can come up to the animal's head without having to go around his heels. If you do find yourself in the unfortunate predicament of having to enter the stall with such a vicious animal, there are one or two methods which can be used with safety. In the first method, shown in Figure 8, the trainer goes into the stall leading another horse, keeping this horse between himself and the bad-mannered animal until he can reach under his protector's neck and grasp the halter of the recalcitrant animal. This is not in any way cruel, since rarely if ever does a vicious horse attack both man and his fellows. A horse that is fighting out of fright, however, will attack anything. With him it will be necessary to use the method shown in Figure 9. Here the trainer, with the help of several assistants, has passed a rope across the stall, pinning

FIG. 9.   A second method of cornering a vicious horse in the stall.

the culprit against the wall. The method of getting the rope across the stall depends on the construction of the stall. Sometimes a stiff wire can be pushed between the side boards to the opposite side, and sometimes it is necessary to work from above.

MANNERS IN THE PADDOCK

The horse's manners in the paddock are important. He should be trained to come up to the trainer when he calls or whistles. At the very least, he should allow the trainer to walk up to him. The colt that is fondled from babyhood will give no trouble—he is much more apt to make a nuisance of himself trying to crawl into the trainer's pockets looking for tidbits; but the range horse, broken by force after he is full grown, is another matter.

33

Catching the Horse in the Field

To teach a refractory horse to come at a whistle, attach a feed box near the paddock gate. Several times during the day, put a handful of oats into this box and step back, giving whatever call you choose. When the horse finds that he is not going to be caught, he will approach readily. He will soon form the habit of going to the box whenever he hears the call. After a few days, gradually stand nearer and nearer as the horse eats. Before long you will be able to stand beside the horse as he eats, then you will be able to pat him, and finally, to grasp the halter. Soon after this the horse should allow you to come up to him in the paddock when he hears the whistle. If he still shows fear, kneel down and rub your hands together (Figure 10).

FIG. 10.   Catching a timid horse or colt in the field.

Horses are full of curiosity and will often come up to persons so occupied to see why they look different and to find out what the funny noise is about. As time goes on, the horse will get tamer and tamer until one call or whistle will bring him cantering across the pasture to you. You must be prepared to reward him with a tidbit if you wish to keep him in training. Head-shy horses will often come up

34

without trouble, but are afraid when the trainer reaches for the halter or foretop. These horses should have a short length of rope left attached to their halters, making it unnecessary for the trainer to raise his hand very high.

Figure 11 shows another method of catching a timid horse. Here the horse is tempted to put his head through a slip noose into a pail of oats, and the noose is then dropped around his neck. He will probably make several attempts to get the oats before putting his head all

FIG. 11.   Sometimes a horse can be caught this way.

the way in the bucket. Do not try to rush the horse, for if he is not too timid, he will eventually place himself in such a position that you will be able to drop the noose over his poll and slide it up.

Cornering the Outlaw

For the outlaw that has just arrived on the place and has been turned out with the herd but refuses to be caught, several different methods can be used. Bring in the whole herd and he may follow them, as horses are by nature gregarious and do not like to be left alone. Someone should walk quietly along on foot behind to keep the horses moving, but not too close to the outlaw.

If the strange horse is out by himself, take another horse out on a lead rope. Let the loose horse come up to his fellow and talk a moment, then lead the latter into the stable without looking back. Often the other will follow.

If this does not work, you will need two people and a fifty-foot rope. Gradually herd the stubborn animal into a corner, trying to work slowly and keep him calm. Have one person at each end of the rope close in on him, forming a triangle with the walls or fence of the paddock, the corner forming two sides, the rope the third (Figure 12). By gradually shortening up on the rope, you will finally succeed in pinning the horse in the corner, and it will be possible to get hold of him.

Never try to corner a loose horse by walking up to him from behind, or a kick may land in your face; always try to get the horse to come to you. Never try to herd horses into a stable or paddock at a run; a slow walk is the only gait that will be successful. By walking twenty feet behind the animal, and shifting your position from side to side as you see him about to turn, you can usually do a better job than you could from the back of another horse. Make it your goal with every horse to have him willing to come to you at the sound of your special whistle or call.

Charging

This is a vice that is often developed in ponies which are given too many tidbits by hand. The cure is to hit the animal a sharp blow across the muzzle with a stick or stinging whip when he approaches with his teeth bared. One such lesson is usually enough.

LEADING

In leading a horse through a narrow or rough spot, walk backwards, facing the horse, so that you may steer him to some extent (Figure 13). In such cases it will often be necessary to have an assistant urge the animal from behind with a hand on the rump. Try to prevent the horse from coming through too fast, and be prepared to jump quickly to the side should he plunge forward from fright.

Leading across a low barway may sometimes be accomplished best by taking the end of the reins or halter shank and running ahead of the horse, jumping the bar in front of him. Be careful to keep a little to one side so that the horse is not blocked and does not jump on top of you. All horses should be taught to lead over low obstacles. Of course, one should start with a rail flat on the ground and raise it gradually. A reward in the form of a carrot or apple is very helpful.

36

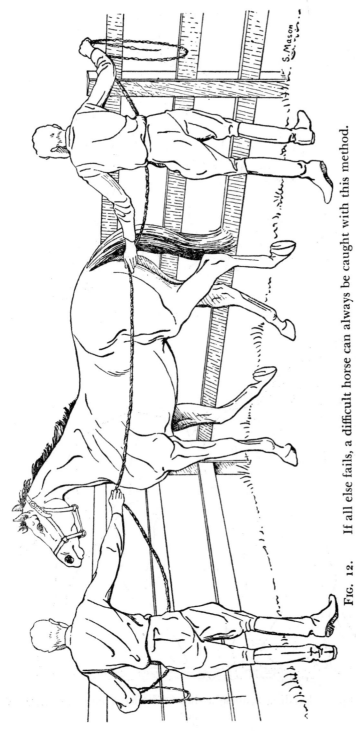

S. Mason

Fig. 12.   If all else fails, a difficult horse can always be caught with this method.

FIG. 13.   Leading a horse through a narrow or rough spot.

FIG. 14.   Leading a horse a short distance (*reins over withers*).

Leading with Bridle

There are two correct techniques to be used in leading a horse that is saddled and bridled. For short distances it is permissible to leave the reins back over the withers. Then take hold of the reins six inches from the bit, forefinger between them to separate the right from the left, and walk forward without looking at the horse (Figure 14). If the horse is to be led some little distance, the reins should be pulled forward over his head to give the trainer more control should the horse try to pull away. Hold the end of the reins in the left hand and grasp them six inches from the bit in the right hand, separating them with the forefinger as in the other method (Figure 15). In both

Fig. 15.   Leading with the reins over the horse's head.

cases, the stirrup irons should be run up on the leathers to prevent them from swinging out and catching in corners or frightening the horse. If the horse does not move or attempts to pull back (Figure 16), his resistance can be overcome by turning the animal abruptly to one side or the other. This will throw him off balance, and he will take a step to regain his footing. Once moving, he will forget his resistance and can be led in any direction.

39

Fig. 16.   The balky horse. *In leading a balky horse if the rider will step backward from this position and turn the horse sharply to the left, the horse will be thrown off balance and will start moving.*

GROOMING MANNERS

Good grooming manners are essential in every horse, yet how seldom does one find them! The goal should be to train the horse to stand quietly without being tied; to pick up each foot in turn and hold it up without the trainer having to touch it; to move readily from side to side, backwards, or forwards on command; to hold his head low to have his poll and ears cleaned; and to stay where he is without moving, should the trainer leave him for a moment. He should also accept the saddle and bridle without demur, not flinching when the girth is tightened, lowering his head and opening his mouth for the bit. Such a horse is a real pleasure, both to groom and to shoe.

To teach a horse grooming manners, cross-tie him. Start by grooming in a routine, methodical manner, always doing everything in the same order. Begin on the near side of the upper neck with the rubber currycomb or the brush. Work down that side, then down the other. Be gentle, but firm. Do nothing to irritate or tickle the horse. The loin, belly, and flanks are particularly sensitive. Be careful in

40

removing caked mud or scabs. Work them loose with your fingers, or, better, apply vaseline and leave it in overnight, then wash with warm water the next morning. Talk constantly to the horse—the words don't matter, as long as they are spoken in a soothing tone of voice. Be very gentle around the head, using only a very soft brush, your hands, or a cloth. Do not use anything rough below the knees or hocks. Be particularly careful to get the backs of the pasterns clean; feel them with your fingers to be sure that nothing adheres there which could cause scratches or other irritations. End with a hand-rubbing all over. This serves two purposes: it stimulates the circulation, and makes the trainer aware of any unusual swellings, lumps, or heat.

When you come to the feet, pick them up in rotation, beginning with the near front and always going in the same order. Use some specific word, such as "up." Lean against the shoulder or haunch, as the case may be, and lift. Work quietly and carefully. Never prick the sensitive heel with the pick; work from the heel toward the toe in cleaning around the frog. Never drop the foot when you have finished with it; put it down quietly. In a few days the horse should pick up his foot when he feels the pressure against his shoulder or haunch and the word of command. Presently you will find that the horse lifts the foot as soon as you take up your position and lean down. Intelligent animals learn to identify the hoof pick and will immediately lift the near forefoot when the trainer approaches carrying the pick.

When the horse stands quietly on the tie reins and has become accustomed to the grooming, try fastening the ropes to each other in front of the horse's chest (Figure 17). The final step in teaching him to stand while the trainer leaves him takes a little patience, but by moving away gradually and giving him the command "stand" in a firm tone, you can soon teach the horse what is required. If he moves forward at all, back him into position and start over. Be ready with praise or reward when the horse has learned his lesson. When the horse will stand in a narrow aisle without tying while another horse is led past him, (Figure 18) the trainer can know that the horse has good grooming and stable manners.

LONGEING

Before the horse is mounted for the first time, he must undergo a long period of training on the longe. This period only too often is hurried or neglected altogether, with the result that when the trainer mounts for the first time, he finds the colt timid, overexcited, or disobedient. This is no reflection on the colt, but on the trainer.

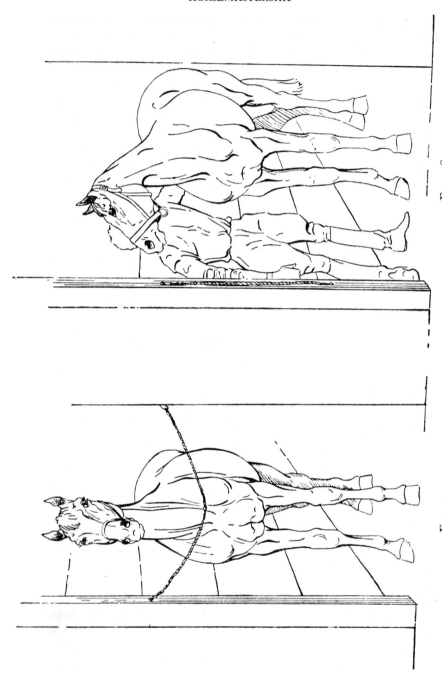

FIG. 18.

FIG. 17.

Teaching the horse to stand without tying.

The purpose of longeing is to exercise the horse, to make him flexible, and to make him obedient to the voice of the trainer. The goals should be to teach the horse to start and stop and turn quietly on command; to teach him to circle equally well to the right or left on a walk, a slow trot, an ordinary trot, and a slow canter; and to teach him to stand on the track without throwing his haunches out, or facing the trainer.

Even after the horse has progressed past the early stages of longeing and is being ridden or even jumped and hunted, a lesson on the tape every now and again is of great value. This is particularly true for high-spirited horses that have been allowed to stand a day or so in their stalls and have developed "stall courage."

Equipment

The equipment needed for this training is a longeing cavesson with side reins, a longe tape or leather strap, a surcingle, and a driving whip. Figure 19 shows the longeing cavesson. The swivel loop on

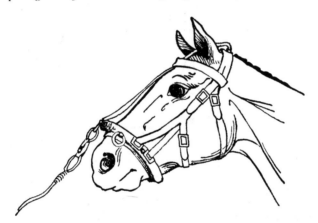

FIG. 19.   A longeing cavesson or bridle with longe attached.

the top of the noseband is mounted on a heavy metal strip and the noseband is lined with felt to prevent chafing. Jaw straps prevent the cheek straps from coming in contact with the animal's eye, should the cavesson be pulled out of place. The whole affair is very strongly made and cannot possibly be broken by the horse. Such a cavesson is not very expensive, will last a lifetime, and is indispensable for proper training.

The surcingle (Figure 20) may be an ordinary web surcingle, a leather one made especially for longeing, or a driving harness saddle. The side reins running from the side loops on the cavesson to the surcingle may be old reins that have been equipped with a snap on one end, a loop through which the surcingle runs on the other, and a buckle somewhere along the side to permit adjustment in length; or they may be real training reins, the front third of which are made of rubber to allow a certain play when the horse throws his head.

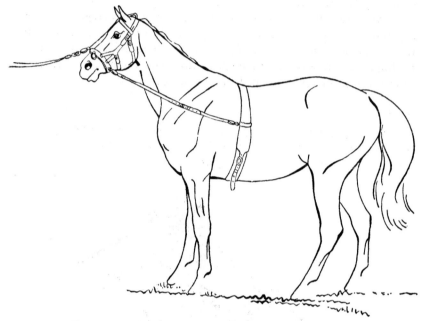

FIG. 20.   A longeing rig made from a surcingle.

The regulation longeing tape is made of webbing with a swivel snap at one end and a loop at the other. One can also use a couple of driving reins buckled together and these, being leather, have the advantage of not picking up the dust as much as the webbing. Most longes are about thirty feet long.

The longeing whip is a driving whip with a twelve-foot lash.

Technique

The longeing technique can be described easily but the novice will have to spend some time practicing it before he gets over his initial awkwardness. Form the tape in a series of loops placed against each other and held between the forefinger and the thumb so that you can release one loop at a time. If you attempt to hold the longe by wrapping it around your hand, you will soon become entangled in it.

44

If the horse is circling to the left the longe is held in the left hand, and vice versa (Figure 21).

The whip is held in the free hand. For a well-schooled horse, the whip is held so that the tip is on the ground behind the trainer, and is raised only if the horse is not immediately obedient to demands for turning or increasing the gait. In schooling green horses or sluggish horses, it is often better to hold the whip more or less horizontally, with the tip pointing toward the buttock point of the horse. The tape runs from the trainer's leading hand to the horse's nose. Place your self about opposite the animal's hip if he is working smoothly, moving with the animal to maintain this position. If the horse goes too

FIG. 21.   Longeing the horse, reins in leading hand.

fast, step toward your leading hand and extend it. This acts as a deterrent to the horse as he sees that you can then block him. If the horse goes too slowly, raise the whip and swing it lightly. If the horse tries to back away, move quickly to maintain your position about opposite the hip-bone. On the longe, the horse turns toward the trainer in reversing direction. Figure 23 shows that the horse and trainer form a triangle, the trainer the apex, the horse the base, and the longe and the whip the two sides. Clever maneuvering on the part of the trainer keeps the horse always working between his two hands, just as later he will learn to work between the hands and legs of his rider.

A second method of holding the longe is shown in Figure 22.

Here the trainer folds the longe in a series of flat loops in the form of a figure-eight. The loops lie across the palm of the hand opposite the croup of the horse. The tape runs through the other hand, which

FIG. 22.   Longeing the horse. *Reins looped in following hand and passing through leading hand.*

feeds it out or draws it in as desired. Some trainers prefer this method of using the longe, as it is easier to keep the tape taut and to let it out smoothly. Others prefer the method previously described, as the whip is more easily handled with the whole tape held in the other hand. With a horse that longes without the use of the whip, the second method is certainly the best. In using this method, if the whip is carried, it should be carried with the point down behind the trainer's back. The horse may be kept moving by waving the loops of the tape.

If the horse is longeing in an enclosed hall or fenced paddock, the walls or the fence may also be used to advantage. Work in one corner so that the angle of the walls forms a barrier when the horse is on that part of the circle (Figure 23). If the horse gets going too fast, it is easy to bring him to a halt by changing your own position in relation to the circle so that he finds himself running headlong into a wall (Figure 24).

In introducing the unschooled horse to the longe, two people are necessary. Hold the tape as described on page 44, looped up in your hand to within a yard of the horse's head. Carry the whip trailing behind you for this initial stage. It is understood that the horse is by now thoroughly halter-broken; that he leads readily, starting and

46

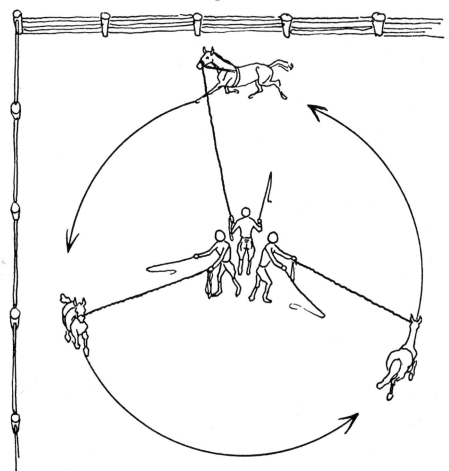

FIG. 23. Longeing. *Note position of trainer and how he always keeps the horse between his two hands.*

stopping at a word; and that he is afraid neither of the trainer nor of the sight of the whip. The assistant walks on the off-side of the horse with his hand on the cheek-strap of the cavesson. Talking quietly to the animal, lead him around in a circle about fifty feet in diameter at a normal walk. Several times, stop and cause the horse to stand on the track while you pat him. Gradually move away from the animal's head, letting the tape out a loop at a time, until you are walking parallel to the horse's shoulder, about four feet away from him. Continue to talk to him and to start and stop him. Then let out another loop or so until you are six feet away, and the horse is describ-

47

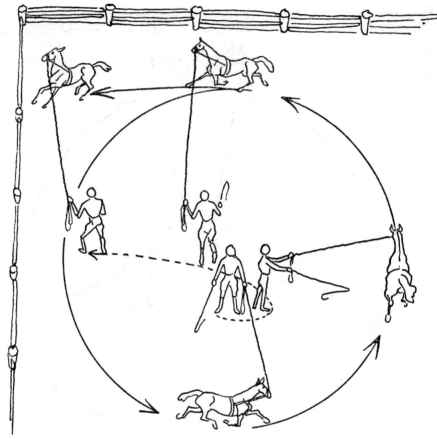

FIG. 24.   Longeing in the corner of the arena, *using the wall to teach the horse to stop.*

ing a circle of about fifty feet. Now move so that you are about opposite the animal's hip, raising the whip quietly, holding the tape taut and well away from your body. You should be beginning to get the animal between your two hands, but the assistant should still walk on the outside of the circle.

The next step is to see if you can halt the colt by giving a voice command. At the same time, step to the left, holding out your left hand and pointing as though to block the horse, and drop the tip of the whip. When the animal will halt in this manner without the help of the assistant and will stand while you come toward him (each time picking up the tape in loops in your hand so that it does not drag on the ground and get in your way), then the assistant can step away from the circle and let the colt work at the walk alone, remaining in readiness in case of disobedience.

Work at the walk on both the left- and right-hand circles. Nearly all horses, after they have been halter-broken and are accustomed to be led, go better to the left than to the right. Some authorities ascribe this to the fact that in leading a horse, the trainer always walks on the left, and consequently the horse makes all his turns to the left. Therefore, the horse's right shoulder muscles become stretched more than the left so that he feels freer and more flexible when turning to the left side.

When you make the first change of direction, go back to the first step and move on the right circle as you did before on the left, with the assistant leading and the trainer close to the horse's head with whip trailing behind.

Most horses catch on to longeing very readily. The hardest part is to teach the horse to move away from the trainer. If there is any hesitation, step back quickly toward the buttock point, raise the whip, and shake the tape.

As in all other aspects of training horses, make haste slowly. Do not attempt the slow trot until you can work the horse at the walk, using the full length of the tape, and can stop him quietly with your voice. The canter, which is the most exciting of the gaits, should not be attempted until the horse is letter-perfect at the two speeds of the trot, and this usually takes several weeks. Do not allow the horse to play on the longe. Check him sharply if he throws up his heels; he is supposed to be working, not playing. If he seems very fresh and it is impossible to get his attention, turn him loose in the hall or paddock and let him run. He will buck and plunge and roll, but, strangely enough, you will find he is more quiet when you put him to work after his play.

SCHOOLING AT LIBERTY

This is a more advanced lesson and a follow-up to longeing. An indoor hall or a corral with high, almost solid, walls is necessary. Most horses learn to free-school quite readily, and I have found it valuable for several reasons, especially for the horse that is to be taught to jump later.

The goal is to teach the horse to circle around the trainer at the walk, slow trot, ordinary trot, and canter; to start and stop quietly on command; and to turn exactly as he did on the longe tape, but without the use of that restraining line to steady him.

49

After the horse has been taught to longe, choose a day when he seems quiet and attentive. After fifteen minutes or so on the tape, un-snap it and ask the horse to walk beside you in a circle while you walk near his head as you did in the first lessons on the longe. Gradu-ally move farther and farther away from the colt and toward the cen-ter of the circle (Figure 25). If the colt attempts to follow, restrain

FIG. 25.   Schooling at liberty.

him by a firm word and by pushing him away with your leading hand. Gradually he learns to work between the whip and the hand as he did before. In changing direction, he should be trained to turn away from the trainer instead of toward you as he did on the longe. You will now have the opportunity of testing the horse's vocabulary. He should understand and obey the following: "walk," "trot," "steady," "slow," "come on," "faster," "canter," "stand," "halt" or "stop," and "turn." When I have finished riding my horses I always have them walk themselves cool while I stand in the center. This refreshes their memory and keeps them obedient to my voice. It is also possible to wipe off my tack and cool out my horse at the same time!

LONG-REIN DRIVING

When the colt works well on the longe, some lessons in long-rein driving will be valuable. This part of the animal's education is nearly always neglected, and while it is not as essential as longeing, it teaches some things which the latter does not.

50

The horse may be started in his cavesson with the side reins and the surcingle. Later a hackamore and then a snaffle bridle can be used. For the first lessons, ordinary driving reins will do; later, ones twenty-five feet long should be substituted for the shorter reins.

The goal is to teach the horse to go forward, to start, to stop, and to turn at the demand of the leading rein. If he receives this training before he is mounted, the horse will have the opportunity to become obedient to the rein effects without being confused or worried by having to learn both to balance under the riders weight and to ignore the feeling of the legs against his sensitive sides at the same time. If you have taught the horse to respond to the rein effects, you will be delighted at his obedience and lack of fear when you mount him for the first time.

FIG. 26.   First lessons in long-rein driving, *reins not through rings.*

The technique of long-rein driving is fairly simple. The reins are held in two hands, the hands well separated. On straight lines, the driver walks directly behind the horse; on turns and circles, he steps toward the inside and leads the inside hand away from the body, using an "active" hand (page 233), thus causing the horse to turn his head in the direction of the movement. At the same time he brings the outside rein along the horse's haunch above the hock line. This helps make the horse follow the track of his forelegs with his hindquarters and also prepares him for the pressure of the rider's legs which will come later.

For the first few lessons, the horse should be kept in the hall or paddock, an assistant leading the animal with a short halter shank. When the horse has learned what is expected of him, the assistant can be dispensed with and the longer reins substituted for the ordinary ones. Then the reins can be run through rings and the horse worked in circles or straight lines (Figure 27). Later you can take the horse

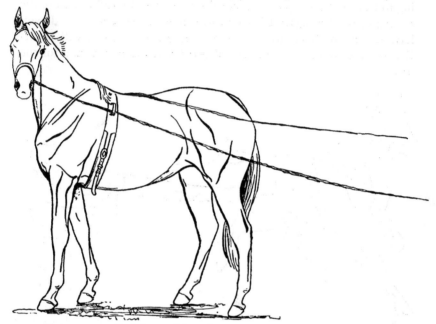

FIG. 27.   Driving with reins through rings of surcingle.

out on the road or across the fields. He should never go at a faster gait than a slow jog. Most of the work on long reins is done at the walk.

At some time during the training, the saddle can be substituted for the surcingle, the side reins dispensed with, and the reins run through the stirrup leathers. The stirrup irons are not run up for this lesson.

In both the longeing and long-rein driving lessons, take care not to let the colt become bored. Fifteen-minute lessons at first, gradually increasing to a half-hour, are best. Two periods of a half-hour a day are better than one long period.

Training the Horse

Many trainers believe that lessons in long-rein driving should be followed by lessons in the breaking cart, even for the horse that is destined to become a hunter or hack and that will never, in all probability, be asked to pull a vehicle again. There is much to be said for this, particularly in working with yearlings and two-year-olds. It permits the trainer to give the young horse adequate exercise without the strain of bearing weight. It teaches the horse flexibility and obedience. It steadies him, and it makes him traffic-wise.

Success or failure with the breaking cart depends largely on the apparatus used. The breaking cart and the harness both must be very strong. Jack Widmer, in his excellent book *Practical Horse Breeding and Training* (Charles Scribner's Sons, 1942), describes a splendid type of breaking cart constructed from two automobile wheels. This conveyance is sturdy, rolls easily without the rattle of wooden-wheeled vehicles, and has brakes on each wheel, enabling the driver to help the horse turn corners readily. If the equipment is available, by all means work your colts in a breaking cart before riding them (Figure 28). The colt can be driven both on a track and on the road

FIG. 28.   The breaking cart.

for longer and longer periods. This helps to muscle him up and enables him to be worked at a faster gait than is possible with the trainer on foot. In introducing the colt to the breaking cart, the trainer should have two assistants. One leads the colt, one walks behind, and the trainer himself sits in the cart or walks beside it holding the reins.

The colt should first be allowed to smell the cart, and it should be moved gently while he is near it. When the animal has lost his fear of the cart, assistants run the cart up to the colt, holding the shafts up high, while the trainer holds him and soothes him. When the shafts are in place, and the hold-backs, traces, and kicking strap fastened, one assistant leads the colt while the other quietly starts the cart rolling. The trainer walks near the animal's croup and guides him with the reins. Gradually the assistant who is pushing the cart from behind allows it to roll along of its own accord so that the colt gets the feel of the pull on his shoulder. He must learn to push against the feeling, although his natural inclination at first will be to stop. In making the first turns, the assistant who is leading keeps the point of the shaft from pressing too hard against the colt's shoulder. The turns should be as wide as possible. When the colt is going quietly, the trainer can get into the cart, but the assistants should remain with him to help until the colt is thoroughly used to the feel and sound of the cart. Above everything, the trainer should not allow the horse to get away with any disobedience, such as bolting or kicking, at this stage. Only when he is well adjusted to the cart should he be driven out on the public road.

INTRODUCTION TO THE SADDLE

The colt's first introduction to the saddle is important. It should not be associated in his mind with either discomfort or fright. If he is stabled in a box stall, he should be introduced to the saddle in this familiar place. If he is stabled in a straight stall, it would be better to show him the saddle for the first time when he is standing in the grooming aisle. Many horses fear having the trainer come into a narrow stall carrying something as big as a saddle.

Carry the saddle across your arm with the throat to the left, the girth tucked in the irons which have been run up on the leathers (Figure 29). Let the colt nuzzle it and smell it. When you put it on the colt's back, do so with the utmost gentleness, talking in a calm voice all the while. Put it a little forward of the withers and slide it back into place, thus making certain that the hairs are not roughed up under the pad. Let it sit in place for a few minutes until the colt gets used to the feel of the weight before you attempt to do up the girth. If the colt seems restless, a helper should hold him so that there is no danger of his plunging suddenly, causing the saddle to fall off, which would really frighten him.

When fastening the girth, tighten it only enough to prevent the saddle from slipping and turning as the colt moves. He is not going to be mounted for some days yet, so it need not be tight. The horse's forelegs should be well forward when the girth is adjusted so that the

54

FIG. 29.　　The proper way to carry a saddle.

skin is stretched and there is no chance of pinching it under the girth. Run your hand down between the girth and the colt's sides to be sure that the hairs are smooth. Be careful to see that, if a pad is used, it is pushed well up into the throat of the saddle and does not cut the withers (Figure 30). A badly adjusted pad can do as

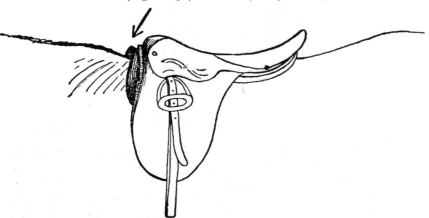

FIG. 30.　　Adjustment of the pommel pad.

much damage as a saddle that does not fit. The colt should be longed, driven in long reins, and free-schooled in the saddle until he is thoroughly accustomed to the feel of it.

INTRODUCTION TO THE SNAFFLE BRIDLE

The bridle will be more of a novelty than the saddle. Before attempting to introduce him to the bit, drive the horse in long reins ir

FIG. 31a.   The hackamore.

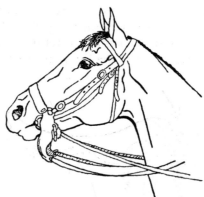

FIG. 31b.   The hackamore with snaffle on separate headstall.

the hackamore. The purpose of the hackamore is, as in the longeing cavesson, to restain the horse by pressure on the nostrils. Figure 31a shows the horse equipped with a simple type of hackamore with plain shanks, not very long. A more severe type has longer shanks that work on a hinge and so give more leverage. This type is not recommended for use with young horses.

56

When the horse is accustomed to working on the hackamore, the snaffle bit may be introduced. It should be adjusted with the hackamore as shown in Figure 31b and the horse allowed to stand in the stall and play with the bit for a half-hour at a time, until he no longer attempts to spit it out.

Trainers differ in their opinions as to the best type of bit to be used at first. Some like the simple snaffle as suggested here, fitted a little low so that the horse becomes accustomed to playing with it and enjoys doing so. Others like to use a very soft rubber bit and rub it with salt or molasses. Still others prefer a regular training bit which has a little bundle of dangles attached to the joint. Some, instead of the ordinary cavesson or hackamore, like to use a dropped noseband at first. This fits below the bit. The purpose of the dropped noseband is to put pressure on a low point of the nostrils, should the horse attempt to get away from the bit by opening his mouth. All these methods have their advantages. It is good to encourage the colt to enjoy playing with the bit, but the bit should be adjusted so that he cannot get his tongue over it. He should certainly be bridled and allowed to become accustomed to the feel of the bit while in his stall. Then he can be longed and driven on long reins with the bit in his mouth but with the reins attached to the hackamore. When the horse is thoroughly accustomed to this, the reins may be attached to the bit with perhaps side reins from hackamore to surcingle.

BITTING AND FLEXING EXERCISES

Some authorities recommend a series of suppling and flexing exercises designed to increase the flexibility of the horse's neck, poll, and jaw. Others feel that the horse develops this best while being ridden. Personally, I have found these exercises very practical if not overdone to such a point that the horse becomes bored.

Lateral Flexion

Stand to the horse's left, opposite his shoulder as shown, with a rein in each hand (Figure 32). Reach over the horse's neck with your right arm, grasping the rein on that side. With little vibrations, achieved by opening and closing the fingers of your left hand, encourage the horse to turn his head toward you, hold it there a moment, and then return it. Do this five or six times, then go to the far side of the horse and repeat the exercise with the other hand. Later, when the horse has been introduced to the full bridle or to the pelham, the flexion of the neck may be increased in the following manner. Standing on the left, take the left snaffle in your left hand and

FIG. 32.   Teaching lateral flexion with the snaffle bridle.

the other three reins in your right, holding the right hand up and over the horse's neck (Figure 33). With vibrations on all four reins, gradually move your hands further and further apart, inducing the horse to bend his head to the left by the vibration of the leading rein (the left snaffle). At the same time, the left curb, which, with the two right reins, is being carried to the right, pushes against the horse's neck, causing him to stabilize the neck at that point, bending only the front half of it. This is also his first lesson in the use of the indirect rein effect (see page 219). Repeat the same exercise from the other side with three reins in the left hand and only the right snaffle in the right hand.

Freedom of Movement and Vertical Flexion.

This is encouraged by standing directly in front of the animal, a rein in each hand, and raising and lowering his head.

Vertical Flexion of the Poll and Jaw

This is taught by grasping the reins under the animal's chin about six inches behind the bit, and with vibrations, inducing him to

Fig. 33.   Teaching lateral flexion with the full bridle.

bend at the poll until his face is vertical (Figure 34) never bent in toward the chest. The horse should relax his jaw and chew the bit. When he does so, immediately release the pressure of the reins and reward him with a pat or a tidbit.

Mobility of the Haunches

To teach mobility of the haunches, the following exercises are useful. Hold the reins on top of the withers in your left hand and stand about opposite the animal's shoulder. Touch the horse with the right forefinger or with a whip just behind the girth, at about the point where your legs will later make contact (Figure 35). The touch should be very, very light. The goal is to cause the horse to take one step with his haunches and one step only away from the trainer. Immediately reward him with a pat. Then demand another step, and a third. Now go around to the far side and cause the horse, by the same methods, to return to position. Later he will learn to do a complete half-pivot.

To teach the horse to bring his legs under him and so stretch the long muscle at the loin, grasp the reins over the withers, and with a

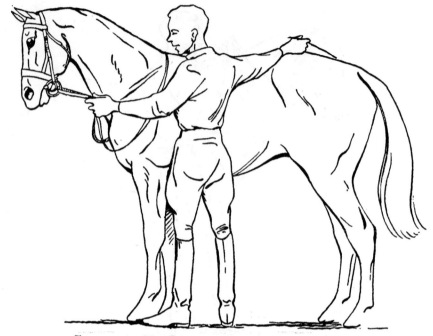

FIG. 34.   Teaching vertical flexion of the poll.

light whip, tap the animal's croup until he moves his back legs forward (Figure 36). The reins prevent any forward movement of the forehand. Until the loin muscle has been stretched, this is tiring for the horse, and he should not be asked to move the back feet more than an inch or so.

If you have been thorough and patient in following the steps of training described in these pages, keeping in mind always the trainer's goals of obedience, calmness, attentiveness, relaxation, flexibility, and confidence, you will be faced with no resistance when you give your colt his next lesson, that of learning to bear the trainer's weight in the saddle.

METHODS OF TEACHING GOOD MANNERS IN COMPANY

Horses fight when being ridden in close formation for one of two reasons: from vice or from fear. Two different systems can be used to combat kicking and biting in horses when ridden side by side. In the case of the young horse, that is acting up from fear, choose a very quiet old horse as a companion. Put the old horse on the wall side of the arena. Ride the young horse near him but not quite abreast. The head of the young horse can come about opposite the middle of the

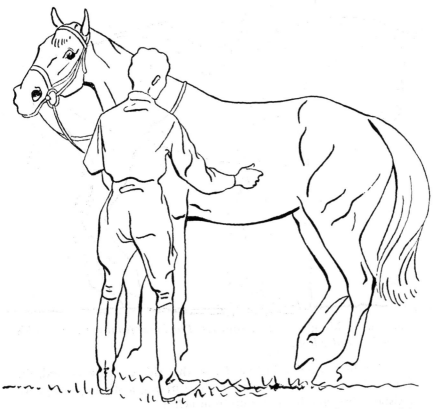

FIG. 35.   Mobilizing the haunches. *The horse is taught to move his haunches one step away from the trainer.*

neck of the old horse. After a few lessons, when the youngster finds that the other horse is not going to kick him he will probably settle down. Now a third horse, also quiet, can be brought in and the youngster ridden between the two until he acquires confidence.

In the case of the horse that is kicking or biting from viciousness choose two horses that are not timid and that will kick back immediately if attacked. Ride the bad actor between these two, good riders being on all three. Ride with as little interval between riders as possible and keep the horses going at a good ordinary trot followed by a good canter. The fact that there is a horse on each side of him, each of which will stand no nonsense, has a wonderful psychological effect on the bad actor. He knows if he kicks or bites one he will not be able to avoid retaliation since the horse on the other side will not stand any nonsense either.

61

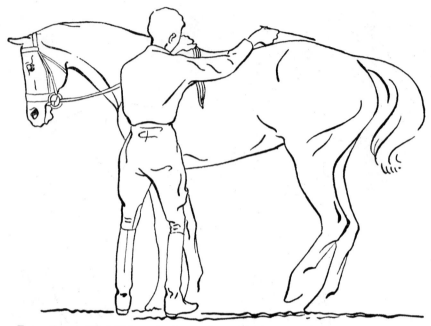

FIG. 36.   Mobilizing the haunches. *The horse is taught to bring his haunches under him.*

For the horse that kicks at horses that ride too close behind, the cure is for the trainer to mount him carrying a stinging whip. An assistant rides another horse up from behind.

The instant the ears of the vicious horse go back and he starts to misbehave, the trainer must jerk (this is the only time when the rider is permitted to be rough) the horse's head up and punish him with the whip. This is repeated until the vicious horse has learned his lesson. The best cure for the horse that runs up and bites the horse in front is to ride him behind a known kicker and let him try his tricks.

Note that many horses that get a reputation for misbehaving are only attempting to tell the riders that they are uncomfortable. Substitute hackamores for bridles and teach the riders to sit quietly and much of the misbehavior will disappear.

Chapter 5

MOUNTING

The day the trainer mounts the young horse for the first time is a red-letter day and one not to be approached carelessly. Everything should be done to insure the successful completion of this lesson. The horse's memory and ability to associate ideas must be taken into consideration. If the trainer succeeds in backing him (this term, in trainers' parlance, means "getting on his back," not "causing him to move backwards") for the first time without causing excitement or fear, he will have accomplished a great deal.

The day chosen for the first mounting should be clear, calm, and not too brisk. It should be a day on which the horse, in his regular longeing or driving in long reins workout, has behaved quietly and has been attentive. The trainer should be assisted by two helpers. One helper stands on the off-side of the colt, holding the cheek strap with his right hand and the stirrup leather with his left. Talking in a quiet voice, the trainer gathers the reins in his left hand on the colt's neck until he has a light contact with his mouth. The other assistant, when the colt seems relaxed, gives the trainer a hand up. The trainer should drop into the saddle as lightly and quietly as possible, being careful not to brush the young horse's off-flank with his leg. He should catch the stirrups, which should have been adjusted previously to his regular length, immediately, and the assistant holding the horse should move around to the near side and lead the colt forward at a walk. It is much more difficult for a horse to adjust his balance to the weight of the rider while standing than while moving, so he should be moved forward quietly as soon as the rider is firm in the saddle. Whether the trainer dismounts at the end of a few steps or continues

63

to walk the horse around for several minutes depends on how the horse takes his lesson. If he has had the preliminary work described, he will not be excited and will be responsive to the bit. The trainer should not attempt to use his leg aids until the colt is fully adjusted to the feel of the rider at the walk and slow trot. If the horse has been longed and driven in long reins he will be well confirmed on the voice commands for moving forward, and any use of the legs for increasing his gait at this point will only frighten him.

On the second day it may not be necessary for the trainer to have a leg up; the colt will probably stand quite quietly. He has not had enough experience to develop any fixed defense against being mounted, and if carefully handled, he never will. This, unfortunately, is not true of horses that have been treated more carelessly. Yet, no horse can be said to be well schooled if he will not stand immobile, with the reins hanging on his neck, while the trainer mounts.

COMMON DEFENSES AND THEIR CORRECTION

There are four types of defenses against being mounted common among horses that either have never been properly trained or that have found the experience of having a rider climb on their backs a disagreeable one, to be avoided, if possible.

Bolting Forward

A vice common in Western-trained horses is bolting forward when the rider puts his foot in the stirrup. To correct it, stand at the horse's shoulder point facing the rear with a carrot in your hand. Take the reins up very short and flex the horse slightly at the poll. Then put your toe in the stirrup, saying, "Stand!" and forcibly prevent the horse from moving forward by means of the tight reins. In this position, without putting any weight in the stirrup and without changing the tension on the reins, reach forward with your right hand and feed the horse a bit of the carrot. Then put your weight into the stirrup and spring up, but remain standing on the foot in the left stirrup without swinging the right leg over. It will be necessary at this point to raise the hand holding the reins. Carry it a little toward the rear to increase the tension, as the horse will almost certainly try to move forward. If this happens, steady yourself with a hand on the cantle. The important thing is to get the horse to remain immobile before and while you swing your right leg across. Having settled lightly into the saddle, lean forward and *immediately* give the horse another bit of carrot. Without allowing the horse to move forward, dismount and repeat the whole performance several times. Within ten minutes, the horse should have learned his lesson well and be will ing to stand and wait for his reward. The value of the technique lies in not moving quickly and in insisting that the horse remain quiet after each step of mounting.

Backing Away

For the horse that backs away from the rider, the same general method is used, but in this case the trainer stands behind the saddle facing front, right hip against the horse's flank. In this position, you can give the animal a sharp slap on the croup or buttock point if he attempts to back away, maintaining your relative position by backing up as the animal moves. When the horse is quiet, transfer the reins to your right hand and mount in stages, giving rewards at each stage as described.

Spinning and Snapping

Many horses have the habit of swinging their hindquarters away from the rider and spinning around on the forehand. Others lay their ears back and try to snap as the rider takes up the reins. The cure for both these habits is the same—namely, to stand at the horse's shoulder point facing the rear and shorten the off-rein so that the horse's head is bent far to the right and held there. He can thus neither snap at the trainer nor swing his quarters away from him.

For the horse that swings his quarters toward the rider and tries to kick at him, the near rein must be shortened, with the rider standing well forward. In every case the immediate reward in the form of the tidbit is what is important.

It goes without saying that, in mounting any kind of horse, the trainer must make things as pleasant as possible if he expects cooperation from his mount. One cannot expect any animal to remain passive if the rider digs him in the elbow with his toe, yanks the saddle out of place in swinging up, kicks the horse in the flanks with his right foot as he brings it over the animal's rump, or lands with a thump on the horse's kidneys.

Chapter 6

THE SECOND STAGE OF TRAINING

*A*lthough authorities such as Chamberlin, Santini, and Müseler have different opinions as to the final objectives of training the
horse and on details of the position of the rider, they all agree that the
second stage of schooling consists in making the horse obedient to the
natural aids *without collection.*

The goals at this stage should be to teach the horse the following:
to move forward willingly at the behest of the rider's legs; to reach
well under him with his hind legs and well forward with his forelegs;
to extend his head and neck, with his balance largely on his forehand;
to go on the bit at the walk, the slow trot, the ordinary trot, and the
ordinary gallop; and to be confirmed on these gaits on the normal
rein with normal tension, the long (stretched) rein with light tension,
and the floating rein. He should be taught to travel on straight lines,
keeping his body in a straight line, except at the gallop. (Keeping
the body in a perfectly straight line at the gallop is a difficult exercise
and should not be demanded until later in the training program.)
He should be able to turn in large circles at the different gaits, following the direction of the movement, with his spine, beginning at
the poll, bent on the circle; his head turned so that he can look in the
direction in which he is going; and his hindquarters tracking the forelegs. He should obey the leading and the indirect rein effects (see
pages 217 to 219) with his back in a straight line, and he should obey
the bilateral and unilateral leg and weight aids (pages 213 and 214),
enabling the rider to range the haunches to either side or to keep them
in line with the forehand. The horse should know how to increase or

66

decrease the rate of speed, to change from one gait to another, and to come to a halt calmly and without excitement.

An indoor hall is very valuable at this stage of training. The horse is more attentive when his horizon is limited. The sides of the hall may be marked with letters and the overhead trusses or supports may be utilized by the rider as guides in riding on straight lines, and also as limiting points in describing circles. In addition, by studying the prints of his horse's feet on the newly raked surface, the rider can determine whether or not the hindquarters are really tracking the forehand, and what the overreach is at the different gaits. If no indoor arena is available, the fence of the outdoor ring may be marked and the rider can watch these marks as he rides, but this method is not as satisfactory.

THE SYSTEM OF REWARD AND PUNISHMENT

Now is the time especially to keep in mind the fact that a horse can and should be taught not only to respect the trainer but to have confidence in him, and to depend on the firm feel of the bit as well as on the steadying of the trainer's legs in moments of stress and excitement. This can only be accomplished if the lessons are painless and pleasant, and are never carried to the point where the horse becomes bored or restive. In the early stages of training, when the trainer was on foot and the horse was being longed or driven on long reins, he was never disciplined or made uncomfortable unless he demanded such treatment by disobedience, but when training under the saddle begins, the horse is at the mercy of the careless rider. The rider whose shoulders and elbows are not relaxed and whose wrists and fingers are rigid, punishes his horse at every stride, except when he is riding on a floating rein, for by failing to follow the oscillations of the horse's head, he jabs the tender bars of the mouth. The rider who cannot maintain contact with his saddle at the slow trot, and who exaggerates his posting, springing too high and landing roughly, punishes his horse on the loins. Such riders should never attempt to train a green horse.

Our young horse is now accustomed to the feel of the rider on his back. He will move forward, turn, and stop without excitement, but he is still awkward. The trainer, up to this point, has relied on the already-learned voice commands, assisted by a lightly active hand (see pages 233 and 234), in asking the horse to halt, and on a light use of the direct rein in asking him to turn. The time has now come to teach the horse to seek and accept the bit; to prefer a light tension on the rein, and to depend upon it at the faster gaits; to lower and extend his head and neck, "reaching for the ground"; to accept the pressure of the legs and to understand it; to obey the use of the rider's weight, both as a ballast and as a command; and to move forward, to halt, or to turn easily.

The system of "reward and punishment" should be strictly adhered to, in this as in the later stages of training. When mounted, lift your reins and slightly increase the tension on them to attract the horse's attention. Ask the horse to move forward, then squeeze your legs very gently, and brace your back (see page 214) for an instant. These movements, in asking the horse to move forward, constitute the "punishment." The instant the horse obeys, the back and leg aids are relaxed, and the hand follows the movement of the head of the animal in motion, the elbows opening and closing smoothly, the fingers and wrists relaxed. This constitutes the "reward." Make every effort to maintain a light contact with the horse's mouth. In reducing the gait, use an active hand (the punishment) followed by a relaxed, following or passive hand (the reward). The important thing is to reward the horse's obedience the instant he begins to obey, not to wait until the turn, change of gait, or halt has been completed. After each halt, pat the horse and drop the reins for a moment, then move off in a different direction. If the horse chews the bit and drops his head, he is relaxed, but if he fights the rider's hands, tries to spit the bit out, tosses his head, or switches his tail violently, he is uncomfortable. In this case, it might be wise to go back to the long-rein driving in the bit, using the hackamore for the mounted work.

USE OF THE LEGS

As the hands are passive except when rating the horse or turning, and then are only lightly active, it follows that the real work of getting the horse to accept the bit and to push forward with free-swinging, cadenced strides rests on the trainer's ability to use his legs and his weight properly. Closing the legs on the horse's sides tells the horse to move on. Pushing or "bracing" the back also encourages him to stride out. If you weight one stirrup, closing your legs as the fore-leg of the horse on that side is planted, lessening the pressure on the other stirrup and pushing that foot a little forward as the horse's shoulder moves forward, it will help both to cadence and to extend the stride of the horse. This is called "walking with the horse." The horse in the early stages of training may be asked to go at the extended walk for a few strides, but for only a few, as this is a tiring exercise, requiring a strong use of the loin muscles. At the ordinary walk, trot, and canter, his energy should be kept up and, particularly if the horse is sluggish, he should be made to work a little faster than he wants to. This puts the horse "on the bit" and improves his responsiveness to the aids. For the horse that is over-sensitive and over-excited, your first goal should be to get him to cadence his strides on the stretched rein and on the floating rein. The work at the slow gaits with a horse of this sort is most important and should not be rushed.

The horse will tend to travel with his hindquarters a little off the track. This is natural in all quadrupeds, but, as time goes on, you can correct this by using the leg on the side toward which the horse is pushing his quarters. The leg should not maintain a steady pressure but should be used lightly and intermittently in cadence with the stride.

WORK ON STRAIGHT LINES

Learning to walk and trot with an even cadence, with his body traveling in a straight line, and squaring his corners at the turns, is one of the most difficult as well as one of the most important lessons for the young horse. In learning this, he must be made to extend his head and neck and to reach for the bit, traveling on his forehand.

The most common mistake made by trainers at this stage is in trying to develop a good head carriage too soon by lightening the forehand or raising the horse's head. Lifting the animal's head with the hands or by the use of check reins does not improve the head carriage. A good head carriage results from good balance, and this begins with the stretching of the loin muscle and a lowering of the croup by the extension and pushing-under of the hind legs. This in turn cannot be done until the horse has first learned to reach for the bit, to push against it, to extend the head and neck, and to take long-reaching strides with the forelegs. If begun too soon, work on collection or vertical flexion produces a horse that drops the bit and gets behind it, that jigs, moves crabwise, tosses his head, backs up and refuses to go forward, or rears. Too much work on lateral flexion before the horse is confirmed on straight lines and large circles leads to the development of a "rubber-necked" animal.

PUTTING THE HORSE ON THE BIT

As time goes on, the trainer should push the horse more and more on the bit, using his leg aids and his back to keep the forward impulse of movement going against what, to the horse, is a contradictory command of the reins. Although the horse should accept the bit and lean a little against it, he should not "bore" on it. A horse that bores is one that pushes against the bit with a hard, "dead" feel, going faster and faster as the rider exerts more tension, overbending his crest and bringing his muzzle in to his chest, or opening his mouth and pushing forward. The rider can tell if the horse is on the bit without boring when he changes from a following to an active or fixed hand to stop or rate the horse. If the horse offers no resistance, he is not boring, even though his head may be low and extended. The old advice, "Ride as though your reins were made of paper," should be kept constantly in mind.

European trainers, especially those of the German and Austrian school, bring out the point that when a horse has been ridden correctly on the bit, he will, if allowed a floating rein, extend his head and neck and "reach for the ground." All authorities agree that free, forward-reaching, energetic strides and a forward extension of the neck and head are the test of whether the horse, at his stage of his training, is being correctly "put to the aids." All agree that this is best attained at the trot. Generally speaking, it is advisable for the trainer to sit the trot, since, by so doing, he is in constant contact with his horse and is therefore able to apply his aids with greater discrimination. It is also advised that the rider sit the trot in teaching the gallop depart, in rating the horse, and in demanding turns. On the other hand, it takes a very expert rider to sit a rough-gaited horse without tiring both himself and his mount.

WORK ON LARGE CIRCLES

When the horse is moving freely, he may be introduced to work on large circles. The purpose of the work on circles is to make the horse flexible in his body, to lengthen and strengthen the muscles of his loins and shoulders, to teach the horse to adjust his balance to the rider's weight on turns, and to make him obedient to the unilateral weight and leg aids.

Some animals—those with much natural impulsion and a certain stiffness of the neck—may begin this work almost at once. Horses that tend to get behind the bit and that have little natural forward impulsion should work longer on straight lines. Horses that are slow in developing physically, that are weedy and narrow-chested, should not be circled too early either. Circling, even on large circles, calls for a redistribution of equilibrium on the part of the horse. He will automatically tend to shorten his strides and slow his cadence. The action of the rider's hands in asking for the turns gives him an excuse for dropping the bit or overflexing the neck laterally. However, for the horse that is strong and perhaps overbalanced on the forehand, or bold and stiff-necked, early work on large circles is very beneficial.

For the sluggard or the over-sensitive horse, the work must be delayed until he is no longer afraid of the bit and will move forward readily on the leg aids. The "volte," or small circle, is used only as a corrective measure at this stage of training. It is the sure way of controlling the "puller" and the runaway. Generally, the leading rein with an active, but never a pulling, hand is used. In emergencies, or with the confirmed outlaw, the "pulley" hand (see page 238) may be used.

Keep in mind the outline of the circle as you describe it and try to follow this outline exactly. In riding two circles with a change of hands between (a figure-eight), keep the circles of equal size and roundness, and see that the horse's body is straightened for an instant at the point where he changes direction. It is better to measure the circle by looking forward or up rather than down on the ground, since lowering the eyes affects the equilibrium of the rider and consequently affects the balance of the horse. Watch the markers which limit the size of the circle. As you go under one marker, fix your eyes on the next, never on the ground and never on the horse, except perhaps for a brief instant to check the position of the animal's neck and head. These circles should not be less than fifty feet in diameter. Begin by using the leading or opening rein with no opposition, with the hand carried forward and a little toward the inside of the circle, working actively in cadence with the horse's stride and ceasing to be active the instant the horse begins to obey. Any straightening of the horse's neck or looking away from the circle to the outside is a disobedience and a sign that the horse is not really obeying the aids of the rider.

The legs are used to keep up the impulsion. If the horse shows no abnormal resistance, the outside leg may be used a little behind the girth to keep the haunches following the track. If the horse tends to be excited and to resist by carrying his head too high, use the inside leg to push his haunches to the outside of the circle. The horse will then have to travel farther with his hind legs than with his forehand and will consequently weight his forehand in order to free the haunches.

Follow the horse's head with your hands. The most common mistake of unskilled riders is in lowering the hand when the horse raises his head. This breaks the required line from elbow to bit and makes a stiff resistance which the horse can fight. Raising the hand and maintaining light contact with the mouth shows the horse that he cannot escape the tension of the bit by raising his head. The minute he gives up fighting and lowers his head, reward him by letting him work for a moment on a floating rein and by patting him. However, there is danger in applying this method of teaching the horse to lower his head if the rider is unskillful or inattentive. If the raised rein is not released the instant the horse *begins* to drop his head, he will not associate the reward of the floating rein with his action of obedience and so will continue to fight the bit. During the work on circles, allowing one hand to act more strongly than the other, "leading" the head in the direction of the movement, or, particularly in a later stage of training, the work on circles with the haunches pushed out, distracts the horse's attention, breaks up his resistance, throws his weight on his forehand, and so encourages him to lower his head.

CADENCE

Learning to maintain an even cadence is extremely important at this stage of the training (see page 68). The unschooled horse moves forward in fits and starts. He weaves from side to side in an effort to keep his balance under the unaccustomed burden of the rider. If he is nervous, he may take out his nervousness in short, snappy strides. A flat-footed, evenly cadenced walk is the hardest of the gaits for the youngster to master. Working him with an older horse that has perfected such a walk is often very helpful. The young horse will copy the manners and methods of the older animal, and the presence of the other horse will give him confidence in himself. Riding to music at the trot and the canter will also help to cadence the strides of the horse. Horses have a good sense of rhythm, and it is interesting to note how they will change cadence voluntarily when the music changes.

In certain instances, listening to the cadence of the horse's stride will help the rider to apply his aids at the desired moment. This is true in demanding gallop departs and the change of lead. Do not use any of the aids with constant tension, but be sure to keep repeated vibrations of the hands and the intermittent squeezings of the legs in cadence with the stride.

RATING THE HORSE

Regulating the gait of the horse is known as "rating" him. This exercise is of the utmost importance in training any horse that is to be used for jumping, hunting, or polo; yet it is one which is often completely ignored and neglected. Most trainers of steeplechasers give almost no attention to this important lesson; yet history shows that such contests as the Maryland Hunt Cup and the English Grand

National are nearly always won by horses that have been schooled to carry ladies to hounds, and that have therefore been taught to rate. In a race over jumps or a point-to-point, the horse so schooled can be readily made to save himself or expend himself at the rider's will, to be easily maneuverable on sharp turns and over difficult obstacles. No wonder it is the quiet "ladies' hunter" that shows up the average steeplechaser!

Halting with the Fixed Hand

The work on rating begins at the walk. The goal is to teach the horse to slow his gait or to come to a halt from any gait with no resist- ance and at a very slight indication on the part of the rider. The horse is put into motion on the bit. When he is walking freely, the rider fixes his hands, braces his back, and slightly increases the leg pressure. The effect of this is to push the horse forward from behind but, at the same time, to restrain the forward movement by the fixing of the hand. The horse pushes himself against the bit and, on meeting this opposition, he stops. By stopping in this manner, it will be found that he has stopped in balance, and can move off in any direction without having to shift his weight.

The principle of the fixed hand must be clearly understood by the rider. He does not oppose the forward movement by pulling; he simply keeps his hand in one position, and the forward movement of the horse, plus the oscillations of his head, cause the horse to push against the hand. It may clarify this point to state that if the hand were a pulling hand and the rein were to be cut, the rider's hands would keep on moving backwards. With a fixed hand, however, cut- ting of the rein would in no way affect the position of the hand. Great delicacy must be used in the employment of the fixed hand, which should be instantly relaxed when the horse *begins* to slow down or stop. There should be no tension on the rein at the cessation of move- ment. The horse must learn to obey willingly, not by force. When the horse comes to a stop, drop the reins on his neck for a moment and pat him, then pick up the reins again and move out at the walk for perhaps ten steps before asking again for a halt. This exercise should be repeated again and again in every lesson period, after the work on straight lines and circles at the walk and trot have calmed the horse and brought him to attention. The rider must become more and more particular in demanding the halt. He should decide on dif- ferent points around the hall where his horse will stop. The first few times he may have to begin asking for the halt some little distance from these points, but eventually he should be able to give his signal for the halt at a distance of less than a foot from the spot where he wishes to be when halted.

Halting with the Active Hand

The horse can also be halted with the active instead of the fixed hand. In this case both reins are used in "direct opposition" (see page 224), but only for an instant. They are released and the signal is given again, thus slowing the horse up gradually but without pulling him in by main force. In using the hands, turn them with palms up, little fingers raised toward the chin. The period of the halt should be decreased more and more in length until it lasts only a fraction of a second. Eventually the halt can be changed to a half-halt (see page 93), but both movements should be practiced.

Advanced Rating

The next step is to put the horse into the slow trot, and from that to decrease to a walk, and then to a halt, rewarding the horse by patting him while he is standing with the rein dropped. Then progress from the halt through the walk and slow trot to the ordinary trot and back to the halt. This step in training takes a long time. The bold horse is reluctant to return immediately to the slower gaits on a light application of the aids. The horse should be worked on straight lines and also on big circles. As he becomes more and more obedient, reduce the number of walking steps until the horse can be asked to take up the slow trot directly from the halt and to halt from the slow trot. The slow gallop (canter) can now be included in these rating exercises, the progression being halt, walk, slow trot, trot, canter, trot, slow trot, walk, halt. When this is performed smoothly, the lesson of taking up the slow trot from the halt and returning to it can be combined with the progression through the trot to the canter and back. Only when this is smooth can the rider begin teaching the horse to halt directly from the ordinary trot, and finally to halt from the canter and take up the canter again from the halt, or to back a few steps and take up the canter immediately without a forward step.

It must be emphasized again that these lessons should be repeated over and over, but not to the point where the horse becomes bored. Calmness, attentiveness and obedience are what the trainer is striving to develop in his horse, and these *must* be preserved.

THE INDIRECT REIN

When the horse has become obedient to the leading rein in turning and to the direct reins of opposition, he may be taught the use of the indirect rein effect. The horse learns this rein effect very easily. The leg aids and the placing of the rider's weight assist the horse to understand, and the leading rein can, in the early stages of the training, give the signal to start the turn. In riding in a hall with rounded corners, the indirect rein and the inside leg push the horse against the wall at the corners and make him flex his body to the curve. This is also the introductory exercise to the "shoulder-in" movement, discussed on page 113.

WORK OUT OF DOORS

When the weather is good, the young horse in his secondary stage of training should receive a good deal of work on trails and through fields. This will keep him interested and will give the trainer a chance to discover just how successful he has been in obtaining cooperation and attention from his mount at the different gaits and in the face of distractions or things that might frighten him. At first, the horse should have the company of an older horse to steady him and make him willing. Do not, however, make the mistake of allowing the older horse always to lead—past objects that are terrifying to the colt, yes, but otherwise, the young horse should be taught to stride out on his own and to be bold. Another great advantage of outdoor work is that it muscles and supples the horse's body and develops his stamina. Slow work up and down hill is particularly beneficial to the loins and hocks of the horse. The question may sometime arise as to how steep a hill a horse may be asked to negotiate while carrying a rider. The old rule is that any grade which is not too steep for a man on foot to climb or descend without using his hands to balance himself is within the powers of the horse to negotiate while carrying a rider. It is assumed that the rider knows enough to leave the animal's head perfectly free and to balance all his weight on the forehand when going either up or down hill.

In turning toward home, the horse should be kept at the free-striding walk. This will bring him in cool and will teach him not to rush for the stable. If the distance is so far that the horse cannot keep the walk all the way, he should be walked when first turned toward home, allowed to trot awhile, then brought back to the walk, and walked for the last mile. He should not be galloped. No gait should be maintained for more than seven or eight minutes without changing to another gait or giving the horse a rest on a floating rein, and the horse must never be ridden so long or so far that he becomes exhausted.

FIRST STEPS IN THE GALLOP DEPART

Although the gallop as a gait has already been mentioned in relation to the exercises of circling and rating the horse, no detailed description of how he is to be put into the gallop has yet been given. The slow gallop (canter) is an exciting gait for the young horse, and he should be eased into it gently. Do not attempt to teach the gallop depart from a walk or halt at this stage of the training; rather, let the horse take it up from the trot. Thus he can be led into it, hardly aware that he is changing gaits.

General Chamberlin suggests two ways of accomplishing this. In the first method, the rider turns the horse's head very slightly to the outside of the circle—to the right if the horse is moving on the left track, to the left if he is moving on the right. If the horse is moving on the left track, turning his head to the right impedes his right shoulder and frees the left. The rider then applies his right leg behind the girth and pushes the haunches off the track toward the center. The rider's weight is carried to the left. The rider should post on the outside (in this case, the right) diagonal, and should use his aids as he settles into the saddle. If sitting the trot, he should use the aids as the inside shoulder moves forward. If the trainer makes the mistake of turning the horse's head too far to the right, the horse will push his left shoulder forward to maintain his balance, and the result will be a false lead.

The second method is almost the same, except that both the hands and the weight are carried forward and to the left as the leg aids are applied. The most common error here is for the rider to throw his weight over the inside shoulder to such an extent that, instead of over-balancing the colt in that direction, he weights the shoulder.

Neither of these methods of asking for a gallop depart is in any way desirable as an end in itself. They are merely the simplest means of getting a green horse into the gallop on the correct lead without excitement. The gallop depart is demanded first on circles, next on the return to the wall after crossing the hall, and finally on straight lines. Since the rider is more in contact with his horse at the sitting trot than at the posting trot, and is able to use his aids more delicately and more harmoniously, he should try to be sitting at the trot when asking for this type of gallop depart. However, if he is confused as to exactly when in the stride he should give the aids, he had better post and remember to use them just as he is settling in the saddle and the outside foreleg is being planted.

LEG-YIELDING

The exercise of "Leg-yielding" recommended by German train-ers helps make the horse responsive to the unilateral leg aids and prepares him for more advanced training. In this exercise the horse's head is turned toward the wall and the hindquarters are pushed to the inside by the action of the rider's outside leg. The rider moves the horse along the wall as shown in Figure 37. The right leg is active in

Fig. 37.   Leg-yielding.

cadence with the stride, and the right leading rein turns the horse's head toward the wall. The wall acts as a barrier preventing the horse from moving forwards, as he must move a little to the side. The angle formed by the horse's body and the wall should not be too wide.

This exercise is not designed to flex the horse's whole body as does the more difficult and advanced movement of the shoulder-in (page 113); it is simply designed to make the horse responsive to the unilateral action of the legs, thus making it possible for the rider to mobilize the haunches at will. The action of the legs should, as always, be intermittent and in cadence with the stride, and an active, not a pulling, hand is used to restrain the horse's head. It goes without saying that the horse must be worked equally in both directions and that he is given this exercise only at the walk until he can execute it calmly. Then the slow trot can be introduced.

DEFENSES AND VICES COMMON AT THIS STAGE

Should the horse show resistance to the progressively active hand demanding the halt, his head can be turned a little to one side or the

FIG. 38.   The sliding rein.

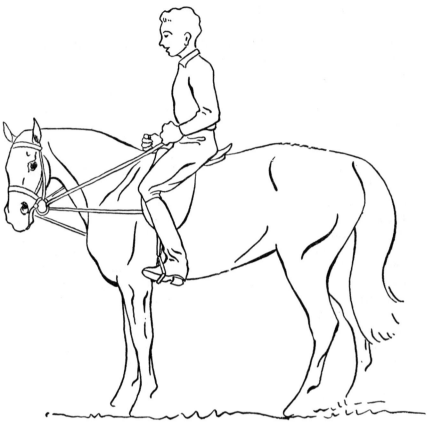

FIG. 39.   The sliding rein used for lateral flexion.

other. This will counteract the resistance by changing the position of
the bit and makes it possible for the trainer to use a lighter hand. For
the horse that, from previous schooling or from bad conformation,
absolutely refuses to flex his poll, a sliding rein (Figures 38, 39), can
be tried. This rein should be used with great care, and only if other
methods have proved inadequate. The hand should be as light as
possible, and must be relaxed the instant flexion is obtained.

To correct lateral stiffness, put the horse through the exercises
recommended on page 103.

Jogging and Refusing to Step Out at the Walk

To correct these faults, the horse must be halted and held at attention. Use your legs strongly to force the horse's hind legs forward
and restrain his forward movement with your hands. The hands fol-

low the movement of the head, but the horse must be induced to push against the bit hard. If he raises his head to get away from the bit, raise your hand, keep contact, and push hard with your legs. Each time he breaks the stride, halt the horse again, and cause him to move forward on the bit. Most riders think that by loosening the reins they can induce the horse to lower his head and accept the bit, but the contrary is true. The horse must be made to push into the bit through a steady feel on the reins plus great impulsion of the hindquarters.

Refusing to Move Out

This vice is usually found in spoiled horses rather than in young ones. Some horses back up when the rider uses his legs; others just stand still. Some buck; some rear. It is a vice often displayed when the horse is asked to do something he doesn't want to do or something he fears. The horse that has been trained thoroughly in easy stages to respond immediately to the pressure of the rider's legs will never develop these vices, but they are very common in horses that have been incorrectly trained, and nearly every trainer finds himself faced with such a problem at some time or other.

The most important factor in breaking a horse of this vice is the trainer's determination to make his horse go forward, in one way or another. The second necessary factor is the trainer's control over his temper. Punishment may have to be used, but it should not be angry punishment. The horse must understand that the rider's will is stronger than his own, and that the trainer is in complete control of the situation, which he will not be if he is goaded into losing his temper.

The methods employed to correct these vices are used one after the other, in regular succession according to their severity, beginning with the mildest.

The horse that is backing away, or that, through stubbornness rather than fear, is bracing his legs against moving forward, may be asked to leave the stable alone, to take a turn that leads away from home, or to move away from his companions who are lined up in the middle of the show ring, and take the track by himself. The rider should first shorten his rein and try to push the horse forward with his legs. If this fails, use a strong leading rein, bending the animal's head sharply to the right or left, and then, using the outside leg vigorously, cause the horse to turn in small circles until he is slightly dizzy. Straightening his head, together with a vigorous use of both spurs, will usually move him forward. Another method is to use a schooling whip hard behind the buttocks. Once moving, the animal must on no account be permitted to stop, or it will be all to do over again.

For the horse with the vice of rearing, it is best to loosen the rein, throwing the weight forward, and, at the same time, using both the spurs and the whip. Or turn him in very close circles, bringing the horse's head around to your toe before he can get off the ground.

For the horse that refuses to go forward because of fright, the approach is somewhat different. Here the trainer must count on his ability to gain the horse's confidence by talking to the animal in a quiet and soothing voice. If it is water or a rough place that the horse fears, get him as near to the edge of the feared object or area as possible, and give him all the time he wants to smell it and investigate it. Use the aids only to keep the horse facing the terrain of which he is afraid or the direction in which he is to go. If there is an older horse along, by all means let him go first, and in all probability, the youngster will follow behind. Quiet persistence, and gentle yet firm use of the aids, should prevail. Take care not to put that particular horse in a similar situation until he has become better confirmed on the bit and the leg aids.

If the horse has been taught the shoulder-in movement (page 113), put him into this movement, keeping in the shoulder away from the object being passed. His head will thus be turned away from the thing he fears and the lateral flexion of his body will break up his resistance.

Most of these habits and vices are not the fault of the horse but of hurried or unskillful schooling. This is particularly true of horses that display such vices when entering the jumping ring. In every case the cause can be traced to the trainer, who has either caused the animal pain or has asked him to jump obstacles for which he was not yet ready.

Uneven Cadence at the Various Gaits

This fault can be caused by improper shoeing, lameness, nervousness, too much feed and too little work, or insufficient schooling at the slow gaits on straight lines and large circles. If the horse is sound, well shod, well fitted as to saddle and bridle, well worked out, and ridden by a good rider who is not making him uncomfortable, yet he continues to bounce and break his cadence, the trainer will have to go back a few steps in his schooling and devote more time to getting the horse to extend his neck and take the bit. In later schooling, the shoulder-in movement can be employed to calm and distract him.

Traveling Crabwise

This fault can be cured as soon as the horse understands and obeys the indirect rein. He should have work on straight lines along a wall if possible. At the corners, the indirect rein becomes the leading rein for an instant to cause the horse to change direction, but again is applied indirectly together with the inside leg aid to push the horse into the corner on the turn. The shoulder-in movement can be used to advantage with horses that have learned it and is very helpful in correcting a horse's tendency to swing the haunches off the track and move crabwise. For horses with this vice, the gallop depart should be taught with diagonal aids as early as possible in the training, since the lateral aids will only accentuate the tendency.

Tossing the Head

This is a very common vice, most often caused by wolf teeth, a too-heavy bit, a badly adjusted curb chain, heavy or unresponsive hands of the rider, insufficient work, general nervousness, or insufficient education in going on the bit. When the habit has become a vice, the horse resorts to it as a defense. Attaching side reins to the girth is sometimes effective in breaking the animal of this vice. A better method is to take the bit away entirely and go back to work on the longe in a hackamore and on long reins, followed by work on circles ranging the haunches out. These methods, however, take time. Martingales should not be used since they do not really prevent the animal from tossing his head and are a serious restriction in jumping.

Refusal to Stay Out to the Wall, Refusal To Turn Square Corners, Cutting the Corners

The horse that has these vices must first be made responsive to the bit and legs. He can then be cured by a stronger use of the inside leg coupled with the indirect rein effect. Riding in pairs with a quiet horse on the inside will calm him and give him confidence, but the inside horse must be kept about six inches behind the nervous horse at the turns; otherwise the nervous animal will be frightened and will back away.

Too Much Weight on the Forehand

Pay no attention to this habit in a colt. If the mature horse that has been under the saddle for some time has this defect, he must receive a thorough schooling in light and intermediate dressage, with particular attention to those movements which throw the weight on the haunches, such as the half-halt, circles and turns on the haunches, and the pirouettes.

Chapter 7

THE THIRD STAGE OF TRAINING

The purpose of all dressage or training, beginning with the first steps of teaching the horse to go on the bit and extend himself, is to make the horse "agreeable" to ride, i.e., keen, but submissive, and to make him athletically strong. There must be freedom in his paces; grace, lightness, and ease in his movements; and above all, harmony with his rider. His body must be straight from poll to tail when executing movements that require that he be straight, and bent symmetrically in the direction of the movement when executing figures on curves. His cadence must be even and smooth. His changes from one gait or speed of gait to another must be smooth and exact. He must be calm and relaxed and must show no sign of resistance. He should execute the movements as demanded by the rider with no obvious commands.

COLLECTION

We now come to the point at which the advocates of the various systems of training the horse part company. Santini, as representative of the Italian system, teaches that the cross-country horse, in which he is primarily interested, should be trained only on the stretched rein, with the balance on the forehand. He states that there is no possible reason for asking that a horse reduce the speed of his natural gait— that all animals are by nature balanced, and that man can do nothing to improve that balance.

The American system, which is based on the French system as taught at Saumur, and whose best-known authority is General Chamberlin, teaches that all field horses—hunters, hacks, jumpers, and polo ponies—need to be "lightly collected"; that, just as a boxer or ballet dancer improves his natural balance and agility by gymnastic exercises, so the horse, in undergoing a system of training which includes certain schooled movements, will improve his carriage, his balance, his obedience, and his agility.

The German system, as advocated by Müseler, has the same objective as the American system—to produce a horse and rider in perfect harmony with each other. Müseler puts more emphasis on collection than does Chamberlin, but continually reiterates that the horse must at all times be calm and relaxed. Since the German school of riding is very much interested, not only in intermediate dressage, but also in heavy dressage and *haute école* training, it is understandable that Müseler desires more collection than does the trainer whose objective is cross-country work alone. Chamberlin, in commenting on heavy dressage and *haute école*, recommends this training very highly from the point of view of developing the rider, but does not feel it is essential for the field horse.

Still another point of view is represented by the "Old Timer," the advocate of the Western or cowboy method of training a horse. "What's all this fancy stuff for?" he asks in his articles in *The Horse*. "If you want to teach a cow pony to turn, turn him. If you want to teach him to back, back him. Ain't no use in all this other stuff. If them methods was good they'd have the best horses, their horses would be the highest jumpers. Where are these fancy horses?" So says the "Old Timer," who can hardly be said to have a "system," but who might be compared to the musician of talent who plays by ear and feels that any more exact knowledge of music is unnecessary. Of course, the answer to his question, "Where are these horses that ought to be so good?" is "In the Olympics and other international competitions," where the system of careful training in flexible, calm obedience proves its worth.

The German, Italian, and American or French systems often are not as far apart in their goals and methods as the casual reader might think. For example, although Santini states in his book *The Forward Impulse* that *il systema* employs an entirely new method of using the hands and reins, and that it is on this method that the Italian forward-seat position depends, a study of his book and the diagrams in it shows that what he is advocating is a passive or following hand when the horse is going at the desired gait and rate in the desired direction, and an active hand when the horse is to be asked to do something different. These methods of using the hands are well recognized and agree with the principles of many other riding masters, German, American, and French.

Training the Horse

The Italian method of assuming a forward position over jumps was a real contribution to horsemanship, and has been adopted by virtually all schools of riding. Taking the weight off the back and putting it on the forehand while giving the horse a free use of his head and neck is the basic principle of the forward seat. The American jockey, Ted Sloan, was the first to use this position in flat racing. The Italian Caprilli spent his lifetime studying the movements of the horse at liberty and figuring out how the rider might ride and give his horse the most possible freedom. He developed the forward position from his studies, and Santini's writings popularized this seat. The analysis of the forward, balanced, and classical or academic seats is given in Part II, Chapter I, pages 168 to 171.

In his book *Training Hunters, Jumpers, and Hacks*, General Chamberlin says that the extreme or heavy collection, in which the croup is lowered and the head is brought to a vertical position, should not be used in training the cross-country horse and the jumper, as it tends to shorten their strides and take away impulsion. Yet, the pictures of both the shoulder-in movement and the two-track which appear in his book show the collected horse. One is led to believe, therefore, that what General Chamberlin really means is that the horse, though trained to be collected at the behest of the rider for the purpose of executing certain movements, should not always be so ridden. He does not, as some of his readers feel, deny the value of collection.

The most famous exponents of the *haute école* are, of course, the horsemen of the Spanish Riding School of Vienna. Careful study of their method of training shows that, although they do demand high collection when executing both the school figures and the *haute école* figures, at the commencement of every training period, the horses enter the ring on stretched reins and are ridden so for at least fifteen minutes, head and neck extended, legs low and reaching forward. There is no indication of a lack of forward impulse in these horses when they are ridden in this manner; they do not wait for the rider to urge them on, but extend themselves of their own accord. When collected there is no sign of stiffness anywhere in the horse— not in the poll, the jaw, the loin, or the croup. Obviously no strong tension of the reins is necessary at any time, even in off-the-ground movements such as the levade, where the horse puts all his balance on his haunches and holds the position shown in Plate XIV. The reproduction of the print of the early rider shown in Plate X depicts the horse doing the levade in full collection, but with the reins floating.

In comparing the results of the systems of training in relation to the field horse and the open jumper, it is interesting to note that only once has Italy placed first in the Olympic trials. That was in the Prix des Nations individual high jumping contest in 1920, when Lt. Lequio on Trebecco captured the first award. In 1924 Italy placed second with the same horse and rider in the same competition; eleventh, twelfth, and twenty-fourth in the Prix des Nations; and fourteenth and twenty-third in the Three-day Event. In 1932 she did not compete. In 1936 she placed fifteenth in the Prix des Nations. That year none of her horses competed in the Three-day Event. Germany, France, Sweden, Holland, and the United States have all placed consistently in the first three places between 1912 and 1936, with Mexico coming to the fore in 1948. All of these nations emphasize the importance of improving the horse's natural balance, agility, and muscular strength through the application of the principles of collection and dressage. One is led to suppose, then, that *il systema*, correct and important as we know it to be in regard to the rider's position and the horse's balance in cross-country work and over jumps, is not, by itself, so successful when it comes to preparing the horse for competition in these fields. The Mexicans, who certainly have been outstanding recently in international competition, exemplify the application of a system which combines the forward impulse in jumping with a great deal of dressage training, in both the preparatory training and the daily exercising of the horses.

Variations in Terminology

In studying the works of various authorities, one is struck by the wide variety of terms used, and the lack of clear definition of these terms. This accounts for much apparent disagreement which is really not disagreement at all.

Let us take the word collection. Chamberlin refers to "light" or "natural" collection and to "heavy" collection. Other authorities use the expressions "to gather," "to put the horse on the aids," "to get the horse in hand," "to get the horse between the rider's hands and legs," or "to bring the horse to attention." All these terms mean collecting the horse to some degree. Yet to the layman they might each be expressing a completely different idea; hence confusion results.

As we have seen, the degree of collection demanded at any given time depends on the type of movement being executed and on the stage of training of the horse. Rather than setting rules of desired position of the animal's head, neck, or croup, one should follow Müseler's principle. He draws attention to the fact that when a horse

86

is properly "put to the aids" (collected, gathered, in hand, etc.), the observer should see the horse and the rider together as a harmonious whole. The rider should be quiet, supple, and in continuous and light contact with his horse, both through his reins and through his legs. Certainly this agrees with all other authorities, although they may express themselves differently. Müseller says that the horse must show quiet, regular, and lively steps; and complete relaxation and acceptance of the bit, his head carried quietly, his body on a straight line when traveling on straight lines, his head and neck turned slightly inward when traveling in a curved line. The rider thus in harmony with his horse is enabled both to feel what his mount is doing and to influence him with the least amount of effort. Harmony between horse and rider is the principle emphasized by this authority, and one which is generally omitted in the mind and eye of the average observer.

One frequently hears the expression "on the aids," and there may be some confusion in the horseman's mind as to exactly what this term means. One cannot state that a horse in a certain degree of collection is "on the aids," since horses may be on the aids at extended as well as collected gaits. One cannot say that a horse taking a feel of the bit is necessarily "on the aids," since a horse that bores and pushes against the bit is certainly not "on the aids." Nor can one say that a horse that is very "leg-worthy" and goes forward at the slightest touch is "on the aids," for such a horse might also be a runaway. A horse that is "on the aids" responds to the desires of the rider as expressed to him through an application of the aids which does not entail force. Such a horse is obedient in increasing and decreasing the gaits, starting and stopping, turning, backing, and performing whatever other movements he has been taught. The strength with which the aids are used will depend on the sensitivity of the horse, but the horse that needs to be kicked to increase his speed, pulled up sharply to decrease it, or who resists the attempts of the rider to turn him, is not "on the aids." In like manner, a horse may give the appearance of being ridden so lightly that he is not on the aids, but if he will halt and turn with a delicate shifting of the rider's weight or a momentary use of his back, the horse is certainly on the aids.

DRESSAGE

Another often misconstrued word is the term "dressage." To some this means a series of special, difficult, and, to them, artificial movements in which the horse is trained for the specific purpose of

87

giving exhibitions or competing in shows or meets such as the Olympic Games. To some, "dressage" means *haute école* training only. The literal translation of the word "dressage" is "training." Light dressage, or early training, comprises making the horse obedient to the rider on straight lines and large circles, as described in Chapter VI. General Chamberlin uses the term "breaking" to denote this period in the education of the horse. Müseler calls it "putting the horse to the aids," i.e., getting the horse to accept the rider's legs, weight, and hands. "Intermediate dressage" or training, as opposed to "breaking," consists of not only getting the horse to accept the rider's aids but of making him obedient to them by means of certain schooling figures such as the pivots on the forehand, pivots on the haunches, half-turns, half-turns in reverse, turns and circles on the forehand and haunches, the serpentine, the broken lines, the voltes (small circles), the two-track (half-pass), the travers (pass), the renvers, the shoulder-in, the zig-zag (counter-change of hands on the two-track), the remener (placing of the head), the extension and collection of gaits, the gallop depart with the diagonal and outside lateral aids or the inside lateral aids on circles and straight lines, the false gallop, and the half-halt. Some include the pirouette and the change of lead in this category. Others place them with the advanced (heavy) dressage or *haute école* movements such as the passage, the piaffe, and the above-the-ground movements taught by the Spanish Riding School— the levade, the croupade, the corbette, the ballotade, the capriole, and others. The 1948 Individual Dressage Test did not include the piaffe or the passage, but it did include the pirouette, the change of lead at every stride, and the false gallop.

Dressage training as described by most authorities does not include the "circus" or trick type of movement, such as the Spanish walk and trot with extreme forward and horizontal extension of the forelegs or the three-step. A few authors such as Beudant, a French writer, do include the artificial movements in dressage training, but most authorities draw the line between the movements that a horse at liberty will execute and those which are contrary to nature. Their contention is that all the movements of the three stages of dressage training as they advocate it, even such movements as the levade and capriole, are natural; that the horse knows how to make these movements of his own free will; but that in order to utilize them as gymnastic exercises, he must be taught to execute them at the behest of the rider, who must learn how to demand them and how to get a harmonious performance from the horse in their execution.

General Chamberlin describes a number of cardinal principles

88

which should be observed in this stage of training the horse to be flex ible and balanced, principles which are advocated by many authori ties but frequently forgotten by the average rider. The first is that it is not the actual execution of a movement which is important but the horse's attitude in executing it—his lack of stiffness and resistance. A second important principle in all the schooling is the preservation of the horse's forward impulsion. He must invariably go forward in re sponse to the rider's legs. If he has been well schooled in this, the maintenance of his cadence and speed on turns and difficult move ments will be at the disposal of the rider.

General Chamberlin admonishes the trainer never to start teach ing a new movement at the beginning of a training period but to put the horse through the lessons he has already learned, waiting until he is worked out, relaxed, and calm before beginning something new. If, in beginning a new movement, the horse shows much excitement and refuses to be calmed, the general inference is that his previous training has not been sufficiently thorough, and that he should be re turned to simpler work. Very early writers such as Xenophon also un derstood and advocated this principle.

Horses of different temperaments react differently to difficult les sons. Those that are timid by nature are sometimes made more ex citable by movements such as the two-track and the shoulder-in. With horses of this nature, only a step or two at a time should be demanded, and the horse should be rewarded with many pats and a complete relaxation of the aids. Bolder horses, whose inattention and excitement is not due to fear but to high spirits, often can be calmed by being required to execute a difficult movement. This seems to get their attention and gives them something to think about. Some horses will fight the rider stubbornly when asked to perform a new movement. Such horses must not be allowed to win the battle, but, since they are of the type that becomes bored easily, the trainer should take care not to demand too long a period of collection. He should stop his work just before the horse becomes bored and puts up resistance. If the horse is really spoiled, resistance must be met with resistance until the horse finds out that he is not the master.

The real test of the trainer's tact and knowledge is his ability to judge when to introduce new work, when to stop working on a par ticular problem, and how to gauge the progress of his pupil. No horse remains static in his education; he either goes forward or backward. If he is going forward, the trainer must decide whether the progress is normal; if he is retrogressing, the trainer must find out why. Very often, if a horse that has been progressing satisfactorily suddenly has a setback, the cause is sore or tender feet. Any pain causes excitement, and a horse that starts a training period with more than ordinary excitement should be carefully checked physically. It may be no more than a pinching shoe or a badly fitted pad or saddle; it may be a touch of thrush that is not severe enough to cause lameness; it may be a bruised heel or sole; or it may be something really serious.

FLEXION

There are two types of flexion: longitudinal, which includes the vertical flexion of the poll; and lateral flexion. Longitudinal flexion of the horse is attained by the erection of his head, the bending and relaxation of his poll and jaw, the lowering of his croup, and the bringing up of his hind legs under his body. This type of flexion,

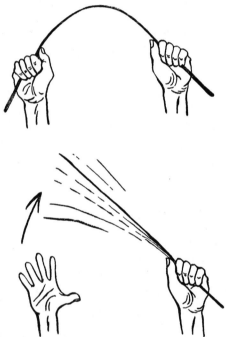

FIG. 40.   Demonstrating the principle of collection with a bent switch.

which embodies the principle of collection in it, can be demonstrated by taking a straight switch and bending the two ends toward each other as shown in Figure 40. Power is thus put at the disposal of the holder. The switch becomes a spring, and if either end is released, there is impulsion in that direction. In a similar manner, when the horse is put to the aids and is held between the rider's hands and legs, his longitudinal axis is shortened by this collection, just as was the longitudinal axis of the switch, and his forces are thereby put at the disposal of the rider (Figure 41). The rider can ask his mount to move in any direction, to increase, decrease, or change his gait, or to halt. The horse, being alertly balanced, can obey quickly and easily.

In lateral flexion, the horse is taught to be supple in neck, ribs, loin, and haunches. His changes of direction become fluid and smooth instead of rough and jerky. His muscles are stretched and strengthened, particularly the long muscle of the loin, which influences all the other muscles.

In addition to flexion, the horse must learn mobility of the haunches and forehand. The rider must be able to move either the forehand or the hindquarters of the horse in any direction, without the opposite half moving with it. He must gain obedience of each individual leg so that he can command its movements as he wishes. It is this that enables him to cause the horse to execute such movements as the two-track.

SCHOOLING MOVEMENTS TO DEVELOP LONGITUDINAL FLEXION

The exercises described in Part I, Chapter VI, pages 72 to 74, for increasing and decreasing the gaits and for starting from a halt on the various gaits are the most important and useful exercises for improving the longitudinal flexion of the horse. The greatest mistake made by mediocre horsemen is to suppose that the horse's head carriage, balance, and longitudinal flexion can be improved by pulling on the reins. The valuable work of teaching the horse to extend and collect the gaits too often is wasted because the trainer does not understand the principle of the application of the aids to decrease the gait and to halt. It must be clearly understood that it is the activity of the rider's legs and weight which drives the horse on to the bit. There he finds himself opposed by the rider's fixed hand, and, meeting this resistance, he decreases the gait or stops. Without the activity of the legs and weight, the horse will not oppose the hand. If the rider brings him to a halt on the bit by the hands alone he is using a pulling hand to do so. Although the horse may stop, he will not do so correctly, with his legs under him and his head and neck in a good position. The young horse is stopped with an active instead of a fixed hand and without the use of the legs, but this is only the elementary training, and no attempt is being made at this time to improve the longitudinal flexion. If this exercise is to be of value in improving flexion, the trainer must understand the principle of the active legs

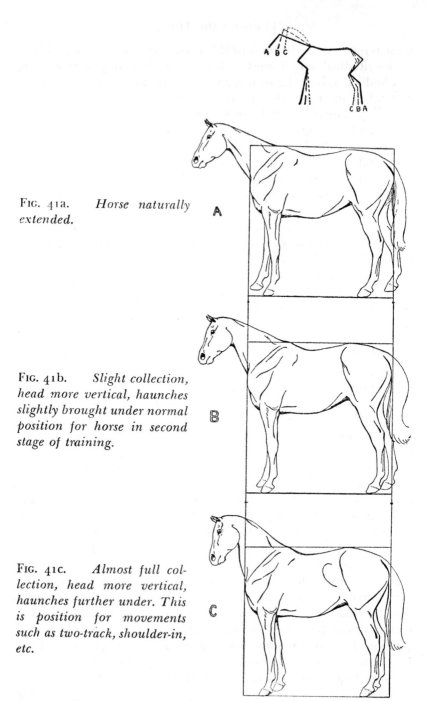

FIG. 41a.   *Horse naturally extended.*

A

FIG. 41b.   *Slight collection, head more vertical, haunches slightly brought under normal position for horse in second stage of training.*

B

FIG. 41C.   *Almost full collection, head more vertical, haunches further under. This is position for movements such as two-track, shoulder-in, etc.*

C

FIG. 41.   Longitudinal flexion and collection.

and weight in opposition to the fixed hand. He must apply this each time he asks the horse to decrease his gait. He must use the active legs with the following hand to demand the extension of gait. He must realize that in both extending and collecting, in decreasing and in halting, the legs move the same way—i.e., they urge the horse forward—but the hand, either by opposing the movement or by not opposing it, decides what the horse is to do. Naturally, the fixed hand, which is new to the horse, must be used with great tact. The rider with educated hands knows exactly how long to resist the horse and how much tension to use in this resistance. His hand gives the instant the horse begins to obey, to be fixed again if the movement is not completed correctly. In using the fixed hand, the rider, on feeling the tension of the rein, should ask himself, "If this rein were to be cut, would my hand fly back?" If the answer is "yes," he is using a pulling hand, not a fixed hand.

The use of the loin in demanding forward impulsion is described in detail in Part II, Chapter 8, pages 242 to 243. The reader is urged to study this description and the accompanying diagrams, and to make use of the exercises suggested. He should then try to make his horse more and more responsive to the bracing of the back in opposition to the fixed hand when demanding a decrease in gait and a halt. When the horse will come quietly to a halt from an ordinary walk on the demand of the briefly braced back and the fixed hand, with his croup lowered, his legs under him, his head brought in almost to the vertical (but never beyond it), his jaw light and relaxed; when the horse will do this calmly and gracefully, the trainer knows that the animal is well flexed longitudinally and that he is properly "put to the aids."

The Half-halt

Another extremely valuable exercise for improving collection and vertical flexion is the half-halt. This movement is used a great deal more in the German system than in other methods, but all authorities except the Italians include it in training. The Germans use it as a preliminary movement before asking the horse to change direction, gait, speed, or to execute a new movement of any kind. It is like saying "Attention!" to the soldier, and serves to put the horse on the aids and to tell him that something new is to be demanded of him.

The half-halt is a momentary pause on the part of the horse, at which time this balance is shifted a little more to the rear. To the onlooker, it is as though the horse had hesitated in his stride, but without losing forward impulsion, and then continued on at the same rate, cadence, and gait as before. The execution is as follows: The trainer fixes his hands and braces his back, squeezing his legs. At the same time, he gives a little upward twist to the hands, bringing the little fingers toward the chest, the palms of the hands turned upward (Figure 42). The instant he feels the horse check, and before he can

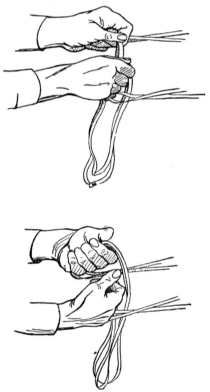

FIG. 42.   Use of the hands in the half-halt.

halt, the trainer's hands become following, and the legs keep up the forward movement. This use of the hands is for the early or elementary stages of training only. Gradually the aids are refined until the rider can demand and achieve a half-halt at any gait with only the briefest tightening of the fingers and a single bracing of the back. The half-halt may be demanded with both reins, or with one only. It may be used not only to bring the horse to attention, but also to steady the overambitious horse. In the latter case, one rein only, usually the outside rein, is used. The half-halt may be used also to correct the head carriage of a horse that likes to travel on straight lines with

94

his head bent to one side. Frequent half-halts given on the side away from that toward which the horse bends will correct this bad habit.

The half-halt is particularly useful for improving horses that are too heavy in the forehand and tend to hang on the bit and bore. With horses of this type, the trainer should demand the half-halt every few minutes throughout each lesson. However, it should not be used so frequently on horses that tend to overflex and get behind the bit, throwing their weight too far back on the haunches.

Reining Back

Collection and vertical flexion can be improved by reining back. The horse is first brought to attention, his head nearing the vertical

FIG. 43.   The correct way to rein back.

FIG. 44.   Incorrect way to rein back. *Rider is not using legs, is pulling with stiff wrists and shoulders, so horse resists by overbending.*

but not overbent or lowered. The rider squeezes his legs and braces his back to demand impulsion, which is directed rearward by the hands acting with direct opposition. The legs cease as the hands act. The hands, however, do not pull; they remain fixed in place and resist the forward impulse, which is the result of the use of the legs. The hands may also be used actively, vibrating the bit by opening and closing the fingers. The instant the horse begins to obey, the aids must cease to act. The action of the aids is resumed immediately as another step is asked. The horse must move backward in the following manner: the diagonal legs move simultaneously, making the movement a two-beat gait; the neck and head are placed as described; the haunches must be in line with the ears, neither hind leg moving off the track. The horse steps backward as the rider demands the steps, without hesitation but without running backward. He must be ready to step immediately forward again without halting if the leg aids are applied and the hand changed to a following instead of a resisting hand. Figure 43 illustrates a correctly performed reining-back movement.

The most common mistake in demanding a rein-back is that the rider ceases to resist before the horse ceases to resist. The horse is

FIG. 45.   Incorrect way to rein back. *Rider has failed to get bend at poll before starting and is using only his hands. Horse's head is very high.*

97

not to be moved back with a series of jerks. The hand is fixed in place and the legs push the horse into the bit. If the rider stops his resistance before the horse gives, he will lose the benefit of the impulsion of the legs, and if anything, the horse will move forward. Unskilled riders try to rein back by jerking or pulling without using the leg aids. Instead of coming into the bit, the horse throws his head up or braces his neck. If the horse is to learn to back smoothly and willingly, he must be rewarded by the relaxation of the aids as he obeys; otherwise he will become confused and will fight the aids. Figures 44-45 illustrate incorrectly performed rein-backs.

Reining back is particularly good for horses that are unresponsive to the legs or stubborn. It is sometimes a terrifying movement to a young, excitable horse, and should not be introduced too early in the training schedule, either of this type of animal or of the "rubbernecked" variety.

Turns on the Haunches

There are a variety of turns on the haunches which may be executed separately or as part of a school figure. In any turn on the haunches, the horse wheels his forehand around his haunches, bringing his weight back (Figure 46).

Pivot

If the turn is to be done in place (pivot on the haunches), the inside back leg is the pivot, and is lifted and put down again in approximately the same spot. If the horse is moving, the hind legs describe a small arc while the forelegs describe a larger arc around them. The aids used to demand the turns on the haunches are as follows: Both legs are applied, the inside leg against the girth to maintain impulsion and limit the movement of the quarters, the outside leg a hand's breadth behind the girth to prevent the horse from pushing his haunches away from the pivot leg. The inside hand acts as a leading hand to start the horse turning, and is immediately assisted by the outside indirect rein of opposition in front of the withers, which throws the horse's weight toward his rear and pushes the inside shoulder over. The rider's weight is directed back over the holding haunch (the inside back leg). There is longitudinal but not lateral flexion in this movement. The horse wheels as a gate, crossing his forelegs, the outside crossing in front of the inside leg.

Should the horse attempt to move forward instead of remaining in place, both reins are used with opposition, the legs squeezing to

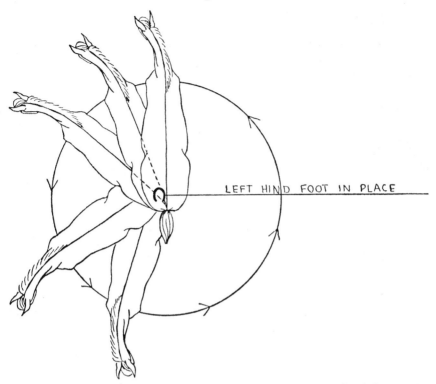

LEFT HIND FOOT IN PLACE

FIG. 46.   Pivot on the haunches, forehand to the left.

push the horse into the bit and against the fixed hand. If the horse steps too far, the indirect rein changes to a direct rein to check the movement and the leading rein either ceases to act or is used as an assisting indirect rein. In other words, in turning to the left, both hands are used to the left, but if the horse moves too far or refuses to be checked, both hands are carried to the right. Only enough opposition is used to prevent the horse from moving forward, as one of the most common defenses of the horse in learning this movement is to attempt to escape the aids by moving backward. In judging the execution of the turns on the haunches, a step backward is considered very serious, while a step forward is penalized much more lightly.

Phlegmatic horses take readily to the pivots whereas excitable horses are sometimes very much upset by them. The horse must execute each step calmly and only at the behest of the trainer; he must not whirl around the instant he receives the first indication from the aids.

Pivot on the Forehand

The aids for demanding the pivot on the forehand are as follows: (Figure 47). The horse's outside foreleg is the pivot. In turning the haunches to the right, the horse's left shoulder is weighted by carrying both hands toward it, the left hand carrying a leading and the right a bearing rein. Enough opposition is used in the reins to prevent the

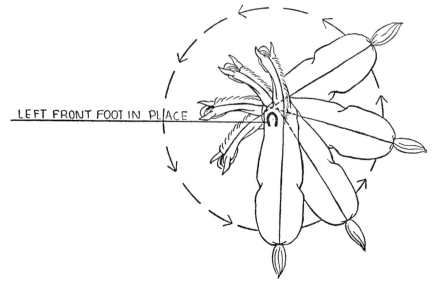

LEFT FRONT FOOT IN PLACE

FIG. 47.   Pivot on the forehand. Haunches to the right.

horse from stepping forward. The rider then applies his left leg behind the girth to cause the hindquarters to move. Only one step at a time is demanded, and the aids are relaxed between each step. If the horse moves his haunches too fast, they must be opposed by the direct rein on the side toward which the movement is directed (in this case, the right). If the horse is reluctant to move his quarters, the leading rein on the opposite side (in this case, the left) is used to flex the horse's head slightly to the left. The rider's weight is carried in the direction of the movement. Each aid must be ready to assist or to oppose the others as the action of the horse indicates. Great tact is necessary, and the rider must learn to feel the correctness of the movement.

Broken Lines

Although as a rule it is best to teach the pivots before the turns on the haunches while the horse is moving, I have known horses that

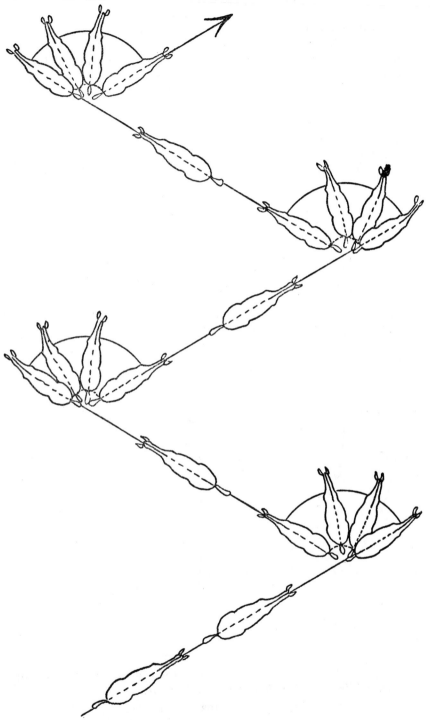

FIG. 48.   Executing broken lines with turns on the haunches.

learned best if the turns while moving at a walk were introduced first. The schooling figure known as the "broken lines" (Figure 48) is the best for introducing the turn on the haunches while the horse is moving, since in this figure the horse turns only two or three steps before moving off in the new direction. It is executed as follows: When the horse has entered the long wall of the arena on the right track, he turns and rides as shown. To turn, the rider applies the following aids: left hand lightly active to flex the horse's head to the left, followed immediately by the right indirect rein; left leg against the girth, right leg behind the girth; legs and hands both used in ca-

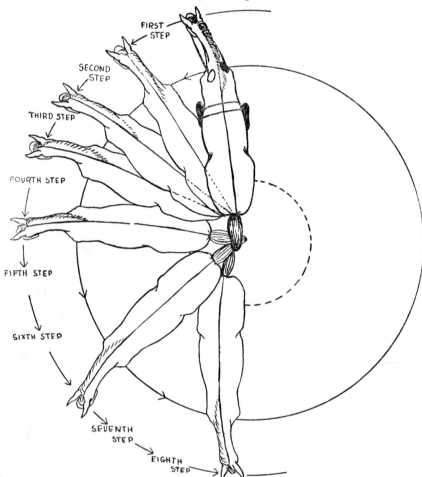

FIRST STEP
SECOND STEP
THIRD STEP
FOURTH STEP
FIFTH STEP
SIXTH STEP
SEVENTH STEP
EIGHTH STEP

FIG. 49.   Circles around haunches. *Horse's forelegs describe a large cirlce while haunches describe a small circle.*

dence with the movement. The weight is pushed to the left, and the rider sits on his left pelvic bone. The horse should swing his body smoothly to the left without interrupting the cadence, then proceed forward in the new direction until the movement is repeated to the right. The rider must use his aids with great tact and must learn to "feel" the correctness of the movement without looking down to see what the horse's legs are doing. This feel is characterized by a swinging, pendulum-like motion of the horse's body with little lateral flexion except at the head in the beginning of the movement

After the horse has learned the turn on the haunches on the broken lines, the rider may do half-turns (Figures 54a, b and c). The horse performs a half-circle in this movement and then goes back to the wall in one of three ways—on an oblique, on a two-track, or on a shoulder-in.

Circles around the Haunches

The pattern of the circle around the haunches with the forehand moving to the left is shown in Figure 49. The dotted line represents the path traveled by the back feet; the solid line, that traveled by the front feet. The aids used are essentially the same for the circle with the haunches ranged in as those described for the pivots (page 98), but the movement should be very fluid and the horse should not be stationary. In both the pivots and the circles, the difficult steps are the fourth and fifth, and the horse should practice the first three steps only a number of times before he is asked to complete the turn. If the horse tries to back up or loses his calmness, he must be brought to a standstill on the bit and the movement begun again. Do not stop applying the legs and hands if the horse drops the bit; they must be applied more strongly to push him into the bit.

Figure 50 shows circles with the haunches ranging slightly in and out. In the circles with the haunches ranged out, essentially the same aids are used as in the pivot on the forehand (page 100), with the horse wheeling as shown in Figure 47. The half-turn in reverse, shown in Figure 55, page 111, can be executed with the haunches ranged out and is a good preliminary exercise for the circles.

SCHOOLING MOVEMENTS TO DEVELOP LATERAL FLEXION

Bending the horse's neck and head to the side is known as lateral flexion. Some authorities use the term "lateral flexion" to mear bending the whole body as well as the head and neck.

It is important that the horse be supple throughout, but before he can become so, his muscles must be stretched. There are certain

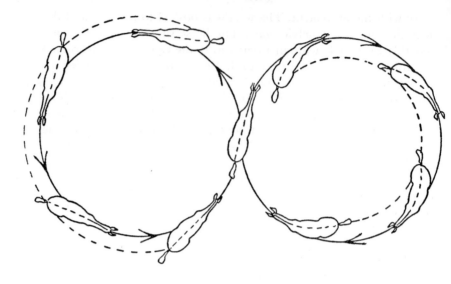

Haunches Ranged out   Haunches Ranged In

Fig. 50.   Ranging the haunches slightly in and slightly out on circles.

schooling figures which are especially designed to increase this lateral flexion and bending. In the first stages of training, not much work on lateral flexion was advised, since horses with a tendency toward "rubber necking" will sometimes refuse to stay on the bit when lateral flexion is demanded, instead bending their necks too much. However, as soon as the young horse is confirmed on the bit and turns only as much as the rider demands in following the big circles, he should be given movements to supple him laterally. The following schooling movements are considered the most useful for developing lateral flexion in the poll, neck, and body of the horse: the turns and half-turns, the voltes, the serpentine with the horse's body following the direction of the movement, and above all, the shoulder-in.

The average horse will turn his head readily to one side or the other on the demand of the leading rein, particularly if the trainer places his hand a little higher and further forward as well as further to the side than usual, and uses the active hand. Later the hand may be placed and fixed, with the back and legs driving the horse into the bit, and the fixed hand determining the direction of the movement. The hand is relaxed as soon as the horse obeys, but remains in position to be fixed again if the horse loses his flexion. The general tendency of inexperienced trainers in demanding movements in which the horse's head is to be bent in a certain direction is to have the head and neck bent too much, so that it is out of harmony with the rest of the body. It requires great judgment to use the hand just enough so that the head and neck complete the curve of the spine, which begins where the tail joins the body.

In executing circles and voltes (small circles), half-turns and serpentines, unless the rider is purposely ranging the haunches in or out, the horse's whole body—his four feet and his head and neck—should trace the pattern of the movement. If a plumb-line with a weight on the end were to be suspended from the throttle so that the tip touched the ground and left a mark, this line or mark would be in the exact center of the tracks made by the feet. The hind feet should follow in the trace of the front feet, and the curve should be harmonious in its bending, not angular with the animal's body first straightened out and then suddenly rebent. Such perfection of riding comes only to a few, but everyone will benefit by striving for it.

The opposite of the horse that overbends his neck is the one that deliberately stiffens and braces his neck against the rider's hand, sometimes going so far as to turn away from the leading rein. Only horses that have been broken roughly will do this. If you go into a straight stall and, standing beside a horse at about opposite his flanks, hold out a tidbit, the horse will have no difficulty in bending his neck and reaching for it. Horses at liberty often turn their heads and necks so far that they can bite their own flanks. Only a horse that has been injured so that his neck muscles have atrophied is unable to do this, but horses that have been cruelly handled will, through fright, often appear to be completely inflexible in the neck. For such a horse, the method of using the reins described and pictured on Figures 32 and 33, is very effective. In asking for lateral flexion to the left (Figure 51), take the right snaffle and both curb reins in the right hand, the left snaffle in the left hand. As the horse, while moving quietly along the wall on the left track, approaches a corner of the arena, carry both hands a little forward and, with vibrating movements of the fingers, gradually separate them, carrying the right hand to the right and the left hand to the left. The effect is to turn the muzzle to the inside with the single rein. At the same time, the other reins act against the neck in the opposite direction and give a little leverage. Sometimes carrying the single rein a little higher or lower than the others is effective. Some trainers prefer to carry the left curb alone in one hand and the other three reins in the other hand. The inside leg against the girth should assist in keeping the horse out to the wall and in not allowing him to turn his whole body stiffly in response to the demands of the leading rein. The outside leg assists in keeping up the impulsion. The weight is used unilaterally with the inner pelvic bone pushed forward.

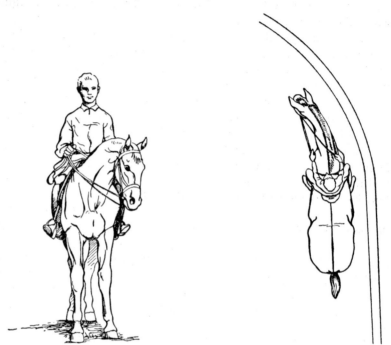

FIG. 51.   Exercise to teach lateral flexion in riding hall.

Although this method of demanding flexion is usually most effective while the animal is moving at the walk, slow trot, or ordinary trot, sometimes it can be utilized to good advantage while the animal is standing. Obedience should always be followed instantly by a pat or some other form of reward and the animal should be allowed to relax on a stretched rein.

If a horse, through fright or other causes, shows extreme rigidity to lateral flexion, it may be wise to long-rein drive him for a while before progressing to work under the saddle. He can be asked to do turns and voltes or serpentines, and will often respond much more willingly without the rider on his back.

Keeping in mind the goal of having the horse bend willingly but not overbend, the trainer should now devote some of each schooling period to exercises to develop lateral flexion.

The Volte

The size of the volte (or turn on a small circle) for general schooling purposes is fixed according to the gait at which the horse is traveling. At the walk, the volte (Figure 52) is executed on a radius of two yards; at a trot, the radius is four yards; and at a canter, six

FOUR YARDS

Fig. 52.   The volte at a trot.

yards. Circles of this size cause the horse to flex sufficiently for schooling purposes but do not overflex him. In competitions such as the Olympic Games, the circles may be smaller. In the 1948 Games the circles at the trot and the canter were three yards in radius. For developing lateral flexion, the voltes may be ridden with the horse's body bent in a matching curve, the hindquarters exactly tracking the forehand. The inside rein "leads" the horse on the circle, while the inside leg against the girth acts as a holding leg and prevents him from narrowing the circle. The outside leg acts behind the girth to keep the hindquarters on the track. The outside rein is an assisting rein and helps to determine the size of the circle. It acts as a bearing rein against the neck, but since the predominating rein is the inside rein, the outside rein does not bend the horse's muzzle. The experienced rider places the horse in position for the circle and maintains that position so that the horse describes his own circle. While the rider is developing the "feel" necessary to achieve this, he can test himself by drawing a path in the loose surface of the riding ring and then seeing if, without looking down at it, he can ride the circle twice and stay on the track.

The voltes can also be utilized to increase the mobility of the haunches by ranging them in or out, as described on page 103. As illustrated in Figure 50, page 104, the hind feet should be only slightly off the track. If the horse is heavy in the forehand, ranging the haunches in is useful; for the horse that gets behind the bit, ranging the haunches out will help.

The Figure of Eight

The voltes with a change of hands (change of direction) constitute a figure of eight. It is most essential that the rider bear in mind the pattern which he wishes to ride and that he bend and flex the animal so that the horse follows this pattern without having to be returned to it constantly. In exhibition work, the figure of eight is always placed so that the beginning and completion of each circle is opposite the short wall, as shown in Figure 53. As the rider on the right-hand circle closes that circle at point A, he straightens his horse's body for a stride, then shifts his aids to demand flexion to the left, thus beginning the new circle. Observe that the horse's body is straightened as the first circle is closed or completed, not when the new circle is opening. This rule holds on all figure-eights, at whatever size and gait they are executed.

In the change of lead and hand at the gallop with intervening trotting steps, the trotting steps come when the horse's body is straight. On asking for the flying change, the horse is first straightened, then the aids demanding the change are employed.

Half-turns

The voltes are described in this chapter before the half-turns and half-turns in reverse are discussed, although these are less difficult and are usually taught first. The reason is that it is easier for the reader to visualize a circle, a pattern with which he is familiar, than to visualize

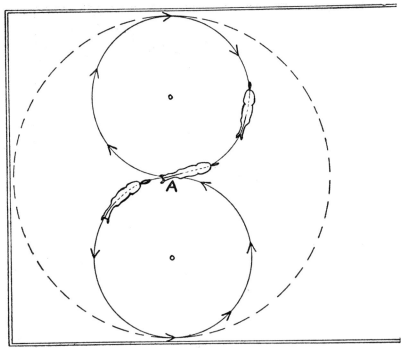

FIG. 53.   The volte figure of eight.

the less familiar patterns of the half-turn and the half-turn in reverse, illustrated in Figures 54a, b, c and 55.

The half-circle may be made with the hindquarters following the track, as shown in Figure 54a; with the haunches ranged slightly out, as illustrated in Figure 54b; or slightly in, as in Figure 54c. In returning to the wall from the half-turn, the rider has the choice of returning on a simple oblique as in Figure 54a (for elementary school-ing and beginner riders), with the horse's body straight, on a two-track (Figure 54b), or on a shoulder-in (Figure 54c).

The half-turn in reverse (Figure 55) is usually begun with an oblique, but may be performed with the oblique line leading away from the wall being executed on a two-track. In executing the half-turn in reverse, care must be taken to move the horse the correct dis-tance from the wall before demanding the half-volte, which will re-turn him to the wall. The half-voltes which are part of these move-ments have the same diameters as the voltes executed at the different gaits (see page 107). When the half-turn is executed as in Figure 54c with a half-circle ranging the haunches in, followed by a shoulder-in movement, it serves to supple the haunches, lighten the forehand, and

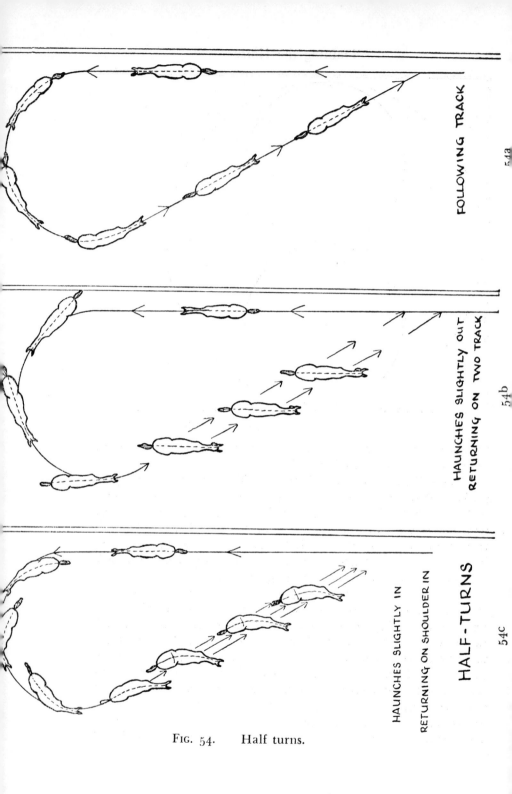

FOLLOWING TRACK

54a

HAUNCHES SLIGHTLY OUT
RETURNING ON TWO TRACK

54b

HAUNCHES SLIGHTLY IN
RETURNING ON SHOULDER IN

HALF-TURNS

54c

Fig. 54.   Half turns.

supple the body laterally as the horse comes back to the wall. When it is executed as in Figure 54b, it helps to flex the neck, poll, and loin, and to get the horse on the bit. The half-turn in reverse may be executed with the haunches pushed out, the inside leg and the inside di·

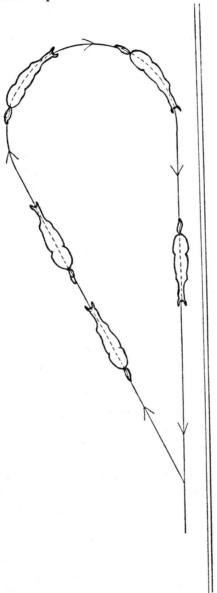

FIG. 55.   Half-turn in reverse. *Simple oblique away from wall.*

rect rein of opposition predominating. This lightens the croup, puts the horse on the forehand, and gives him practice in turning on the direct rein of opposition.

The Serpentine

The serpentine (Figure 56) is a series of half-circles which may be executed either with the horse's body bent in the direction of the movement, with the haunches ranged in, or with the haunches ranged

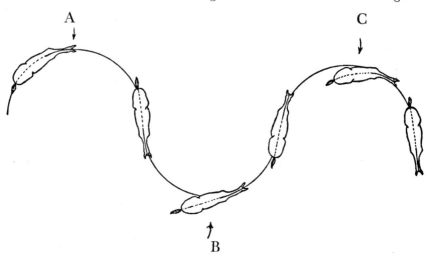

Fɪɢ. 56.   The serpentine. A *haunches following the track*. B *haunches ranged out*. C *haunches ranged in*.

out. The importance of this movement lies in the smoothness of the turns and the exactness of the pattern. The same aids are used as those which are described for turns, half-turns, and voltes. The horse must be straightened before each succeeding turn. Horses that need lateral flexion should work on the serpentine with the body following the direction of the movement, the hind legs exactly tracking the forehand. Those that are heavy on the forehand should work on it with the haunches ranged in; those that get behind the bit and have too high a head carriage will profit by executing the serpentine with the haunches ranged out.

Another form of the serpentine (Figure 57), which is really just a series of flat loops, is used in the initial stages of training the green horse to be responsive to the aids in changing direction. It may also be used in the later stages of training to teach the horse to maintain a lead even though he is bent slightly the other way. It is therefore the introductory exercise for teaching the false gallop.

FIG. 57.   The flat serpentine. *Used in teaching the false canter.*

The Shoulder-in

Most authorities agree that of all the schooling movements designed to supple the horse laterally, make him attentive, teach him to
go on the bit, calm him, and make him generally obedient, the
shoulder-in is the most important. In addition to its value as an exercise, the movement may be employed to correct vices and defenses
and in close-order mounted drill. The horse that is shying may be
taken past the frightening object by being put into the shoulder-in,
the shoulder away from the object being carried in. The horse that
tries to rub the rider against a wall may be circumvented by being
flexed toward the wall in a shoulder-in. The horse that refuses to ride
close to his companion in close-order drill may be flexed to the side
away from his partner and so pushed against him. This is particularly

useful with horses that bite or kick when ridden close beside another animal.

Figure 58 shows the position of the horse's body when executing the shoulder-in. Notice that the rider's inside leg, against the girth, is

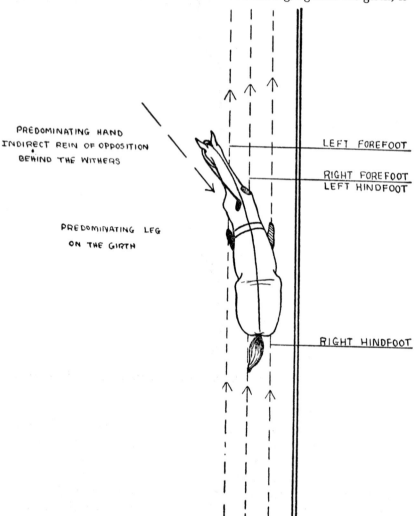

FIG. 58.   The shoulder-in.

the center of the curve around which the horse's body is bent. This curve must be harmonious. The neck and head must not be turned too much, and there must be bending at the loin. The pattern or track which the feet follow is shown in Figure 59. Note that, whereas the hind feet parallel the long line of the hall as indicated, the inside foreleg is pulled off the track and the outside foreleg is tracked by the inside hind leg. There is a good deal of difference of opinion among the various authorities as to whether or not the legs actually cross

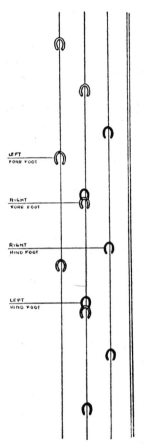

LEFT
FORE FOOT

RIGHT
FORE FOOT

RIGHT
HIND FOOT

LEFT
HIND FOOT

FIG. 59.   Trace of the shoulder-in.

each other. I have watched this movement being executed by a number of different riders and have come to the conclusion that, because of the position of the horse's body, which is not in line with the direction of the movement, the legs appear to cross but actually do not. It is the curving of the body away from the direction of the movement which causes the appearance of crossing as seen from the front. Obviously, since the hind legs are on the track, they cannot actually cross. However, Müseler, Chamberlin, and others all refer to the shoulder-in as a movement in which the legs cross.

The aids employed in the shoulder-in are as follows: When the rider has crossed the short side and has entered the long side of the hall, he uses the inside leading rein to draw the forehand a little off the track and to flex the neck and head to the inside, thus turning the head away from the direction of the movement. The inside leg is pressed firmly against the girth to move the horse along the track. The outside leg, a holding leg, is carried a little behind the girth to prevent the haunches from being turned off the track and to flex the horse at the loin around the inside leg. The rider then changes the rein effect from a leading rein to an indirect rein of opposition *behind* the withers, thus pushing the horse toward his outside or leading shoulder while his inside shoulder is held off the track. The horse moves fluidly along in a straight line, making three rows of prints with his feet. The line of prints nearest the wall is made by his outside hind foot alone; the middle line of prints is made by his inside hind leg and his outside foreleg; and the inside line of prints is made by his inside foreleg alone. This is one of the very few movements in which the horse is not required to look in the direction of the movement. The bending of his body serves to lengthen and supple the muscle of the loin. Any resistance in the neck is broken up, and the general flexibility and athletic agility of the horse is developed.

The German school recommends that the shoulder-in be executed on straight lines only. General Chamberlin recommends that the movement be executed also on circles. When executed on circles, the effect is to enlarge the circle. I have found that many horses which resist when asked to execute the shoulder-in on straight lines show less resistance when the movement is introduced while working on a circle. Having become obedient on the circles, they readily accept the work on straight lines. Other animals seem confused by the circles, and learn best on the straight lines first. The shoulder-in on the oblique, called the *appuyer*, is sometimes easier for the novice to start with as this form of the movement is less demanding. The trainer must keep his mind open to other people's methods, in this as in other phases of training. He should profit by suggestions and use them to advantage.

The shoulder-in is extremely useful in calming an excited animal that jigs and sidesteps and tries to get away from the bit. Since it is a movement which is carried out in only one direction, it may be utilized by the rider when riding along the side of the road or along a trail. For the horse that gets excited at the sight of the in-gate of a show ring, a few steps of the shoulder-in will often bring him to attention as nothing else will.

From an athletic standpoint, the execution of the shoulder-in at the ordinary trot is most valuable. Compare with position of leg-yielding, Figure 37, which is much simpler.

The Travers

The travers or pass (sometimes called the *passage*, but not to be confused with the *passage* movement of the *haute école* described on page 135) is shown in Figure 60. Note that in this movement the

Fig. 60.   The travers (*Haunches in*).

horse's shoulders are parallel to the wall, his neck and head are flexed slightly inwards toward the direction of the movement, his quarters are pushed away from the wall, and the horse is again bent around the rider's inside leg. Whereas in the shoulder-in the horse was looking away from the direction of the movement, now he is looking in the direction of the movement. In the shoulder-in, his quarters were kept on the track, and the forehand was moved off it; in the travers, the shoulders and forehand are on the track and the hind-quarters are pushed away from it. Do not confuse this movement with the leg-yielding exercise shown in Figure 37, page 77, in which the quarters are also pushed off the track, but the bend of the horse is in the other direction. The horse moving to the left, for example, is bent with the inside of the curve to the left in the travers. In the leg-yielding movement, he is bent the opposite way, with the outside of the curve to the left in the direction of the movement.

The Renvers

The renvers is shown in Figure 61. The horse is moving on the same track as in the travers—that is, to the left (the center of the arena is on his left)—but he is bent the other way. This time his

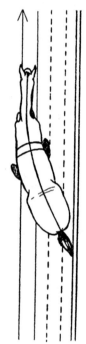

Fig. 61.   The renvers (*Haunches out*).

quarters are kept near the wall, but are not parallel to it; his shoulders are parallel to the wall, but are pushed away from it. Compare the position of the quarters in the renvers to the position of the quarters in the shoulder-in.

In both the travers and the renvers, the rider's predominating leg is the one on the outside of the curve of the horse's body. The inside leg is a holding leg and is pushed against the girth. The horse's neck and poll are flexed slightly in the direction of the movement, with a light use of the inside leading rein. The other rein gives to allow the neck to bend but remains in contact with the mouth when

Training the Horse

the proper position of the head and neck is achieved so that both reins maintain and control the direction of the movement and the position of the head and neck. The rider's inside pelvic bone is pushed forward. The pass travers and renvers may be practiced at all gaits.

The Two-Track

The two-track is also called the half-pass. In fact, certain European schools refer to all movements in which the horse does not follow the same track with his hindlegs as with his forelegs as a two-track. Readers of foreign books should keep this in mind. In American and English publications, the two-track refers only to the half-pass shown in Figure 62. In this movement the horse moves in two directions at once: forward and to the side. If the rider starts the two-track from the southeast corner of the hall, he will end up in the northwest corner. The front and back legs cross completely and pass each other, those away from the direction of the movement crossing in front of the others. The steps should be smooth and precise with no stiffness or awkwardness. The horse's body is held quite straight and almost parallel to the wall, but with the forehand leading slightly. It is considered more graceful if the head is bent slightly in the direction of the movement. Since the horse's body is not flexed as it is in the travers, renvers, and shoulder-in, this movement is used principally to make the horse's quarters and forehand obedient to the aids and to give him balance. The aids used are as follows: When the rider has entered the long wall on the left track and has gone one horse-length along the wall, he leads his horse off the track by employing his inside (left) leading rein. This is supported immediately by the right bearing or indirect rein, which pushes the horse onto his left shoulder and causes him to cross his right foreleg in front of his left. As this occurs, the rider employs his right (outside) leg behind the girth to push the hindquarters in the direction of the center of the arena, thus causing the horse to cross his right hind leg in front of the left and to keep both legs almost in line with the forehand. The horse does not move directly to the side but forward as well. The diagram of the tracks (Figure 62) makes this clear. The amount of opposition employed in the reins depends on the forward impulse of the horse. If too much opposition is used, the horse will not move forward, and may even cross his outside legs *behind* the leading legs. If not enough is used, the horse will take steps which are too long and too rapid in the forward direction and which do not cross enough. The rider's weight follows the direction of the movement. This is accomplished best by weighting the stirrup slightly on the leading side.

119

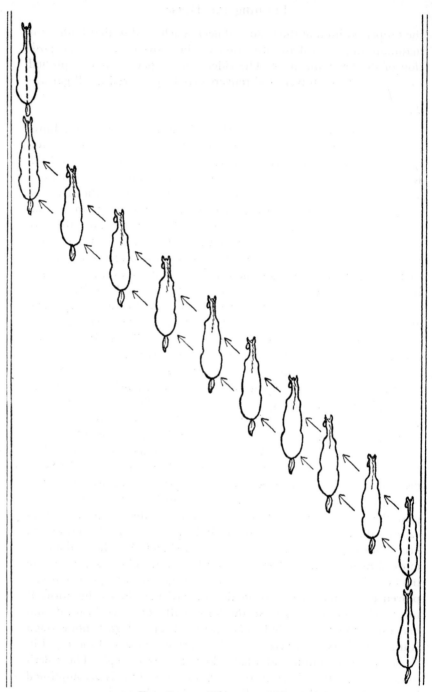

FIG. 62.   The two-track.

Training the Horse

There is no more graceful movement than the two-track, and none that makes the rider more aware of the independent use of his aids, both to command and to correct. He must feel whether or not the horse is crossing properly and use his aids accordingly. The most difficult part of this movement is schooling green horses to keep the haunches moving actively, and yet not to let them get ahead of the forehand. It is also difficult to teach the horse not to bend his head away from the direction of the movement. If this happens, the horse should be halted and put in the correct position before he is allowed to proceed.

Some horses yield the haunches more readily in one direction than in the other, even though they may have been well schooled in leg-yielding in both directions. A light switch may be employed to assist the leg aids until the horse becomes more responsive. It should be tapped very lightly well behind the girth just once as each step is demanded. In teaching the two-track, move only a few steps at first, then straighten the horse and move him back to the wall on the two-track going the other way, with the aids reversed. The next step is to combine the two-track with the half-turn (Figure 54b). When the horse becomes proficient in this movement, he may be asked to two-track from the wall to the center of the arena, and then to return. When he is sure of himself and thoroughly responsive at the walk, he can learn to two-track at the slow trot, the ordinary trot, and the canter. In the latter, he is put on the canter with the correct lead on the track and the movement is begun after the rider has entered the long wall. The two-track is continued across the hall to the opposite corner, where the horse turns, still maintaining the lead, and continues on the track. Some very talented horses learn to combine the two-track with the *haute école* passage movement.

The Counter-Change of Hands

The counter-change of hands on the two-track, also called the zig-zag, is executed as follows (Figure 63): The rider moves forward on a straight line, then off that line on a two-track for a designated number of steps (from two to six). Without pause in cadence, he reverses the direction of the two-track and moves back across his original line, going an equal number of steps beyond it. Here he reverses again and moves as he did at first. On the changes of direction, the haunches are held while the forehand moves across in front of them. The rider experiences a smooth, swinging feel of the horse under him as he gracefully changes direction. The exercise is first taught by moving away from and back toward the wall, but when it is

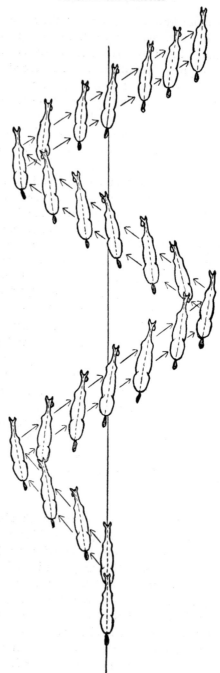

FIG. 63. The counter change of hands on the two-track.

learned, it should be executed down the center of the arena. The change-over of the aids must be exceedingly subtle; otherwise the too-eager horse will jerk as he reverses his direction. His head must always be kept looking in the direction of his movement, and with each change the forehand must be in the lead when the haunches start moving. The counter-change of hands on the two-track at the gallop is one of the most difficult of all movements, since it involves a change of lead as well as a change of direction, and can only be attempted by the most skilled riders and the most perfectly schooled horses. At the slower gaits, however, it is not so difficult, and can be attempted as soon as the horse is proficient at the simple two-track.

The travers, renvers, shoulder-in, two-track, turns, and pivots, once thoroughly understood by both rider and horse, may be employed in a variety of sequences. Such combinations of movements may be compared to the combinations of the inner and outer edges, backwards and forwards, which the figure skater employs. All figure-skating patterns are based entirely on these four movements, yet tremendous variety is achieved. By demanding the dressage figures in different sequences, the rider can render his horse enormously sensitive and responsive to the aids, and can increase his own ability to "feel" and to "influence" to an astounding degree. To do this there must be complete harmony between horse and rider. The rider must be virtually "glued" to his saddle, and must use his aids with the utmost tact and understanding. He should always remember that all his aids must be in readiness at all times, and that when and how they are employed will depend entirely on how the horse reacts.

Gallop Departs

An elementary method of demanding the gallop depart from the green colt was described in Chapter VI. The horse more advanced in his schooling can be taught a more advanced method, based on the idea that the horse should normally look in the direction in which he is going. Therefore, in taking a gallop right, he should not first bend his head slightly to the left, as previously advocated, but should bend it slightly to the right. This means employing the right rein either as a leading rein or as an indirect rein. Since the right indirect rein of opposition has the effect of weighting and limiting the movement of the left shoulder, and at the same time, freeing the right shoulder and permitting the horse to lead with that shoulder, this is the better rein effect to apply. The indirect rein is assisted by the outside rein, also working slightly in opposition. The instant the reins have been used in this manner, the legs urge the horse forward, with the outside leg carried a little behind to push the haunches in toward the center of the ring. As the legs act, the hands give, since the forward movement must not be impeded. For the first lessons, the horse should be on a trot and working in a circle. If the rider is posting, he should be posting on the outside diagonal, and should apply the leg aids as he settles into his saddle. If he is sitting the trot, the legs are used as the outside shoulder comes back. The rider should push with his inside pelvic bone. Gradually the aids can be refined as the horse becomes more sensitive to them. Finally it will be necessary only for the rider to indicate slightly with his hands and to give a little push with his pelvic bone and the horse will canter. Horses become almost psychic, and the well-schooled animal appears to read his rider's mind. He can take the canter on the desired lead with the rider hardly being aware of having demanded the movement.

This use of the aids to demand the gallop depart is known as using the *diagonal* aids. The method described on page 76, in which the rider uses his leg and hand on the same side, is known as using the outside lateral. A still more refined method of demanding the gallop depart involves the use of the *inside lateral* aids. In this method, the rider uses his inside leg in front of the girth to indicate to the horse that he is to push that foreleg forward. At the same time, he uses the inside indirect rein or the inside leading rein.

Each horse differs in his ability to understand the various aids. I am working at present on two horses of very different temperaments. Their initial schooling was the same through the employment of the diagonal aids for the gallop depart. Both horses have become very sensitive, but while one works most smoothly if I simply close my fingers on the inside rein for an instant and do nothing with my legs to demand the gallop depart, the other understands best if I carry the outside leg back an inch without pressing it and do nothing with my hands!

Sometimes a horse that has been thoroughly schooled to take the canter on the outside lateral aids becomes very confused, and will persistently gallop false when the diagonal aids are used, even though he is bent in a very small circle. For such a horse, the following method is often useful. When the horse is on the track to the left, a half-turn is executed at the slow trot. At the exact instant that he returns to the wall on a diagonal, (Figure 64 Point A), with the haunches still pushed to the center, the inside indirect rein is used to move him along the wall in the new direction and the legs are applied with force to push him into the gallop.

When the horse is thoroughly schooled to take the gallop on the

124

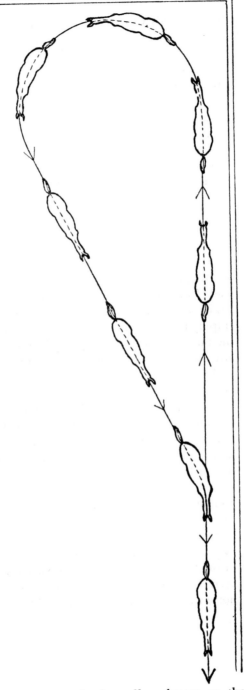

FIG. 64.   Using the half-turn to teach the gallop depart on the diagonal aids.

diagonal aids while traveling in a circle, both at the walk and trot and from a halt, he should then be trained to gallop right or left on these aids while traveling in a straight line. At first it may be necessary to push his quarters a little to one side or the other, but eventually he should respond with his body in a perfectly straight line.

The greatest mistakes made by mediocre riders in demanding the gallop depart are to over-use the aids and to throw the weight forward over the leading shoulder. Since the aim is to free this shoulder and not to impede it, is easy to understand why this is wrong. The forward push of the inside pelvic bone does not impede the shoulder, but increases the impulsion on that side.

The Change of Lead

When the horse has learned the gallop depart with the diagonal aids, he may be taught the flying change, or change of leads without interruption. Working on a large figure of eight with each circle at least thirty feet in diameter, circle at a canter to the right on the right lead. As the first circle is completed, bring the horse down to a trot, straighten him, and, after putting him in position for the left circle, employ the necessary aids to demand the left lead. Gradually reduce the number of trotting steps until you sense that the horse is ready to attempt the flying change. To accomplish this, when the horse is galloping right on the right circle, commence to apply the rein aids just as he is closing the circle. Then use the legs strongly in cadence with the stride, the right leg a little behind the girth, keeping the horse's head bent to the right for an instant before it is changed over to the new direction. The legs should act as you are farthest down in the saddle (the "hard" of the canter). Some authorities advocate that the weight be kept a little out of the saddle to free the haunches since it is in the back legs that the change takes place, but the rider must be ever careful not to throw his weight over onto the shoulder which is to become the leading shoulder. As time goes on, the aids are used more and more tactfully, until the horse understands what is expected of him with only a slight indication. Do not allow him to get in the habit of making a flying change without your command, however. This would be desirable in a polo pony, but not in a dressage horse which is going to be required to gallop false.

Chapter 8

HEAVY DRESSAGE AND HAUTE ÉCOLE

by Fritz Stecken

The schooling of a horse along more advanced lines than have been described in the preceding chapters is called *haute école* or High School. It is a logical continuation of that primary training and is carried on in sequence to it. As we have seen, we begin with the elementary school, the "breaking" period, followed by the intermediary and advanced stages including two-tracking, increasing and decreasing of gaits, turns, circling, serpentines and jumping.

Then, when our horse can perform these simpler movements with perfection we are ready to start the final phase of training—the High School. The High School includes these very special movements or "airs": the piaffe, the passage, the flying change on every stride, and the pirouette. When these movements are properly achieved they represent the highest possible degree of suppleness, flexibility and collection.

There are two different schools of horse training that use the same technical terms but are fundamentally different from each other in method and purpose, consequently before starting High School training the rider must have a clear picture in his mind of the goal he hopes to achieve.

The first of these schools (and the one with which we are *not* concerned in this book) is that of the circus. Here the purpose is to put on a show, to amuse and impress the uneducated spectator with a display of great excitement, flashy gaits and artificial movements. Certainly one of the greatest experts in this line was James Fillis, who described the principles of this school in his well-known book, *Breaking and Training*. Circus movements take considerable skill to perform, but have little or nothing in common with the classical school.

The classical school required in the Olympic Equestrian games has a more ancient tradition. The knowledge, the experience, and the artistic ability of many great riding masters of the past are brought together in the principles of this classical art of riding. Here the trainer's aim is to obtain absolute correctness and perfection in all gaits and at all figures. He rides for the discriminating taste of the judges' trained eyes—the average spectator will be unimpressed by what he shows.

Many authorities from all over the world have tried to find a better word for "dressage"—until now without success. In one sense, dressage means to train any four-footed animal to perform, with visible signals, certain tricks. In a classical sense the word dressage means something entirely different—it means the suppling and gymnastic training of the horse's body.

The fundamental necessity is the suppleness and mobility of the horse's back and hindquarters. The manual of the Fort Riley Cavalry School points this out in Part II, paragraph 103:

"The hindquarters are the seat of impulsion and at the same time they form a sort of rudder in the changes of direction.

"The mechanism of impulsion lies in the play of the hip joint. The closing of this joint leads to the engagement of the hocks under the mass and allows the horse to cover more or less ground according to the energy of the extension of the propellers. Such engagement of the hocks under the mass leads to a lowering of the hindquarters—a position which greatly facilitates rapid changes of direction.

"The hindquarters should be able to move with facility in a lateral direction as well, but because of his construction the horse can execute this movement only by passing the right hind foot, for example, in front of the left hind. Here again the horse must lower his croup and draw his hocks under the mass.

"The movements which cause this engagement and this mobility of the hindquarters are: extending and collecting the gaits, halts, the broken lines, the serpentine, the circle, the half turn and the half turn in reverse with a smaller and smaller radius, the false gallop, backing, two tracks and shoulder-in."

This indeed is the key to riding and training a horse in the principle of the classical school. Lateral flexion of the horse's body is de-

128

veloped through the rider's legs in riding two-tracks and figures in the ring. The proper longitudinal flexion of the horse's body can never be obtained by the rider's hands or legs; it comes only as a result of many hours of cross-country riding and jumping. I would like to stress the importance of starting to train a prospective dressage horse first as a hunter or jumper. The training for a dressage horse should begin after he has learned to go well-balanced in a hunt or over jumps. Only with this foundation is it possible to start to train a horse for the Olympic dressage test.

The result of this training will be a supple horse. His gaits and movements will be perfect and the entire performance will be in perfect harmony. He will show the highest degree of collection as well as the greatest degree of extension (Plates XVII and XIX). The better a horse shows this, the better his performance will be judged. The Olympic dressage judge looks for this suppleness and flexibility. He is not interested in flashy gaits and a spectacular effect.

A supple horse will extend or collect promptly at the rider's command. He will perform with ease the most difficult movements, such as the piaffe and passage, flying change on every stride, and pirouette. The performance of both horse and rider will look as if the horse is performing the movements of his own will. This perfection of horsemanship is the requirement for the Olympics.

COLLECTED CANTER

Before it is possible for the horse to make flying changes and pirouettes, he must be able to make a really correct collected canter. Collected canter does not mean just a slow canter. The mobility of the hind legs must be as great as in the extended canter; the tempo of the two gaits is practically the same. The difference is only in covering more or less ground; consequently the silhouette of the horse is shorter or longer. Compare Plates XVII and XVIII.

To obtain this very high collection without losing the mobility of the hind legs or shortening the horse's neck, the best exercise is the canter on the counter lead. In order to keep his balance in the counter lead, the horse will find it necessary to carry his weight more on the outside hind leg; this will result in his bringing both hind legs farther under. It should be made clear here that when the horse goes on the counter lead, what was previously the outside becomes the inside and vice versa; for example, when going on the left hand the left side of the horse is the outside, while the right side, since the horse is cantering on the right lead, becomes the inside.

When the horse has learned to balance himself in the counter canter, and to carry himself correctly without losing any of his forward impulsion, it should be possible for him to perform figures and turns which he previously could perform only on the ordinary lead.

In the counter lead the trainer must be very particular about the straightness of the horse; that is, the animal must follow with his hind feet in the tracks of the front feet, and he must be bent to the right when on the right lead and to the left on the left lead, regardless of the turn he is making.

In general, to make the hind legs and ribs more flexible, the next step is to start the pirouette. At the same time, the trainer may start working on the flying change. Whether he decides to work on both movements at the same time, or one or the other first, depends on his own feeling and on the individual horse.

PIROUETTE

The suppleness and willingness of the horse in the counter lead will make it easy for the trainer to decide in which way he can develop the pirouette. Usually the easiest way to start is to go on the counter lead about nine or twelve feet away from the wall, then make a small circle toward the wall in each corner. Because the horse in this exercise is turning toward the wall most of the time, it takes away his tendency to pull, and to avoid carrying his weight with his hind legs. With practice, any horse will perform this exercise willingly.

When the rider has developed the horse on both hands in this exercise, he can start to make a pirouette away from the wall by cantering on the ordinary lead in a smaller and smaller circle. This preparatory exercise of making small turns in the corners will give the horse the feeling of making turns on the hindquarters, and he will understand that the more active legs of the rider don't mean more extension, but more collection.

These preliminary exercises are the suppling work for developing the pirouette, and if the horse should show resistance later in performing a half or full pirouette, the trainer should always go back to these exercises. The expression of the highest collection in the trot is the piaffe; in the canter, the pirouette, for this is really a canter in place with a turn on the haunches.

Through increasing and decreasing the collection of the canter it will be possible for the horse to go in higher and higher collection; so high that he can almost perform a canter in place. When the rider has reached this stage it will be very easy for him to bring about a pirouette simply by bringing his weight a trifle to the left or the right; then in order to balance himself the horse will follow the rider's weight and make a turn on the haunches. (See Plate XIX) The proof of the correctness of the pirouette will be that the rider will be able, at any point, to go straight ahead at the greatest extension.

FLYING CHANGE

There are many ways of teaching the flying change, but first it is important for the horse to attain sufficient suppleness and collection from practice at the counter lead.

One of the easiest methods is to canter on the counter lead, giving the signal for a flying change as one reaches the corner. Also, one can practice the flying change in a figure eight, in the serpentine, or in crossing the ring, giving the signal to change on reaching the opposite wall.

It is generally advisable at first to practice changing leads by bringing the horse back to a walk for a few steps, then starting the canter again on the other lead. After the horse learns this simple change of lead, the rider should try the first flying change.

In order to avoid interfering with the forward impulsion, the rider must be careful not to try to help the horse with his hands. Another important point is to keep from moving the upper part either forward or sideward; this throws the horse off balance. The rider's legs are all that give the signal for the flying change. Only during the split second of suspension between strides is it possible for the horse to make a flying change; this is the moment when the rider's legs must act.

Most horses will be nervous at first from this unaccustomed aid. Only long practice and experience will give the horse the ability to make flying changes with calmness and quietness. After every try, whether successful or not, the trainer must give the horse a rest period. Otherwise the horse becomes more and more excited and soon will surely start to fight. With suppling exercise in the counter lead, every horse will sooner or later learn to make a correct flying change.

When the horse can make a flying change correctly and quietly in the figures described above, then the trainer may start to make a flying change going straight ahead. First he should practice changing every ten strides, then every nine, eight, etc. on down to two strides, being careful to work as much on one lead as the other. If the horse has had sufficient preliminary suppling work and really goes on the rider's aids, there will generally be no difficulty in going right on down to changes every two strides.

Flying change on every stride, depending on the individual horse, will always take a longer time; for a long while the trainer must be satisfied with one stride left and one stride right. Then he must stop immediately, pet the horse, and finish all work for the day. He should only try this after a long limbering-up period.

As in all work requiring very high collection, it is never force which brings the horse under the rider's control, but the rider's feeling, his understanding of his horse, and the horse's suppleness and ability to work willingly under the rider. When horses show resistance against high collection, only more suppling exercise can bring eventual success.

One of the most important things for the horse, and one which is too often forgotten by dressage trainers, is plenty of work at extended gaits. The rider can never overdo extension, but he can very quickly overdo collection. He should give the horse a chance to stretch out completely in rest periods, in the walk, trot and canter. This complete extension will be instrumental in bringing success at collected gaits without resistance or fighting. After work in high collection, the trainer must always give at least an equal amount of work in complete extension.

The proof for the correct collection is that the rider must be able to go from the highest collection to the greatest extension in one stride, and at all gaits. The center of gravity is never regulated by the rider's hands, but by the horse's hind legs, controlled by the rider's legs and back. Otherwise it would be artificial collection, which has no place in the classical art of dressage. For this reason, all of this schooling must be done only on the snaffle bit to avoid any tendency of the rider to use his hands too much.

In the correct flying change the rider must sit straight and firmly so as not to interfere with the horse's movements, his hands should be steady and motionless, and the legs should give the aids effectively but invisibly; only thus is it possible for a horse to make a flying change straight ahead, supple, collected, without hesitation and with forward impulsion. In perfection, regardless of what figures the horse may be performing, he must always give the impression of being at ease, as if he were making a natural canter straight ahead.

THE PIAFFE

It requires a skillful trainer to develop the piaffe, or trot in place. The easiest way is to start this work from the ground—then the horse does not have to cope with the rider's weight, and too, it will be easier for him to understand what is asked of him.

I cannot overemphasize the importance of a thorough and correct schooling in the preliminary and the advanced school before the trainer undertakes to ask of his horse the difficult and exacting piaffe. If he tries to begin this work before the horse has attained sufficient suppleness, calmness, flexibility and balance, the inevitable result will be a fight with the horse. Unfortunately, through lack of knowledge and understanding about the principle of the classical art of riding this happens all too often.

To start the work from the ground the trainer needs a cavesson, longe line, and side reins. The side reins are attached at one end to the girth, at about the height of the rider's knee, and at the other end to the rings of the snaffle. Both reins should be of an even length, long enough not to shorten the horse's neck, but short enough to have a light tension, with the horse's face a trifle out beyond the perpendicular. The longe line is attached to the ring of the cavesson, its length looped up in the trainer's hand so that he is holding the line about a foot from the horse's nose.

Now the trainer leads the horse to the wall of the indoor ring and stands at his head, facing the hindquarters. In his right hand he carries a whip long enough to reach the hind legs easily.

The purpose of the first few lessons should only be to let the horse understand the meaning of the whip, and to react correctly, promptly, and calmly at its use. The trainer should handle his whip so that the horse learns to move in a free walk as the whip touches his croup and slides down over the hind legs to the fetlocks. As the horse moves forward the trainer walks with him, moving backwards.

If the horse does not react to the touch of the whip, it may be necessary to tap him gently with it. Some horses, on the other hand, are afraid of the whip and will be nervous at the first few lessons. With this type it is essential to proceed with extreme quietness, patience and gentleness, rewarding the horse with lavish praise for a few correct steps, and being satisfied with very little at each lesson until the horse is able to have confidence in the trainer and to maintain a calmer attitude.

When the horse has learned to walk forward willingly and quietly at the signal from the whip, the trainer may start to make him trot at the same signal. After a few steps of trot, the trainer with his left hand brings the horse to a full stop. He must never forget to pet and praise the horse for every correct response to the whip and to the hand. He should stop this work after two or three successful tries, and never make the lesson longer than a few minutes. The inclination of many horses to move the hind legs in toward the middle of the ring should be corrected only by increasing the forward movement.

After several lessons, providing, as was pointed out before, the horse has had the proper foundation, and if in each lesson it has been made clear to him what he is supposed to do, he will reward the trainer by showing a few piaffe-like steps. When he does this it is important to praise the horse lavishly and stop this work immediately until the next lesson.

When, after weeks of this work, the horse shows more piaffe steps, it is time to put a rider on his back. At first the rider is completely passive, acting only as a dead weight while the trainer continues with the lessons as before. Only after such time as the horse shows his willingness and ability to work under the rider's weight as well as he did previously, should the trainer mount and try to obtain a few piaffe steps from the saddle. This is done by urging the horse vigorously forward with the back and both legs, while preventing his gaining ground by giving half-halts on the snaffle. It is most important to be satisfied for many weeks with only a few steps; one should keep in mind that the piaffe is very difficult for the horse to do and he will easily become angry and disgusted if asked to do too much. It is well to let the horse advance a little in the piaffe until he becomes really adept at it; only then should one try to obtain it exactly in place.

If the horse resists this schooling, it is most likely not because he does not like his work, but because it is difficult for him. When this happens, one should never start to fight with the horse; more suppling exercise, quietness, rest periods, and plenty of praise for every small success will obtain much better results. The mobility of the hind legs, the ability of the horse to flex and bend his hocks, hip joints and back, and to arch and erect his head and neck are what make it possible for him to perform the piaffe.

Since the piaffe is an individual gait, every horse will show a slightly different way of performing it. Some horses will show higher action, some less; some horses have to move a little forward, very few can do it exactly in place. But characteristic of every correct piaffe is the lowering of the hindquarters, the regularity of the steps, the cadence, the supple motion of the back, the erection of the neck and head. Bobbing up and down of the croup, or balancing from side to side behind, is proof of stiff hind legs and back, and especially shows that the horse is incapable of bending his hip joint. Generally in addition to these faults in the incorrectly suppled horse there will be an unsteady connection between the rider's hand and the horse's mouth. In other words, the horse moves his head up and down, goes behind the bit or against the rider's hand, but does not really have his balance, and so is not capable of staying steady on the bit.

As was explained regarding the collected and extended canter, the principle difference between the trot movements—the extended and collected trots, the passage and the piaffe—again is in the silhouette of the horse, as can readily be seen by comparing Plates XX, XXI and XXII. The piaffe shows the highest degree of collection; in the passage the horse covers less ground than in the collected trot, showing instead higher elevation with his legs; in the extended trot the horse covers the most ground and takes the longest strides.

Psychological understanding of the horse is the primary requisite for the trainer in the classical art of dressage. It is up to him to realize if, due to conformation or temperament, some particular horse is not able to give the highest degree of collection; then he should stop working him in it and keep this horse only as a hunter or a hack, rather than persisting until he ruins an otherwise useful horse.

THE PASSAGE

The development of the passage can be made from the piaffe, through letting the horse go farther forward until he is able to show more elevation in his legs. From the experience of many riding masters, a much more effective method for lazy horses is to develop this only from the extended trot. There can be no rule about it. This kind of work is individual to each horse.

In either case, it is always better to teach the piaffe first because it is easier to prepare a horse for carrying his weight with his hind legs through piaffe work; this paves the way for the passage, so to speak, and the trainer will find that the horse learns it much more easily than he did the piaffe.

Whichever method of teaching the passage the trainer decides to use, he must remember again to be satisfied with only a few steps at each lesson—the horse will find it most difficult at first to keep his balance for a longer period. Only practice and experience will make it possible for the horse to carry himself by lowering his hindquarters and erecting the forehand to keep balance and elevation. The rider should use both legs simultaneously to avoid a balancing from side to side of the horse's hind legs. As in the piaffe, uneven steps or this balancing is evidence of stiffness in the hindquarters and back. Correctness is far more important than high action.

After long practice the horse will perform the passage with even steps, the hind legs reaching well under, helped by a light steady tension on the reins. Then, at this point, the rider may change from piaffe to passage and passage to piaffe. These changes should be fluid and without hesitation or interruption.

To increase the flexibility and suppleness of the horse, the rider can later on practice shoulder-in, haunches-in, haunches-out, and traversers in the passage. The more grace and elegance the horse shows in all this performance the more it will look as though horse and rider are united as a statue; it will be the perfection of the classical art of riding, for the nature of art is to show clearness, beauty, and harmony. Art should and will speak only for itself.

Plate I
THE HITTITE HORSEMAN

The earliest representation of a mounted horseman. Date about 1400 B.C. The leg and foot position are interesting since they show that the Hittites realized the value of the depressed heel. No stirrups of course at this period of history.

Plate II
EGYPTIAN, 1300 B.C.

This Egyptian Lady looks entirely at home on her tiny pony that is obviously of Arabian breeding.

Plate III
ASSYRIAN HUNTSMEN, 800 B.C.

Note the beautifully balanced positions of these riders. There is no stiffness and there is definite forward impulsion, especially in the leader's seat. The American Indian's seat was much the same. The horses were obviously trained to weight and knee signals.

Plate IV

GREEK RIDERS

From a bas-relief on the Parthenon by Phidias. Period about 350 B.C.
The horse is executing the difficult "corbette" yet the rider is perfectly
balanced and relaxed. These horses must have been only about twelve
hands high judging by the standing figure.

Plate V

THE MONGOLIAN SCHOOL

Period 1310 A.D. The Mongolian and Arab riders were the only ones
to use the extremely short stirrup shown here.

Plate VI
THE PERSIAN SHAH TAHNRASP, HUNTING
About 1540. The seat used here is similar to the Spanish or Arabian School of the *Jineta*. See text, Part II, Chapter 1.

Plate VII
A KNIGHT OF THE MIDDLE AGES
(XVth Century)

Heavy, inflexible armour was responsible for the popularity of this seat which came to be known as the *Estradiota*.

Plate VIII
PERSIAN, XVIIth CENTURY (?)

Portrait of Shagista Khan executing the levade. This seat is between the straight kneed *Estradiota* (Plate VII) and the short stirruped Mongolian seat (Plate V).

Plate IX

MIDDLE AGES

Even when not impeded by armour the knights and squires of England and Northern Europe rode with the straight knee and the down pointed toe.

Plate X

THE LEVADE, 1600 A.D.

This seat, universal throughout Europe at this time, was the forerunner of the classical or academic seat.

Plate XI

THE CORBETTE

In this illustration taken from Pluvinel's book, 1660, we see the horse executing the corbette. Compare with Plate IV showing the Greek horse on the Parthenon (350 B.C.) executing the same figure. In Pluvinel's book we find that although the knee is still quite straight the horseman must now keep his heels well depressed.

Plate XII

THE CAPRIOLE

Pluvinel was the first man to use the pillars in training the horse. He used both one and two pillars. This method is still used by the Spanish Riding School.

Plate XIII
THE LEVADE ON THE LONG REINS

This beautifully graceful painting taken from a Greek amphora (vase) which was executed 500 years before the birth of Christ proves that the Greeks had developed a systematic method of dressage training which included work on the long reins. No improvement on their methods of training has ever been made.

Plate XIV
A LIPIZZAN STALLION EXECUTING
THE LEVADE ON THE LONG REINS

Compare with Plate XIII.

Plate XV

PIAFFE

Dr. Archie Dean on Noble, dressage stallion owned and trained by
Fritz Stecken.

Plate XVI

DRESSAGE TRAINING DOES NOT
RUIN A HORSE FOR JUMPING

Dr. Archie Dean puts Noble over an "oxer," a type of spread jump
which requires full extension of the horse.

Plate XVII

THE EXTENDED CANTER

Dr. Archie Dean on Oakledge Spotlight. Compare the profile with that of the horse at the collected canter, see Plate XVIII.

Plate XVIII

THE COLLECTED CANTER

Fritz Stecken on Noble executing the collected canter, the basis of all advanced dressage training. Compare with Plate XVII.

Plate XIX

PIROUETTE TO THE RIGHT

Richard Waetjan, internationally known Olympic rider, on Burgs-dorf.

Plate XX

COLLECTED TROT

Fritz Stecken on Noble.

Plate XXI

PIAFFE

Developed after the horse has learned the collected trot. In the Piaffe the horse "marks time" in place. It is first taught by the trainer walking beside and a little in front of the horse. This movement requires great engagement of the haunches and suppleness of the loins. Note the shortness from front to rear of the horse.

Plate **XXII**

THE PASSAGE

To many this is the most beautiful of the dressage movements. Developed either from the Piaffe or from the extended trot the horse
moves in a rhythmic balanced fashion, his body rising and falling as
the joints of his legs close and open. There is a perceptible hesitation
as each pair of diagonal legs are lifted. Not to be confused with the
"Spanish Trot," an artificial gait seen in circus riding which requires
horizontal extension of the front legs.

Plate XXIII
PYRAMIDS
A mounted gymnastics team from the McDonough Troop.

Chapter 9

EARLY TRAINING IN JUMPING

*F*or horses of three years or more, early training in jumping may begin toward the end of the second phase of training, the "breaking" period. The trainer should understand clearly the gymnastics through which the horse puts himself in taking a barrier. In Figures 65a and b page 138, the horse is seen approaching the jump. His ears are pricked up and he is gauging his strides; his neck and head are extended; he is on the bit. He must be allowed this free approach, and should be placed in such a position that he can see the jump in advance so that he may measure his strides subconsciously and take the obstacle without awkwardness. Any interference which would cause the horse to throw his head up at this point would limit his power to judge the position of the barrier and its height or breadth.

When he reaches the obstacle, (Figure 65b) the horse is beginning to fold his front legs, arch his crest, and lower his head; the haunches are brought well under him so that he can use them as a spring when he pushes off. In Figure 65c his forehand rises to maximum height and the hocks are beginning to straighten, but the horse has not yet left the ground. In Figure 65d the hocks are fully extended, their thrust projecting the entire mass over and beyond the obstacle; the head is descending; the crest is well curved. The horse is now going to use his head and neck as a man jumping a high barrier would use dumbbells, pushing the dumbbells, or, in the case of the horse, his head and neck, out in front of him as he goes over the barrier and utilizing their weight to carry him over.

Figures 65e and 65f show the horse in various stages of suspension. His head continues to descend as his croup rises. Then in

65g, the profile suddenly changes. The horse, still off the ground but about to land with his forelegs outstretched, now raises his head to help elevate the croup to its highest point of ascension, and also to help his descension. It is this lowering of the forehand and raising of

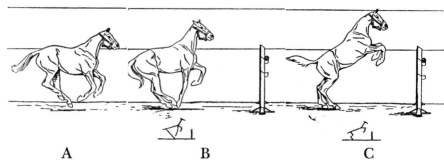

A   B   C

Figs. 65a, b, c.   *The approach and take-off.*

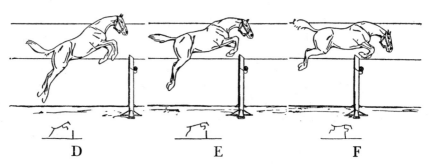

D   E   F

Figs. 65d, e, f.   *The flight.*

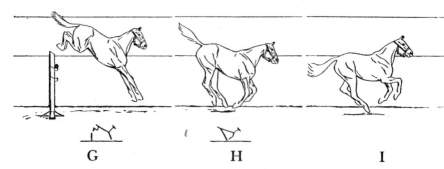

G   H   I

Figs. 65g, h, i.   *The landing and departure.*

Fig. 65.   The mechanics of the jump.

the head and crest, keeping the horse from getting his center of gravity too far forward and so losing his balance to the front, that permits him to clear the obstacle with his croup. This is a most important factor in the gymnastics of the jump and one which is rarely understood. It shows the illogic of using a standing martingale on a horse that is expected to jump high. Many horsemen contend that a standing martingale is allowable in jumping since it permits the horse to extend and lower his neck. They forget the descent of the jump, in which the horse, in order to maintain his balance and at the same time throw his croup high, must have complete freedom to raise his head.

This movement of the horse is also important to the skillful rider who wishes to maintain contact with his horse's mouth throughout the jump so that he may direct or turn him as he wishes. It is comparatively easy to learn to follow the lowering of the horse's head as he rises and begins to descend, but to have enough independence of the hands to continue the light contact as the horse raises his head again before lowering it for the second time is extremely difficult. I fancy that it was this motion of the head and neck which led to the practice, now discarded, of trying to "lift" the horse over the jump. Unfortunately, horsemen who had not studied the gymnastics of the jump always used the lift at the wrong time—while the horse was rising—instead of while he was descending. But I was interested to note that Señora Valdes, who was a member of the Mexican jumping team at the National Horse Show in the fall of 1950, did lift her horse's head just as he reached the peak of his jump. By that I judge that her horse had a bad habit of dropping his hindquarters. Such a method of helping the horse takes a very expert rider and is necessary or desirable only for a horse that for some reason cannot jump normally. To definitely "lift" is one thing; to try to follow the natural movement without impeding it is another, and it is for this ability that the horseman must strive.

Figure 65h shows that the horse, having landed, once more lowers his head and neck in preparation for resuming the gallop. Note, too, that the forelegs touch the ground and then leave it before the hind feet touch. This is a delicate feat of balancing on the part of the horse, and he must not be interfered with either by having his head pulled suddenly upward or by having the rider land with a thud on his loins.

We may deduce from these pictures that the horse that jumps the best is the one which can be given complete freedom by the rider. Such a horse must be willing, calm, and sufficiently experienced to know what he is doing. He must accept a light contact with the bit throughout, for though the horse needs freedom to use his forces over the jumps, it is the rider who knows what jumps to take and, from having gone over the course, what types of obstacles are presented, and who therefore can help the horse by the way he places his mount and by the way he rates him in between the obstacles.

Although the mechanics of the jump are always the same, horses differ in the way they like to jump. Some come up to the obstacle very slowly and pop over it; others jump better if allowed to go faster. Horses that have not had a long preliminary training over jumps without carrying a rider will seldom jump calmly. Horses that have not learned to go on the bit and to place their confidence in the rider through this means—those which have not both lateral and longitudinal flexion and that will not respond instantly to the aids—are useless, no matter how good natural jumpers they may be. All modern jumping courses require sudden turns and changes of direction. The horse must be ever ready to obey the rider so that he may negotiate these courses. In the hunt field too, it is the rider who decides where the horse is to jump. Many times, because of bad footing, wire, a fallen rider, etc., it is necessary to place the horse at a high point in a wall rather than at a low point.

The ideal hunter or jumper is the horse that, accepting the light contact of the bit and submitting to the rider's will in regard to such matters as changes of direction, will jump of his own free will and to the best of his ability any obstacle at which the rider faces him. He will jump calmly and in his stride, with plenty of impulsion, but he will not waste his strength by over-jumping. The ideal horseman over jumps is the one who can follow every movement of the horse without interfering with the movement, and who uses his own weight in such a fashion that it least impedes the horse. At the same time he never loses contact with his horse's mouth and is thus able to signal changes of direction to him at any time, even while the horse is in suspension.

WORK ON THE LONGE

Some trainers prefer to start the jumping training of the young horse in the chute with the horse at liberty, but since the horse is more excited and less controllable in the chute, I have found that a more satisfactory method is to start with work on the longe, where the trainer maintains physical contact with his horse and so can prevent disobedience.

The jump, which at first should be simply a bar flat on the

ground, should be placed in the hall as shown in Figure 66. A light rail runs from the top of the jumping standard, which is set in from the wall, to ground on both sides. This is to prevent the longeing tape from catching on the standard as the horse jumps. The trainer begins by longeing the horse at a quiet trot in a circle placed in rela-

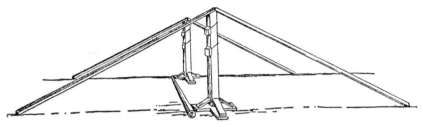

FIG. 66.   A jump set up for longeing.

tion to the jump as shown in Figure 67. The position of the circle is all-important. The trainer must be careful to place himself exactly in line with the jumping standard so that the circle is actually centered on it. If the horse is longed on a circle placed as in Figure 68, as he circles he will be going *away* from the jump, and as he nears it, he will be going in exactly the same track that he would take if he were shying out deliberately. If he circles as in Figure 69, he will not be placed so as to get a good look at his jump and will be jumping it on an angle.

When the trainer has trotted the horse quietly past the jump on the longe in both directions a number of times so that the jump no longer looks strange to the horse, he includes the jump in the longeing circle in the following manner: As the horse reaches point *A* (Figure 67) in the longeing circle, the trainer walks toward the jumping standard. He thus moves the circle toward the wall, and so places the horse in the correct position to include the jump in the circle. Most horses will not be surprised by this maneuver but will trot quietly over the bar with only a slight hesitation, if any. A horse that is either very timid or dull and inattentive may stop suddenly when he realizes that the bar is right in front of him. Having stopped, he may put his nose down and smell it. This the trainer should allow. If the horse gives a sudden and tremendous leap over the bar, going into a canter with signs of excitement, the trainer should step back to his original position, calm the horse with his voice, and get him working quietly at the trot again before once more moving forward to include the jump in the pattern of the movement. One thing only must the trainer never permit. If the horse, having stopped and nuz-

*t*led the bar, shows signs of reversing his direction in order to avoid it, the trainer must step quickly up to his shoulder and lead him over the bar. It is unlikely that the horse, if he has had the preliminary training advocated, will attempt to evade a bar which is flat on the ground, but a horse sent for reschooling or one that has been badly mishandled over jumps may do so. In leading the horse over the

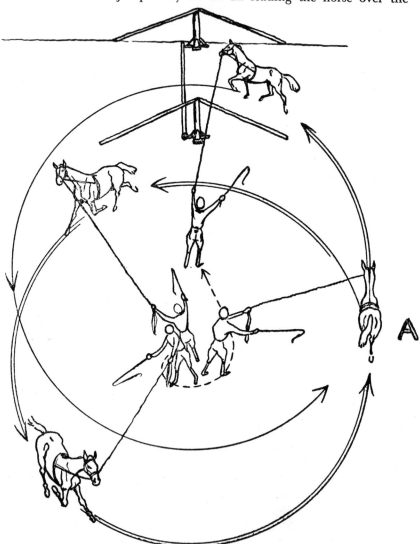

A

FIG. 67.   Correct method of longeing over jumps. *The diameter of the longeing circle is in line with the jump standard.*

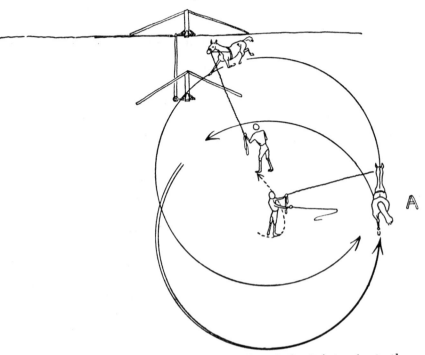

FIG. 68.   Incorrect placing of the longeing circle. *It is too far to the right in relation to the jump.*

jump, the trainer must be sure not to place himself in line with the horse's movement, or the horse may come across the bar unexpectedly and land on top of the trainer.

Having gone around the circle and over the jump several times, the horse should be made to change hands and circle the other way. The trainer should go back to circling inside the jump a few times so that the horse can look it over from this angle before including it in the circle. The horse should not be kept too long at this routine, but by the time the lesson is ended, the bar should not seem unusual, frightening, or even of much interest to him.

The second day's lesson begins by repeating the previous one, the bar flat on the ground, the horse first circling inside it, and, when he is calm, including it while coming from both directions. If he is calm and takes the bar without hesitation, one end of it—the end resting on the standard toward the center of the ring or corral—may be raised to about four inches above the ground. Again the colt is longed inside the jump until he has had a chance to look at it, then the circle may be moved toward the wall as before and the horse

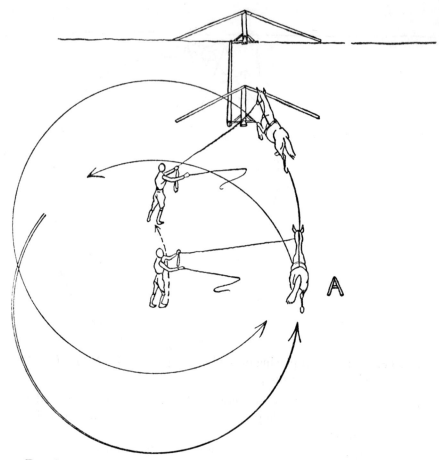

FIG. 69.   Incorrect method of longeing over a jump. *Longeing circle is too far to the left.*

asked to include the jump. If he is young, he will probably jump very high. This will give the trainer a good chance to judge how well the horse uses his forces in jumping—whether he jumps with an arched back, whether he uses his head well, etc. Some horses are very awkward at first and simply spring straight up, flattening their backs instead of arching them, and coming down with a jolt. These horses will need much work over spread jumps without a rider. Colts that have been jumped prematurely with weight on their back often show this tendency.

Each horse progresses at his own rate of learning. His intelligence, his previous training, and his confidence in his trainer determine how quickly the jumps may be raised. Many trainers say the horse should not be asked to jump higher than three feet during the first year of training. Some say that if he can carry a rider with ease and confidence over a three-foot bar, he may be longed or free schooled over obstacles about eleven inches higher than this. Whatever you do, you must make the horse's attitude the deciding factor. Keep him on one height jump until he is absolutely calm and obedient, then raise the bar, but not more than three inches at a time. The Italian Cavalry School advocates starting with a bar on the ground and raising it one inch a week.

Although a horse should not be asked to jump very high at this stage of his training, he should be trained to trot over a wide variety of obstacles, each one flat on the ground to start with. Striped rails, one, two, or three, laid side by side with from six to eighteen inches between them, are good. A row of balloons, a row of folded coats or feed sacks, a row of newspapers, anything and everything that the trainer can lay his hands on, should be utilized. Thus the horse learns to take strange-looking obstacles without fear.

If the jump is something that is completely foreign to him—a row of balloons, for example—the colt should first be led up to it and allowed to smell and nuzzle it as long as he likes. Then the trainer should step across it and tactfully persuade the horse to follow. If necessary, a helper may assist him by urging the horse from behind, but the horse should jump because of his confidence in the trainer, not from fear of the helper behind him. The assistant should soothe and pat the horse with his hand on the animal's rump rather than shout at him or use a whip. When he has crossed the strange obstacle several times in this fashion, the horse may be put on the longeing circle and asked to take it as described.

As the education of the horse proceeds and the jumps become higher, he may be longed over them at a quiet canter. It is easier and more natural for the horse to jump from a canter, since the movements of the horse in going over a jump are more similar in sequence to the canter than to the trot; but since the canter is a more exciting gait, it should not be introduced too early in the jumping schedule. Also, jumping from a trot is a good gymnastic exercise.

JUMPING AT LIBERTY

There are three methods of training a horse to jump at liberty. One is by means of a chute, which should be an oval measuring from fifty to sixty feet at its widest diameter. The walls must be very high, ten feet at least, and as solid as possible so that the horse, in trying to evade the jumps in the chute, is tempted neither to try to jump the wall nor to crash it. Generally there are two jumps with fixed standards in a chute of this size. Figure 70 shows an excellent method of constructing these jumps and standards. Since the object is for the horse to learn to respect the jump, clearing it without knocking it down, the jumps must be solid. At the same time, it must be possible to raise the jumps one inch at a time; if they are the type that will give a little without falling when hit, there will be less possibility that the horse will hurt himself. The type of construction shown in Figure 70 presents a good solution to the prob-

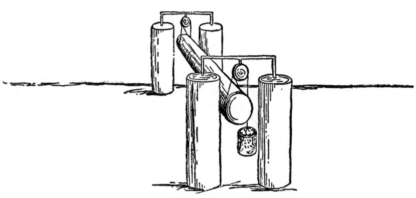

Fig. 70.   A good method of constructing permanent jumps in a chute.

lem. With the poles flat on the ground, the horse is turned loose in the chute and allowed to walk around it at will. When the horse has investigated the poles and gotten the playfulness out of him, the trainer takes his position in the center of the chute with his longeing whip in hand. As the horse starts the course, the trainer follows parallel to him, about opposite his middle and ten feet inside the jumping standards, holding his whip in the hand nearest the croup. His other hand is extended so that he is really free-schooling the horse and is able to step forward or backward to prevent disobediences. The horse should be free-jumped in both directions. His attitude should determine how soon the jumps should be raised.

The second method of free-jumping the horse is by means of a "jumping lane." This is a lane bordered by high fences or walls with jumps which extend completely across, from one side to the other.

146

The young horse is started at one end, usually with another horse that has been schooled previously or with a mounted horse as leader. He is then urged from behind to take the series of jumps. The jumping lane teaches the horse to jump freely and willingly in his stride, and to keep going from one jump to the next. A wide variety of jumps can be introduced and the distances between them can be varied. However, the trainer has not as much control in the jumping lane as he has with the longe or in the chute, and the horse can therefore get away with more disobediences than he can when in the smaller chute or on the tape. For this reason it is better to start with the longeing technique, graduate to the chute if you have one, and then go on to the lane. The jumping lane is very useful in training the rider, as with its assistance, he can learn to jump a schooled horse over a series of obstacles with his reins tied, and so can get his balance without hurting the horse or having to control him.

The third method of free-schooling over jumps is to train the horse to take the jumps on the command of the trainer in the ordinary indoor arena or schooling corral (Figure 71). If this is a very large affair, two or three people will be necessary at first to prevent the horse from running out in between the jumps, but it is surprising how quickly a horse of average intelligence can be taught to take a course

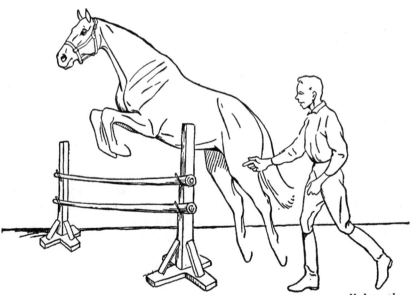

FIG. 71.   Free jumping in an arena. *Trainer moves parallel to the horse to keep him on jumping track.*

147

of jumps set up along the walls at the word of the trainer. The objection to this type of free-schooling is that the jumps cannot be permanent and so the horse may get into the habit of knocking them down. To correct this, when the horse has learned to take the simple jumps, he should have much work over the spread jumps and over jumps made of strange materials, as he will have more respect for these than for the simple bar that he knows is easily knocked down.

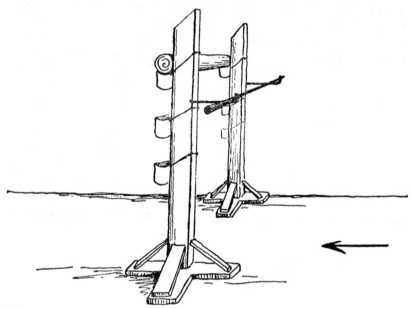

FIG. 72.   A good type of schooling jump to teach the horse to jump clean.

The type of jump illustrated in Figure 72 is also good to encourage the horse to jump clean. If the horse hits the iron bar, causing it to roll toward the standard, he receives a slight rap, which is unpleasant enough to make him stand away from his jumps and take them more carefully. Some trainers fasten a strand of light wire to the bar about six inches higher than the top plane of the jump. If this is done, the wire should be fastened so that it will break if the horse hits it hard. The purpose of this is to fool the horse into thinking he must clear all obstacles by six or more inches.

CONFIRMING THE HORSE ON THE FLOATING REIN

When the horse jumps two or three feet readily without the rider and arches his back correctly, the next stage of training—carrying the

148

rider over obstacles—may be introduced. He should be started as he was in his first lessons on the longe, with a single jump set up from the wall, the bar flat on the ground. The rider begins by circling at a slow trot in the center of the arena, the circle placed in relation to the jump as in Figure 67. Do not use the side rails running from the standards to the ground, since a longeing tape is not being used, and the horse must not become dependent on wings. Be careful not to "signal your punches" by changing the pattern of the circle when going for the jump. You do not want the horse to think something different is being introduced, and he will think so if you approach the bar from a distance and go straight at it.

Start the horse at the quiet trot, but if he breaks into a canter as he jumps, let him do so. Then bring him back to the trot, circle a few times without including the bar, and take it again. Have the rein stretched, even floating. The horse must be confirmed on the loose rein at the slow trot on each type of jump before more difficult obstacles are introduced. If he is placed in his circle so that it is easier for him to jump than to refuse, he will jump without the rider having to use his reins for control. Remain out of the saddle for at least a stride after the horse has landed. Coming back hard on his loins will frighten and confuse him and will make for later disobedience. Don't try to maintain contact with the mouth at this stage of training. Green horses jump awkwardly and peculiarly, and even the best horseman will find himself out of rhythm with such a horse on occasion. Besides, part of the training is to teach the horse to take the jump of his own accord, to pace himself and measure his own strides with no help from the rider. He is not being asked to take a series of obstacles with sudden changes of direction. Maintain only enough contact with the mouth to keep the horse circling and to place him on the approach so that the jump is included in the circle. Having landed, he should continue the pattern.

Work from both directions. Place the jump in different locations on the walls of the arena. Follow the same routine as advocated for the longeing period of training, first raising the bar at one end only, then very gradually letting it go up an inch or so at a time. Let the horse's attitude, his calmness, willingness, and confidence, determine how soon the jump may be raised. The horse must never be allowed to become bored or tired, nor should he show any excitement.

When the horse takes obstacles of two feet in height readily and on a floating rein without any signs of excitement or disobedience, you can begin to introduce a series of obstacles. These should be scattered around the ring in such a manner that the horse can be worked

in and out among them and can take all obstacles from both directions. Some should be set in line with each other, some at angles,
some along the wall, some in the center. The horse should first be
trotted around and between them without being allowed to jump.
When he is calm, pick the lowest obstacle placed against the wall and
allow him to hop over it from a trot, continuing the gait on the other
side without taking the next obstacle, even though it is in line with
the first. Each obstacle should be jumped at least once from both directions before the horse is permitted to take two in succession. The
purpose of this schooling is to teach the horse to be obedient to the
rider—not to feel that he must rush madly at a row of jumps as soon
as he sees them, yet to be willing to take any at which he is put. Occasionally, approach a jump and pull up as you reach it. Have the horse
stand a moment, then back him up three or four steps and ask him to
take the jump from that position. As he becomes more and more
obedient, he may be allowed to canter quietly in and out around the
jumps and then over them, but never take the series in the same order
twice. On no account should the horse be punished by rough hands
or legs or by a wrong use of the rider's weight. If you want to see how
much the distribution of weight controls your balance and ability to
walk forward, lift a child "piggy-back" fashion, and then ask him to
swing from side to side as you attempt to run along a straight line.
A young, immature horse is greatly disturbed by a badly balanced
rider, and it can easily sour him on jumping.

As in the earlier training, different types of jumps may now be
introduced. A good type for this kind of work is shown in Figure 73.

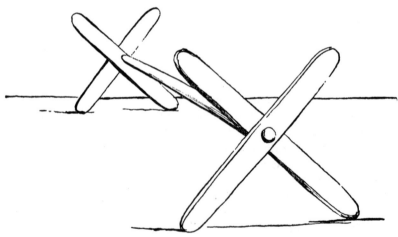

FIG. 73.   A useful type of jump which rights itself.

This jump will simply roll over if the horse strikes it; it does not need to be set up again, and it is light and easy to carry around. By all means, have as many "mental hazard" jumps (balloons, coats, wheelbarrows) as you can. Just give your horse a chance by letting him move around them freely and become accustomed to the sight of them before you ask him to jump them.

The horse should not be jumped every day lest he become soured or bored. Rather his jumping lessons should be alternated with his general schooling and his work out of doors on the trails. On the days when he does jump, he should first be warmed up by going through the schooling figures that he knows at the slow gaits. When the lesson is over, he should be walked on a floating rein and rewarded with pats or a tidbit.

Chapter 10

ADVANCED JUMPING

*A*gain we come to a point in the horse's education where he has completed his "basic training" and must become a specialist. There are three types of jumping horses for which classes are provided in the shows. The professional trainer bears this in mind, and the higher education of his horse in jumping is adjusted to the purpose for which he intends it.

TYPES OF JUMPERS

The *conformation hunter* is the first of these types of jumpers. This horse must have good conformation, no serious blemishes, a nice way of going, and good manners. He may be a lightweight, capable of carrying up to 160 pounds; a middleweight, capable of carrying 180 pounds; or a heavyweight, capable of carrying over 180. The hunter is expected to jump in his stride without hesitation, galloping on at a steady pace. He must not weave coming into his jumps. A light tick is not considered a serious fault in hunter classes, but poor jumping form is, and the horse that lands heavily, "buck jumps," rushes, misjudges and comes in too close, looks hard to hold, needs urging with a whip, or the one that cannot jump off his hocks stands no chance in a hunter class. If he is to go into the ladies' hunter classes, his manners must be impeccable. He must be calm, preferably snaffle-mouthed, and must pull up readily.

The *working hunter* classes call for the same type of jumping and manners required in the conformation classes, but conformation is not counted. The horse must be sound, but "honorable blemishes" such as wire scratches are not considered by the judges. Another classification in the working hunter division is the *handy hunter*. This horse must not only have a good way of going and good manners, but he must show that he is exceptionally handy and docile. In such classes the judges may ask the rider to knock a bar off a jump, dismount and lead over the obstacle, open and close a gate, or take certain obstacles at a trot.

SCHOOLING THE HUNTER IN THE FIELD

In preparing a horse to show or to be sold as a hunter, or to be actually hunted, the trainer must keep the goal in mind. His horse should have training in galloping both up and down hill as well as on the level. He must be schooled to follow behind another horse, waiting quietly at a panel, keeping his distance, or going in the lead. If enough outdoor space is available, the trainer should provide a wide variety of jumps of the type to be met in the hunt field and in the hunting classes of the show ring—chicken-coops, post-and-rails, gates, picket fences, stone walls, hedges, hitchcocks, drop jumps and landing jumps, ditches, and combinations of poles and ditches. As many as possible of these should be movable so that the courses can be varied. If their height and width can be adjusted, so much the better (Figure 74)

Horses jump much better and more freely on outside courses and in company than alone in the ring. The horse that can jump three feet in the schooling ring will take four feet and better with no hesitation in the hunt field.

If there is an adjacent hunt, the best schooling for the hunter, once he has learned to respond to the aids, to be rated, and to jump up to three feet cleanly and without awkwardness, is hunting. The cubbing season starts in August as a rule, and this is the time to introduce the young horse. His misbehavior, if any, will be forgiven; the field will not be big; and the runs will not be too long or fast.

If there is no adjacent hunt, and if there is open country, I strongly advise the trainer of hunters to get himself a couple of bloodhounds and have his own hunt. This breed of dog, generally misunderstood in this country, is the gentlest, most sagacious animal imaginable. Through the centuries, he has been trained for one purpose: to trail. He will trail anything, and once on the scent, he will not depart from it. He need not be kennelled but can be kept as a house pet. It is not necessary to lay any kind of drag. The hound will follow the scent of a man on a horse. It is necessary only to teach him that the horse and man are his quarry. The procedure is simple. A

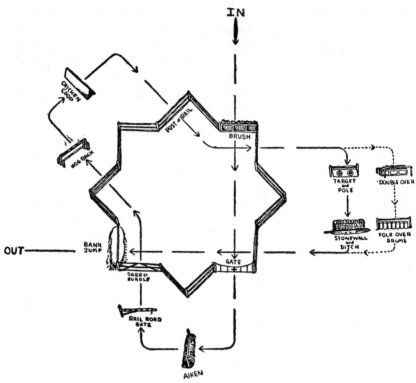

IN

CHICKEN LOOP

POST + RAIL

BRUSH

HOG BACK

TARGET and POLE

DOUBLE OXER

STONEWALL and DITCH

POLE OVER DRUMS

OUT

BANK JUMP

GATE

SHEEP HURDLE

RAIL ROAD GATE

AIKEN

FIG. 74.   A jumping course which can be set up in a comparatively small area but which will provide a great variety of obstacles. *The jumps are so arranged that they may be taken in any sequence, thus lessening the probability of the horse becoming bored. The possibility of introducing sharp turns will teach him to be flexible and to rate easily. A tentative course is shown.*

man representing the fox rides away from the group of riders, calling the hounds. After a few minutes' grace, the hounds are released. They pick up the scent and gallop across the country, baying with a full-throated cry. If there is any wind, they will pick up the scent as it drifts back, and will take short-cuts. The riders will be put to it to stay with hounds in any country that is at all rough or wooded. Other game, water, or hard roads will not throw these hounds off the scent. When they come up to the quarry, they lick him affectionately.

The young hunter should be trained to the hunting thong early. Carry one with you always and make a practice of swinging and cracking it at unexpected moments. The horse should also learn not to fear the hunting horn, and not to kick at hounds or to be nervous when they run around his heels. He must not kick at other horses and must stand quietly to be mounted and dismounted, even when other riders are in the process of riding away. If he is to be used by one of the hunt staff, he should be trained like the handy hunter, and must be willing to scramble over awkward places, to push himself through undergrowth, and to wade streams and boggy places.

Having finished his day's work, he must be willing to walk home quietly on a long rein. He should van easily, as most hunts go to invitation fixtures many miles away.

If his destination is the show ring, start him in the small local shows as soon as he has finished the secondary stage of his training and has had some jumping. Try not to let him have any disagreeable experiences until he is well confirmed in the ring. If it is a question of winning a cup or saving your horse, by all means save the horse.

This variety of training for a hunter makes him less likely to sour than an open jumper but he must not be over-jumped. Don't put him over jumps higher than three feet more often than twice a week. Don't take more than ten or twelve jumps in one schooling period without doing something else in between. Give him as much open-air and field work as possible. Careful physical conditioning as well as consistent work on the intermediate schooling and dressage figures will produce a horse that is a delight to ride and a valuable animal in any market.

THE OPEN JUMPER

The open jumper must be a horse with tremendous heart, outstanding gymnastic ability, and strong nerves. He may be of any breed. His advanced training is a continuation of the course pursued in his elementary training—gradually raising the jumps, and introducing more and more variety into the course. It takes about a year of showing to settle a young open jumper and get him over his stage fright. Don't expect too much. Keep the jumps down and raise them only gradually. Go back to free-jumping him every so often, and give him plenty of cross-country work. Don't jump him high more than twice a week. Jumping higher than three feet is a strain on any horse, and once he is injured, it is hard to get and keep an open jumper sound.

To prepare an open jumper for the show ring, the general rule is that, if the horse is green, he should be schooled up until two days before the show, but need not be asked always to scale jumps of the height that he will be expected to face in the ring. If he is a well-schooled, experienced horse, he should be exercised only lightly for the week previous to the show. Any extra energy that he can build up during this time will show in greater jumping ability when he gets in the ring.

In choosing your classes, be contented with three classes per show, especially with a young horse. There may be jump-offs in each of these, and the number of jumps will add up surprisingly fast. One of the greatest curses of the modern show ring is the custom of awarding championships to horses that have won the most points in a given division. With these in mind the professional will often put his horses into class after class with no regard whatsoever for their physical condition.

The open jumper is quite a different animal from the hunter. Soundness is required of him, but he can have any type of conformation. His main attribute is his ability to get up in the air. The American Horse Shows Association Rules penalize the horse for ticking a jump, and for this reason the mercenary trainer sometimes goes to the utmost of cruelty to make his horse jump clean. The advocates of the F.E.I. rules of judging jumpers, which penalize only knockdowns, falls of horse or rider, refusals, shy-outs, or getting off the course, claim that if all shows were judged by these rules the fate of the jumper would be more happy; unfortunately, however, in this country, the F.E.I. rules do not help a great deal.

In international competitions and in national competitions abroad, the jumping courses are far stiffer than those in America. The jumps are big, wide, and placed so that a horse must be able to turn sharply on the bit in order to clear them. Because they are so stiff, there are not as many jump-offs as there are in the simpler courses in this country. In competitions judged on F.E.I. rules in this country, sometimes nearly half the class goes clean. Since time often is not taken into consideration until the jump-off, that means a great many jump-offs. When courses are not stiff enough and time *is* taken into consideration, one often sees horses being galloped madly, with no attempt made to place or rate them properly, and with a consequent danger to the life and limbs both of the rider, who deserves no pity since he rides from choice, and to the horse, who deserves all our pity since he has nothing to say about it.

If all open jumpers could receive the careful schooling that is given the international show teams, there would be little to complain about, but unfortunately, in this country anyway, the open jumper lives a horrible life.

Training the Horse

In selecting or preparing horses for international competition, one must take into consideration their speed over jumps, their flexibility and obedience, their high- and broad-jumping ability, and their stamina. Of all the varieties of show horses, the field horse destined for international competition is the best trained, the best treated, and, as a result, the strongest and most athletic. Many of our Olympic team horses have competed successfully at eighteen years of age, but it is rare that the average open jumper goes more than a few years without serious injury or going sour. Records have shown that horses with dressage training have been the most consistent winners over jumps in the various international events. There is no regulation as to size, breed, or type. With the doing away of the American Army team, both trainers and breeders are becoming more and more aware of the market for Olympic horses and of the type of training which will suit them for international competition. It is to be hoped that the general lot of the open jumper will be improved through this form of education.

PART II

Training the Rider

Chapter 1

HISTORY AND EVOLUTION
OF THE SEAT

The earliest reported records of horseback riding are in the stone tablets of the Hittites, chiseled out some fourteen hundred years before Christ. Saddles were unknown at that time, and continued to be unknown for many centuries. Two thousand years later, the Greeks had learned to ride on pads or saddle cloths, it is true, but stirrups were a much later innovation.

The Hittite tablets show the warrior sitting with his heels down, toes raised (Plate I). The horse in this illustration is very small, which is typical of other pictures of the horses of the ancients. The horse is apparently doing a form of the levade, although it is questionable whether the horses of that era actually were trained to do this movement or whether it was a position which appealed to the artist. The reins are held in one hand and the spear in the other.

The next picture (Plate II) shows an Egyptian lady in 1300 B.C. Judging by the absence of riding habit, the climate must have been extremely humid. The horse is very tiny, probably only eleven hands or less, the size of an ordinary Shetland pony; but it has the dished face and the poll of an Arab. The lady appears to be an expert rider, since the hand holding the rein is well relaxed while the other brandishes a whip. One cannot see how her feet are held, but there is a very definite bend in the knees.

The position of the Assyrian riders of 800 B.C., as shown in the picture in Plate III, reminds one strongly of the seat used by the American Indians. Apparently, like the Indians, the Assyrians trained their horses to respond to pressure of the knees so that the warrior or hunter could have both hands free to use his bow. The riders look like excellent horsemen. There is a definite feeling of forward impulse in the leading figure; the lower legs are completely relaxed, with no sign of gripping with the knees, as was true in the picture of the Egyptian damsel. These men rode on balance alone.

The illustration in Plate IV is a reproduction of one of the figures sculptured on the Parthenon by Phidias. One could profitably spend hours studying these figures, which portray so beautifully the anatomy and movements of the horse. In this picture the horse appears to be executing a corbette, a movement in which the animal first balances on his haunches and then leaps off the ground. The rider is sitting perfectly relaxed with a straight back, and is in complete balance with his horse. He must have been a very excellent horseman indeed, since to sit this movement is extremely difficult. Here again one is struck by the small size of the animal. The horses of the Greeks were stocky and strong, but certainly no more than thirteen hands high.

In addition to the sculptures of Phidias, we have the beautifully clear text of Xenophon, who exhorts his pupils in this fashion:

"Whether he uses a cloth or rides upon the bareback, we would not have him [the rider] sit in the attitude of one who drives a chariot, but as if he were standing erect with his legs somewhat astride, for thus his thighs will cling closer to the horse and, being upright, he will be better able to wield his lance and strike with more force.

"The leg below the knee must hang loose and easy. If it is kept stiff and should strike against anything, it might be hurt or broken, but being at liberty, whatever it encounters, it will give way while the thigh remains unmoved. Indeed, the whole of the rider's body should be, above the knees, as pliant as possible, that he may be able to endure more fatigue, and be less liable, when he is attacked, to be either pulled or pushed from his feet."

From this passage it is clear that the Greeks understood the use of a relaxed, balanced seat as opposed to the theory of riding on grip, which came later. It is interesting also to note that the translator used as a decoration on his title page the figure of a centaur, thus expressing the oft-repeated admonition that a man should ride as though he were one with the horse.

The saddle and stirrups were invented in about 300 A.D., and were largely responsible for the development of a school of horsemanship known as the *Estradiota*, a word which means mercenary soldier. The school of the *Estradiota* called for very long stirrup leathers, and

162

no bend in the knee. This seat was adopted in Germany and France and continued in use in these countries throughout the Middle Ages. Such a position was made necessary by the heavy armour worn by the knights.

A different school of horsemanship, known as the *Jineta*, developed in Spain after the Arabs invaded that country in 711. Under the Arabian influence, the Spaniards changed their method of riding (the *Estradiota*) to this new method, which called for a much shorter stirrup.

The earliest mention of *balance* as being the most important factor in the seat in riding is to be found in an Arabian manuscript *The Ornament of the Cavaliers and Banner of Gallants* by one *Ibn Hudayl*. This book, written in Arabic about fourteen hundred was translated for me for the first time by the daughter of Mr. Marius de Zayas this past summer (1951) and proves beyond a doubt that contrary to the opinion of some authorities the Arabs were great students of horsemanship. The writer states as follows:

And you must know God guide you to correctness, that the principle of equitation is to acquire *balance* on the horse. And the beginning of this knowledge lies solely in learning to ride without saddle. And whosoever does not try repeatedly at first to ride without saddle will most times not be able to consolidate the steadiness of his position on the horse and will remain unsteady on his saddle, especially when trotting and galloping and will be unable to save himself from falling if his horse becomes unruly or if some accident befalls him [the horse] . . .

Whether Hudayl was familiar with the principles of Xenophon one does not know, but the two had come to the same conclusions regarding the importance of smoothness and lightness of the rider's seat and non-abuse of the horse in his way of handling him. For example in regard to mounting the Arabian says as follows:

And he should take the reins in his left hand (and) with [the same hand take hold of] the pommel of the saddle-bow, or the mane of the horse if he sees that this is easier for him. He should shorten the reins in his hand in order to control the head of the horse, for so long as the horse does not feel the bit he may become nervous and he [the rider] must not be careless of his [the horse's] unruliness but should go around him and deal with him gently.

163

We see from this that Hudayl understood two of the fundamental traits of the horse, his ability to develop confidence in his rider and to depend on him, and the rule of working quietly around him to prevent his becoming frightened.

Mounting is described in great detail including the admonition that the rider should extend his toe toward the horse's shoulder in order not to dig him in the belly in mounting, that it is a good idea for someone to hold the off stirrup to keep the saddle in place and that the rider should spring up "quickly and lightly."

Great emphasis is put on keeping the reins exactly even and maintaining a light and never jerky contact with the horse's mouth. The horse must not carry his nose pointed out nor must it be drawn in to his chin, and the rider should take care that the bit is as light as possible for that particular horse and is comfortable for him. In fact quietness and equestrian tact together with the importance of learning to ride by balance and of studying the fundamental principles behind the art of equitation are most carefully stressed by this Arabian writer and horseman, who ends his treatise with the following:

> And for all emergencies there are rules according to the conditions [to be dealt with] at the time and the person must meet each emergency to the best of his ability and possibilities with the help of Almighty Allah.

The Arabian influence extended to Mongolia and Persia, where riders did not use heavy armour and did a great deal of mounted work in the form of hunting, contests with lances, and games such as polo, which originated in Persia. In such contests and in hunting, the riders did not need to wear armour, and a shorter stirrup made it possible for them to rise in their stirrups in order to get a good thrust with the spear. Plates VII and IX show in the photo section the position of the rider as developed by the school of the *Estradiota*. In contrast, note the position of the riders in Plates V, VI, and VIII, which show the Persian and Mongolian riders of about the same period.

A third school of riding, called the *Bastarda* or *Brida,* was also popular in Spain after the Arab invasion. This school adopted a position which was a compromise between that of the *Estradiota* and the *Jineta*. Probably the Persian rider shown in Plate VIII has about the same seat taught by the school of the *Brida*.

That this Arabian influence was recognized as a good one is demonstrated by the fact that in 965, Pope Juan XIII asked the king of Spain to designate Spanish soldiers to instruct Italian soldiers in equitation. The Arabian influence thus spread to Italy, where the system was called the *Jineta,* or Spanish Riding School. The horses used by these riders were Arabians, far superior to the Italian horses in obedience, flexibility, and training.

FIG. 75. The seat used in the Middle Ages.

FIG. 76.   Classical or academic seat. *Used in dressage and* haute école.

In France and England, riders continued to use the long stirrup as shown in the illustration in Plate XI, taken from Pluvinel's book, but in Spain, the *Jineta* school of riding predominated. Gradually, however, the long stirrup became popular even in Spain, for one finds in a book written by Luis de Bañuelos in 1605, *Libro de la Gineta,* that the author deplores the fact that the art of horsemanship is deteriorating in Spain, and that it has become the fashion to ride with the "stirrup so long that the rider can barely reach it with his toe." De Bañuelos claims that money is at the root of the decline in the art of horsemanship—that the cavalieros prefer to sell their highly trained horses rather than to ride them, and that even the young ladies care more for the presents that the money will buy than for seeing their suitors executing difficult feats of horsemanship!

In regard to the seat, de Bañuelos tells the prospective rider that he should take his horse to a flat field with no holes or rocks and, having mounted, rise in his stirrups at a gallop. Furthermore, the pupil is instructed to keep relaxed and not to grip with his knees and thighs. This is the earliest mention of what might be called the for-

Fig. 77. Old-fashioned English hunting seat as pictured in English hunting prints. *One sometimes sees modified versions of this in the hunt fields today.*

ward seat, and is the only recommendation of such a seat until modern times.

In England, France, and Germany during the eighteenth and nineteenth centuries, we see the same seat that was popular earlier —the legs and hands are quite straight, and the body is perfectly vertical (Plate X). Pictures of the famous master of the Spanish Riding School, Max von Weyrother, done in the early 1800's also show this position. By the end of this century the classical, or academic seat, as it is called, had undergone some important changes (Figure 76). The stirrups were shortened so that there was a very definite bend in the knee, and were carried on the toe for dressage work to enable the rider to touch his horse with his spurs without changing the position of his leg. The body is extremely vertical, with the hands just in front of the body. This seat, pictured by de Souza, is certainly far more logical than the so-called English hunting seat, shown in Figure 82, in which the rider has his stirrup leathers pushed forward, his weight all on his buttocks, and no lightness in his loin or chest.

In France, the importance of the supple loin, sometimes referred to as "stretching" the loin, is first mentioned in the Cavalry Regulations of 1829, which tells the soldier to "sustain his loin without rigidity." It is in the French school also that one first comes across instructions that include holding the hands "about six inches apart." Great emphasis is put on elevating the "bust." As the years went on, more and more emphasis was put on relaxation and suppleness in both the German and the French schools—the same principle expounded by Xenophon in 400 B.C.

At the beginning of the twentieth century, there was still a divergence in the seats used in various countries. The English country gentleman rode over his wide ditches with his feet thrust out before him. He admonished his children to "grip with their knees," and, unless he was inclined toward traveling in foreign countries, he knew little and cared less about the higher forms of riding.

In America, the situation was much the same. The rider was told to keep his body always perpendicular to the ground in riding over jumps, regardless of the position of his horse's body. Thus he leaned forward as the horse rose on the aids, and far back as he landed. No one had thought of relieving the horse of the rider's weight on his back during the flight, so the rider sat as far down in his saddle as he could. It took a good horseman to do this and still absorb the shock of the landing so that he was not thrown off balance.

THE ACADEMIC SEAT

In Europe, the art of dressage and *haute école* was continued both at the Spanish Riding School in Vienna and at Saumur, the French cavalry school. The present-day academic seat, shown in Figure 76, was standardized. In this seat the rider sits in the middle of his saddle, his body upright. His legs are bent at the knees, and the stirrup leathers are vertical. His arms form a straight line from elbow to bit as seen from the side. Since several different rein positions can be used, the hands are not carried as far apart as they would be in either the balanced or the forward seat. The reins are somewhat longer than in riding the two latter seats, but the principle of relaxation remains the same. The stirrup in the academic seat is carried more on the toe than in the balanced seat. This, as explained before, is to enable the rider to use his spurs without carrying his foot back.

De Souza, Müseler, and Podhajsky all recommend this seat. The Germans put more emphasis on the flexibility of the loin to keep the rider in contact with his horse and as an aid to making him execute

168

his movements, than do the French. The French put more emphasis on the elevation of the chest. All European schools emphasized the importance of harmony between rider and horse and of "style." Even in 1605, de Bañuelos remarked that to be a good horseman one should have three things: *aire* (air or style), *mano* (hands) and *dar los pies con mucha soltura en la silla* (firmness and deepness of seat due to a strong placing of the feet). The first two, he goes on to say, are given to each one of us by God; the last can be learned at the riding school.

THE FORWARD SEAT

Between 1897 and 1907, the first really important change in the position of a rider over jumps was developed by Federico Caprilli. An American jockey, Ted Sloan, noticed that the boys who watered the horses occasionally were run away with. Some of these boys, to keep from falling off, leaned far forward and hung onto the manes of their horses. The horses so ridden always went faster than they had ever been able to go before. Sloan shortened his stirrups, climbed up his horse's neck, and proceeded to bring down on himself hoots of laughter from the audience, but a gratifying number of trophies as well. Sloan made no study of the scientific reasons for the horse's behavior; it remained for the Italian, Caprilli, after years of study, to develop and formalize what is now known as the "forward seat."

This seat was a real innovation, based on a different principle and used for different purposes than the academic seat. The forward seat, contrary to the beliefs of the uninitiated, does not mean merely leaning forward; it means making the animal free to extend himself and to move forward without interference from his rider. The rider's weight is placed so that the horse can bear it in the easiest possible manner, and his hands are used so that they control without impeding the forward impulse.

The position of the horseman in the forward seat is shown in Figure 78. Note the slant of the sole of the rider's boot, accomplished by a breaking inward of the ankle bone. This serves to keep the knees, legs, and thighs against the horse *automatically*. The leg, to achieve this position, is rotated at the hip, and this rotation, together with the position of the feet and ankles, places the inside of the calf and leg against the horse and holds it there with no effort on the part of the rider. The rider sits on his pelvic bones, not on the fleshy parts of his buttocks. His upper body is inclined slightly forward, even at the walk, and very much so at the faster gaits. As his body inclines forward, he rolls more on his thighs, maintaining a three-point contact with his horse—crotch and thighs. In the flight of the jump, or at the racing gallop, he raises his pelvis and crotch out of the saddle and maintains a two-point contact with the horse, with his weight placed mainly on his stirrups.

FIG. 78.   The forward seat.

The hands are very important in riding the forward seat. Instead of carrying them a few inches in front of the body and close together as recommended by de Souza, the rider carries them several inches in front of the pommel of the saddle, and the width of the horse's shoulder's apart (six to ten inches). Thus the rein does not touch the horse's neck, and there is always a straight line from the rider's elbow to the bit when viewed from the side or from above. The hand must be a following hand as long as the horse is going at the desired rate of speed at the gait and in the direction chosen by the rider. There is always light contact with the mouth. To change direction or decrease the speed, the rider uses an active hand.

    This seat has been adopted by all nations for show jumping and for galloping and racing (Figure 79). In America it has been adopted by the younger generation for hunting, but in England and Ireland, the old-fashioned hunting seat is preferred. Americans who learned to ride before the forward seat came into popularity also tend to ride the hunting seat.

FIG. 79. The forward seat over jumps. *Driving rein method of holding rein, used with beginners and green horses since rein slips through hand easily.*

THE BALANCED SEAT

Santini contends in his book *The Forward Impulse* that there is no such thing as a "modified" forward seat. One either rides forward or one doesn't. But the American cavalry seat, sometimes called the "balanced" or "military" seat, is a modified form of the Italian seat (Figure 80).

There are four elements of the balanced seat: the upper body, which comprises the head, chest, arms, loin, and back; the base of support, consisting of all parts of the rider's body which touch any part of the saddle (or the horse, if the rider is bareback)—the crotch, that portion of the buttocks which is under the pelvic bones, the inside of the thighs, the knees, the upper part of the leg, and the soles of the feet; the lower leg, which is free to be used as an aid; and the equilibrium. The rider must be able to use these four elements independently as he wishes. The lower leg, for example, cannot be dependent upon the position of the upper body, nor must the latter depend upon the position of the base of support. The rider must be able to place his equilibrium (weight and balance) where and when he wishes, regardless of what the rest of him is doing or what the horse is doing.

171

FIG. 80.   The balanced seat. *Also called the military seat.*

The American government spent many thousands of dollars and years of research to develop this seat. It sent its best riders to Europe to study the different methods of riding. The best-known exponent of the balanced seat is, of course, General Chamberlin. The American Army contends that the balanced seat is a correct seat from the mathematical and mechanical point of view, that it gives the greatest ease to the horse with the least effort on the part of the rider, and that it can be adapted for any type of work.

In dressage work, the rider must be in close and relaxed contact with his horse. The extreme forward position of the Italian seat prevents this, but the balanced seat does not. The balanced seat is a very flexible seat. The rider is told that he may use one of three lengths of stirrup, depending upon the kind of work he is doing. For training horses and for dressage and schooling movements, he rides with a stirrup that hangs a little below his ankle bone. This enables him to keep his whole lower leg in contact with his horse. For ordinary hacking, he raises the stirrup until it knocks the point of the ankle bone. This makes it easy for him to ride forward at the gallop and so take the weight off his horse, yet it is not uncomfortable for him at the other gaits where he sits down at the saddle. For high jumping, the stirrup is again raised to well above the ankle bone. Here the rider wants to be able to keep his weight entirely out of the saddle and so to relieve his horse. He is not going to demand complicated movements and steps from his horse, and so does not need to "feel" as delicately or use his aids as precisely.

At the halt in the balanced seat, the rider is vertical. At the walk, jog trot, and the canter, he is very slightly forward. At the ordinary and extended trot, and at the gallop, he is as far forward as is the rider of the Italian seat. The thigh, leg, and foot positions, as well as the position and use of the arms and hands, are the same in both the balanced and forward seats. The only real difference between the two seats is that in the balanced seat, the rider sits down in the saddle at the canter and slow trot and maintains a more vertical position of the body. In the balanced seat, too, the rider has a variation in the permissible length of stirrup.

Fig. 81.   The saddle seat.

173

OTHER AMERICAN SEATS

There are two other seats used in America and recognized by the American Horse Shows Association as desirable. To the horseman who has studied the principles behind the academic, balanced, and forward seats, it seems ludicrous that these two seats are permitted, since they help neither the rider nor the horse. The first of these seats is the "saddle" seat, illustrated in Figure 81, in which the rider is pushed back in the saddle. The lower arms are not in line with the line from elbow to bit, and the legs are pushed forward. This seat means that, to maintain his position, especially at the posting trot, the rider either must use his hands, or he must use much more effort than is usually necessary with his back, since he is not and cannot be in natural balance. Ask a rider using the saddle seat to rise in his stirrups and maintain his position without using his hands and he will not be able to do so. Yet each time the rider posts, he must rise in his saddle!

FIG. 82.   The hunting seat. *Compare with Figure 83.*

The "hunting seat," as shown in Figure 82, permits the rider to ride with his hands on his stomach, his feet pushed forward and all his weight on his buttocks. This rider is not and cannot get in true balance, especially if his horse is moving, since he must inevitably be "behind" the horse. He cannot use his hands correctly and lightly, since his reins are too long, his hands flattened, and too close together.

Not until the Horse Shows authorities recognize the illogic of these two seats, and not until their judges stop awarding prizes to riders who use them, will the American civilian begin to compare with European riders. Fortunately, the admission of civilian riders to the Olympic Games contests is stimulating interest in the academic, balanced, and forward seats, and I have no doubt that in another twenty years all other positions will be forgotten as far as horsemanship competitions go.

Chapter 2

THE RIDING INSTRUCTOR

A person who is considering becoming a riding instructor with the idea of making it his or her life's work should have certain qualifications and characteristics, without which he stands very little chance of being successful. Unfortunately, the average camp counsellor in charge of riding and the average "instructor" at a hacking stable are totally lacking in these characteristics. This accounts for the deplorably low standards of riding in many sections of the country, and also for many of the riding accidents.

No one would be allowed to teach any subject in a public school without first having studied methods of teaching, as well as having been well grounded in the subject that he proposes to teach. If he fails as a teacher, the pupils may not learn much, but at least they are in no physical danger. The safety of the beginner on a horse, however, no matter how gentle the horse may be, depends entirely on the knowledge and ability of the instructor. Since teaching riding presents many problems not encountered in the ordinary classroom, the riding instructor not only must know how to teach his subject, but he must be able to handle his class in such a way that, as far as possible, all potential dangers are eliminated. At the same time, by his attitude, he must keep his pupils from becoming frightened. He can do this only if he understands the horse and his reactions, and also knows how to handle a group of children or adults, watching them and thinking for them, sensing the coming of trouble and preventing its occurrence.

Every instructor should have a definite set of goals in mind for his pupils, both specific and general. He should strive to teach each student to love his horse, and to consider him always; to be relaxed and unafraid; to learn to feel, interpret, and influence the horse's movements; to want to improve his riding ability and to improve it until he gets to the point where he can take any ordinarily well-trained horse and control him readily; and, above all, to develop educated hands. If the pupil is studying jumping, he should be able not only to get his horse over the jump in good form, but also to manage his mount in the hunt field.

PHYSICAL AND TEMPERAMENTAL CHARACTERISTICS

Teaching riding is one of the most tiring and nerve racking of professions, as well as one of the most rewarding. The prospective riding instructor must be strong physically, agile and alert, with quick reactions. He must not tire easily, either physically or nervously. He must have great self-control in the event of emergencies. He must think, at such times, not only of the child involved in the accident but also of the others in the group. He must, of course, help the injured or frightened child, and he must also give some instruction to the others in the class that will make them realize that they are still under discipline. Above all things, he must make them realize that in emergencies they are still expected to keep their heads and to obey. If he does not maintain this discipline, he may have several injured children on his hands instead of one. The ability to control one's own reactions to the extent of appearing perfectly calm and unworried when the exact opposite is the truth is difficult; for some people, it is impossible. Such people should never try to teach riding.

The riding instructor must have both tact and humor, and he must be able to use his humor in such a way that the child learns to take things lightly and to laugh at mishaps *with* the instructor. It is taken for granted that no instructor worthy of the name would ever laugh *at* the mistakes of a pupil or allow others to do so. He will need tact both for handling the children whom he teaches and for handling their parents. Every parent seems to feel that his child must be at the head of the class. In placing his pupils in groups for instruction, the instructor tries to put those with the same experience, learning, and aptitude together, but invariably one or two children in each group will either advance too rapidly for the group or get behind it. The child who gets too far ahead of his group is being held back in his advancement if he stays with the class, since, for safety's sake, the class can work only on problems within the capabilities of all. The child who gets behind the group holds the group back, and generally becomes discouraged and timid. Putting the child with high aptitude into a more advanced group presents no problem as far as handling the parent goes since every parent is delighted to learn that his child makes better-than-average progress. It is wise, however, when explaining why the child is being moved to a new group, also to explain that the work in the new group will be harder and that the child, after having been at the head of the previous class, will now find himself one of the poorest learners, that this is apt to be discouraging, and that the parent must not expect to have his child be as capable as some of the others in the more advanced group.

Handling the parent of the child who has not made normal progress is a more difficult problem. No parent wants to be told that his child is not up to average, particularly if it is a case of mental aptitude. It is best to try to find some reason for the child's slowness which does not reflect on his natural ability in other ways, or which is beyond his control. Perhaps he is overweight, or slightly younger, a little smaller or taller than average. Perhaps he is a naturally apprehensive child, one who has lived always in the city or one that has never had animals around. Perhaps he is an only child who has not had the advantage of rough-and-tumble play. Whatever the handicap, the instructor should explain to the parent that the child is doing well but needs a little extra help which the instructor can give him by putting him into a smaller group, and that as soon as he catches up a bit, he can go back to his original class.

The riding instructor must be able to organize. He will have to group his classes according to the ages, experiences, and aptitudes of his pupils, the schools they attend, and their other engagements, also taking into consideration their friends and the localities in which they live so that car pools can be arranged. He will have to organize his work and teaching schedules, allowing time for schooling the horses that need it. Although he must have this organizational ability, he must also be a flexible and adaptable person, willing to change a routine to suit the occasion.

Imagination is a very essential element in the make-up of the successful riding instructor. Unless he can use his imagination to catch and hold the attention of his pupils and to vary his teaching, the riding lesson will be a very dull affair.

The riding instructor must have, as well as a thorough knowledge of horses, a love of them; otherwise he will not pass this love on to his pupils. If he does not make his pupils feel that the horse comes first, and that everything they do with or on the horse must be done with an eye to his comfort and with sympathy for the animal, the riding instructor has failed, no matter how proficient at riding his pupils may have become.

It goes without saying that anyone who proposes to handle children must love and understand them. With this attitude goes the ability to inspire confidence in himself as a teacher, to lead as well as to control. Only in this way will the instructor obtain obedience. The child will obey only if he believes that the person teaching him knows more than he does, and that he, the child, can have a better time with the help of the instructor than he can without it. Unless the instructor can be certain of absolute obedience from every pupil at all times, he will run the risk of grave accidents. He cannot obtain this obedience either by punishment or by threat; he must obtain it by making the child eager to learn from him. The personality of the arithmetic teacher, while it may not please the pupil, is not considered a legitimate excuse for his dropping arithmetic; but if a child does not like his riding instructor, he will quickly drop his riding lessons.

In handling his pupils, impartiality is all-important. Each pupil must be carefully studied, and the instructor must not appear to show more interest in or favoritism toward the apt pupil than toward those not so apt. If he has to deny a request, he should do so in such a fashion that the pupil feels the justice of the refusal and understands the reason behind it. In granting a request, the instructor should show by his manner that he is glad to grant the request, but that he has agreed to do so not because he likes this pupil more than any other, but because the request was a legitimate one that he would have granted as readily to anyone else. Particularly must the instructor be impartial in assigning horses. If more than one child in a class wants the same horse, the children should take turns. If a rider asks for a horse that is unsuitable for him, either because it is too much for him or because it is too easy for him, the instructor must make clear to the child why he is refused, and try to give him another horse that he will like.

EDUCATIONAL BACKGROUND

The more broadly educated the riding instructor is, the better teacher he will be. A college education is therefore most desirable, especially if the prospective teacher has taken courses which will help him later in his chosen profession. A knowledge of languages, although not essential, is very useful, since there are many valuable books on the art of equitation in Italian, French, Spanish, and German which have never been translated. Reading these in the original is both interesting and instructive, and serves to increase the knowledge of the instructor, thus making him better able to teach his subject.

A course in child psychology is valuable for the prospective riding instructor. One of the things he will have to do is to size up and classify his riders quickly. Some will need to be put into groups in which they can be among the best; others will do better if put into groups which offer a challenge. Some children try to get attention by pretending stupidity; others will say they understand because they are afraid they will be thought stupid if they say they don't. Some children do best if given extra help; others will take advantage of such treatment, and must be made to stand on their own feet. The more education and experience he has in handling children, the fewer mistakes the riding instructor will make.

A knowledge of sports other than riding makes it possible for the riding instructor to interest his pupils by comparing what he is teaching them with what they may have learned already in connection with some other activity.

Many times young students applying for entrance in schools for training riding instructors say, "My one interest is riding," under the mistaken notion that this statement will please the directors of the school. On the contrary, such a prospective student is always urged to continue his or her general education, and to try to develop other interests. This is important for several reasons. A riding instructor in a school or camp often finds himself the only member of the teaching staff with any knowledge of or interest in horses. Unless he has some other interest, he will find nothing in common with the other members of the faculty. The riding instructor planning on starting his own school in a community where he is not known will need ways of becoming acquainted with the members of the community. If he plays some musical instrument, if he likes to act, if he is interested in any of the other arts, he will find many doors open to him that would otherwise be closed. And the riding instructor whose interests range far out of his field will be a better teacher, and will understand his pupils more thoroughly.

One of the most valuable courses which a person intending to teach riding can take is a course in public speaking. It is by our voices that we are first judged. Regional accents are irritating to people not native to the particular region. Little habits of speech, such as slurring words together or hesitating, detract from the effectiveness of the teaching, as they distract the pupil's attention. The riding instructor must be able to make his voice carry several hundred feet without effort. When it reaches the ears of the class, it must not sound harsh or strained—it must sound like an ordinary speaking voice, distinct and easily understood. The riding instructor must learn to put his own confidence, enthusiasm, and sympathy into his voice. There must be no feeling of impatience, discouragement, disappointment, or boredom in it. The tempo of his speech must be neither too fast nor too slow. His words must be carefully chosen with regard to the age and knowledge of the class. He must be able to explain his points clearly, in a few words and without unnecessary repetition. Even though he may have taken classes in elocution or public speaking, the inexperienced riding instructor can also benefit by practicing with a wire or tape recorder. He should plan a lesson and then give it in front of the recorder, talking exactly as though he were conducting a class. As he listens to the play-back, he will note many little faults in his delivery which he had not noticed before, and can then work to improve these.

The ability to use a typewriter is almost essential if one plans to run a riding program. Schedules, lists of riders, horse-show programs, time sheets, monthly bills, general instructions to be posted on the bulletin board, all will have to be typed. Even though he does not become professionally expert in the use of the typewriter, every instructor should own one and should be able to use it with some facility.

The riding instructor should never consider his own education in riding complete. He should visit other establishments, read books and other publications, and try to keep abreast of modern ideas and changes of thought regarding his subject. The more training he can get from recognized masters of equitation, the better. He may find that the authorities differ in their techniques. This is to be expected. While he is working with them, he should not argue about or discuss these differences, other than to find out, if he can, what fundamental principles lie behind them. Later he can compare one method with another and so have a broader knowledge to pass along to his pupils.

ABILITY AS A HORSEMAN

The riding instructor must be so at home on his mount that, no matter what the horse tries to do, the instructor is able to control him automatically, carrying on his own teaching at the same time. He must be able to school new horses coming to the stable and to re-school those that have acquired vices. He must be able to feel what a horse is about to do, not only when he is on him, but also when he is watching him being ridden in the class. He must be able to quiet a horse that is acting up. If he plans to teach jumping, he must know how to school jumpers and how to cure them of vices which have to do with jumping. The same applies to the other branches of equitation. He must be able not only to demonstrate what he is teaching, but to answer any questions pertaining to the lesson.

STANDARDS OF DRESS

In addition to the many specific factors of pedagogical technique, pupil-teacher relationships, and the development of his own personality, experience, and training, the riding instructor should bear one other thing in mind: the impression which he makes on pupils, parents, and the public at large. Unless a riding instructor presents a professional appearance, his establishment will be rightly classed as second-rate.

The riding instructor does not need to wear expensive clothes, but what he does wear while teaching should be neat, well fitting, and clean. In summer, either jodhpurs or breeches and boots with a cotton shirt are excellent garb. Female instructors should beware of an over-liberal use of make-up. If any sort of riding jewelry is worn, such as collar or tie pin, it should be perfectly plain. The instructor's hair must be neat and trim.

The coat or jacket worn in winter should be suitable to the climate. Regular riding coats look the best, but are rarely warm enough. Leather jackets with a smooth finish are excellent since they do not catch the hair of the horse nor retain the smell.

Bright-colored breeches, sleeveless vests worn without a jacket, and other flashy articles of clothing all proclaim the amateur. Blue jeans, denim jackets, and rubbers or rubber boots may be worn while cleaning the stable, doing tack, or rubbing down horses, but they should be discarded when conducting the class. A denim apron such as carpenters wear is excellent protection while grooming and is more easily removed than blue jeans.

The instructor also should require a neat appearance in his pupils. This does not mean that all the riders need to wear expensive clothes. It does mean that they should keep their shirts tucked in, that they should wear cotton jodhpurs rather than dungarees if possible, and that they should wear suitable shoes or boots. If a child's clothes are uncomfortable, he will not be able to sit well on his horse. Dungarees pull up and bunch at the knee. A flying shirt tail prevents the instructor from seeing whether or not the child is sitting well. One of the advantages of a Junior Cavalry or Scout unit is that the children all dress correctly and alike. Not only do the uniforms of these groups give the children a better appearance, but with everyone dressed alike, any awkwardness of posture is quickly noted by the instructor, whereas in a class where the clothing varies considerably as to cut and color, the instructor may attribute the awkwardness to a blowing shirt or loosely fitting jeans.

STANDARDS IN STABLE MANAGEMENT

From the day he begins his job in a school or camp or opens his own establishment, the riding instructor must set up desirable standards of stable management and must adhere to them. Parents bringing their children to ride will carry away with them a general impression. If the stable appears to be clean, the horses in good condition and well kept, the tack clean and orderly, if there is a feeling of well-organized activity rather than confusion, the parents will be favorably impressed. But if things are not so organized, it will be only a matter of time before the instructor will lose his position or the parents will withdraw their children.

Certain rules are of utmost importance. A definite routine must be followed in the care of the stable and the horses, planned so that the animals and equipment will be ready and properly turned out when they are required. In regard to visitors and pupils, there are also rules to be observed. Smoking should be prohibited in the stable area, and signs to this effect must be posted. There should be no shouting or running allowed in the stable, riding hall, or ring. Children should not be permitted to take out their mounts until they have first reported to the adult in charge of assigning them. Either the instructor or one of the assistants should check each horse and the fitting of his equipment before he is mounted, and check him again before he is returned to his stall. Any minor injuries or unusual behavior in any horse should be reported at once to the instructor.

It is hard to get good grooms and stablemen and even harder to keep them. The riding instructor should make every effort to find suitable ones and to make things pleasant for them. At the same time, no one is perfect and a great deal of tactful supervision will be necessary. Few men of the stableman caliber are willing to accept new ideas, and fewer still have had proper training. The riding instructor will have to be constantly on the lookout for unintentional mistreatment or neglect. Grooms and stablemen like to be held responsible to one person only. If it is necessary to give an order regarding the horses, it should be the instructor and not one of the assistants that gives it. Complaints should be heard with patience, and explanations should be given when there is a difference of opinion.

A bulletin board should be provided on which to post the list of horses to be prepared by certain hours, notices to the riders, and articles and pictures of interest to the pupils.

A riding stable is like any other business: it should present a picture of good organization, and, since it has to do with children, there should be an atmosphere of happiness and good will.

Chapter 3

THE PUPIL

*E*ach child that comes to ride must be studied as an individual. Even though there may be fifteen or more in a group, all riding at the same time, the riding instructor must be aware not only of the capabilities of each rider but of his temperament, his personal problems in regard to his relationship with his horse, his reactions to emergencies, his ability to accept instruction, his attitude toward the others in the class, and his willingness or ability to continue trying.

In addition to temperamental handicaps and aptitudes, each rider has certain physical handicaps and aptitudes. These the instructor must understand and take into account when he is grouping the riders, planning the program, and assigning horses.

FEAR OF THE UNKNOWN

One of the most common characteristics of the young beginner, particularly if he is an only child or one of a small family, is a general apprehension regarding anything new—the common "fear of the unknown." My own belief is that this fear begins early in babyhood. The child who is over-protected, who is allowed little freedom to take ordinary tumbles and make mistakes, who has feeding problems, whose mother or nurse is apprehensive about colds, fatigue, or minor mishaps of all kinds, will usually have fear of the unknown. Unfortunately, the advent of the machine age has made supervision of children necessary in cases where it was not necessary before. Our highways are dangerous and most parents feel that they cannot allow their children to play unsupervised. Usually they include in this supervision the making of all decisions and the prevention of little mistakes. If the two-year-old is allowed to run on rough ground, to tumble, pick himself up, and run and tumble again with no comment from an adult, he learns that tumbling is part of life and not to be feared; but if mother always holds his hand and sympathizes with him, making much of a bumped nose, the bumped nose comes to be something very important, and mother's hand a necessity. Little children should be allowed to explore, even though their explorations may be limited to the confines of their own rooms or front yards. It is through mistakes and failure that we learn. Failure in itself is unimportant, provided that one keeps on trying. By not giving the child a chance to fail and then to try again and finally to succeed, the parent is depriving him of his principal opportunity to learn.

The child who has a fear of the unknown can be spotted easily by the riding instructor. He is the child who dreads being assigned a new horse; who never wants to try a new game or have the jump raised a little higher; who, having become used to the riding hall, is worried by the idea of riding on the trail. Inquiry will disclose that this child is also afraid of swimming, of changing schools or going to birthday parties where he does not know the other children, or of new foods. One cannot hope to take away this deep-rooted fear of the unknown; one can hope only to give such a child as much experience as possible in every field so that there will be fewer things left for him to fear.

Fear is abolished only by successful experience. Every effort must be made to see that the timid child has no accident, no matter how slight, in the early days of his riding. Unfortunately, such children are even more frightened by an accident to another member of the group. If the timid child falls off and does not hurt himself he may not be very frightened, but if another child falls off, the timid one has no way of knowing just how badly that child was hurt, and he identifies himself with the victim in every case.

Even more frightening than a fall is the misbehavior of a horse, whether his own or someone else's. Only the quietest and most reliable mounts should be used in groups with timid riders, and the program must be carried forward very slowly. The instructor should spend as much time as possible telling little anecdotes and stories which will amuse the children and give them an idea of what to expect from their mounts. He should never give any impression that he is even aware of the child's timidity; rather he should show by his manner that he has confidence in the child's ability to carry on the program. If a child says openly that he is afraid, the instructor should tell him that many people are afraid until they learn how to do a thing and that then they lose their fear. He should be careful never to ask the child to do anything of which he is not fully capable, but having asked it, he must see that it is accomplished.

In grouping timid children, the instructor should put with them one or two very much younger children who are bold. Boldness in a child as large or larger than himself will not give the timid child confidence, but when a timid eight-year-old sees a tiny five-year-old trying things which the older child fears, he will sometimes be encouraged.

If a child seems very timid because he is mounted on a horse he has never ridden before, the instructor should stay near him, but unobtrusively so, keeping a close eye on him, ready to prevent any mishap. If the child loses his fear during the lesson, the instructor should tell him at the end how well he has done, and should draw attention to the good qualities of his new mount. At the same time, he might add that there are other ponies or horses in the stable which the child might like to ride another day.

In working with the timid child, the instructor must watch the child's shoulders and wrists for any stiffness, which will indicate fear. He may keep him at a slow gait, doing the suppling exercises, answering questions, or playing simple games such as halting at a given spot or touching indicated numbers until this stiffness disappears. In very extreme cases, he may have to resort to having the child take off his jacket and put it on again, put his cap on backwards, and similar actions. Going through familiar movements while mounted will do more to relax the tense rider than anything else.

As the child becomes more experienced, the instructor may be fooled into thinking that he has taken away his fear entirely. But, unfortunately, in most cases, it will come back as soon as the child finds himself in an emergency or is asked to do something different. The instructor must accept this, and as the child improves, seek to give him as much varied experience as he can. Practicing vaulting off a moving horse or pony is the best method to cure the fear of falling. "Monkey Drill" (see page 294ff.) will give confidence faster than other exercise. Games distract the timid child, but they must not be beyond his ability as a rider, nor must he be the poorest in the group. Handling the horse in the stable teaches him what to expect from the animal, and the more of this that he does, the better.

Timid children should be mounted on horses or ponies that have good manners, easy gaits, and not too much forward impulsion. The smaller the animal, the more sure of himself the rider will be, but stubborn ponies are worse than better-mannered big horses. On the other hand, a well-mannered small pony will give an awkward or timid child a tremendous amount of confidence, since he will feel himself near the ground and more capable of handling the smaller animal.

FEAR OF FAILURE

A second basic fear in riders is the fear of failure. Children with this fear rarely enjoy competition. It is not that they feel they must win; rather they are afraid of not putting on a creditable performance. They should be encouraged to compete with the idea of improving themselves and their mounts. Emphasis should be put on their individual performances in relation to their capabilities rather than on their standing in the class. They should be given the opportunity of training a mount for a specific class, and careful note should be made of the improvement in the animal. If possible, these children should be called upon in class to demonstrate or explain some point. They should be grouped with other riders so that they are near the top in ability. They should be given easy mounts until they have passed the beginner stages, then they may be mounted on animals that offer a challenge, but a challenge which they are capable of meeting.

It is children of this temperament who benefit most by an organized program such as a Junior Cavalry unit where they can be given authority and may be assigned to helping younger and less experienced children. Even in groups that are not so well-organized, they can be assigned little jobs such as helping a younger child get his horse out or put him away. Any work of this sort will help the child to build up self-confidence and will make him less afraid of appearing conspicuous. Incidentally, these children are often much more successful as leaders and helpers than the more confident and less conscientious children.

PHYSICAL HANDICAPS

Children who are handicapped physically by poor coordination, excessive weight, or awkward conformation generally have more fear of being hurt than the average child. About all that the instructor can do is to mount such a child on as small and comfortable an animal as possible and give him as much in the way of Monkey Drill, suppling exercises, and slow work bareback as he can. The child should be put with a group which is expected to progress rather slowly, but he should not be allowed to shirk and give up trying. Such children will often ask for help in things which do not involve danger at all, such as adjusting stirrups, but unless the instructor can establish good habits of making a serious effort and carrying out orders in these simple things, he will never get the child to put enough effort into riding and controlling his horse to get him over his awkwardness and fear.

FEAR OF THE HORSE

It is rare for a child to be afraid of the pony or horse as an animal unless he has had some previous experience which has set up such a fear. If such is the case, the instructor must spend much time having the child handle the horse, lead him, saddle him, water him, etc. Only by becoming so familiar with his mount on foot that he is no longer afraid of him will the child be able to develop any confidence while mounted.

THE FOOLHARDY CHILD

The opposite of the timid child is the foolhardy child. This type is generally a "know-it-all," unwilling to pay attention to instruction because he thinks he knows more than the instructor. He is often an only child with indulgent or not too alert parents. He is apt to be very bright mentally, well coordinated, and with excellent capabilities both in riding and in leadership. He is usually very unpopular with the other children in the group and, because of his unpopularity, may develop unsocial habits such as bullying or sneakiness.

The foolhardy child is easy to handle. All one needs to do is to overmount him slightly and put him with a group more capable than he. One does not wish to make him afraid, only to instill a little normal caution. The instructor should take advantage of his capabilities as a leader and should allow him to use them, but should not allow him to monopolize class time. It is better, when handling a class in which there are one or more such children, to ask questions in rotation rather than to call for a show of hands. Children who are overconfident need a constant challenge. They like competition, but often lack patience. Games are not important for them, although they prefer them to anything else. It is up to the instructor to set very high standards for such children and to work to keep their interest.

THE CHILD WHO WON'T TRY

Certain children seem incapable of making any real effort to improve. Sometimes this is due to fear, sometimes to a desire to attract attention, sometimes to an unusually short attention span. The instructor must decide what is the basic cause and then try to correct it. With the child who makes no effort because he wants to attract attention to himself, the best solution is to take him aside quietly and tell him that unless he shows more improvement he either will be dropped from the class or will be put with a younger group. At the same time he should be mounted on an animal that requires him to pay attention. He should be given as little help with his horse as possible, and should be required to mount without assistance and to adjust his stirrups alone. He can be asked to help a younger child and should be praised for his help. This type of child usually likes competition and will try to win. He should be put in a group where he can win occasionally, but not always.

ATTENTION SPANS

The child who has an unusually short attention span for his age will have to be placed in a group of younger children. The work should be planned so that there is a constant change of activity with as much pupil participation as possible.

The average length of attention for very young children is about three minutes. Using this as a guide, the instructor should plan to change the activity or vary it slightly at the end of every three minutes. The lesson plan for children of this age on page 275 shows how such a program can be handled. It is no use going into long explanations with these children. After the first few words, the child's mind closes and he starts to think about other things. Questions and answers to impart information are the best teaching technique to use with such children. In teaching something new, the instructor should ask the question first to get the child's attention. For example, in teaching the difference between the extended and collected gaits, the teacher can start by asking, "If you make your horse trot slowly around the ring once and then go fast, will he take more steps when he goes fast or when he goes slowly?" Not having thought the question out, most children will say, "More when he goes fast." The teacher, on foot, demonstrates by taking "baby" steps to get from one point to another, then "giant" steps, with the children watching and counting the steps. He lets the children experiment by taking a slow trot first, counting the strides of the horse, and then an extended trot. Thus the teacher can explain a relatively complicated fact to children with short attention spans without their losing interest.

THE CHILD WITH UNUSUAL APTITUDE

The child who has both aptitude and patience is rare indeed, but what a pleasure it is to come across such a pupil! Such a child, mentally alert, physically well coordinated, with an intense desire to learn and the ability to work at detail, will go ahead three or four times as fast as the child who has some but not all of these attributes. The teacher must advance such a child as rapidly as possible, and must constantly hold out future projects and goals, for the one thing to guard against is that such a pupil may stop his lessons too soon. For this reason, every instructor should plan some new project each year for his advanced riders. Such projects are discussed on page 255.

It can be seen from the above analysis that there is no "average" child. Each group, however, will settle into a more or less steady rate of learning, and it is up to the instructor, having studied the different personalities of his pupils, to advance or put back those who do not seem happy with the group to which they have been assigned.

Chapter 4

GENERAL TEACHING TECHNIQUES

The first goal of the riding instructor is to keep the child interested and improving in his ability as a horseman. To do this, it is necessary to develop the pupil's confidence in his instructor, the horse, and himself. Where the first two of these attributes have been developed, self-confidence will follow.

DEVELOPING CONFIDENCE IN THE TEACHER

A good relationship between the pupil and the teacher is all-important, and must be established at the very first lesson. It is on this relationship that the success of the teacher in imparting knowledge, maintaining discipline, preventing accidents, and developing a love of horses, the idea of sportsmanship, and the ability of the group to work together, depends. Once he has established a good pupil-teacher relationship, the teacher need worry no further, for incoming pupils will pick up the attitude of the children who are already members of the group.

In a group with good *esprit de corps,* such as units of the Junior Cavalry of America, the instructor can leave the class at any time, fully confident that the children will carry on exactly as though he were there. The disciplinary training a child receives in such a group is almost as important as the riding instruction. This discipline is a *positive* discipline. Each member of the group has his own duties and responsibilities. In carrying out these duties, he comes to take for granted that he is to obey the instant he is asked to do something. During the riding period, the children are relaxed and at ease, delighted to answer questions or to make suggestions, but if an officer calls them to attention or blows a whistle, they are instantly alert and ready to do what they are told. A parent of a child in a Junior Cavalry troop once said to me, "I think that if you asked one of the children to ride a horse off a twenty-foot cliff he would not only obey you but would do so with the utmost confidence in his own ability to succeed without getting hurt."

Developing Confidence in Beginners

In teaching beginners, it is very easy for the instructor to establish a good relationship. It is necessary for him only to help his pupil, through explanation and instruction, to understand a little about the character of his mount so that he is no longer afraid of him, and by showing him how to sit properly and how to post, to make him more comfortable than he would be without that instruction. If the child, with the help of the instructor, has had a better time and has been more successful than he would have been without the instructor's help, he will not only have confidence in his teacher, but he will also be ready to obey him. Unless something happens to destroy this confidence, the instructor need never worry about whether or not his pupil respects him, nor about the discipline of the class as a whole.

However, the instructor must be careful, if he is to keep this confidence, never to make a statement that is not based on either fact or experience. If he is not absolutely sure that something is going to happen, he should say not "It will," but "It may." For example, if one tells a child that riding with his heels up and digging his horse in the side will cause the animal to go too fast, and if that child then is mounted on a sluggish horse that is not very "leg-worthy" and pays no attention to the digging in of his heels, the child will lose respect for the instructor, for he has made a statement which the pupil has found to be untrue. Instead, one should say, "John, when you ride a horse like Slowpoke, carrying your feet the way you do, you may not get into trouble, but if I were to let you ride Rocket, you wouldn't be able to keep him going quietly because you would make him very uncomfortable." If the child persists in the habit in spite of his ability to do otherwise, he should be put on a more sensitive horse for a few minutes, and the point proved. In the same way, it is better to tell a child who sits hunched up with his eyes down that if the horse should stumble or kick he will *probably* fall off—because miracles do happen, the horse might stumble, and the child might just manage to stay on!

A child will have more confidence and respect both for the judgment of the teacher and for his knowledge if he is made to un-

193

derstand the reasons for the teacher's corrections or instructions. If the child is told merely that it is easier to post when he carries his feet under, he may think this is just a notion of the instructor, and not important; but if the point is proved to him by having him try to balance in his stirrups with his legs held in place by the instructor, then with the instructor holding his feet forward, he will understand the reasons for the teacher's suggestion and will try much harder to keep a good leg position. Also, he will know, from his own experience, that what the instructor says is true, and will have more belief in the instructor.

Attitude of the Teacher

The basic factor in obtaining such confidence and obedience is the teacher's attitude toward the child. He must never begin a lesson with the assumption in his own mind that the child whom he tells to do something may not do it. Of course, he must be careful never to ask the impossible. If you expect a child to be slack, impudent, timid, or a failure, you are bound to get exactly what you expect. If you take for granted that every child will be willing and obedient, you will generally get willingness and obedience.

The teacher, or the parent, sets standards for the child's behavior and attitudes. These standards cannot be artificial; they must be true beliefs and practices. The parent or teacher who is impatient himself will never develop patience in his child, no matter how he attempts to conceal his own impatience and preaches the value of patience. He who is at heart dishonest, unsportsmanlike, selfish, or timid will develop the same qualities in his children, for they will sense his true standards and will pay no attention to the artificial ones which he tries to set up. So the teacher of riding must be true to himself; he must believe in and live up to what he teaches; and if he cannot do so, he had better not take up this profession.

The teacher should have a friendly relationship with his pupils, but not an overly familiar one. The pupil must not lose his respect for his instructor. Fear of an instructor is a thing to be deplored, but respect is essential if one is to obtain obedience.

The cheerful teacher makes the cheerful pupil. The bored teacher soon passes on his boredom to his class. Learning to ride is fun, and the teacher must enjoy teaching the class or the class will not enjoy learning. The teacher can find much more satisfaction in his work if he puts everything he has into it, studying his pupils, holding out goals and projects for them, planning his lessons. If the teacher finds satisfaction in the lessons, the pupils will also find satisfaction, but not otherwise. The pupils must at all times feel that the teacher is working for them, trying his best to increase their enjoyment, that he is there to help them, and that his criticisms are never destructive.

Punishment and Rewards

Children take criticism more readily than adults, but the criticism should always be worded so that the child's feelings are not hurt and he does not become resentful. One punishes a horse only if he is purposely vicious, never because he is ignorant. One punishes a child only when he is purposely disobedient, not because he is unable to do as well as one would wish. Speaking sternly or in a humiliating fashion to a child before other children is a severe punishment. Only if a child has been willfully disobedient or has done something anti-social does one ever correct him before the other children.

In the case of a child who deliberately annoys another child— something which occasionally occurs with a child who has been very timid and has suddenly acquired confidence—I have found that the most successful method of punishment is to say quietly, "Mary, you know that you are not supposed to do anything to make anyone else uncomfortable or to distract their attention. Since you are obviously not paying attention to the lesson and so are not learning anything, you had better dismount, put your horse away, and go and sit by yourself over there for the remainder of the hour." I then devote the rest of the period to something which I know the child who is being punished likes to do. I have never had to punish the same child twice in this fashion, and often years go by without the necessity for such a lesson.

Rewards are a tremendous incentive to children. With young children, it is best to have a non-competitive type of award, whereby any child who passes a given test receives a prize, not just the best four or five of the group. A simple game employing this type of award is to place little candies on posts and have the members of the class try to pick them off as they walk or trot past. There should be enough candy to go around, and no child should take more than one. Competitive awards in which the winner is the child who pays the best attention are good as they are within the grasp of all. An award to the group as a whole, such as a picnic ride, is a good incentive to effort if it is announced that, when everyone in the class has reached a certain stage in their riding, it will be given. The reward to the group also instills a certain amount of cooperative spirit.

To teach children to control their horses and not to be afraid to ride close together, the teacher can offer a candy or a penny to every child who can hold hands with a partner and trot to music for a full three and a half minutes—the length of time it takes to play a phonograph record. Such rewards will do far more to instill confidence and encourage effort than will destructive criticism aimed at a child who is unable to ride in pairs or who cannot control his horse enough to ride out the corners.

Impartiality

As discussed in Part II, Chapter II, impartiality of the teacher toward the children is all-important. No child will work well for a teacher whom he believes to be unfair or partial to another child. I have never found that the children who worked under me felt that any impartiality was shown, but sometimes parents cannot understand why someone else's child is promoted to officership in the Troop before their child is, or why theirs is not picked to ride on an exhibition team. It sometimes requires great tact to explain to a parent that Johnny has been made a lieutenant because he has more leadership qualities, is popular with his fellows, and has the ability to inspire confidence, whereas their Peter, although just as good a rider, shows little sense of responsibility and is not looked up to by the other children. Although the children coming into the Troop quickly settle down and adopt the group spirit, it sometimes takes the parents a year or two to do likewise.

DEVELOPING CONFIDENCE IN AND CONSIDERATION OF THE HORSE

The second most important relationship which must be established is that between the child and his horse. Horses are no longer a familiar feature of everyday life. Because they are vehicles of transportation, the average modern child (and often the adult) is prone to look upon a horse as he would upon a car. The horse is expected to go forward when the rider uses the accelerator (his heels), to stop when he applies the brake (reins), and otherwise to be passive. It is up to the instructor to change this attitude, to make the child aware of the horse as a living creature entirely dependent upon his master for care and comfort. The first and foremost goal of every rider, from his first lesson to his last, should be to cause his horse to perform well without abusing him.

There are several means for the instructor to develop this consideration and love of his mount in the child. The most important is to make the animal real to him as a personality. All children love stories about animals, and horse books are among the most popular of any on the juvenile shelves. Knowing this, the instructor should make a point of relating little incidents and anecdotes about horses and ponies which will amuse the children and encourage in them an attitude of sympathy toward their mounts.

An important factor in instilling this sympathy for the horse is the instructor's own attitude toward the animals. He should make a point of talking to them when he holds them for the children to mount, showing by his voice that he loves them and looks on them as companions and friends, rather than as machines. When a rest period in the lesson comes, the children should be told to let their reins out and pat their horses. Not only does this familiarizing of the child with his mount make him more sympathetic, but it also takes away any fear of the unknown. When a child is mounted on a new animal for the first time, the instructor should tell him what to expect. If the horse has a rough trot but a good canter, the rider should be told this. If he is a horse that tends to run up on the rider in front or to get too far behind, the instructor can bring this to the rider's attention, telling him how he can best prevent these habits. In this manner the child learns that not all horses are alike, that each has his good and his bad points, and he will learn to look for these, to correct or encourage them, and so to become a wiser and a better horseman.

Another way in which an instructor can develop in his pupils a sense of the importance of non-abuse of the horse is by gradually teaching them as much as he can about the horse's temperamental and physical characteristics, his sensitivity to ailments or injury, and how these may be prevented. For example, from the very beginning, the child should be made to walk his horse for the first and last ten minutes of the lesson, and should be told the reason behind this rule.

Horses that come into the stable in very poor condition or with vices due to mistreatment, such as head-shyness, should be used to demonstrate to the children how the horse depends on his master not only for the care of his body, but also for the development of his disposition. Again and again, the point should be made that misbehavior of the horse is a result either of ignorance and mistreatment on the part of the rider, or of his lack of skill. He may be asking too much of the horse, or he simply may not be a good enough rider to get what he wants from his mount.

The abuse of horses in this country is appalling. There are hacking stables which allow their horses to stand in cramped stalls for five days a week without exercise, then rent them out to ignorant riders for eight hours on Saturdays and Sundays, riders whose one idea is to get the most speed possible out of their hired hack during the time they ride him. And there are "high-class" horse shows with open jumpers being prodded with battery-charged or nail-studded poles, saddle horses with ginger under their tails, whipped before entering the ring to make them appear animated. The child is constantly exposed to incidents involving cruelty. Unless the instructor does something to counteract this, the child becomes callous and thoughtless of his mount. The callous rider will never become a real horseman, no matter how well he may be able to stick on the animal's back.

CONSIDERATION FOR OTHER RIDERS

The third relationship to be established is that between the rider and his companions. The expert horseman not only has consideration for his horse, but also for his fellow horsemen. These courtesies and considerations are important from the point of view of safety. The careless rider who holds a branch back too long and then lets it swing in the face of the horseman behind him may cause a serious accident. So too may the rider who pulls off the path to allow the huntsman to pass, with his horse's tail to the path. The rider who, meeting up with a group of beginners, gallops past them with no regard for their ability to control their horses, may someday have a lawsuit on his hands. The instructor should teach and insist upon the observance of all rules of courtesy. No child should be allowed to speak rudely to another in class, or to act roughly toward either his horse or his companions. Rudeness and roughness breed callousness and carelessness, neither of which are traits of the accomplished horseman. As in instilling confidence in the horse, the teacher must set the example. He must never be rude to a child himself, for his voice and his manner will be imitated.

SUPERVISION

The child who rides on his own horse at home and who is an accomplished rider needs no supervision, but the child who is sent to school for riding instruction should be supervised throughout his riding period, except in a few instances. Unless the beginner is under supervision, he may get hurt, and he will certainly form bad habits. The intermediate rider who may have more confidence than judgment is apt to mistreat his horse unknowingly, taking him over the same jump over and over, or galloping him for too long at a time. Also, he too is apt to form bad habits in posture and uses of the aids. The advanced rider who knows what he is doing may be assigned a problem such as training a colt to execute definite movements and may be left alone to practice, but he should have frequent criticisms and check-ups on his progress.

Training the Rider

The teacher who conducts a ring class while mounted himself rarely can do as good a job as the one who instructs from the ground. With beginners, the instructor must be able to stand or walk beside the child and to help him with his position by holding his hands or legs for a moment. An instructor on foot can prevent trouble by signaling unobtrusively to a lazy pony to catch up before he gets too far behind, or by blocking off a horse that suddenly bolts out of line. It is much easier to shift one's position while standing on foot to watch a given rider circle the ring than to turn a horse around. In jumping classes, someone must remain on foot to set up jumps and replace rails, and this the instructor can do if he is not mounted. Also, he can place himself so that he may discourage the horse that intends to shy out, or urge on the sticky horse. In musical rides, exercises such as circling in the middle, or practicing riding straight lines with square corners, the instructor who is on foot places himself in the ring in order to give the riders something to guide on and also to watch them from different angles.

There are certain conditions, however, under which the instructor should not be on foot while teaching in a ring. If the ring is so large that he cannot get from one end to the other readily, and if he is using all of it, he will do better mounted. If he is teaching beginners and the ring is being used by other riders, he may have to take his pupils on lead reins. And if he is teaching beginners and has no rider who can act as leader for them, he will have to combine leading the group with teaching it. This, however, should be avoided whenever possible. In mounted drill work, he may prefer to ride at the end of the line where he can see that the commands are given correctly and that the rate of speed is correct.

DIVIDING THE RIDING PERIOD

Generally speaking, each riding period should be divided into three or four parts, as described in detail in Part II, Chapter 13. During the first part, the rider is mounted; he moves off at a walk while the instructor checks his length of stirrup and makes sure that he is comfortable and able to control his horse; and he then receives instruction in position or control, beginning with a review of the previous lesson. This part of the lesson may also include suppling exercises or school movements at the slower gaits. The second period of the lesson can be devoted to formation riding, such as mounted drill or musical rides, or to equitation exercises at the faster gaits. Any new work is taken up at this time. In the case of very young children, the second period may include a guessing game or suppling exercises while the pony is standing still. The last part of the class, except for the final ten minutes, can be a game, jumping, or riding at will (free time), depending upon the level of ability of the class. During the last ten minutes, the horses are walked and the riders encouraged to ask questions. By breaking up each period of instruction in this way, the teacher will avoid boring his class and will be sure of giving his pupils a well-rounded program.

ASSISTANTS

The fortunate teacher will have several experienced children to help him. These children must be capable of tacking up a horse and handling him in the stall, mounting and dismounting a beginner, adjusting stirrups, leading a pony while balancing the rider's knee with their hand, riding in the lead of the line, and maintaining the desired gait. Children as young as nine or ten are often very capable and will gladly run around the ring helping a six-year-old learn to post, if they can have a free ride in return. In addition to making use of these children in the ring, the instructor can develop traits of responsibility and dependability in them by giving them certain jobs such as checking the tack and the adjustment of stable blankets, or helping a beginner to tack up his pony and lead him into the ring. The child comes to feel his own importance and will take pride in the correct accomplishment of his assignment.

In a group in which older children have authority over younger children, the instructor must be careful, in choosing his leaders, to make sure that they are youngsters who have real ability as leaders, who are trustworthy and well liked, and who will not play favorites. Having chosen these leaders, he should give them some instruction in leading. He should explain both to them and to the other children that these leaders are chosen because they know more than the children whom they are to help. Knowing more, their sole duty is to be of service to those placed under them. They have not been made leaders so that they can "boss around" the other children but so that the others can come to them for help and advice. The instructor should then be prepared to stand behind his leaders. He should not countermand their decisions except in matters involving the safety of a child or animal. If it is necessary to countermand an order given by a student leader, the instructor should do it tactfully, so that the other children will not lose respect for the cadet leader.

These cadet officers are often amazingly conscientious and will take great trouble to see that their group is correctly mounted and that every child has a fair chance to ride the horse best suited to him. I have never found any of these student leaders to show favoritism or to be other than tactful in handling the younger children. I wish that some of the instructors that I have watched would handle their pupils as well, and develop as good a relationship with them.

A junior instructor working under a senior instructor must be careful to do nothing that will detract from the respect the children have either for himself or for the older instructor. If he does not agree with something the older instructor says, or if he does not instantly follow out what he is told to do without argument, one of two things will happen. If the children like the senior instructor, they will think the junior instructor stupid for contradicting him. If they do not like the senior instructor, they will follow the pattern set by the junior and will begin to disobey either or both instructors when they see fit. It is perfectly all right for the junior instructor to choose some moment when the senior instructor is alone to discuss a question on which he may have a different opinion.

TEACHING NEW MOVEMENTS

In teaching a new movement or rein effect, or the correct placing of a saddle, the teacher should follow the principle of breaking up the teaching into three parts. First comes the explanation of the movement, which includes the description of what it is, what it is supposed to accomplish, and the reason behind its use. In the second phase, the instructor demonstrates the movement or has another pupil do so. In the last phase, the pupil tries the movement, and is corrected and helped by the instructor. For example, in teaching the rider to use his back and keep down in the saddle at the canter, the teacher first explains that bouncing up and down as he canters makes the rider insecure and abuses the horse. He may ask the riders to pound themselves on the back so that they will know how it feels. He describes the movement of the back, comparing it to the pumping of a swing. At the same time, he describes the movements of the horse at the canter, showing how he rocks back and forth like a see-saw, and demonstrating that not only the rider's back must follow but his arms and hands as well. Then he either demonstrates himself or has his assistant on a horse demonstrate the difference between sitting tight at the canter and, because of stiffness, bouncing. When he is certain that the riders understand, he has each one try in turn while the others watch, making corrections and trying to improve each one. If this is not successful, he may put his class at a walk and ask each member to try to follow the movement of the horse with his body. If there is a mirror available, the pupils can be asked to look at their positions as they pass it, then to canter again, with the idea of maintaining the position and contact with the saddle. The teacher should not leave the subject of the lesson until he is sure that every rider at least understands the principle. At the next lesson, he should review whatever was taught at the previous meeting to be sure that the pupils have not forgotten.

ADAPTING TECHNIQUES TO DIFFERENT AGE GROUPS

The teaching technique described above can be applied to all age groups, but the instructor will have to adapt his methods somewhat to the particular age group he is teaching. He must, for example, use words which are comprehensible to the children, yet not patronizing.

Children hate to be talked down to. Instructors sometimes make the mistake of using similes to a ten- or twelve-year-old group which would be perfect for the six-year-olds, but which sound silly to older children. Little children appreciate the bringing in of everyday matters to the riding hall. In teaching the suppling exercises described in Figures 118 and 119, in which the riders first lean down and touch their toes, then lean back until they are lying flat with their heads on their ponies' rumps, I tell the little fellows that in the first position they are going down to breakfast, and they tell me what they are eating. Then when they lie back, they are taking their morning naps. When they come forward again, they are going down to lunch, and so on, ending with a raid on the ice box at midnight. One mother was quite astounded when her little girl came home and said she had had the best time at her lesson—she had had green peas and lamb chops and mashed potatoes and ice cream for lunch! This technique, of course, is useless with older children.

Children easily learn new words and phrases. If the instructor makes a point of introducing one or two technical terms at each lesson, explaining their meaning carefully and then repeatedly using these terms, the children will soon develop a good horseman's vocabulary. This will save a great deal of class time, and the instructor can be sure that the child knows exactly what he is talking about. The "Guessing Game" described on page 288 is an excellent means of teaching children the vocabulary of horsemanship.

In giving instruction to all age groups, the instructor must speak with authority in his voice, but not with the type of authority which makes for friction. He must explain his points clearly, but he must not be wordy. He must be quick to sense when his class is bored or overtired. He must be sure to end each lesson with some activity which will give the children a feeling of accomplishment and the desire to come back again.

The intelligent riding instructor is prepared at all times to adapt his methods of teaching and his program to the reactions of his pupils. He is forever striving for new and better methods of accomplishing his goal—keeping his pupils interested and improving their skill as horsemen.

Chapter 5

BASIC PRINCIPLES OF HORSEMANSHIP

The horseman must be able *to feel, to interpret,* and *to influence* the horse's movements. Through his base of support and his reins, he *feels* what the horse is about to do. From past experience, he is able *to interpret* what he feels. And, through the correct use of the aids, he is able *to influence* his horse and cause him to obey. In these three attributes lie the whole of the art of horsemanship. It is possible to explain these basic principles of equitation, and it is possible for the intelligent pupil to understand what he is to try to do, but only experience and practice will bring their achievement within the reach of the rider.

LEARNING TO FEEL

In order to feel what the horse is about to do, one must be completely relaxed. A blind person running his hand over a sculptured head in order to determine its shape relaxes his hand and fingers, making them as soft as possible, so that they can follow the contours of the marble. If he stiffens his hand and fingers, they will not follow the curves but will bounce from the crest of one to the next, and he will not get a true impression. In riding the horse, the same principle applies. Unless the muscles of the thighs, loin, legs, ankles, etc., are relaxed, they will not be in close contact with the horse, and so will not be able to feel his muscular tensions and interpret them. Any stiffness in the upper part of the body will necessitate stiffness in the legs in order to maintain balance. Such stiffness will make it impossible for the rider to use refined aids or to ride a sensitive, highly trained horse, since, by that very tension in his own body, he is telling the horse to increase his gait.

In addition to detracting from the tactile sensitivity, hardening the muscles of the legs and stiffening the loin and back forces the rider's seat and makes it impossible for him to sit down in the saddle and remain in contact with the horse. A partly deflated balloon placed on a board will not bounce off when the board is raised and lowered, but if the balloon is hardened by being inflated, the slightest movement of the board serves to throw it into the air.

LEARNING TO INTERPRET

While he is learning to feel, the beginner is, consciously or subconsciously, learning to interpret. The intelligent instructor can help him to acquire this ability by watching the horse closely, anticipating its actions, and explaining to the rider what these mean and how to interpret them. For example, let us take the pupil that has learned to maintain his position at the canter while following another horse. Now he must learn to maintain the canter while working individually. When he takes the track at the canter, the horse probably will canter for a few steps and then begin to show signs of breaking the gait. Just as the instructor sees that the horse is about to break, he calls out, "Now use your legs!" The horse continues the canter, then the instructor brings the pupil down to a walk and says, "Did you feel when he was about to break?" He has the pupil repeat the exercise, and tells him to try to feel the moment when the horse is about to break, and to see if he can use his leg aids just strongly enough to maintain the canter. He asks the pupil to circle around him, watching him hold up his fingers and counting the number held up to draw the pupil's attention to his own ability to feel and to interpret the horse's movements without looking down at his mount. The pupil will use his aids automatically to keep his horse moving in the circle, even though his eyes are fixed on the instructor's fingers. For advanced riders, riding over jumps with eyes closed makes them aware of their skill in feeling and interpreting, since they will discover at once that they really do know without looking when the horse is going to jump. Taking the canter with the eyes closed and then telling which lead the horse is on emphasizes feel and interpretation, as does taking the trot with the eyes closed and telling which diagonal the rider is posting on. These are exercises for advanced riders, but any rider needs such exercises all through his riding career to make him remember the basic principles of feeling and interpreting the horse's movements in order to influence them.

LEARNING TO INFLUENCE

The pupil cannot learn to influence and so to control the horse until he has attained some measure of relaxation, since the use of the aids depends on the rider's ability to use his hands and legs independently, and this he cannot do as long as he depends on either his knee or leg grip or on his hands to maintain his balance. However, he will acquire relaxation at the walk very soon in his riding career, so the instructor can begin work on the correct use of the hands and on the simple rein and leg effects at this gait from the beginning.

Part II, Chapter 7, gives the accepted uses of the aids and a definition of the following, active, and fixed hand, as well as the meaning of the rough or pulling hand, the light hand, and the educated hand. The instructor must make himself thoroughly familiar with these principles and terms. He must teach them to his pupils little by little, starting with the simplest principle and making sure that the pupil understands the terminology and the effects. The chapters dealing with the progression of lessons give methods and exercises for teaching the aids, and the chapters on the intermediate and advanced training of the colt give the application of the aids in all the schooling movements and dressage figures. The instructor, in making up his lesson plans, should have a clear picture in his mind of the movements he is working on, and should choose movements which will serve to teach the use of the aids being emphasized at the moment. He will be able to test his pupils' progress by the way the horses respond and he should make every effort to bring this improvement to his pupils' attention and to encourage them to refine their aids further and to develop the abilities of feeling, interpreting, and influencing.

DEVELOPING GOOD POSITION

Balancing oneself on a horse is not a natural position; it is completely different from any position assumed in performing any other sport. In effect, it is a combination of balancing oneself while standing, and, at the same time, taking a seated position (Figure 83). To do this, one has to learn to use certain muscles never used before, and to place the skeletal structure of the body in unaccustomed positions. All of this is made necessary by the movements of the horse. The rider's body must be able to absorb the shocks and thrusts caused by the movements of the horse in such a way that he can maintain his balance without effort and does not become fatigued; at the same time, he must be able to apply his aids independently.

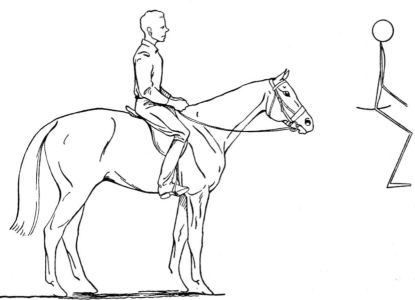

FIG. 83.   The balanced seat at the halt.

It might seem possible for anyone to acquire a close seat simply by getting on a horse and relaxing completely. Unfortunately, this is not true. Not only must the rider be relaxed, but he must be at the same time light, not heavy, in his saddle. There must be elevation of his chest without stiffness of the spine, and there must be no unnecessary motion in any part of his body. All movements of the rider's hands, trunk, or legs must be intentional, for the slightest unintentional movement disturbs and confuses the horse. The relaxation must be controlled. The rider, while relaxed, must follow the movements of the horse with his body, consciously at first and then subconsciously, so that the two are virtually welded together. He must be able to direct these movements through his hands, legs, and weight, modifying his own uses of these aids to suit the reactions of the particular horse he is riding.

Before the beginner can acquire the ability to adjust his body lightly and smoothly to the horse's movements, he must learn to supple his loin, the lumbar region of the back. Before he can learn to keep what to him is an unnatural leg position without stiffness, he must lengthen and flatten his thigh muscles. Before he can apply his aids with accuracy, he must first interpret through an acquired sensitivity of legs, body, and hands.

In standing and walking positions, the center of gravity runs from the ear down through the hip joint, through the front of the knee to the ankle. The ischia (pelvic bones) are behind the hip joint. In sitting, the pelvic bones become the base of support, and the position of the legs is unimportant since no weight is put on them. In riding a horse, however, the legs must be placed so that the ankle and side of the knee remain in line with the center of gravity, just as they do when standing. Since the man in the saddle is to sit on the pelvic bones, these too must be brought in line with the center of gravity, not pushed behind, as in sitting. It is the *front* of the pelvic bones on which the rider rests, however, not the fleshy part of the buttocks; these must be pushed to the rear.

In order to put his body in the position described above, the rider pushes his knee downward and forward toward the horse's shoulder point. His lower leg is carried back in order that the point of the knee and the toe may be on a line. The upper body is carried erect with the chest elevated and the loin kept supple. Here is where the trouble starts for the beginner. He can raise his chest, but in so doing he stiffens his spine in the lumbar region (Figure 84). Until

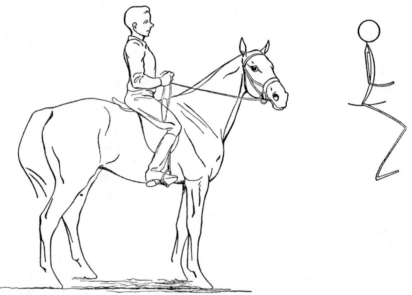

FIG. 84.   Bad Posture. *A common error of beginners when told to sit up straight.*

he can utilize the articulation of the joints of the hip, knee, ankle, and, above all, of the vertebrae in the lumbar region, to absorb the shock of the horse's movements, he will not be able to maintain his equilibrium without effort, and so make his legs and arms independent. A position which is too relaxed (Figure 85) will also make it difficult for the rider to maintain his seat.

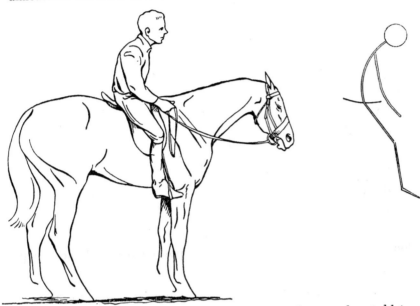

FIG. 85.   Bad posture. *A common error of beginners when told to relax.*

Even though the instructor cannot expect the beginner to be able to follow the movements of the horse immediately, he must work toward this goal by devising special suppling exercises and games to develop relaxation in the pupil. He must analyze the position of his rider and decide which part of his body needs correction first, trying at every lesson to help the beginner to understand how he can improve. On no account should the instructor discourage the pupil, or, by his words or tone, make him more frightened than he already is. Fear itself engenders stiffness and makes it impossible to develop relaxation. Some riding instructors advance the theory of making the pupil so afraid of the teacher that he forgets to be afraid of the horse, but this is basically wrong. Fear can be conquered only by successful experience.

The instructor must remember that a certain amount of fear or, at least, uncertainty, is inevitable. Mounted for the first time, the beginner finds himself upon a creature far bigger and stronger than himself. This creature has a mind and will of its own, and the begin-

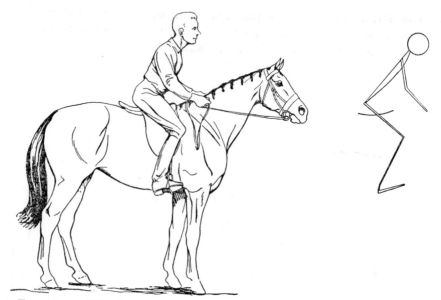

FIG. 86.   The balanced seat at the posting trot and the gallop.
Compare with Figure 83.

ner has no way of knowing what the animal is about to do or of communicating intelligently with it. The movements of this great body under him are surprising and uncomfortable. He can no more adjust himself to them than the pedestrian can adjust his balance to the tremors of an earthquake. The beginner is faced with that primeval and overpowering fear, the fear of the unknown. He has no idea what to expect. He has probably watched countless pictures of cowboys galloping, or steeplechasers leaping over enormous obstacles. These are his only criteria, and although while watching the pictures he may have had delightful visions of himself going through the same motions, when he actually finds himself aboard a horse, his reactions are apt to be very different from his preconceived ideas. Finding that even a walk has a good deal of motion in it and that a jog trot is uncomfortable in the extreme, the thought of a gallop or a jump terrifies him. Yet, from his previous education via television and motion pictures, he believes that the gallop is the horse's ordinary gait, and that the jump can be expected at any time. Many times has a little seven-year-old, on his second and third lesson, come into the hall before the jumps from the previous class have been removed, and, with his eyes bulging, asked, "Are we going to jump today?"

So, before the instructor can expect relaxation, he must remove fear and tensions through successful experience. In Chapter XIV, exercises are given for suppling the loin, improving the balance, and relaxing the rider generally. Gradually, as the pupil loses his initial fears and begins to have confidence in himself and in his mount, the instructor tries to get him into the correct position. However, he must not put too much emphasis on position, as with beginning riders, this will only increase stiffness. The correct position can best be learned through exercises which make it impossible for the rider to be in any but the correct position, since he cannot maintain his balance otherwise. The exercise illustrated on page 269 (Figure 115) can be used at frequent intervals for short periods during every lesson period. Beginners practice it at the halt and the walk. A little later they can learn to do it at the trot. It should not be introduced at the canter until the rider can sit close to the saddle at that gait, since a too early introduction of balancing in the stirrups at the canter will prevent the rider from learning to sit down and follow the movements of the horse.

The instructor must remember that, though the beginner after a time will be able to place his body and legs in the correct position, he will not always maintain this position. It will be the instructor's responsibility to remind him of his mistakes without either boring or discouraging him. This is where work with a group is superior to work with an individual, for the instructor can use the stimulus of competition in work on, for example, heel position.

THE MECHANICS OF THE GAITS

The instructor must understand something of the mechanics of the gaits, and why it is that until one has learned to absorb the shock of the horse's movements, there will be reiterated separations of the rider from the saddle in cadence with the stride. This is the "bouncing" which is so uncomfortable to the beginner.

There are two movements of the horse's body to which the rider must learn to react—the vertical movement and the horizontal movement. Let us first examine the vertical movement.

Vertical Movements

In every gait except the walk and including the jump, there is a period of suspension, or "flight," when all four of the horse's feet are off the ground. Before the gaits were studied carefully, it was thought that during the flight the horse's body was pushed suddenly upward, and that this was what thrust the rider out of the saddle. On the contrary, slow-motion pictures have brought to light the fact that the period of suspension is attained by the *flexing* of the joints of the horse's legs. They are drawn up under him, and consequently the body of the horse is *lowered*. Thus it appears that the bouncing is not caused by the rider's inability to stick to the saddle when the straightening of the horse's legs raises the croup and the withers, but by his inability to follow with his body when the flexing of the animal's legs causes the body to drop suddenly out from under him. The rider must learn to follow this flexing movement, and this he can do in two ways. The first method is by relaxing the muscles of his base of support so that they do not react independently of the horse. As explained on page 205, a balloon which is inflated until it is rigid will bounce higher and come down more slowly when placed on a plank and subjected to sudden upward thrusts than will a balloon that is only partially inflated and relatively limp. The second method of following the horse's movements is by utilizing the joints of the knee, ankle, hip, and lumbar vertebrae.

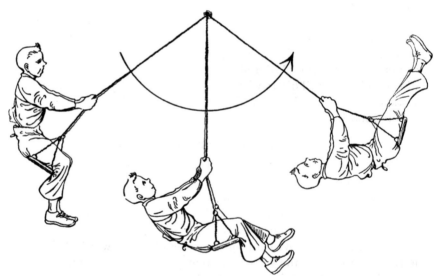

FIG. 87.   Suppling the loin. *As the boy pumps, the loin is stretched.*

There are several exercises designed to develop this suppleness of loin. A child pumping a swing (Figures 87, 88) stretches his vertebrae vertically to make the swing go higher, then shortens it in swinging back. Pushing a book forward on a table (Figures 89, 90) also performs this stretching function. Raising the loin off the floor (Figure 91) is another valuable exercise. In all of these movements, the pelvic bones are pushed forward—the same position which is neces-

FIG. 88.   Suppling the loin. *As the boy swings back, the loin is shortened.*

sary to maintain a balanced position on the horse. Note that in Figure 90, only one pelvic bone is pushed forward. This is called the "unilateral" (one-sided) use of the back, and is used in executing many movements on the horse, such as the gallop depart and turns. The "bilateral" use of the back refers to the vertical suppling of the

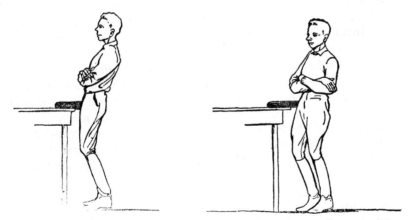

FIG. 89.   Exercises to supple the loin. *Bilateral suppling of the loin. Pushing the book straight forward with neither hip advanced.*
FIG. 90.   Unilateral suppling of the loin. *Pushing the book sideways by advancing the hip.*

loin without pushing one of the ischia farther forward than the other. It is this movement which the rider must learn in order to be able to adapt to the sudden lowering of the horse's body at the moment of suspension. Thus he can follow the horse's body with his own, and there will be no separation or "bounce."

FIG. 91.   Another exercise to supple the loin. *Also to teach the pupil what muscles to use in bracing the back.*

Horizontal Movements

At the walk, there is no period of suspension, and consequently, little necessity for vertical suppling of the loin. However, there is considerable horizontal motion of the horse's body. Because the cadence of the walk is comparatively slow, the instructor should utilize this gait to teach the rider to relax his buttock muscles and supple his loin, feeling the movement of the horse under him and following that movement with his body.

The horizontal movements of the horse are less violent than the vertical movements, and to counteract them it is necessary for the rider only to move his body with the forward movement of the horse. Unfortunately, the forward movement of the horse in the faster gaits is not even or sustained. In the period of suspension, it slackens; as the legs again push the horse forward, it accelerates. To a very minor degree, this is like a trolley car that goes ahead in fits and starts, causing the passengers to swing and sway. Since there is no period of suspension at the walk, the forward movement is much more even and therefore the rider is able to follow the motion very easily. At the sitting trot, he will have to learn to absorb the vertical thrusts and falling away of the horse's body before he can combat the horizontal movements and stay with his horse.

At the posting trot the rider has a choice of two methods of moving with the horse, both of which he must know and understand, for he will want to use them both. The first is posting behind the trot. In this movement, the rider first allows himself to be pushed up vertically by the thrust of the horse, then pushes himself forward,

214

and comes down again. In the second method, he posts with the movement of the horse by inclining his upper body forward, rolling forward on his thighs, and pushing forward, then up. This method, although it is more difficult to learn, is easier on both the horse and rider, and much smoother. However, it cannot be used on horses that are difficult to rate, since the pushing forward of the rider's body has the effect of making the horse go faster, and therefore, makes it necessary for the rider to use his reins more strongly. The trainer uses the method of posting behind the trot in rating overambitious horses.

Some authorities believe that the slow trot is preferable to the fast trot in covering distance, since they consider the fast trot a more tiring gait for the speed attained than the gallop. I feel that there are arguments to be found in favor of both theories. The fact that the Pony Express riders always used the gallop, and that there are some extraordinary records of remarkable distances covered by ponies used for this purpose would appear to sustain the theory that the horse tires less easily at the gallop. Colonel Richard I. Dodge, in his book *Riders of Many Lands* (Houghton Mifflin, 1901), mentions a Pony Express rider who carried the mail each week between El Paso and Chihuahua, a distance of three hundred miles. Since the country was infested with Indians, he rode only at night, covering one hundred miles a night for the first three nights of each week and resting the remainder of the week. He used only one pony and kept it up for six months, at the end of which time neither man nor pony was the worse for it.

On the other hand, it is the trotting horse that is subjected to the greatest tests of endurance in racing. Whereas the runner and steeplechaser are required to go from one to four miles at full speed, the harness horse usually races three heats and is "scored" as much as twelve miles previous to the race. In the early days, trotting and pacing races, both under the saddle and in harness, were extraordinarily long. According to old records, "Bishop's Mare" trotted sixteen miles on the Epsom road in sixty-eight minutes and thirty seconds; "Ogden's Mare" trotted thirty miles in two hours and ten minutes; and in 1793, "Crocket's Mare" trotted a hundred miles in eleven hours and fifty minutes.

In the Vermont Trail Ride, it has been found that horses that are walked on the grades and rough places and trotted where the going is good but that are not galloped, finish in the best condition. In long military marches, the cavalry uses the walk and the ordinary trot, but seldom the gallop.

Unquestionably, the slow trot is less tiring to the horse than the extended walk, which requires much more energy on the part of the horse than the slow trot does.

At the gallop, the rider is faced with the necessity of adjusting his equilibrium to strong vertical thrusts and sudden lowerings of the croup and forehand due to the periods of suspension, as well as to very irregular forward movements. This is the most difficult of all the movements for the rider to learn, and for many months, the beginner who can negotiate the slower gaits very creditably takes terrific punishment at the canter. I have found that the suppling and relaxation necessary can best be acquired by riding at the canter without stirrups. The rider should be told to "pump" as in swinging. The horse or pony chosen should be one with a very even and slow cadence at the canter, preferably one that has been trained to take the gait on a voice command. The rider should go only a short distance, and the instructor should be prepared to stop the animal if the rider gets off balance. Methods of teaching the canter are discussed in Part II, Chapter 14.

Chapter 6

THE AIDS: THE REIN EFFECTS

The rider's natural aids are his hands, his legs, his voice, and his weight. His artificial aids include his spurs, his whip, and such limiting pieces of equipment as types of martingales.

The rider should think of his horse as having two divisions: the forehand—that part of the animal which is in front of the rider; and the hindquarters—the area behind him. These two parts must be coordinated by the rider by means of the aids. The action of the rider's legs and weight on the hindquarters gives the forward impulse; the reins control the speed with which the horse advances, the direction and the degree of collection.

The horse is taught on a system of "reward" and "punishment," as mentioned previously. His response to the aids is essentially a movement *away* from the pressure of a leg, toward the action of a rein. Therefore, the use of the aids should be stopped the instant the horse has obeyed the rider's will. In stopping the horse, for example, the pressure of the bit on the horse's bars is "punishment"; the relaxing of the reins when he has obeyed is "reward."

With his hands, through the reins, the rider directs his horse. To do this he uses one of five rein effects: the leading, or opening, rein, called the direct rein by some authorities; the bearing, or indirect, rein; the direct rein of opposition; the indirect rein of opposition in front of the withers; and the indirect rein of opposition behind the withers.

THE LEADING REIN

The direct rein of opposition which halts the horse is the first rein effect the beginner learns, but the leading rein (Figure 92) is the most important. It is easy for the beginner to learn this term, since the instructor explains that by carrying his hand out to the side and forward, the rider is leading the horse's head to one side and that the horse will naturally follow his own nose. The leading rein effect can also be demonstrated on foot, showing the pupil how bending the horse's head toward the leader causes him to turn. It is best in teach-

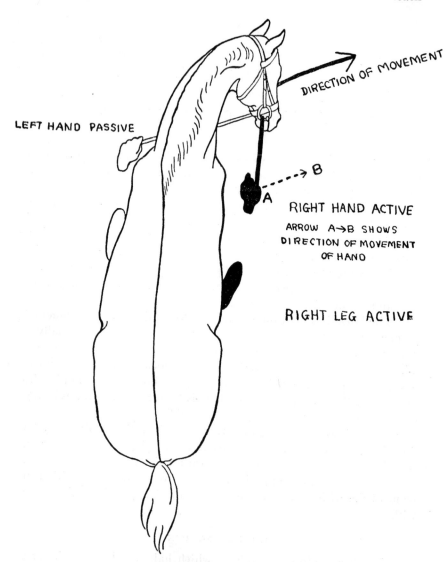

FIG. 92.   Right opening, or leading rein.

ing the leading rein effect to review the use of the active hand, then to have the rider, carrying his hand forward and to the side, fix his eyes on where he is going.

The exercise which is known as riding from front to rear is an excellent one for teaching the use of the leading rein. The pupil at the head of a line of riders executes a half-turn (see Figure 54), using his inside leading rein and his outside leg, and looking over his shoulder at the last horse in the line as he makes his turn. He then continues along the line, going in the opposite direction from the other riders and as close to them as possible until he reaches the end of the line, when he executes a half-turn in reverse (Figure 55) and takes his place behind the last rider. Each rider in turn executes the movement of riding from front to rear. Beginners should ride from front to rear at a walk, with particular emphasis on the use of the active hand and outside leg. The rider's weight should be on the inside stirrup, and his eyes must look up and in the direction of the movement. If this movement is executed at a jog trot while the rest of the line is walking, the rider, who is at the head of the line, should take up the jog trot and go straight forward for a few paces before beginning the turn. He should maintain this gait throughout the movement, coming down to a walk only when he is back in place at the end of the line.

Circles and voltes are excellent exercises for teaching the use of the leading rein. The desired position of the horse's head and neck is brought to the attention of the pupil, who is then asked to apply his aids, to leave the line of riders, and to circle around the instructor in the center of the arena. The instructor then holds up his fingers in sequence and asks the rider to count the number he is holding up. As long as the pupil keeps his eyes fixed on the instructor's hands, uses an active outside leg, and uses his inside hand actively but well forward with no opposition, the horse will circle willingly enough. Horses, being gregarious, like to work in the line rather than as individuals, and a stubborn horse will often leave the center and return to the line the minute the rider stops looking at the instructor's fingers and looks down at the horse. Beginners do this exercise at the walk, intermediates at the slow trot, more advanced riders at the canter.

THE INDIRECT REIN

The third rein effect to be taught is the indirect, or bearing, rein (Figure 93). The instructor can explain this best by walking beside

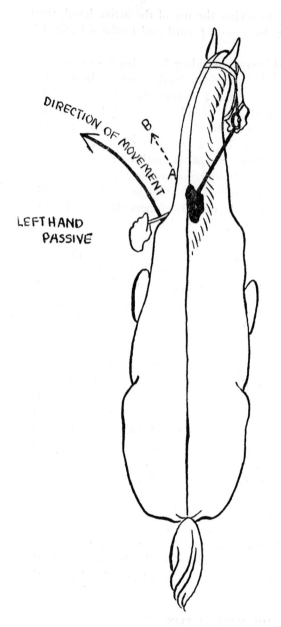

DIRECTION OF MOVEMENT

B

A

LEFT HAND
PASSIVE

RIGHT HAND ACTIVE
ARROWS A → B SHOWS
DIRECTION OF MOVEMENT
OF HAND

FIG. 93.   Right indirect or bearing rein.

the rider as he travels along the wall and placing his hand over his pupil's inside hand, showing him how he can push his horse against the wall by pushing on the upper half of the horse's neck with an active hand. At the same time, the pupil uses the inside leg and puts his weight over on the outside stirrup. In this way he is able to "ride out his corners," going well out on each turn, bending his horse's neck and head a little to the inside as he pushes him out against the wall.

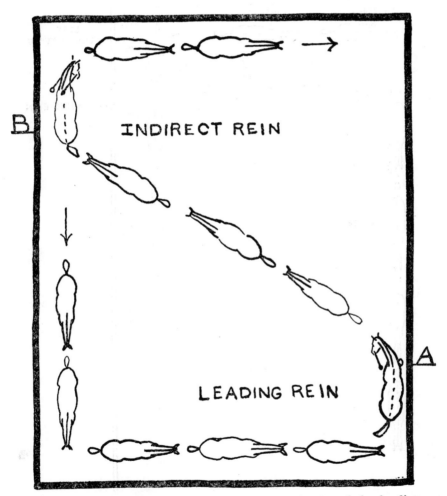

FIG. 94.   Changing hands across hall to teach uses of the leading and indirect-rein effects.

TEACHING THE DIFFERENCE BETWEEN THE LEADING-
AND INDIRECT-REIN EFFECTS

The difference between the uses of the leading rein and the indirect rein may be demonstrated by the following exercises.

(1) The rider on the track going to the left is told to use the indirect rein to push the horse into the corner, touching the point in the ring marked *A* in Figure 94. Using the same rein (the left), he

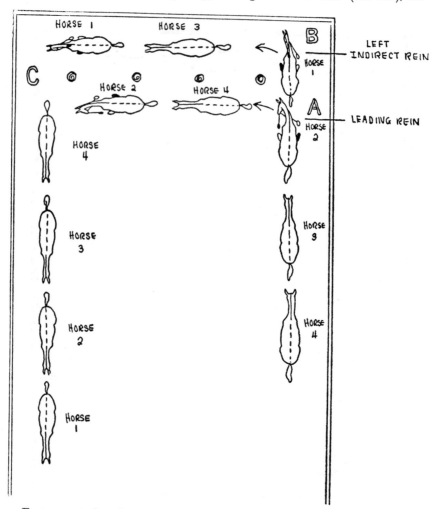

FIG. 95.   Another exercise to teach the riders to distinguish between the leading- and indirect-rein effects.

is to change it to a leading-rein effect and move the horse off the track, crossing the hall on the oblique to point *B*. As he nears this point, he is to use first a right leading rein to turn his horse, then a right indirect rein to push him against the wall so that the rider can touch point *B*.

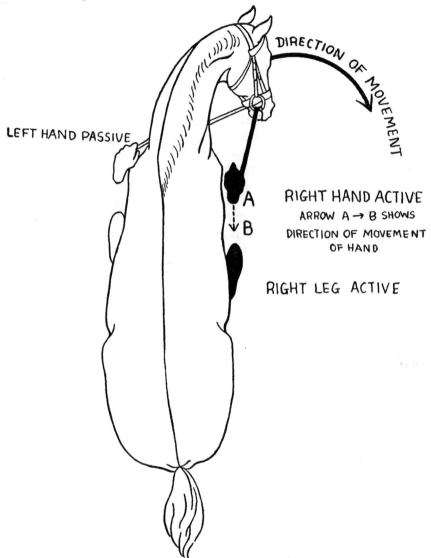

DIRECTION OF MOVEMENT

LEFT HAND PASSIVE

A
B

RIGHT HAND ACTIVE
ARROW A → B SHOWS
DIRECTION OF MOVEMENT
OF HAND

RIGHT LEG ACTIVE

FIG. 96.   Right direct rein of opposition.

(2) In the second exercise, a row of posts or jump standards are placed as shown in Figure 95. The riders move along the track to the left or right as designated. They are told to number off by fours. The instructor explains that this is an exercise to demonstrate the different uses of the rein, reviews the leading- and indirect-rein effects, and, by asking questions, makes certain that all riders understand them. He then directs all the odd-numbered riders to use their inside indirect rein and push their horses into the corner at *A,* so that they can touch point *B* and follow along the track as close to the wall as possible. Meanwhile, all the even-numbered riders, as they reach point *A,* are to use the inside leading rein and come inside the line of posts, following a new track as indicated. After he passes point *C,* each even-numbered rider goes back to his original position. All riders must watch those in the other line and maintain their distances so that they can go smoothly into place. The riders on the outside track will have to go a little faster than those who have come inside the line of posts. When the reassembled line again reaches point *A,* the odd-numbered riders, using the leading-rein effect, take the inside track and vice versa. Beginners execute this exercise at the walk, intermediate riders at the slow trot, advanced riders at the canter.

(3) The simple half-turn (Figure 54, page 110) can be executed by all riders in unison, if they are first spaced out properly in the ring. The riders are told to use the leading rein to make the turn and the indirect rein to move back to the wall on the oblique.

THE DIRECT REIN OF OPPOSITION

In teaching young children the rein effects in opposition, the instructor first explains that the word "opposition" means to "go against," and that in this case it is the horse's forward movement that is being opposed. Therefore, any rein effect that has the term "opposition" in it necessarily means that the horse will be either slowed down or stopped by the effect of the reins. The beginner usually learns to execute the direct rein of opposition (Figure 96) long before he is aware of its name, since he learns early in his riding career to stop his horse by means of the active hand.

The following exercise is useful for teaching the direct rein of opposition. It is usually not introduced until the riders have learned to stop their horses quietly and at will. With the riders on the track, each one is told to consider a certain number, marked on the walls of the ring, as his "home spot." The "home spots" are assigned in sequence, according to the position of the rider in the column. After going once around the ring, each rider, using both direct reins of opposition with the active hand, is to stop his horse so that the horse is against the wall and the rider's knee is on the home spot. The riders are to see how seldom it is necessary for them to open and close their fingers before the horse comes to a halt.

When the uses of the leading, indirect, and direct rein of opposition are clearly understood, the indirect rein of opposition in front of the withers (Figure 97) may be taught. The rein effect is explained to the rider when he is at the walk. He is asked to halt at a given spot, using only the inside rein of opposition in front of the withers. It will be found that his horse will halt with his body very close and parallel to the wall, whereas if the rider is asked to stop his horse by using only the inside direct rein of opposition, the horse will turn toward the center as he stops.

An excellent exercise for teaching the application of and the difference between the indirect rein and the indirect rein of opposition in front of the withers is to have the pupils ride in pairs. As each pair approaches a corner of the ring, the inside rider is to use his inside rein of opposition in front of the withers, while his partner against the wall uses his outside indirect rein without opposition. The effect will be to keep the horses close together and to slow down the inside horse, which must move more slowly on the corners than the horse against the wall.

The indirect rein of opposition in front of the withers is used in any schooling figures that require that the horse turn on his haunches, such as the broken lines, the serpentines, ranging the haunches in, and the circles with the haunches ranged out. When the pupil becomes sufficiently advanced to practice these figures, he will find this rein effect essential to their correct execution.

This rein effect (Figure 98) is not used as much as the indirect rein of opposition in front of the withers. It is a very strong rein effect, and its most common use is in the shoulder-in (see Figure 58). It is also used for very sharp turns on the haunches, such as are required in polo.

The indirect rein of opposition should not be taught too soon. The riders should become very familiar with both the names and the applications of the first three rein effects first. When the class is ready

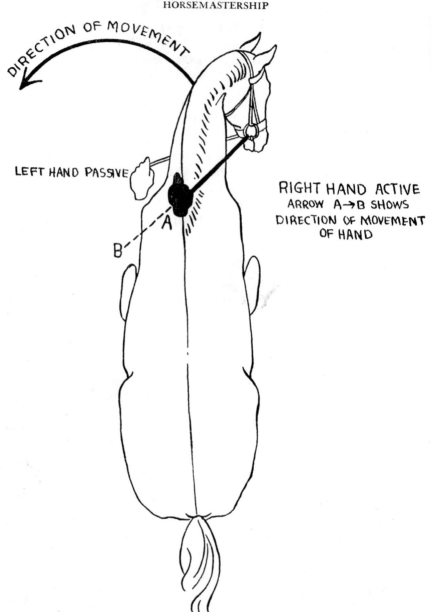

DIRECTION OF MOVEMENT

LEFT HAND PASSIVE

RIGHT HAND ACTIVE
ARROW A→B SHOWS
DIRECTION OF MOVEMENT
OF HAND

A

B

FIG. 97.   Indirect rein of opposition in front of withers.

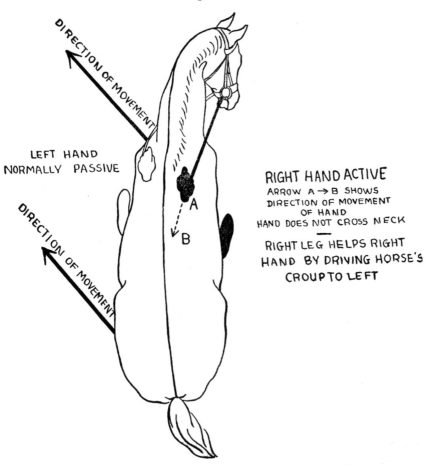

LEFT HAND
NORMALLY PASSIVE

RIGHT HAND ACTIVE
ARROW A → B SHOWS
DIRECTION OF MOVEMENT
OF HAND
HAND DOES NOT CROSS NECK
—
RIGHT LEG HELPS RIGHT
HAND BY DRIVING HORSE'S
CROUP TO LEFT

FIG. 98.   Indirect rein of opposition in rear of withers.

to do mounted drill or musical rides, it can be taught the indirect rein of opposition in front of the withers. Riders can then apply it as they learn to do the schooling movements which immobilize the haunches. The time to teach the indirect rein of opposition behind the withers is when the pupil is ready for the shoulder-in. Enlarged charts will serve to make the rein effects clear. If they are drawn with the horses in solid black, they will show up better to a mounted rider. The schooling figures may be drawn the same way.

Chapter 7

THE AIDS: THE HANDS

*T*he beginner invariably employs what is known as a "pulling" hand. In so doing, he punishes his horse unnecessarily, and we say that he has "rough" or "heavy" hands. In judging horsemanship classes or in evaluating a new pupil, the instructor looks first at the hands of the rider. If they bounce up and down, allowing the reins to become slack and then to tighten with a jerk when he posts; if he raises them suddenly with a hard pull so that the horse opens his mouth in stopping; if he breaks the wrist downward (Figure 103), causing the horse to push his nose out when he stops; or if the tendons on the backs of his hands stand out, with the fingers tightly closed, the elbows and wrists stiff and unyielding; the instructor classifies the rider as having "heavy" hands, and knows that his first duty is to lighten them. In all probability the rider is using his reins as a means of maintaining his position and balance. The instructor will be careful not to put such a rider on a sensitive horse. If possible, he will bit the mount of this pupil in a hackamore to save his mouth. He will have this rider spend much of his riding time with his hands on his waist while his reins are knotted and allowed to hang on the animal's neck. The instructor will work to achieve relaxation and balance, for he knows that only when the rider can maintain his seat without using his hands will he improve the use of his hands. He will keep him working at slow gaits on easy-gaited horses. When the pupil has gained his balance, the instructor will put him on an animal that responds very readily to the bit, and will teach him to use his hands ever so lightly to control his mount. There is nothing worse for the rider with heavy hands than to ride a pulling horse.

When the rider has learned not to interfere with his horse, he can be said to have "light" hands. Such a rider will not hurt his mount, and it is in this category that most so-called "advanced" riders may be classified. If, at the end of a year's instruction, the instructor can say that all his riders have "light" hands, he can congratulate himself. Nor is this goal beyond his reach. When the theory of riding by balance is understood and applied, when the rider is taught to use the "active" hand to control his horse, he will soon develop light hands. Riders with light hands may be mounted upon sensitive horses without fear of their ruining them. They are not yet ready to ride a spirited horse, to reclaim a spoiled horse, or to train a green one.

The experienced rider, he who is capable of riding the most sensitive and spirited horses, and who can train a green colt without ruining him, must have what are known as "educated" hands. The educated hand is the hand that knows exactly how much tension to apply in order to resist the tension of the horse or to demand a movement from him, and the exact instant to release that tension. Since every horse differs in his reactions, it is easy to see why few riders may be said to have educated hands, but such a rider is readily recognized by the attitude of the horse he rides. Entering a ring, his horse looks alert, yet calm. He executes the most difficult movements without any obvious use of the aids. His transitions from one gait to another and his changes of speed are exact and smooth. The rein is slightly stretched but never flapping if the horse is extended. The horse flexes at the poll as the rider demands, with no signs of discomfort, and the rider's hands follow the movement, the rein always maintaining the same light contact. Rarely does any horse under such a rider misbehave, even those horses which are noted for their bad manners.

THE PULLING HAND

So much for the classification of the rider's hands. Let us now consider the ways in which the rider uses his hands. The beginner, or the rider who has had poor instruction, rides with a *pulling* hand (Figure 99). He exerts tension to the rear or upward which continues even after the horse has responded. Should someone cut the rein when the rider with pulling hands is in the act of stopping, his hands would fly backward and hit him in the stomach. Pupils should be instructed from the very beginning that they must *never* use a pulling hand.

FIG. 99.   The pulling hand.

THE PASSIVE HAND

The *passive* or *following* hand (Figure 100) describes the action of the rider's hand when the horse is going in the desired direction at the desired gait and rate of speed. The following hand does just what its name implies: it "follows" the movement of the animal's head and neck, and always maintains a light contact with the bit. The principle of the passive hand, together with that of the active hand, is explained to the rider at his very first lesson.

To develop a passive or following hand, the rider must study the movements of the horse's head and neck at the various gaits. He must also know that at the posting trot, his elbows must be relaxed, their angles opening and straightening as he rises in the saddle, closing as he settles down in it. The following demonstration and exercise is useful for explaining and teaching the relaxation of the elbows to the rider.

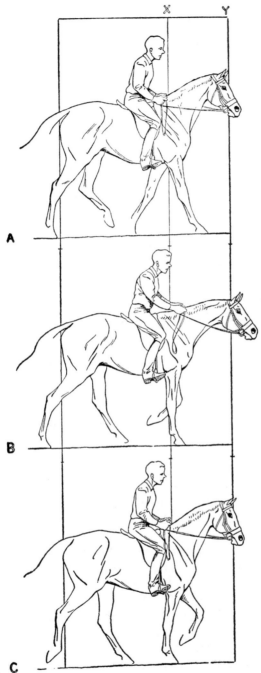

FIG. 100.   The passive or following hand. *Rein remains lightly stretched and follows the movement of the horse's head. Figure 100a shows the head as it is raised, 100b as it is extended, and 100c as it is raised again.*

The instructor stands on the ground with his knees bent as though he were sitting in the saddle. He bends his elbows and holds his hands as though they were holding reins. He then imitates the posting motion, keeping his elbows stiff, and draws attention to the manner in which his hands rise up and down with the movement of his body. Next he slows the cadence of his movements, and each time he straightens his knees, he also straightens his elbows, showing the pupil how, in this fashion, he can keep his hands in one position. The pupil is now told to take the track at a walk, and to rest the tips of his little fingers on the horse's neck just in front of the withers. He is then to rise and balance in his stirrups for a few steps and sink again into the saddle without moving his hands. When he succeeds in this, he is to put his horse into a trot and again balance in the stirrups for several steps, resting the tips of his little fingers on the animal's neck. Then he is asked to post, consciously straightening his elbows at each step of the horse, and maintaining the light contact of the fingers on the neck. This exercise should be repeated at frequent intervals until the pupil's hands no longer bounce up and down when he posts.

In teaching the rider to ride at each new gait, the instructor should allow him to rest his hands on the neck or hold the neck strap with the reins very loose until he has gotten his balance and is able to follow the movements of the horse with his body. Then the movements of the neck and head are explained to him, and he is asked to follow these movements consciously, without allowing the reins to become too tight or too slack. It is particularly difficult for the inexperienced rider to learn to sit the canter, so at this gait especially he will need first to hold the neck strap and later to realize how the horse moves and to follow this movement with his hands as his body rocks to stay with the motion.

It is comparatively easy to develop a following hand at the various gaits, but much more difficult at the jump, because of the sudden changes of position of the horse's head and neck, and because of the sudden thrust of the horse's body which throws the rider off balance. The instructor should not attempt to teach the following hand over jumps until the rider has become very experienced. He should be content to have the rider first hold a neck strap and later rest his hands lightly on the animal's neck with his fingers spread. When the rider is entirely balanced and automatically adjusts himself to the movement of the jump, the instructor can begin to teach the following hand, in which the rider maintains a light contact throughout the three phases of the jump. Eventually, he must learn to do so, as only thus can he maintain control.

Training the Rider

In using the *active* hand (Figure 101), the rider is taught to slow, halt, and turn his horse by first establishing a light contact with the mouth, and then opening and closing his fingers in cadence with the stride. Since many beginners cannot conceive of how such a mild method of using the hands could possibly be effective, the instructor should take hold of the reins himself near the bit while his pupils hold the other end in the usual fashion. The instructor asks the pupil to close his eyes while he himself opens and closes his fingers on the reins. The beginner is able to feel this very easily, and it can be pointed out that the horse's bars are even more sensitive than the rider's hands, so he will be well aware of what the rider is doing. The instructor explains that, besides acting as a signal to the horse, the use of the active hand actually prevents the horse from bracing his neck and poll and pitting his great strength against the puny strength of the rider. He demonstrates this by taking hold of the reins as before, and asking the rider to pull steadily while he pulls against him. Then, without warning, the instructor suddenly relaxes his hold. The pupil, finding that he has nothing to pull against, will relax, and the instructor can easily apply a quick tension which will cause the rider's hands to give and come forward. This can be compared to a tug-of-war between two people of unequal strength. As long as the weaker person maintains a steady pull, the stronger one can easily pull him across the line; but if the weaker person lets go suddenly, he can often get the stronger one a little off balance and be the winner himself.

The beginner is first shown how to halt the horse on an active hand, and then how to turn him, using only one hand carried forward and to the side.

These two simple uses of the hand, the following and the active, are the only ones which are taught the rider through the beginning and early intermediate stages of his riding. By using the following hand, the rider learns to feel what the horse is doing or is about to do, and by using the active hand, he can influence the horse in the least severe way possible.

THE FIXED HAND

Another method of using the hands is the use of the *fixed* hand. This method is difficult to understand, difficult to apply, and even more difficult to explain. For this reason its use is reserved for the more experienced rider.

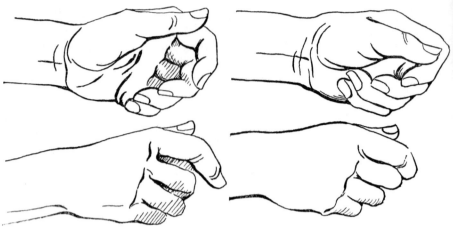

FIG. 101a. *The hand starts by being passive.*

FIG. 101b. *It becomes active as fingers begin to close on reins.*

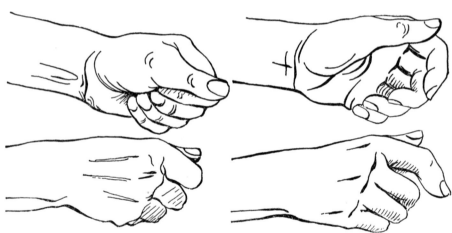

FIG. 101c. *Fingers are now tightly closed for an instant.*

FIG. 101d. *Fingers relax and hand again becomes passive. Hand is used actively in cadence with the stride. Only the fingers are used; the hand does not change position. Action is repeated if necessary.*

FIG. 101. Using the hand actively.

To apply the fixed hand (Figure 102), the rider first places his hand in contact with the horse's mouth, the rein stretched. He next "fixes" it there by closing his fingers firmly, stiffening his wrist and his shoulders. At the same time he pushes the horse forward into the bit with his legs and his loin. Responding to the forward urge, the horse pushes against the resisting bit and brings himself to a halt or slows down. With a sensitive horse, the movements described above are ever so slight, a second's fixing of the hands and a little push with the loin being sufficient to push the horse into the bit and stop him. In turning with the fixed hand, the rider carries the hand to the side, establishes contact, and fixes it. He then pushes forward with the inside pelvic bone (unilateral use of the back) and presses his outside

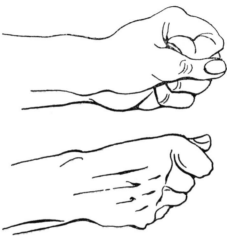

Fig. 102.   The fixed hand. *Fingers are closed tightly and hand is fixed in position. With the use of the legs the horse is pushed into the bit and meets the resistance of the fixed hand. In movements such as the walk, the natural movement of the horse's head is enough to bring him against the bit and cause him to stop on the fixed hand.*

leg. The horse will turn and keep turning as long as the rider continues to use these aids.

The danger in the use of the fixed hand is that the rider who fixes his hand with tension to the rear may go on pulling when the horse gives. The fixed hand never moves from its position, no matter what the horse does. It is not a pulling effect of the reins which stops the horse, but the action of being pushed forward by the rider against the bit.

If, after fixing the hand, the rider finds that the horse still pulls against him, he should shorten his reins and again fix his hands, bracing them, if need be, on the animal's neck. If the horse, attempting to get away from the fixed hand, brings his muzzle in and pushes it out again, the reins will flap against his neck, showing that the rider is indeed using a fixed (Figure 102) and not a pulling (Figure 99) hand.

The principle of the fixed hand is that the rider, through the use of his back and legs, forces the horse to use his own strength against the rider's hands. Thus, the stronger the force, the sharper the disci-

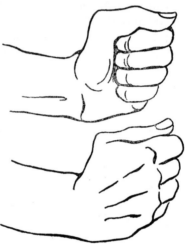

Fig. 103.   Bad position of the hands. *Wrist is broken downward. Rider's whole body will be stiff.*

pline of the hand. This might be compared to the technique of jiu jitsu, in which the fighter's own strength is used by his opponent to overcome him.

The rider who has learned to use the active hand, who can use his legs correctly, and who knows how to brace his back, can be introduced to the principle of the fixed hand, but until he is very experienced and sensitive, he should use this method only to demand the halt or the half-halt from the walk. The instructor explains the principle, demonstrates it himself, and then asks the pupil to apply it, watching carefully to see that his pupil's hands do not move backward when placed, and that the horse does push himself into the bit and thus stop himself.

In demonstrating the uses of the pulling, following, active, and fixed hands, the technique illustrated in Figure 104 is very useful. The instructor holds a belt with a buckle on it above him as shown. He explains to the class that the buckle end of the belt represents the

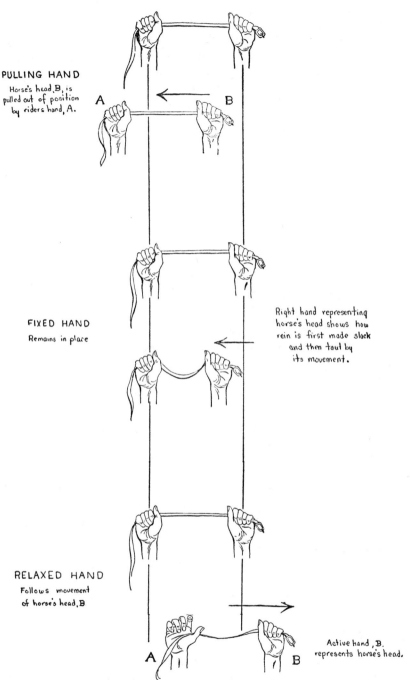

PULLING HAND

Horse's head, B, is
pulled out of position
by riders hand, A.

A ← B

Right hand representing
horse's head shows how
rein is first made slack
and then taut by
its movement.

FIXED HAND

Remains in place

←

RELAXED HAND

Follows movement
of horse's head, B

→

Active hand, B.
represents horse's head.

A   B

FIG. 104.   The instructor demonstrates how the hands are used
with the aid of a belt.

bit; the hand holding that end, the horse's head; and the other hand, the rider's hand, while the length of belt between is the rein. He moves the hand holding the buckle end of the belt to show the movement of the horse's head when he walks. With the other hand, he follows this motion, keeping the rein lightly stretched. Next he pulls against the movement, demonstrating the pulling hand (Figure 104) and showing how it pulls the horse's head out of position and upsets him. Next he shows the active hand and how, by using the fingers actively, he changes the tension of the rein so that the horse feels a little series of vibrations, yet has nothing to pull against. Finally he fixes the hand representing the rider's hand (Figure 104) and continues the backward-and-forward motion of the horse's head, showing how that motion acts on the bit and causes the horse to shop (Figures 105, 106).

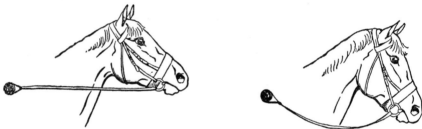

FIG. 105.   Another way to demonstrate the fixed hand. *The ball represents the rider's hand held in position. When the horse flexes at the poll, the rein slackens and the tension automatically ceases. Compare with Figure 106.*

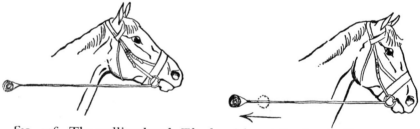

FIG. 106. The pulling hand. *The hand is not fixed as in Figure 105, but flies backward when the horse flexes, thus continuing to punish him, although he has obeyed.*

THE PULLEY HAND

There is still another method of using the hand which is taught only to advanced riders, and which is used only in emergencies. This is the *pulley* hand (Figure 107). Like the fixed hand, this employs the jiu-jitsu principle of pitting the horse's strength against himself. The rider braces one hand on the horse's neck about halfway up toward the poll, holding the rein tight. The other hand is then raised

FIG. 107.   The pulley hand. *A method which can be used effectively to stop a runaway.*

and carried to the side, where it may be fixed or used actively. The effect of this is to bend the neck and muzzle laterally, causing the horse to pull against his own neck. This also throws the horse a little off balance so that he must turn rather sharply. It is used to stop runaways or to pull up very suddenly between jumps.

Chapter 8

THE AIDS: LEGS, BACK
AND EQUILIBRIUM

THE LEGS

*T*he highly schooled horse ridden by an expert rider will obey without any change of leg position on the part of the rider, who keeps his legs and feet always in line with the girth and wears long-shanked, blunt spurs. For dressage and *haute école* riding, the Viennese riders use a special spur which is curved upward in the opposite manner from the hunting spur. To give a signal requiring the horse to move his haunches from one side to the other, the expert rider very lightly touches his horse's side with his spur, without changing the position of his foot. To signal the horse to move the center of his body away from the rider's leg, he uses the side of his leg against the girth. To signal a change of lead or an extension of the forelegs, he touches the horse in front of the girth with his toe. But this delicate use of the leg is for the expert rider and the highly trained horse only; we cannot expect the average school rider on the average school horse or the un-schooled horse to respond to this refined use of the leg aids. Neverthe-less, it is well to bear in mind the old French adage, "The well-trained horse obeys the wind from the rider's boot."

The legs are used progressively—that is, first lightly then more strongly, if the horse does not obey—and never with a steady push. To cause the horse to move his hindquarters, the rider first pushes him gently with the side of his leg. If the horse does not respond, he uses his heel or spur. If the horse is in motion, the rider uses his leg in cadence with the movement, and only until the horse *begins* to obey. If the horse is standing and the rider is working on a pivot, he presses until he feels the horse about to yield, then immediately rewards him by relaxing the aid. Under riders whose legs are used too strongly, phlegmatic horses quickly become so insensitive that they will not obey the legs at all, while excitable horses become unmanageable.

There are three recognized positions of the legs: on the girth, four inches behind the girth, and in front of the girth (Figure 108) All movement of the horse comes from the hindquarters. Whether the rider wants his horse to move forward or backward, to change direction while moving, or to pivot in place, the rider's legs must first be used to put the horse into motion.

A   B.   C.

On the girth.   *Behind the girth.*   *In front of the girth.*

FIG. 108.   The permitted positions of the active and holding legs.

Basically speaking, the horse moves his body away from the pressure of the leg. Pressure from both legs will cause him to move forward in a straight line, unless the forward motion is opposed by the hands. The legs can also be used to prevent the horse from moving his quarters. If the rider wishes the horse to describe a circle with his body bent in the direction of the movement, his hind feet tracking his fore feet, he uses his outside leg behind the girth and his inside leg on the girth. If he wants the horse to turn sharply on his center, he uses his inside leg behind the girth to push the horse's quarters over. If he wants the horse to turn on his haunches as in the broken-line movement, he uses his outside leg strongly to cause the horse to hold his quarters in place.

The rider must learn to feel the effect of his leg aids. Each horse responds differently, and therefore requires a slightly different use of the legs. Horses that have not learned to respond to the legs at all will have to be schooled in the leg-yielding exercise described in Figure 37. It may be necessary to employ a light switch to tap the horse on the flank as the leg is used. Horses that have been well schooled to yield to the leg on turns and circles sometimes become confused when a more difficult movement, such as the two-track, is taken up, and again the switch may have to be resorted to. The role of the assisting or holding leg is also important, and is discussed in detail in Part II, Chapter 9.

The instructor should spend at least a part of each lesson period in stressing the importance of the use of the legs. He should ask his pupils to make sharp turns and circles using the hands as lightly as possible. From the very first lesson, when the use of the leading rein is taught, the pupil should learn to use his outside leg with it and to put his weight over onto the inside stirrup. As soon as the pupil can coordinate his aids at all, he should be asked to turn flank movements and to ride square corners; the use of the legs in these movements must be well understood. Flank movements executed by a group of riders simultaneously, or as an exercise in groups of three, are particularly valuable for teaching the rider to use his legs both to turn and to continue the forward impulse after turning.

It is comparatively easy for the average rider to remember to use his legs correctly when he is working on schooling figures, but when he starts playing games, he is apt to forget that, in turning, the legs and weight are used first, and the reins only lightly, to direct the movement. One often sees fairly competent riders "ying-yanging" their horses around in the excitement of the battle. For this reason, the wise instructor bits his horses in hackamores for games.

THE BACK

The use of the back is extremely important in feeling and in influencing the horse's movements. The European schools put more emphasis on the use of the back, both in riding and in jumping, than do the American authorities. It is rare to find a riding instructor in this country who understands the importance of the use of the back or the method in which it should be used.

As explained previously, it is the flexibility of the rider's loin or lumbar region which enables him to follow the movements of the horse with his body. All children learn to "brace" the back when pushing a swing, but when mounted on a horse and asked to use the same motion to follow the movement of the canter, they cannot do so. The exercises shown in Figures 89 and 90 are valuable for making the rider conscious of the proper use of his back. They should be practiced faithfully between riding instruction periods. The back can be used either bilaterally, as in pushing a book forward on a table, or unilaterally, when one side of the pelvis is pushed forward and the book moves sideways. The back is used bilaterally in following the movements of the horse at the various gaits and at the jump, except at the posting trot, where the rider is not attempting to follow the movements of the horse with his body. It is used unilaterally for turning the horse and for demanding a gallop depart on a specific lead. In using the back unilaterally, the rider must make sure that, sitting in the center of his saddle, he pushes the required pelvic bone forward. Sometimes in demanding a right gallop depart, where the right pelvic bone should be pushed forward, the rider instead pulls the left pelvic bone back, which is not the same thing at all.

Throughout the intermediate stages of training, the instructor should encourage riders to exaggerate the bracing of the back in following the movements of the horse, particularly in the slow trot and the canter. Later this aid, like all the others, should become so refined that the observer cannot tell when it is being employed.

With the use of the fixed hand, the bracing of the back plays a great part in stopping the horse. It should also be used in starting the horse, the only difference being that in one case the hands oppose the movement of the back, and in the other they do not.

As soon as the riders have refined their aids sufficiently to control their horses at the various gaits, and have learned the principles of bracing the back both unilaterally and bilaterally, they should be given exercises in riding in circles and in gallop departs, using the back only. The horse will respond much more readily with these aids than he does when the rider uses his reins and legs to demand these movements, since, in using the back only, the rider cannot possibly annoy the horse, thus making him uncomfortable, stubborn, and disobedient. I have taught children as young as seven or eight years old to leave a line of horses and circle independently by the unilateral use of the back alone, and have found that in so doing they became much more conscious of the refinement of all the natural aids.

The rider must be very careful always to keep his eyes up and to look in the direction of the movement. If he drops his eyes and looks at the ground or at the horse, he will not be able to control the animal by the use of the back, as this will change the weight distribution.

THE WEIGHT

Most horses are very conscious of the distribution of the rider's weight or equilibrium. The instructor who wishes to bring this point home to a pupil can ask him to take a younger child "piggy-back" and walk or run slowly in a straight line. The younger child is then told to swing his weight abruptly from side to side. The pupil who is doing the carrying will be unable to travel in a straight line, and will be made very much aware of the effect of the distribution of his own weight on his horse. The lightly built horse is particularly sensitive to weight, and I have known horses of this type to go completely sour on jumping because the rider did not use his weight correctly.

Generally speaking, the rider places his weight in the direction of the movement. If he is turning to the right, he weights his right stirrup. If he is pushing his horse over toward the wall, with the left leg and the left indirect rein, he again weights his right stirrup. The weight can also be used to immoblize a section of the horse's body. If the rider wishes the horse to turn to the left, pivoting on his left hind foot, he weights his left pelvic bone, rather than the left stirrup. If he wants to immobilize the right foreleg in a pivot with the haunches moving to the left around the forehand, he throws his weight a little forward and to the right. This is why it is always incorrect to demand a change of lead or a gallop depart by "throwing the weight" forward over the inside shoulder, as is so often done by the inexpert rider. In a gallop depart the aim is to free the inside shoulder of the horse, not to weight it. A horse that is circling to the right or left may be made to increase or decrease the size of his circle by the use of the rider's weight. A horse taking a course of jumps that require sharp turns will be best prepared if the rider signals the turn by shifting his weight very slightly in the direction of the turn while the horse is in mid-air over the preceding jump.

Riders who have not yet learned to brace the back should practice the circles, changes of hands, turns, half-turns, and serpentines, using the weight alone to signal the changes of direction. The instructor must go back to these exercises continually throughout his pupil's riding career.

There is some difference of opinion among various authorities in regard to the use of the weight when backing and when halting. The average beginner trying to halt his horse will lean forward, pull his hands back into his stomach, and draw up his legs. This only urges the horse forward. I have found that beginners learn relaxation more quickly and are more successful in stopping their horses without pulling hard on the reins if they are told to let their shoulders come a little back. This does three things: it counteracts the tendency of the beginner to draw up his legs and dig his horse in the flanks with his heels; it gets him down in the saddle; and it has a very mild effect of pushing the horse into the bit. In backing, the same principle applies.

If the rider is allowed to lean forward when asking his horse to back up, he is likely to squeeze too hard with his legs and to look down at his horse. Letting the shoulders come slightly back and sinking down into the saddle makes him more aware of the movements of the horse under him, and so makes it possible for him to feel, interpret, and influence the animal.

Chapter 9

COORDINATION OF THE AIDS

The aids are used both independently and in combination. In combination, they can be used either as assisting or as opposing aids. This statement sounds very confusing to the inexperienced horseman and is the cause of much misunderstanding, since one authority will state that the aids are to be used independently, while another will say that they should always be used in combination with each other.

The rider must be able to use each aid independently from the others in the sense that one leg must be able to act by itself without a reflex action of the other leg, one hand must be able to be used by itself, and so forth. However, legs and weight always act with the hands, and each aid that is not being used actively should be held in readiness to assist the active aid if the horse be sluggish in his responses, or should oppose the active aid, or if the horse responds too much.

In the pivot on the forehand, for example, if the horse is to swing his quarters to the left, the rider uses the left indirect rein of opposition in front of the withers to weight the right shoulder. This rein effect is assisted by the right leading rein or, should the horse try to move forward, by the right direct rein of opposition. The leading rein turns the animal's head slightly to the right and encourages him to move his hindquarters to the left. The rider also applies his right leg behind the girth and follows the direction of the movement with his weight. If the rider uses his aids too strongly, or if the horse is more sensitive than he had supposed, the horse may swing his hindquarters too fast and too far. The rider immediately counteracts this by changing the left indirect rein to a left leading rein, which serves

246

to check the movement of the hindquarters, since turning the horse's head toward his moving haunches automatically opposes the movement of the haunches. At the same time, the rider ceases using the right leg actively and may begin to use the left leg to assist in correcting the reaction of the horse. In this case, the rider has used his aids both independently and in combination. He first used them in combination to assist each other, then used one or more aids independently to oppose and correct when the first application of the aids was found to be too strong.

ANALYZING THE EFFECTS OF THE AIDS

Only too often, a rider supposes that to make a horse perform a given movement, he must always use a certain set of aids in a certain sequence. But very often, either because of the temperament or degree of training of his horse, or because of a lack of skill in himself, he finds that even though he may be following what he thinks is a magic formula, he still does not get the desired result. Instead of trying to memorize a sequence of aids for each movement, the rider must be taught first to analyze what he is asking his horse to do, how the horse is to place each leg, how his head is to be placed, in what direction he should move, and so forth. As he decides what aids he will need to get the horse to perform the movement, he should also decide what corrective aids he may need, or what assisting aids, should the horse not react correctly. Then he should attempt the movement, trying to feel without looking how the horse is responding. In difficult movements he can ask someone to tell him whether the horse is doing the movement correctly—or as nearly correctly as his training permits. Only by thinking and analyzing, by trying to feel and to interpret, will the beginner learn to use the aids correctly and with tact.

THE AIDS IN OPPOSITION

The instructor must not try to teach too many schooling movements too soon; rather he should pick the ones which will demonstrate to the pupil the effect of the particular aids that he wishes him to learn at that time, drawing his attention to the reaction of the horse.

The first and simplest application of the aids in opposition to each other is the fundamental use of the legs to urge the horse forward, and, if he goes too fast, the use of the direct rein of opposition to slow him down or stop him. When, many lessons later, the pupil has learned to rate or stop his horse with the use of the fixed hand

and the bracing of the back, the instructor should point out to him how, in this instance, he has refined his aids, and how differently the horse now responds from the way he did when the pupil knew how to stop only with the active hand.

THE ASSISTING AIDS

The first lesson in using the aids to assist each other should consist of teaching the beginner to circle on the leading rein, using the outside leg to keep the horse's haunches on the track and to keep him going, and putting his weight on the inside stirrup. Somewhat later, the pupil can be taught to enlarge the circle by shifting his weight to the outside stirrup, should the horse be making too small a circle; thus he learns what a corrective aid is.

Another useful exercise in teaching a combined use of the aids to assist each other is the application of the indirect rein and the inside leg to move the horse against the wall at the corners (Figure 95). These two exercises—the circles with the leading rein and the outside leg, and the use of the indirect rein and inside leg—are all that the average beginner can learn about the combined use of the aids. He is not yet skillful enough for a more delicate use of the aids, such as the use of the back and legs in opposition to the hands in stopping. But, even at the very beginning of his training, the rider must be made aware of the independent effect of each aid, and how it is used to demand a certain movement from the horse; also, how it may be used to assist the other aids, and how it may be used as a corrective aid to oppose them.

MORE REFINED USE OF THE AIDS

When the rider has developed enough "feel" so that he can tell what his horse is doing under him and can apply his aids delicately, he may be taught the pivot on the forehand. This is the first lesson in which the pupil is really made aware of the variety of combination of aids, and much time should be spent upon it in order to develop his ability to feel and to interpret, and thus, to develop his ability to influence. He should be given horses of different temperaments to ride, and should be encouraged to work until his mount will pivot calmly and completely around, one step at a time, keeping his outside foreleg as much in place as possible. The beginner works against the wall, and does only a quarter-pivot to begin with, bringing the horse back to his original position after three steps.

To develop awareness and skill in the use of the indirect rein of opposition in front of the withers combined with the holding leg, the rider must work on pivots around the hindquarters, broken lines, circles, half-turns, and serpentines, the last four movements to be executed ranging the haunches in (see pages 98 to 112). The instructor should demonstrate the movement himself and explain carefully what the horse is supposed to do. He should watch the pupil as he attempts to repeat the movement, making corrections and suggestions, and not letting him work alone until he is certain that the rider understands what he is trying to do, and is able both to feel the reactions of the horse under him and to interpret what he is feeling.

The various movements which cause the horse to move on two tracks—the shoulder-in, travers, renvers, half-pass (or two-track)—should be saved until the rider is well along in his training, since these are the most difficult movements for the horse and require great tact in the application of the aids. All these movements are described and illustrated on pages 113 to 123.

DISTINGUISHING BETWEEN THE MOVEMENTS

Since it is often difficult for the pupil to distinguish one movement from another, the instructor must help him by demonstrating each movement and by having him study the charts and analyze the horse's movements himself. He should learn one movement at a time, and each succeeding movement learned should be used in combination with the preceding movement or movements. Only in this manner will he really learn to distinguish one from the other. For example, he can move the horse along the left track on a left shoulder-in starting at the beginning of the long wall of the arena. Then, when he is halfway down the wall, he can change to a two-track to the left and move toward the corner diagonally opposite. In combining these two movements, he will discover that, although the horse remains facing more or less in the same direction, he moves very differently, and the rider has to reverse his aids completely. In the same manner, the horse can be made to do a travers along one wall, followed by a renvers along the next. By riding these schooling or dressage movements in combination, the rider is enabled to compare them with each other, noting the exact difference between them, and how the aids must be used. If he does each movement separately, with the horse walking or trotting on straight lines in between, he is more apt to confuse them and will be unsure of just which he is doing.

The various movements which can be combined into courses for riders of different degrees of skill are given in Appendix G, page 398.

In riding these courses, the instructor emphasizes exactness and smoothness in the execution of each figure, and especially smoothness of transition from one to another.

PRINCIPLES REGARDING USE OF THE AIDS

The instructor should bring to his pupil's attention certain general principles in regard to the application of the aids.

(1) The aids are applied with the very minimum of force required to cause the horse to execute the desired movement. The more highly trained the horse and the more skilled the rider, the lighter will be the aids. If the rider does not know from experience exactly how a given horse will react to the aids, he should apply them very lightly, and then increase their action if the horse does not respond.

(2) The aids should be applied in cadence with the movement and in response to the reactions of the horse, never continuously without release.

(3) The rider must understand the fundamental principles behind the application of each aid, not only how it is to be used actively to demand a movement, but also how it may be used as an assisting aid and as a correcting aid in response to the action of the horse.

In most movements, the rider weights the stirrup that is *not* being used actively, and so throws his weight in the direction of the movement. Thus, in causing a horse to move his body to the left, with the aid of the right indirect rein and the right leg, the rider weights his left stirrup. In work on circles in which the horse follows the pattern of the movement with all four feet, the rider carries his weight toward the center of the arc, unless the horse tends to make the circle too small, in which case he carries it to the outside. In every case, the aid ceases to act when the horse *begins* to obey the movement, and is applied anew if the movement is not completed satisfactorily.

The horse should almost always look in the direction of the movement. The exception to this is the shoulder-in movement, where the horse's head is turned slightly away. In ordinary circles and turns, the horse's spine, beginning at the poll and continuing to the dock, is bent on the same arc as the circle which is being described. This rule is the one most commonly forgotten by ordinary riders, who ride the circles and turns with the horse's body straight, his head often turned to the outside, and his legs changing directions in little jerks.

Chapter 10

PROGRAM PLANNING

*I*f the teacher is to be successful in presenting a well-rounded riding program—one which covers, in succession, the principles and practices of good horsemanship, and which will continue to interest his pupils year after year—he must plan his programs carefully. To do this he must have a good idea of the capabilities of each age group.

AT WHAT AGE SHOULD CHILDREN START TO RIDE?

I am often asked at what age I prefer to start children on their riding careers. There is no exact answer to this question, as it depends on the facilities available and on how the child is to be introduced to riding. If other members of the family ride and can spare time for the lessons, the earlier a child starts after he is able to sit up, the better. A baby who cannot walk can often learn to sit on a moving pony and balance without using his hands. By the time he is two years old he will be able to walk and trot on a quiet pony without a lead rein. He will have good posture, and will be able to post, to use the leading rein for turning, and the direct reins for slowing down. He will have developed a love of horses and will be completely fearless of them. However, this only applies if some older person, experienced as a horseman and a patient teacher, has put in many, many hours walking and running beside the child, keeping up his interest with little games, never letting him become frightened. Such conditions rarely exist. Instead, at frequent intervals parents call me and tell me that they are looking for a pony for their child, and ask me if I know where they can get one. Inquiry usually shows that no other

member of the family rides, that the child is completely inexperienced, and that the pony is to be treated as a pet. Invariably I coun-
sel the parent to put off buying his child a pony or a horse until he is
a fairly accomplished horseman, and then not to get him one unless
there are other children in the neighborhood with whom he can ride.

If there is more than one child in the family, it is generally more
successful to get two ponies than one, especially if the children are
under eight years old. Ponies hate to work alone. A pony taken out
by himself tends to stop and eat grass or to bolt back to the stable.
Two ponies will usually trot along quietly enough. Also, a child who
rides by himself when he is only in the early stages of his riding career soon becomes bored. For the first week or month, the pony is a
novelty; then he becomes just another chore. The child with no companions with whom he may ride had better wait until he is a good
enough horseman to buy an animal which will set up a challenge or a
problem. The advanced young rider, with seven or eight years of riding experience, can take a green colt, train and break him, and finally show him. A group of children good enough to ride and manage well-trained horses or ponies alone can have fun if they have a
"community stable," keeping their horses together. They can have
little gymkhanas, or go on picnic rides. But don't buy the very young
child or the beginner a pony and expect him to become a good rider
and maintain his interest.

WHEN SHOULD RIDING LESSONS BEGIN?

Another question often asked me is, "At what age do you advise
starting the child's regular riding lessons?" This depends on the type
of riding lessons to be had. Children of three and four can get a great
deal of enjoyment out of the "pony ride" type of lesson. In the school
here we have one instructor or assistant for each two children. The
children are mounted on small ponies and taken for a little walk up
the road. The lesson lasts a half-hour. The goal is to make the child
familiar with and unafraid of the pony, to teach him to sit relaxed
at the walk and at the slow trot. Little by way of control is expected,
but the child rides both bareback and in a saddle, and can be taught
to steer, to post, and to start and stop at a walk. A month or so of
this at a time is enough; then the child should have a change of occu-
pation to prevent him from becoming bored.

Occasionally a four-year-old will show special aptitude and is
able to go further with his riding. In this case, he can be classed as a
five-year-old, and can be given work suited to that age.

Training the Rider

The five-, six-, and seven-year-old children progress according to their aptitudes. Some children as young as five can learn to manage a pony at the walk and trot in a group without assistance. They can learn the use of the leading and indirect rein effects and the corresponding assisting leg aids. They can learn to use the following and the active hand. They can play simple games such as "Red Light" or "Touching Numbers." They can learn to have a good position at the walk and trot, and occasionally, on a smooth-gaited pony, at the canter. They can learn to handle a pony on foot, leading him, grooming him, picking up his feet, saddling him, and, if he is very obliging, bridling him. The average six-year-old can be expected to accomplish about as much as the advanced five-year-old.

The six-year-old with particular aptitude will keep up with the average seven-year-old. This age group can be expected to have a good deal more control than the younger group, to ride bareback over one-foot jumps, to ride in pairs, to play "Musical Stalls" and perhaps "Red Rover," to enjoy trail riding, and to be able to control a pony in a ring during "free time" when all are riding at will and there is no leader.

The gifted seven-year-old and the average eight-, nine-, or ten-year-old will make rapid progress. This group has good muscular control and strength. It is at a good age for learning, and is very fearless. Boys of this age have not become so involved with team games such as football and baseball that riding seems too unexciting for them. The child of ten or eleven who has average aptitude and who has started lessons at the age of seven should be a pretty good rider. He should be able to jump, should know all the rein effects and uses of the aids, and should be able to train a horse or pony for light and intermediate dressage. He should be able to canter and jump bareback without reins, and to do mounted drill and musical rides. I am speaking of children who have lessons once or twice a week, not of those who own their own horses and ride every day. These, with proper instruction and the right mounts, are often hunting or show jumping at nine or ten.

Boys can start riding at eleven, twelve, or thirteen, and make good progress. Usually by the age of fourteen or older, they have too many other interests and are unwilling to see children younger than themselves outride them. Girls who start older than the age of twelve seem to have a great deal of difficulty. For one thing, they grow very fast at this age, but the ratio of muscular strength to height and weight does not remain the same. A fourteen-year-old girl is apt to be badly coordinated, self-conscious, and somewhat timid. I have never had a girl start riding over the age of fifteen and turn out to be an expert rider. Boys, however, can make good riders even though they do not start until eighteen or older, as is proved by the Italian Cavalry, which takes its recruits at seventeen or eighteen and makes them into good horsemen in a fairly short time. However, the training is too rugged for the average woman, and without the bareback work with its inevitable falls, no horseman will ever have a completely independent seat.

Adults

Adults present a very different and much more difficult problem as pupils than children. The average man who takes up riding after he has grown up or who returns to it, after having ridden a little in his youth, wants to depend entirely on his strength. He is usually unwilling to spend the long hours at the slow gaits without stirrups necessary to develop a relaxed seat. He finds it hard to use his aids with delicacy. Such riders can learn to stay on a phlegmatic animal, but never have I seen one that I would class as expert.

The woman who starts to learn to ride after she is grown up seldom gets very far. She is usually timid about falling for she has lost the flexibility and agility of youth. While a fall to a ten-year-old, who is always falling off bicycles or swings, is an everyday affair, to a mature woman it is something disturbing. The adult taking up riding is not at an age when learning something is expected. His first reaction is, "I am probably too old to learn." The child, in the midst of learning everything, takes for granted that he will learn.

The adult who takes up riding, having ridden as a child but never having become expert, is almost as much of a problem as the beginner. The beginner expects to fail at first, but the adult who has ridden as a child can't understand why he does so poorly. Riding will be a constant frustration to him. If he has owned his own horse or pony and has ridden only that particular one, he will have forgotten much in regard to that animal's habits and temperament, remembering only that this horse was much, much better than anything the riding school has to offer. An adult who has ridden previously with no instruction or with incorrect instruction cannot understand why the riding teacher is trying to change his ways. He may have been to a dude ranch where he took long, all-day rides on a quiet animal that followed the one in front of him. He either walked or loped, and when he loped, he was instructed by the cowboy to grab the pommel and let the pony alone. Such a rider sees no reason why he can't ride in the East the way he did out West.

Finally, there are adult riders who have had good basic instruction and want to improve their riding. These are a pleasure to teach, for they will improve and remain interested, whereas with the other types of adult riders described above, one cannot have the high goals that one sets for the children.

ADVANCED RIDERS

The success of the advanced rider in shows depends to some extent on how good a mount he can afford. The rider, no matter how competent, who competes in an equitation class in a big show stands no chance unless his horse is easy gaited, well schooled, and the kind that catches the judge's eye. Jumping classes are not really judged on the ability of the rider as a horseman; rather they are "form over fences" classes. The rider who has a balky horse or one that goes too fast or has a rough jump cannot win. However, children should learn to compete in the show ring with the idea of putting on the best performance of which they are capable, regardless of the awarding of the ribbons. Small shows in which children of like ability compete against each other are fun also. Appendix J, pages 407 to 413, discusses horse shows in detail.

One of the most serious problems facing a riding instructor is that of keeping the interest of his pupils beyond the elementary stages of their riding careers. Too often a boy or girl will become fairly capable, able to handle a well-trained animal without trouble, and then, feeling that there is nothing more to be learned, will stop his riding lessons. Pony Clubs, Mounted Scouts, and Junior Cavalry units are one answer to this problem. With these, one combines the fun of team work and intramural competition with the rather dry business of improving riding techniques. The young child in an organized group can see what the older children are doing and can look forward to doing the same when he becomes more skillful.

In planning work for the advanced children, the instructor must vary the program from year to year. One year these children can have the emphasis put on breaking and training young horses or on training well-schooled horses to intermediate dressage. Another year they can be put to work improving their own and their mount's jumping ability, with the idea of entering as many jumping competitions as possible. A bloodhound hunt is a very inexpensive method of providing a stimulus to fox-hunting, and of giving the instructor a chance to teach hunting etiquette. Junior Cavalry units in which the cadets are advanced to higher ranks accompanied by more authority and privileges are fine for keeping up the interest of the advanced riders. The intelligent instructor will not be content to carry his riders only to the point where they look well and can ride the average horse; he will use riding as a means of developing many desirable character traits in his pupils. To do so, he must keep their interest and provide a challenge to the advanced students.

The riding instructor who takes over a group of varied abilities and ages should plan his programs so that the advanced riders review the basic principles each year, and the beginners and intermediate riders progress as far as they are able. In order to do this the instructor will have to make a series of lesson plans covering all the things he wants his riders to know. Examples of such lesson plans are given in detail in Appendix B, page 375. If he will take one objective, such as teaching the use of the indirect rein effect, and concentrate on that one thing with all his classes for a week in rotation, making notes of the children who need more practice, and then work on another definite problem the following week, he will be sure of not skipping anything. When he finishes with the elementary instruction he can go on to the advanced work with his advanced riders, continuing to work on the simpler things with the beginners. Remembering the goals to be expected from each age level, and the differences in aptitude within the groups, the instructor can make out a season's training schedule that will cover the needs of all his pupils.

Chapter 11

THE YOUNG CHILD'S
FIRST LESSON

*T*he goals of the instructor at the young child's first lesson are to make the child familiar with the pony and unafraid of him; to get him to mount willingly and to ride at a walk; to give his pupil confidence in himself, in the teacher, and in the pony; to keep him relaxed and happy; and to make him want to come back for another lesson.

Three or more children should be taught at the same time. One child alone is much more timid and apprehensive. As soon as the children arrive, the instructor finds out their names. He must train himself to remember the names from the beginning as this will have an excellent psychological effect on the child. Being called by name, the child will feel that the instructor knows him apart from the others, and this will give him a sense of security.

INTRODUCING THE CHILD TO THE PONY

A pony of quiet disposition and of a size suitable to the children is brought out. The pony should be one that will stand without moving and has no unpleasant habits such as nipping or shifting sideways when mounted.

An assistant holds the pony while the instructor tells the children about him—his name, and some little thing about his personality that will please and interest them. He draws attention to certain physical characteristics of the pony, such as the silkiness of the coat and the softness of the muzzle. He encourages the children to pat the horse on the shoulder and feel the muzzle. With a timid child, he may find it necessary to put his own hand under the child's hand to give him confidence. He explains to the children that the pony uses his tail to switch away flies and that this is one reason why one always walks around the head of the pony when going to the other side. He picks up the tail in his hand and slaps it lightly on the palm of each child's hand so that the children can feel how it stings, thus without frightening them, impressing them with the importance of moving around the pony's head instead of his heels. He may add that some horses kick, which is another reason why it is best to move around the head, but that of course this horse would never do so.

He now explains a little about the temperament of the pony—how easily he is frightened, and how quiet one must always be around him. He points out the position of the pony's eyes, and explains that the pony can see just as well behind him as in front of him, so that the rider must not do sudden things such as throwing balls up in the air when he is standing behind the pony. He asks the children if they would like to ask any questions.

This period of explanation should take about fifteen minutes. The purpose of it is to get the children accustomed to being near the pony, and to remove their fears.

LEADING THE PONY

The instructor then teaches the children to walk along with the pony. He pulls the reins over the pony's head and leads him himself, the children going with him for perhaps six yards. He shows how it is necessary to keep in step with the pony so that the leader does not put his foot in such a position that the pony might step on it. He explains that the child is not to look at the pony while leading, and demonstrates that when he looks back and turns his shoulders, the pony stops.

"Railroad Stations"

Now he has the assistant hold the pony while he places the children at regular intervals around the riding hall or ring. Each child, he tells them, is a "railroad station," and he gives each a name, using the names of stations familiar to them. One child is selected as the engineer to take the "train" (the pony) from his station to the next station. The instructor allows the child to take the reins in his hands and he himself walks beside him on his left. If the child is unusually timid, the instructor places himself between the child and the pony, but allows the child to hold onto the end of the rein. On reaching the next "station" (child), the one who has been leading the pony turns him over to the new engineer, and himself becomes a station. This is continued, each child leading from one "station" to the next, until all are familiar with the method of leading and none is afraid. If the group is fairly self-confident, the instructor can move away from the child that is leading, staying just near enough to urge the pony on should he stop. This game should take about fifteen minutes.

ADJUSTING THE STIRRUPS

The pony is then brought to a halt and held by the assistant, while the children are lined up, one behind the other, according to height. If the smallest child appears to be bold and self-confident, the line can start with him; if not, the tallest child can have the first turn. The instructor first demonstrates how to pull the stirrups down (they should always be run up on the leathers when leading). Each child in turn steps forward, pulls down the near stirrup, then the far stirrup, and takes his place at the end of the line. He is reminded to go around the pony's head. The instructor and assistant run the stirrups back up after each child has brought them down, explaining to the children that this is done so that when the pony is moving, the stirrups won't swing out and catch on things or frighten him.

MOUNTING AND DISMOUNTING

After the last child has pulled down the stirrups, the instructor leaves them down, and says to the first child, "Now I am going to show you how to get on your pony and how to get right off again." He has the child grasp the reins and the saddle as high as he can reach, and gives him a leg up. As soon as the child is in the saddle, the instructor says, "Now we'll jump off—swing your leg over his back and slide down." He assists the child if he is awkward. The first child then takes his place at the end of the line, and the next is mounted and quickly dismounted.

When the last child has had his turn, the instructor says, "The first time I helped you get up. This time I will show you how to get up by yourself, and you can show me how quickly you can get off." He drops the near stirrup down and shows each child in turn how to put his foot in it and how to spring up. It will probably be necessary to give a bit of a boost to the more awkward ones, but if the pony is small enough, some of the children will be able to manage themselves and should be highly praised when they do.

When each child has done this, the instructor says, "Now this time when you are in the saddle I will show you how to sit and how to put your feet in the stirrups. Then you show me again how quickly you can jump off." As each child is mounted the instructor carefully adjusts the stirrups, explaining just how long they should be. He then has the child raise his hands as high as he can over his head and explains how nice and tall he looks when he sits that way. He must make sure when the child brings his hands down that his shoulders are relaxed, and that his feet are not pushed forward. Each child in turn demonstrates how tall he can sit and how quickly he can jump off.

The instructor next demonstrates how to pick up the reins before mounting. When the child is in the saddle and has shown how tall he can sit, the instructor asks him to see if he can stand in his stirrups, pointing out how easy it is to do this if the feet are carried under the rider and how hard if the feet are pushed forward. Then he shows the child how to pick up the reins at the buckle with the right hand, place the left hand around both reins and slide it down to the withers, and, releasing the right hand, put it beside the left and take a rein in each hand. The child does this several times until he can shorten his reins without awkwardness.

After all the children have done the above exercises, it is time to accustom them to the motion of the pony. By spending so much time in getting on and off and sitting for longer and longer periods on the pony, the children will have lost their apprenhensions about the animal as something unknown, and, in discovering that they can get off easily, they will be less afraid of falling.

The children are told to run as fast as they can to their "railroad stations." The instructor leads the pony to the first station and says, "Now you are going to be a real engineer. Sit on your engine and take him to the next station. Let me see if you remember how to get on and how to hold your reins." The child is then mounted and the instructor, leading the pony by the cheek strap so as not to interfere with the reins, leads him to the second child. The first child then dismounts and takes over the new "station" while the second child becomes the engineer.

The second time around the course, the instructor shows each child how to start his engine by squeezing his legs or giving a little kick, and how to stop him by leaning a little back and opening and closing his fingers on the reins. If the child is very young or badly coordinated, the instructor can help him to balance in the saddle by steadying the near knee, but on no account should he place his hand behind the young rider as that will give him the habit of leaning backwards.

Training the Rider

If there is any lesson time left, the instructor can demonstrate the act of posting in the following manner. He first explains that when the pony trots, his legs spring up and down, and unless the rider rises and sits again, he will bounce. An older child gets on the pony and rides around while the instructor draws attention to his posting, having him occasionally sit and bounce to show the differ-ence. The children are then lined up facing the instructor, who says, "Jump your feet apart like this," while he himself jumps, landing with his feet about twelve inches apart. "Now together," and they all jump and bring their feet together. "Now apart," and they repeat. "Now bend your knees like mine and stand on the inside of the sole of your shoe." He looks to be sure that the children do not lean far forward. "Now, when I say 'up,' straighten your knees, and when I say 'down,' bend them again like this." He demonstrates the posting

FIG. 109.   Teaching the mechanics of posting while standing on the ground. *Riders dismount and stand in front of the instructors as pictured.*

261

motion, the class working in unison with him (Figures 109, 110). One at a time the children are mounted on the standing pony and practice rising and sitting. They are permitted to hold the pommel of the saddle or, if their arms are long enough, they hold a neck strap placed over the withers. If there is time, each is allowed to practice the movement while the pony walks. In some cases, with children as old as five who are bold, it is possible to allow each to trot a few steps with the instructor steadying the rider's knee. Many times the child will pick up the rhythm immediately.

FIG. 110.   Teaching posting, continued. *Riders, on command, spring into this position and then straighten and bend knees to the count of "up-down."*

When the lesson is over, the children go with the instructor while he puts the pony away. The instructor shows each how to walk into the stall in front of the pony and tells them all to say "goodbye," "thank you," and "see you again next (lesson day)" to him.

In this first lesson, the child has acquired a great deal of confidence. If he came with a fear of the unknown, he has conquered it, as far as general handling of the pony goes. He can mount with a little help and dismount alone. He knows how to sit, how to pick up and shorten his reins, how to start and stop his pony, and how to balance at a walk. He may have begun the trot. In giving the instruction, the teacher does not say, "You will or you must do so-and-so," nor does he leave it up to the child by saying, "Would you like to do so-and-so?" Rather he says, "Now I am going to show you how to do so-and-so." This gives the child the idea that the instructor is there to help him, and that he will not be left alone. The instructor also sets a limit or a goal to the activity. He does not say, "We will now practice leading the pony." He says, "We will lead the pony from here to the next 'station.' " He does not say, "I will show you how to get on," leaving the child with no assurance as to what the next step is to be; he says, "I will show you how to get on and get off," so that the child knows that he is not going to be left sitting on the pony. An older group of children learning to trot can be told that they are to "trot once around the ring" or "trot one record," for example.

If the children are very young—under four—an assistant will be needed for each two children. Sometimes, at this age, they get more confidence if they are taken for a little walk up the road with the pony, but usually the first lesson can be as described in this chapter. On the second lesson, each child can be mounted and the group can go for a walk, an assistant walking between each two ponies and leading them.

Chapter 12

INTRODUCING THE SEVEN-YEAR-OLD

TO THE STABLE

*W*hen the class has assembled, the instructor takes the children into the stable and lines them up along the wall behind the straight stalls. If the horses or ponies are stabled in boxes, he has the class line up in front of them. He tells the children how horses sleep on their feet, often with their eyes open, so that it is hard to tell when they are asleep. He explains about their timidity, and how the position of their eyes affects the way we handle them.

ENTERING THE STRAIGHT STALL AND LEADING OUT

The instructor demonstrates the correct way to come up to a stall, first speaking to the horse quietly, then putting a hand on the rump and causing him to move over. If heel chains are used, he shows how they are to be unfastened and fastened up again on the opposite heel post, not dropped in the dirt. He then demonstrates how to go in to the horse and move up to its head. Each child in turn is taken into the stall and shown how to take the reins out from under the stirrups and to take off the halter, if there is one on the horse. It would be wise to have an assistant stand behind the horse to prevent him from coming out.

After each child has had his turn, the instructor demonstrates backing the horse out of the stall and leading him. He draws attention to the way the animal's head is first turned in the direction in which he is to go after he is out of his stall, and explains exactly how the horse is caused to move backwards. Assistants help each child get his own horse out and led into the ring while the instructor goes with the first one. The children are made to continue leading their horses around the ring, going close to the wall, until all children are in the ring. If the walls of the ring or the fence are marked with numbers or letters, each rider, as he enters the hall, can be told to lead to such and such a number, following the track, to stop when he gets there, and to face the center.

If the members of the class are young and there is only one assistant, it would be better to assign one pony to every two children for the first lesson, but if there are older children to help, each child can have his own. The important thing is to have a person to hold each pony as the children are taught to mount. Whenever possible, the animals assigned should be of such a size that the child can learn to mount alone.

CHECKING THE FITTING OF THE TACK

When the class is all in the ring, halted and facing the center, the instructor brings one animal into the center of the ring for demonstration. He first explains that every good horseman checks his equipment before mounting. He points out the throat latch and the bit, their purposes and how they are adjusted. He shows how the girth is fastened on, and that it is almost always necessary to tighten it when the horse is first led out of the stall into the ring. He shows how to run the hand down along the inside of the girth on both sides to smooth down the hair, and how to tell when the girth is tight enough.

Next he demonstrates how to pull down the stirrups, and how to lengthen the left stirrup so that the rider can get his toe in it. It is often necessary to teach children exactly how to open a buckle—many will simply pull the strap upward, instead of holding it straight and pushing the buckle up to open it before letting it down to lengthen the stirrup. Each step is demonstrated before the children go through the motions described by the instructor.

MOUNTING AND DISMOUNTING BY THE NUMBERS

The instructor next demonstrates very carefully, slowly, and clearly the exact method of mounting "by the numbers" (see below). As he gives each command, the instructor performs the movement. When he is in the saddle, he demonstrates dismounting by the numbers. If he prefers, he can have an assistant do the mounting on his commands, pointing out the movements to the children. Particular emphasis should be put on the importance of the spring, of not digging the horse with the toe, of carrying the right leg high over the cantle, and of settling lightly in the saddle. The class then practices.

Routine and Commands for Mounting by the Numbers

Command	Routine
Prepare to mount	Rider grasps buckle of reins in right hand, slides left hand down both reins to horse's mane halfway to poll (Figure 111), grasps mane with reins or, if horse has hogged mane, grasps top of neck, faces rear, takes hold of stirrup in right hand and puts left toe in it, puts right hand on pommel, braces left hip against horse's left shoulder (Figure 112).
Mount . . . one	Rider springs from ball of right foot, straightens left knee, and remains standing in left stirrup, weight on hands (Figure 113).
two	Rider swings right foot high over croup and settles lightly into saddle, catches other stirrup, and picks up reins in both hands (Figure 114).

Fig. 111.   Teaching the beginner to pick up his reins and get them the right length before mounting.

FIG. 112.   Position of a rider at "prepare to mount."

FIG. 113.   Mounting by numbers. Position at the count of "one."

FIG. 114.   Mounting by numbers, position at the count of "two."

Routine and Commands for Dismounting by the Numbers

Prepare to dismount   Rider disengages right stirrup, puts reins into left hand, places left hand on mane, right hand on pommel.

Dismount . . . one   Rider swings leg over croup, straightens left leg, and remains balanced on hands and left foot as in mounting.

two   Rider disengages left stirrup and kicks heels together.

three   Rider drops to the ground, facing front, and pushing a little away from the saddle.

If there are enough leaders to hold all the horses, all children may work at once; if not, half the class mounts while the other half holds the horses. The riders should practice mounting and dismounting at least three times, with the instructor helping those who need help.

Training the Rider

The instructor then demonstrates the correct position in the saddle at the halt, explaining why this position is necessary to maintain balance. All riders stretch their arms high over their heads and drop them, relaxed. Then they stand in their stirrups (Figure 115). The

FIG. 115.   Balancing in the stirrups to get correct leg position.

instructor then demonstrates how the reins are picked up, shortened, and held. He also demonstrates the use of the active hand in stopping. He tells how the legs are used to help to turn the horse. Then he demonstrates and explains how the horse is put into motion.

PUTTING THE HORSE IN MOTION

When all the riders are comfortable and have picked up the reins, the instructor says, "Carry the right hand slightly forward and to the side. Apply the left leg, and use the right hand to cause the horse to turn and take up the track to the left." He himself is on foot, ready to assist anyone who needs help in putting the horse into motion. One assistant rides at the head of the line. The others, if there are any, walk near the riders.

Posts such as jump standards can be placed at intervals in the ring or hall, about twelve feet in from the wall. These serve as markers, and help beginners to keep their horses out on the wall. After the class has walked once around, the instructor repeats the directions for halting the horse with the active hand, asking the riders to carry their shoulders slightly back, to push down on their heels, and not to move their legs forward or to the rear. As soon as all have stopped and distances have been corrected, the riders start the horses forward again. This is repeated several times until the riders know exactly how to start and stop their mounts.

The next exercise is for the riders to drop their stirrups and let their legs relax. This rests their legs and gets them down into the sad-

FIG. 116.   Arm-suppling exercises.

dle. They are then told to "look up at the sky, look down at the ground, turn and say hello to the person behind you." This is repeated several times ending with "look up at the sky." In this position the riders are told to feel for and catch their stirrups. When they have both stirrups, they are to say, "I have them." This little game will do much to distract and relax the riders.

SUPPLING EXERCISES AT THE HALT

The riders are then told to put their reins in the hand toward the wall (the right hand) or to drop them and to extend the left hand in front of them and look at it. Next they extend their arms up over their heads and look at them, then to the rear, looking back and waving to the person behind them (Figures 116, 117). Finally they touch their left knees. When this exercise has been repeated two or three times, the riders are asked to touch first the right knee with the left hand, then the left toe. The class then changes direction (hands) as follows: The leader touches a designated point on the long wall, rides diagonally across to the opposite end of the other long wall, turns to the right, touches a designated spot, and continues on the track to the right. Each rider follows the leader. The suppling exercises described above are then repeated with the right hand, with the reins held in the left. At the end, the riders are told to drop their stirrups, let their horses extend their necks on a long rein, and pat them on the shoulder. While horses and riders are thus resting, the instructor can ask a few questions to check up on how much the class has absorbed. When the riders again pick up their reins, they may be told to take them by the end in the hand toward the wall, putting both hands on their waists. In this position, they pivot from the hips, looking first over one shoulder and then over the other. They can also try balancing on their stirrups, but will probably have to use their hands to help themselves at first.

POSTING

The class is halted and the riders dismount by the numbers as before. The riders stand in front of their horses, holding the reins, facing the instructor, who explains the posting trot, as described in Chapter XI. An experienced rider demonstrates the motion and the class practices it, first on the ground, then on horseback while the horses are standing still, then at a walk. If anyone has difficulty rising in the stirrups, the instructor walks beside him, holds his feet in the correct position, and causes him to stand and remain balanced in the stirrups. The horses should be equipped with neck straps which the riders should grasp with the inside hand, keeping the rein toward the wall in the hand toward the wall, and carrying that hand out a little while using it actively. When all pupils have the motion, the horses can be put into a trot while the riders try to get the motion at that gait. If there are enough leaders or if the horses are trained to follow the assistant riding in the lead, there will be no difficulty, but many animals will take advantage of the beginner and cut in to the center or refuse to trot. Riders on lazy horses should be supplied with switches, as they do not have enough control of their legs at this point for them to be of much use. The instructor, by walking just opposite the rump of the horse that is refusing to move out, can help a great deal. This is the most difficult part of the lesson for the beginner. The class may have to take turns practicing the trot, one child running beside the horse or pony while the other rides.

With good instruction, every child over seven should learn to post a few steps in his first lesson. There will always be a few awkward ones, but the average child picks up the rhythm and motion very quickly, although it will be several lessons before he relinquishes his grip on the neck strap and gets a good position. Many schools of riding feel that the riders should not be allowed to attempt posting until they have learned to sit the slow trot. If the riders were all ten or twelve years old or more, and if they rode every day, I also would feel that this was the best method, but it takes young children too long to learn the necessary flexibility of the loin to sit the trot, and meanwhile they are uncomfortable. The instructor's first goal is to develop in the child enough control so that he can have fun on the horse from the very beginning. If the child rides only once or twice a week, this takes long enough at best. If he can learn to post to the trot, he will be better balanced and will learn the control much sooner. However, beginning with the second lesson, some time should be spent at each lesson at the jog trot without stirrups and reins, and the rider's attention should be drawn to the necessity of suppling his loin and so keeping close to the saddle.

At the end of the first lesson, the riders dismount, run their stirrups up, and lead the horses back into their stalls. They are shown how to unsaddle and unbridle the animals, wash the bits, and hang up the tack.

The goal of the instructor for this first lesson has been to give the children confidence, to teach them how to handle their horses in the stall and how to lead. He wishes to establish a routine of discipline so that the children will learn how to obey automatically. He wishes his class to leave with a sense of accomplishment. He wishes to do all he can to make it easy for each child to mount and dismount without help, as this will save a great deal of time in later lessons. By teaching the class to mount and dismount by the numbers in the form of a drill, the instructor has laid a basis for immediate response to his commands. In learning to dismount actively, the children have gained confidence and a certain amount of agility.

The instructor also wishes to give basic instruction in position, in the use of the active hand, and in the coordination of the leg and hand aids in turning. He knows that this instruction will have to be repeated again and again until the riders learn to apply the aids correctly without thinking, but by starting them correctly, he has done what he can to prevent the formation of bad habits. The suppling exercises have helped to relax the riders and to give them confidence in their mounts. Because of the instructor, the riders have learned more and had a better time than they would have had without his help. For this reason a good basic discipline has been established and there is no reason why there should ever be any problems in that direction. The lesson has been varied enough to be interesting, but no child has been asked to do anything beyond his powers. He should go home with a feeling of success and be anxious to come back to the next lesson.

Chapter 13

THE SECOND LESSON

All lesson periods, after the first one, for all age groups, should be divided into sections, as in the following outline for the second lesson.

First period	Mounting, riding at a walk with supling exercises, questions and answers on work covered in previous lesson, riding at walk without stirrups. Practicing halting with stirrups at specified numbers. Review of use of aids to start, stop, turn horse, and explanation of leading rein.	20 minutes
Second period	New work: Demonstration of posting. Practice posting. For more advanced children this could be mounted drill, etc., and would take twenty minutes.	10 minutes
Third period	Suppling exercises at the halt. Rest period for beginners. For older children there could be a short rest period and then class should take up final activity which could be "free time" (riding at will) or a game or jumping.	15 minutes

Fourth period	New work: instruction in vaulting off at a walk. Start by vaulting off with horse standing still. Ride without stirrups at walk and jog trot (very short distance only), rest on long-rein walk while instructor asks questions on work covered. Final practice in trotting.	20 minutes
Last 10 minutes	Riders walk without stirrups with long reins. Dismount and put horses away.	10 minutes

The above lesson plan makes it plain that the goal of the instructor is first to help his pupils to achieve relaxation and confidence. He does this by starting the work with suppling exercises and with questions on previous lessons to take the rider's mind off his horse and insure his active participation in the lesson. A review of the work covered in the previous lesson helps him to avoid mistakes.

During the second period, some active phase is covered. In the case of the beginners, this is the posting trot. The length of time spent at the trot without resting will depend on the age and ability of the class. When all have learned to post, this trotting could be done to music. When all can post easily without the neck straps, the class could post first with their hands on their waists, then doing the suppling exercises as described in the previous chapter. The instructor should watch very carefully, making corrections in position to make the riders more comfortable, but not worrying them too much. With a group of intermediate riders, this period should be lengthened to twenty minutes or more, and should be utilized for such active work as mounted drill, school figures, practice on musical rides or mounted square dances, practice on gallop departs or the forward position at the trot and canter. The instructor should take advantage of the fact that the student is freshest at this time of the lesson.

After this active period, it will be necessary for beginners to rest, so the suppling exercises at the walk or guessing games can be introduced. For more advanced riders, a short period of relaxation at the walk will suffice before introducing new activities in the fourth period.

After the period of rest, the beginners receive instruction in new movements, in this case vaulting off at a walk. The instructor should explain the importance of learning this movement since it makes the rider active and insures his ability to jump off quickly should something go wrong, teaching him to fall so that he won't be hurt.

The instructor should encourage pupil participation as much as possible in the form of questions and answers. This instruction is followed by one more trot, or, if the riders are slightly more advanced, by a simple game such as "Red Light" (page 293) or "Follow the Leader."

The final few minutes of every class period, no matter how advanced the riders are, is spent at the walk. It is explained that this is necessary for the health of the horse. If the period before this has been very active, the horses are led by the riders and the time utilized for instruction in stable management or care of the horse. The instructor or the assistants go into the stable to help the children put the horses away and check carefully to see that all is in order. Those who really need help are given it, but as far as possible the children should be trained to do everything for themselves.

Chapter 14

PROGRESSIVE STEPS IN
TRAINING: ELEMENTARY

The exercises and games described in this chapter will be found very valuable for developing confidence, suppleness, and skill in the beginner. One or more of the exercises and games should be introduced in every lesson period until the riders are ready to advance to the intermediate class.

EXERCISES TO DEVELOP GOOD POSITION OF THE UPPER BODY

The class is lined up at regular intervals, facing the center of the ring. If the horses are restless, horse holders should be provided. If no horse holders are available, divide the class into two groups and let them take turns.

Exercise 1

With feet in the stirrups, riders stretch their arms as high as possible, looking up at their hands. They breathe deeply and bring their arms down to their sides, palms facing out, shoulders relaxed. Repeat five times.

Exercise 2

Riders reach up as in Exercise 1, then place hands on hips and pivot, first one way and then another, as far as possible, finishing by reaching up again.

Exercise 3

Riders stretch arms overhead and bring them back to a horizontal position. Riders pivot, holding arms in this position, then reach overhead and bring arms down relaxed.

Exercise 4

The rider keeps one hand on hip, the other arm stretched forward with palm down (Figure 117). With eyes fixed on the outstretched hand, the rider slowly carries this hand back horizontally, and forward again. Repeat with other hand.

Exercise 5

Riders describe circles with straight arm swinging, as shown on page 270 Figure 116.

Fig. 117.   Arm-suppling exercises.

278

Training the Rider

One of the greatest fears of the beginner is that the horse will go too fast, or will do something unexpected unless the rider holds on tightly. (It is assumed that any mounts used for beginners are of the type that will follow quietly behind a leader in a ring or hall without attempting to pass. If any of the horses are a little overambitious, side checks can be used.) From the first day, the beginners should be made to drop their reins and ride at a walk. As soon as they have learned to post, they should spend at least a part of each lesson trotting with their hands on their waists. If the pony has any tendency to cut in, the rider can take the end of the rein in the hand toward the wall and put his hands on his waist. This is usually enough to keep the pony out.

By the fourth or fifth lesson, the riders should be secure enough to jog trot without stirrups for a few steps with their hands on their waists. Gradually the suppling exercises described on pages 271 to 278 can be introduced while the horse is moving, first at the walk and later at the trot. When the child finds that the horse does nothing un-

FIG. 118.   Suppling exercise, "going down to breakfast."

expected when the reins are dropped, and that he is able to maintain his balance without them, he will acquire much more confidence, and consequently, will be infinitely more relaxed. Vaulting off the horse at a walk, trot, and later at a canter will also give him confidence and should be practiced frequently.

Exercise 1

Riders reach forward and touch both toes, then lie back so head is resting on horse's croup, and fold arms on chest (Figures 118, 119). On command, they sit up without using their hands. Next they lie back, head on horse's croup.

Exercise 2

Riders swing right leg across in front of them, turn in the saddle, and swing left leg across the croup of the horse so that they sit facing the horse's tail. They continue by swinging right leg across croup, and finally bring left leg across in front and once more face front

FIG. 119.   Suppling exercise, "the morning nap."

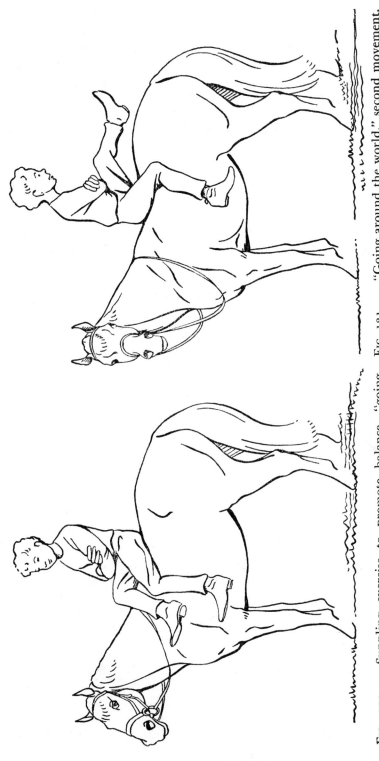

FIG. 120.   Suppling exercise to promote balance, "going around the world," first movement.

FIG. 121.   "Going around the world," second movement. (Arms folded.)

(Figure 120). This exercise is called "Going Around the World." It should be repeated in both directions. When riders have attained some agility, it can be put in the form of a competition for speed, with riders keeping their hands folded while turning (Figure 121).

Exercise 3

On command, riders rest their hands on the pommels of the saddles and draw their feet up as shown in Figure 122. On the next command, they stand (Figure 123). In returning to the sitting position, riders put their hands on the pommels and come down slowly. To teach this exercise, the instructor stands beside the horse and holds one of the rider's hands to steady him. Before learning to bring both feet up under him, the rider can try standing in the off stirrup and putting one foot on the saddle while the instructor steadies him, then putting the other foot on and straightening up.

FIG. 122.   Preparing to stand up.

FIG. 123.   Standing up on the horse.

EXERCISE TO DEVELOP GOOD POSITION OF THE BASE OF SUPPORT

Resting the tips of their fingers on the horse's withers, the riders rise in their stirrups and maintain their balance. This can be done while the horses are standing still and at all the gaits, but it is best not to teach it at the canter until the riders have learned to sit the canter. It should be practiced a number of times at each lesson. This exercise will do more to correct faulty positions of the thigh, knee, and foot than any other, as well as teaching the rider to balance and helping him to learn to post with the horse. In teaching this exercise, the instructor should demonstrate the exact position and then, if possible, the riders should take their positions in front of a mirror so that they can see what they are doing. Emphasis should be put on hollowing the back, lowering the upper body without rounding the shoulders, pushing the fleshy part of the buttocks to the rear, and holding the position of the lower leg. The tendency is for the beginner to straighten the knee and stand almost upright instead of taking the correct position shown in Figure 115.

EXERCISES TO DEVELOP GOOD POSITION OF THE LOWER LEG, ANKLE, AND FOOT

The rider must learn to relax his ankles and make them supple. Dropping the stirrups and describing circles with his toe will help. In extreme cases of inability to lower the heel when the foot is in the stirrup, the following exercises are useful.

FIG. 124.   Exercise to teach the rider to put weight into his heels.

Exercise 1

The rider drops the stirrups and puts his feet back into them from the front, as shown in Figure 124. He attempts to keep this position at a walk and trot.

284

Exercise 2

The rider dismounts and walks once or twice around the ring on his heels.

The exercise of balancing in the stirrups (page 283) will also help the rider to attain correct position of the lower leg, as he cannot maintain his balance unless his feet are carried under him.

EXERCISES TO DEVELOP CORRECT USE OF THE EQUILIBRIUM

For beginners, the exercise of balancing in the stirrups (page 283) is best to develop proper weight distribution. The riders can also try this at different gaits with hands on their waists. For more advanced riders, the following exercises are suggested.

Exercise 1

Riders wind in and out between a row of posts by weighting the stirrup on the side toward which they want to turn.

Exercise 2

By weighting the inside stirrup, riders ride in circles, serpentines, and figure-eights.

EXERCISES TO DEVELOP GOOD POSITION OF THE HEAD AND EYES

From the very first lesson, much emphasis should be put on the position of the rider's head and eyes. To prove to him how important it is to keep looking up, the instructor should have the rider balance in his stirrups at a walk, then look down, dropping his head as he does so. This will throw him off balance. In beginners' classes, the instructor can stand at a corner of the ring and hold up his fingers suddenly as each rider approaches, asking each to tell him how many he is holding up. This exercise is also used in training the rider to look ahead when he jumps.

DEMONSTRATING THE ACTIVE, FOLLOWING, AND PULLING HAND

The instructor explains how sensitive and easily injured the bars of the horse's mouth are, and that when a horse feels pain, he is apt to do something disagreeable to the rider to show his discomfort. He may nip or kick at another horse, or he may come into the center, or he may start to go too fast or to buck. It is therefore up to the rider to keep his mount as comfortable as possible if he wants to have an enjoyable ride.

He talks about the horse's great strength as compared with that of his rider, and asks how many in the group have ever played "tug-of-war." He brings to the attention of the class that when this type of competition takes place between persons of unequal strength, the stronger one will soon pull the weaker one over the line. But if the weaker contestant stops pulling for an instant, and then, when the stronger one is off guard, pulls unexpectedly, he will have much greater success. In riding, the instructor says, the pony or horse is much the stronger, and if the rider attempts to control him by a steady pull, the pony will pull back and thus will win. Instead of a steady pull, therefore, the rider should use something called "the active hand," which tells the pony what the rider wants without hurting him, and at the same time, gives him nothing to pull against.

The instructor holds up a belt, as shown in Figure 104, page 237. He tells the riders that the buckle end represents the horse's head, and the other end, the rider's hands on the reins. He explains about the movement of the horse's head as he walks, and says that when the pony walks the rider should keep his hands, elbows, and shoulders relaxed, letting them follow the movement of the animal's head. He demonstrates the following hand with the belt as shown. Then he says that if the rider wants to stop he can do so by just opening and closing his fingers without moving his hands—that the bobbing of the horse's head, plus the little vibrations of the bit caused by the hands being used thus actively, will cause the pony to stop. He illustrates this with the belt as shown.

The instructor demonstrates a "pulling" hand by showing how the reins remain taut when the rider moves his hands and pulls them back toward his stomach, thus hurting the pony and causing him to act up or pull back. The instructor goes up to each rider and takes hold of a rein near the bit. The rider is to be the pony, and the instructor vibrates the rein with an active hand so that the rider realizes that even though the motion is slight the pony can feel it easily. Next, the instructor, acting as the pony this time, grips the rein firmly, and tells the rider to pull as hard as he can. The instructor pulls against him and shows how, because he is the stronger, the child cannot win.

The class now takes the track at the walk. The terms "active," "following," and "pulling" hand are repeated. The child is told that his hand is to remain following or passive as long as his pony is going in the direction and at the rate of speed that the rider desires. The instructor watches each rider as he passes and makes sure that not only the hands, but the elbows and shoulders as well, are relaxed. The instructor tells the class that he is going to give a command to halt, and that the riders are to see if they can do so without changing the position of their hands—simply by letting their shoulders come back a little and opening and closing the fingers of each hand. He then says, "Prepare to halt . . . halt . . . *now*."

If any child still has difficulty in using the active hand, the instructor should walk beside him and demonstrate the movement by placing his own hands over those of the rider. If the horses tend to turn toward the center as they halt, the riders should be told to shorten the outside rein slightly.

EXERCISES IN THE USE OF THE ACTIVE HAND
FOR STOPPING AND TURNING

Exercise 1: Home Spots

As the riders ride around the ring at a walk, the instructor assigns each a "home spot," each spot about twelve feet from the next on the wall of the ring. The riders are to continue at the walk until the instructor gives the word, then they are to halt the next time they come to their home spot, using the active hand and coming to a stop in such a position that they can reach out and touch the home spot.

Exercise 2

When the riders are on the track at a walk or trot (preferably the latter), they are told to leave the line as their names are called and circle around the instructor, who is standing in the center of the ring holding up his fingers. As he circles, the rider is to call out the number of fingers held up by the instructor. The rider is to use his outside leg, his inside hand actively using a leading rein, and his inside stirrup weighted. The instructor changes the number of fingers he holds up in rapid succession.

Exercise 3

Using the aids described above, each rider, beginning with the first, makes a half-turn toward the center and rides back along the line. At the other end, he makes a half-turn in reverse, falling in at the rear.

USING THE WEIGHT IN STARTING, STOPPING, AND TURNING

Few riders realize the importance of the proper use of the weight in controlling the horse. Carrying the weight forward to start the horse assists him into motion. When the principle of the fixed hand is understood, the rider will also use the weight and back to push the horse against the bit and bring him to a halt.

The beginner cannot learn this technique until later in his training, nor can he be taught to use his back unilaterally, but he can learn to turn his horse by weighting one stirrup. He should also make it a practice to carry his weight forward in starting and to carry his shoulders slightly back in stopping. This method will cure the normal tendency of the beginner to crouch forward and pull his hands in to his stomach, and to carry his heels back and up in stopping. All the exercises described on page 287 for teaching the use of the active hand can be used to teach the proper use of the weight.

USING THE LEG AIDS

From the beginning, the riders should be taught to assist their hands by using the correct leg aids. During the early stages, they should be taught to apply the outside leg when turning and circling. In nearly every case, the beginner uses his reins in opposition in turning instead of simply as leading or indirect reins. Unless the rider uses his legs to keep up the impulsion, the horse will inevitably slow his gait or stop.

The exercises given for the use of the active hand can be used with emphasis on the application of the leg. These are most important at the slow trot, since it is the leg which keeps the horse trotting.

Exercises by the right and left flank are equally important. The procedure is to have the class form in a column of troopers (single file). When the last rider has entered the long wall, the instructor gives the command, "By the right (left) flank . . . *now.*" On the command *now,* all riders turn simultaneously and ride across the hall to the opposite long wall, where they are turned to the other flank, so that they are following the wall on the opposite track. In crossing through the center, they should be made to watch the leader, keeping their horses in line with him. Beginners under seven can make this turn easily at a walk; slightly older or more experienced riders should execute it at the slow trot.

GUESSING GAME TO TEACH THE HORSEMAN'S VOCABULARY

To teach the names of the parts of the horse and his equipment, the instructor, during the first lesson period, emphasizes how important it is for the riders to know the nomenclature. He names each part of the bridle, pointing to each separate piece, explaining its use, and asking all riders to repeat the name after him. For very young riders, he should try to fix the names of the parts in their minds by methods of association—for example, the "cheek-piece" runs along the horse's cheek, the "crown piece" is where the pony would wear a crown if he had one, and so forth. After the parts of the bridle have been named, a guessing game is played using only these parts.

This game is the best method for teaching the child the nomenclature of horsemanship. The riders are halted facing the center. One rider and his mount are brought in to the center and the rider dismounts. He thinks of some part of the horse or his equipment, and the other riders try to guess what he is thinking. As each guess is made, the rider in the center must point to the part or article named. The person guessing the correct answer becomes "It" for a repetition of the game.

After one game has been played using the parts of the bridle, the names of the different parts of the saddle are introduced, and a game is played using these as well as those of the bridle. At the third lesson the children can be taught the parts of the horse's head. Next comes the forehand of the horse. Here it would be well to go into the anatomy of the horse, explaining how the "arm" of the horse differs from the arm of the human being, drawing attention to the fact that the horse's knee corresponds to the rider's wrist, and so forth. The remainder of the parts of the horse may be added at a subsequent lesson. It is amazing how, under this system, even very tiny children acquire a good technical vocabulary which makes later explanations easy.

EXERCISES IN RATING THE HORSE AND CHANGING GAITS

At first the beginner will have no independence in regard to determining the rate of speed or the gait which his horse takes. What the leader does, the beginner's horse will do. To teach the novice rider a little independence, the instructor should start all horses from the walk to the trot at the same time. The instructor first explains that, before taking up the trot, the riders must shorten their reins, not because the horse will go too fast if they do not do so, but because the horse raises his head when he trots, and unless the rider shortens his reins first, he will have to do so while the horse is trotting. He then explains that all the directions or commands which he will give to the class will be in two parts: the first part will tell the riders what they are about to do (the preparatory command); the second will tell them to do it. He says, "Trot . . .," looking to be sure that all riders have shortened their reins, then "*now.*" At the word *now,* all riders urge their mounts into the trot. This will have to be practiced many times before all the riders are able to start together.

The exercises mentioned earlier for teaching the use of the active hand will also help to inculcate independence in the rider, particularly circling individually and riding from front to rear. Before these are introduced, the game of "touching the numbers" can be played. In this game, the riders try to see how many of the markers or numbers along the wall they can touch as they ride past. Beginners can usually get them all at a walk, but they find it difficult to get the corner numbers at a trot as they do not have enough independence of the leg aids at this gait. For a special treat, or as a gymkhana event, the instructor can put little candies wrapped in paper on the window sills or posts and have the riders try to get them as they trot by. It is a good idea to start every riding period with a touching-the-numbers game at a walk to get the riders' attention and to give the instructor a chance to check on their positions and stirrup lengths.

To practice changing gaits independently, the riders are told that each must take up the trot from the walk when he reaches a designated spot, coming back to a walk when he reaches another designated spot. Some riders will have much difficulty keeping their horses from trotting when the rider in front starts. It is too early in the young rider's career to teach him the difference between the slow, ordinary, and extended forms of the various gaits; these will be taken up a little later. Riding without regard to distance—i.e., spacing the riders around the track so that the full ring is used—is also too hard for beginners, but can be taken up when the riders have acquired good balance and a real independence of the aids.

TEACHING THE USE OF THE INDIRECT REIN

As described on page 219, the instructor first explains the purpose of using the rein indirectly, and then, walking beside each rider, shows him exactly how to use his inside rein in a manner to cause the horse to move his body over against the wall or fence. Emphasis is put on having the rider carry his hand forward in using this rein effect, on using the hand actively, and on using the leg on the same side. The games and exercises of "touching the numbers," stopping at the "home spots," and turning by the flanks can be practiced using this rein effect. To learn to differentiate between the two rein effects, the game described on page 222, where the riders first number off by twos and then ride on either side of a line of posts, can be utilized.

BAREBACK RIDING

Children enjoy riding bareback if their mounts are of a suitable size and have correct equipment. There is nothing better to develop a firm seat. In my school in Connecticut, all riders ride bareback for at least three months each winter. The mounts are equipped with heavy saddle pads and surcingles and either halter shanks or neck straps. Since the first purpose of this riding is to get the rider down on his horse and to get him balanced, he should be made to relax his legs, ankles, and feet completely. The toes should dangle, and no attempt should be made to carry them higher than the heel.

Beginners ride bareback in line, one behind the other. All the flexing and suppling exercises mentioned earlier should be rehearsed at the beginning of each lesson at the walk. A phonograph record with a suitable rhythm is then put on, and the riders jog trot for the three and a half minutes it takes to play it. During the next walking period, they practice dismounting at a walk or touching the numbers. The direction is then reversed and the jog trot to music taken up again. Those with good enough balance are encouraged to put one or both hands on their waists, or to look around at the person behind them.

Exercises for control also can be introduced gradually while pupils are riding bareback. Beginners' games of "Red Light" and "Follow the Leader," for example, can be played bareback and will help to relax the players.

Cantering

As soon as the riders have attained a modicum of balance, the canter should be introduced. There are two methods of doing this safely. One is to put a pony or horse with an easy canter on a longe. One by one, the children are mounted. The pony is put first on a walk, then on a jog trot, and finally on a canter. The instructor draws attention to the see-saw motion of the canter. It is far easier for a beginner to canter without stirrups than with them, but since he will be unable to use his aids for control, the longe is necessary.

The second method of introducing the canter is to mount the riders one at a time on a pony or horse that is voice trained and will automatically take up the canter and follow a lead horse around a hall or ring. Cantering once around, and then walking, is enough to begin with. When more than one horse is used, the riders should take up the canter individually as each reaches a given point. This will help prevent the more ambitious horse from starting too fast and running up on the heels of the horse in front. The fact that the horse ahead leaves will spur the sluggard on to emulating him.

bar, squeezing or kicking on the last stride, and being sure to keep their eyes up. "First over the bars" is an exercise based on the advertisement using that slogan. Each rider takes off his cap and makes a bow as he crosses the bar (Figure 126).

Jumps for beginners riding bareback should not exceed two feet. Up to this height, there is little motion and the rider easily can learn to stay with his horse. At higher jumps the horse is apt to go too fast or jump too high.

BEGINNERS' GAMES

"Railroad Stations," "home spots," and "guessing games" have been described earlier in this book. "Red Light" is another favorite for beginners. It helps teach control and gives practice in halting.

Red Light

A leader or instructor—"It"—stands at one end of the ring with his horse's rump toward the other riders. The players line up at the opposite end. The leader counts aloud from one to twenty and says

FIG. 126.   "First over the bars."

292

Jumping

As soon as the riders can maintain their balance easily bareback, a low jump should be put across the center of the hall or ring, consisting of three bars laid end to end. Four-by-fours with rounded corners painted with gay stripes are best as the horse can see them easily. The bars should be laid flat on the ground at first, then arranged as shown in Figure 125. As the riders progress, one section of the jump can be placed with ends resting on the kegs and the other two with one end on the keg and the other end on the ground. Figure 124b. When some of the riders can negotiate the eighteen-inch jump successfully without depending on their hands or grip for balance, one of the panels can be put at two feet, using ordinary jump standards, one at eighteen inches, and one left with one end on the ground.

In teaching the children to negotiate these jumps, relaxation should be emphasized. The class can be given "free time" as soon as the jumps have been laid on the ground and the riders told that they may cross at any time from one end of the ring to the other. A few will walk gingerly across, looking down. The instructor tells them to try it again, and see who can smile the broadest while looking up at the instructor—or they can be asked to look up and clap their hands over their heads or in front of them as they cross. Presently some will begin to jog over the bar. When all seem relaxed, little competitions can be started. Two riders are told to cross side by side or to cross coming from opposite directions, then another pair crosses to see if they can do better. It is amazing how quickly young children will relax and begin to attain a good balance bareback if the bars are used as incentives. When the children begin getting into a canter they should be told to count the strides of the pony as he approaches the

A

B

Fig. 125.   Beginner's jumps.

293

"red light." He turns his head and looks at the players; if any are still moving forward, they must return to the starting point. The first person reaching "It" tags him; then "It" tries to see if he can catch any of the players before they get back behind the starting line. The first rider caught becomes "It."

Musical Stalls

"Musical Stalls" is a game for advanced beginners. Bars are laid on the ground about four feet apart and parallel to each other. The riders take up the track, and when the music stops or a whistle is blown, they ride into the stalls made by the bars. There should be one less stall than there are riders; thus, each time the music stops, a rider is eliminated. As each rider in turn is eliminated, one bar is removed. It is well to put markers in the form of jump standards at either end of the ring and rule that the riders must keep out beyond these posts until the music stops.

Fig. 127.   Monkey drill. *Using the platform to vault onto the pony.*

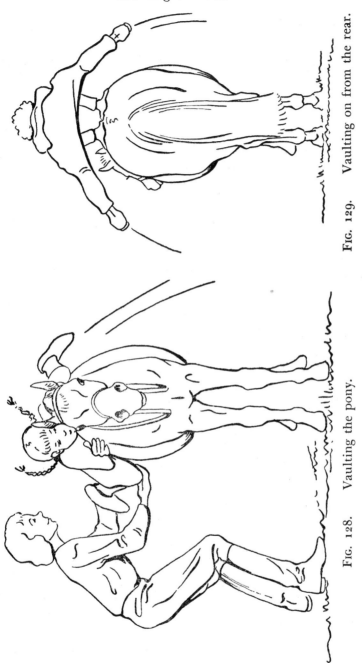

FIG. 129. Vaulting on from the rear.

FIG. 128. Vaulting the pony.

295

Musical Chairs

"Musical Chairs" is similar to the above game, but here chairs are used, and the riders must dismount and run and sit in a chair without letting the horse go.

MONKEY DRILL

Monkey drill, or mounted gymnastics, is one of the best ways to develop confidence and agility in riders. All riders can do the easier movements, and some can do the more advanced ones. For exhibition purposes, a team can be picked. A drill with the riders doing the movements in unison makes a very spectacular event. Small horses or ponies that do not mind being mounted from the rear, having riders turn somersaults on their backs or stand up on them, are used. If a horse is restless, an assistant can hold up one front foot, but it is sur-

FIG. 130.   Vaulting into position from the side, "no hands."

prising how many will stand quietly without even being held by the reins.

Beginners can do all the suppling exercises described on pages 277 to 283. Each turn or movement should be done to a whistle signal. Two riders are assigned to each pony. One holds the pony while the other performs. They then change places.

Vaulting on from the Side (Figure 127).

Beginners should first practice running and vaulting onto a rail or gymnasium horse. The performer runs toward the obstacle, places his hands on it, and springs upward, putting his weight on his hands and straightening his arms. He then swings his legs over and lands sitting on the rail. After he has become proficient at this, he can try it on a pony, but he will find this somewhat harder, partly because of the "mental hazard" of jumping onto something animate, and partly because of the bulge of the horse's barrel. A low ramp can be utilized to teach the vaulting. It should be about two feet wide and three feet long, and should be sloped up to a height of six or eight inches. This is placed in position beside the pony, and the class lines up one behind the other to take turns running up the ramp and vaulting onto the pony.

Vaulting over the Pony (Figure 128).

This is done as above, but the rider carries his legs clear over the rump, landing on the other side. The instructor should stand on the opposite side from the take-off in order to catch any rider who forgets to steady himself with his hands. Overambitious vaulters will sometimes do an unexpected nose dive.

Vaulting on from the Rear (Figure 129).

The performer runs up from behind, puts both hands on the pony's rump, and leap-frogs onto his back. He should try to push himself as far forward as possible so that he does not land on the loin, and should close his knees as he settles into place, letting them absorb the shock of the landing.

Vaulting on Without the Use of the Hands (Figure 130).

Only active riders can do this one. The performer runs from the near side on an oblique. As he reaches the pony, he springs in the air, throws his right foot in front of him and across the withers, landing in a sitting position.

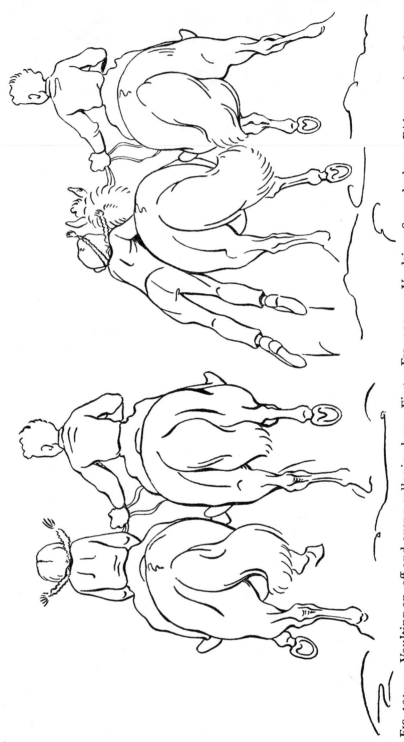

Fig. 131. Vaulting on, off and over a galloping horse. First phase. Riders ride side by side, rider on right controlling both horses;

Fig. 132. Vaulting. Second phase. Rider vaults off horse and bounces once on the balls of her feet on the ground.

Vaulting on and Landing Backwards

The performer vaults on over the rump, but turns in mid-air and lands sitting backwards.

Vaulting on and Landing Upright

The rider vaults on over the rump, but lands standing up on the horse.

Vaulting on a Galloping Horse (Figures 131, 132, 133).

This is not difficult provided the performer can do all the vaults described above, but it is sometimes difficult to find a horse that will

FIG. 133.   Vaulting. Third phase. *Rider, impelled by movement of horse, springs over her own horse onto the other one. In learning this movement, the rider should first practice springing back onto her own horse. Horses may be coupled together at the bits to help keep them together.*

keep the canter going. The rider can start mounted, get into a canter, vault off, and, as his feet hit the ground, spring up again onto the animal's back—or he can start by running beside the horse. This can also be done over jumps, the rider jumping off as the animal takes off and allowing his spring to return him to the animal's back. An active rider can also vault over the galloping horse, landing on the other side, and back again. Two riders can work in pairs, riding side by side. At a signal, one rider vaults off his horse onto the ground, then back up and over his horse, onto the horse of the other rider, who controls both horses.

FIG. 134.   Turning a somersault off rump of pony. *Instructor helps with a quick lift on the back of the boy's head if he does not spring hard enough.*

Somersault off a Standing Horse (Figure 134).

The performer puts his head down on the rump of the animal, bringing his knees close to his chest, and pushes off as in an ordinary somersault. In teaching this, the instructor should stand beside the horse, placing his hand under the performer's head in order to assist him by giving an extra push if the performer loses his nerve and doesn't give a hard enough spring.

Vaulting off the Rump (Figure 135).

The performer, standing on the back of the horse where the saddle would be placed, and facing rear, puts one foot squarely on the point of the croup and steps off.

FIG. 135.   Stepping onto point of croup before jumping off.

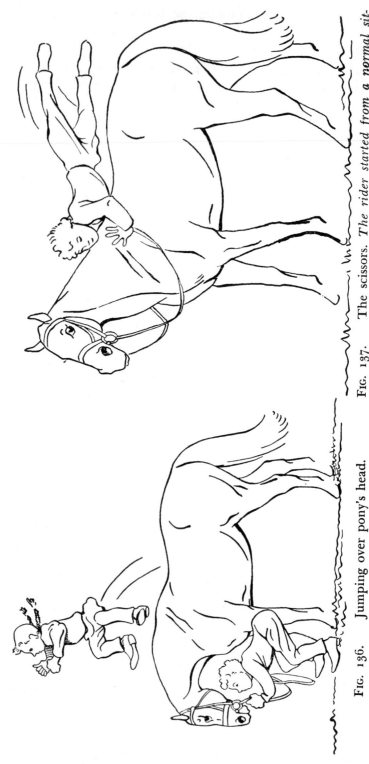

FIG. 137. The scissors. The rider started from a normal sitting position facing front.

FIG. 136. Jumping over pony's head.

Training the Rider

Vaulting over the Head (Figure 136).

The performer, standing on the horse's back facing front, springs up, spreads his legs, and jumps over the horse's head to the ground.

The Scissors (Figures 137, 138, 139, 140, 141).

This movement is a little difficult to describe and hard to perform at first until the rider gets the knack. The performer sits on the horse facing front and places his hands on the animal's withers. He throws his legs up behind him, crosses them, twists his head and

FIG. 138.   The scissors completed. *Rider is now facing the rear. He repeats the movement from this position and ends facing front again.*

303

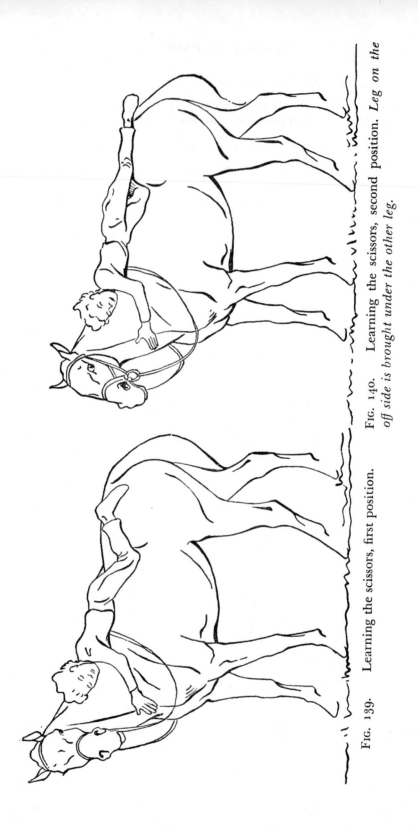

FIG. 139.   Learning the scissors, first position.

FIG. 140.   Learning the scissors, second position. *Leg on the off side is brought under the other leg.*

FIG. 141.   Learning the scissors, third position. *Rider now pushes hard with his hands and sits up.*

body, and ends up sitting backwards. To return to position, he places his hands on the animal's rump and repeats the movement. In teaching this movement, the instructor stands on the near side of the horse while the rider lies on his stomach on the animal's back, his head toward the horse's head. The rider turns his head to face the instructor, who reaches across for the rider's opposite leg and pulls it *under* the leg on the near side. As he does so, the rider turns and sits up. He will then be facing the horse's rear.

Jumping Around (Figures 142, 143, 144, 145).

The rider comes to a standing position on his horse as described on page 282 and does an "about face" by jumping about in place to face the opposite direction. To teach this, the instructor stands on the near side of the horse, takes the performer's outside hand, and stead-

FIG. 142.   Standing by ready to jump around.

ies him as he jumps. To return the rider to position, the instructor
moves to the other side of the pony or reaches behind the pupil, who
is now facing the rear, and again takes the outside hand. When the
performer can turn fairly readily, the instructor no longer holds his
hand but instead places his own hand in such a position that the performer can grasp it as he completes his jump.

Roman Riding

In Roman riding, the performer places a foot on each of two
horses being ridden by other riders and coupled together at the head.

306

FIG. 143. Learning to jump, the instructor helping.

He rests his hands on the other riders' shoulders to get his balance, but later will be able to balance alone. If the horses are very well trained, he will be able to ride Roman without the assistance of the seated riders. Two riders can also ride one horse, one seated and controlling the horse, the other standing behind him.

Pyramids

In a pyramid, three horses and six riders are used. Plate XXIII shows how they are mounted.

FIG. 144.   Preparing to jump back, instructor helping from near side.

FIG. 145.   Jumping back, instructor helping from off side

Chapter 15

PROGRESSIVE STEPS IN
TRAINING: INTERMEDIATE

*T*he exercises and techniques which follow may be taught to riders who have passed through the beginning class and who can execute successfully the movements described in Chapter 14.

TRAIL RIDING

As soon as the beginner has learned to keep his horse in line at the walk and slow trot, trail riding may be introduced. In some ways trail riding is easier for riders at this stage of development than riding in a ring, since there is no problem of keeping the mounts in motion or of keeping them from cutting in on the corners. One instructor and an assistant can handle as many as seven pupils, provided the horses are well mannered. If more riders go out together, there should be more than one assistant. It will be found that intermediate riders relax much more readily on the trail than in the ring. The long periods of trotting which are possible will confirm their ability to post. The unevenness of the ground and the inclines and declines which they will be called upon to negotiate will improve their balance.

Hazards of Trail Riding

On the other hand, there are certain negative factors to be considered in trail riding which do not occur in the ring. The first of these is the sight of unusual objects—dogs running out over stone walls, workmen carrying tools, bits of paper, birds flying up—which are bound to be met with occasionally and which might frighten the horses. Normally well-schooled horses will not pay attention to such objects, but since the horse's eyes function differently from those of a human being, even the steadiest animal will disgrace himself occasionally by showing fear. The instructor can prevent many such occurrences by keeping alert himself. When he sees the approach of something which he thinks might frighten a horse, he should bring the group down to a walk and be prepared to block the path of any animal that might get out of line and try to pass.

Except in camps located in the woods, it will be necessary for the class to ride some distance on the edge of traveled roads before entering the trail. For beginners this is often easier than riding the trails themselves. The going is smoother, and the horses are not tempted to go too fast. Few horses nowadays are afraid of the ordinary automobile or truck. Unfortunately, there are some drivers who will deliberately try to frighten horses they meet just for the excitement, not realizing how serious the consequences may be. For this reason it is always best to bring the class down to a walk when a motor vehicle is passing. Bicycles, especially if they are being pushed and not ridden, are often more frightening to horses than cars, as are motorcycles, baby carriages, and children on roller skates.

Another hazard in trail riding is the propensity of beginners' mounts, especially ponies, to stop and eat grass. The beginner who is caught unaware will often be pulled off over his pony's head. Even if this does not happen, there is the possibility that the pony, having finished his stolen tidbit, and finding himself some distance behind his fellows, may try to catch up at a gait too fast for the rider. The best method of preventing this vice is to provide old offenders with muzzles or check reins. Muzzles are best, since the pony with a check rein can still eat off a bank. The muzzles can be made of wire, leather, or webbing. They should fit over the bit and be held in place with a strap or rope running over the poll. Shipping muzzles are good, or similar ones can be improvised, using a fine mesh wire or canvas webbing. If a check rein is used, it should be an overhead check fastened to the crown piece of the bridle and to a strap running in front of the pommel. A check rein should not be used on low-withered ponies unless a crupper strap is also provided. Otherwise the rider will be sitting on the pony's neck.

Riding on Roads and Narrow Trails

On narrow trails, the instructor should ride at the head of the line and the assistant should ride last. If the road is wide enough for cars to pass each other, the assistant can ride in the lead and the instructor on the opposite side of the road. From this position he can watch the whole line of riders and make corrections on position, maintenance of distance, and alignment of the riders. Cars seeing riders on both sides of the road will be much more careful in passing and the instructor can always get entirely off the road if necessary. Furthermore, with both the assistant and the instructor up at the front, they can easily block any incipient runaway. When there is more than one assistant, they may be spaced along the flank on the left behind the instructor, and each should be assigned to watch specific children.

Before taking a class on the trail or road for the first time, the instructor should explain to the riders the importance of keeping in line and riding neither too close to nor too far behind the person in front. If there are more than six riders, they should number off by fours and the number one riders should repeat all the instructions. Children riding ponies with short strides should be provided with switches if necessary. Riders should be cautioned in coming down hills to maintain a *slow* walk when they reach level ground so that those still on the hill will not get behind and be tempted to catch up at a trot.

Girths and lengths of stirrups should all be checked in the ring before the class goes out on the trail or road. It is best to have a trot in the ring to be sure everyone is comfortable. The instructor and assistant then take their positions and the class goes out at a walk, maintaining this gait for at least five minutes. Trots should not be too fast since small mounts and those at the end of the line will have to go faster than the leaders and those on long-legged mounts in order to keep up. The instructor should keep looking back to be sure that no one has gotten too far behind. Corners and downhill grades should be negotiated at a walk, and the leader must keep at a collected walk until all riders are around the corner or down the hill. If the class is able to canter, the instructor and assistant should ride as a pair in the lead to block off incipient runaways. Grassy trails on the up-grade are ideal for beginners and intermediates to canter on. The rider is automatically thrown a little back, the horse moves smoothly and willingly, and if the leaders take care not to go too fast, everything will go well.

Jumping on the Trail

If the class has reached the jumping stage, the riders can be allowed to hop over logs, but should be made to maintain their correct distance so as not to jump on the rider in front. The assistant should remain at the jump to give instruction while the instructor leads the line of riders, rating his horse according to the progress of those behind him.

If a class of beginners comes across an unexpected obstacle, such as a fallen log or a boggy place, the instructor should caution the riders to hold on to the mane or pommel, and should lead the line very slowly, looking back to see that the riders maintain a walk. In crossing muddy places or streams, it is best to keep moving at a rapid walk and to caution the riders to use their legs to keep their horses going. Otherwise some may try to stop and drink or to lie down.

If the leader or instructor notices a hole or a loose wire in the riders' path, he should call back " 'ware hole" or " 'ware wire," which should be repeated back through the line. If it is necessary to go through a gate, the assistant should hold the gate open until all riders are through. In catching up to the line after fastening it, he should not take up too fast a gait.

Passing Other Riders

If a group of riders overtakes another group on a narrow trail going at a slower gait, the group wishing to pass should first ask permission and then should pass with as little excitement as possible. The group being passed should pull off the trail, keeping their horses' heads turned toward the passing riders to prevent kicking, and the leader of that group should maintain a walk until the other riders are out of sight.

Picnic Rides

Intermediate riders enjoy a picnic ride. It is possible to combine two groups at a time for this occasion. One group rides out from the stable, and the second group follows in a car with the lunch. At the appointed spot, the mounts are tethered, stabled, or turned loose in a corral, both groups lunch together, and the second group rides the horses home. Rides such as this give the instructor a chance to teach proper handling of horses in regard to tying and watering on the trail. They also give the riders a chance to explore country that may be too distant to be reached in the ordinary riding period.

The End of the Ride

Toward the end of the ride, the riders can walk without stirrups to rest themselves, but should not slouch in the saddle. Conversation between riders should be encouraged as this makes for relaxation and adds to the pleasure of the ride. Little children like to pretend that they are hunting Indians or bears when they go through woody places. Intermediate riders can ride in pairs or fours if riding on roads where there is little traffic. They must first have learned to do elementary mounted drill (pages 324 to 333) so that they can be gotten back into "troopers" (single file) quickly, should that be necessary. In all trail riding, the last mile homeward should be negotiated at a walk, both as a method of training for the horses and for their conservation.

EMERGENCIES ON THE TRAIL

Either the instructor or the assistant should always carry a spare halter shank which can be used as a lead rein in case of trouble. One or the other, preferably the assistant, should be mounted on an animal that will stand quietly for mounting, even when his fellow horses leave him, and that will allow another animal to be led beside him.

Falls

Falls are the most common emergencies in trail riding. Rarely is a rider hurt; the problem is to get him on his horse and back into line with as little confusion as possible. If the rider has had the presence of mind to hold onto his reins, the problem is comparatively simple. The assistant dismounts, puts the child back on, takes the horse or pony on a lead line, remounts himself, and catches up to the rest of the class at an ordinary trot. The instructor, meanwhile, has gone ahead with the remainder of the class at a walk. It is much better to handle the emergency in this way than to have the whole class stop, since it is at such times that horses get out of position and may eat grass, kick, or bite.

If the child has fallen off the pony and has let go his reins, the whole class will have to stop. All riders line up on the shoulder of the road, facing the road. Even though the loose pony may pass and run ahead, he will almost invariably stop when he sees that the other mounts are not coming with him. The assistant will have to dismount and turn his horse over to the child who has fallen off or to the instructor. He should then place himself in such a position that the loose pony is between him and the class. He should pick a little grass and walk up quietly to the loose animal's head. If the horse moves, the assistant can herd him quietly back to the line, where he will probably stop.

If the class is near home when the accident occurs, the stray pony may run home, in which case the dismounted child will either have to walk back or can perhaps ride double with the instructor or the assistant.

If the accident occurs on the trail and the loose pony runs on ahead, the class is halted in line, while the leader or the instructor faces the line or stands sideways across the trail to prevent any of the other mounts from following the loose pony. The assistant goes ahead on foot and herds the stray back to his companions.

If a child falls off and is hurt, the instructor must make every effort to prevent the other children from getting excited. If possible, the instructor or assistant should go ahead with the group, while the other, having caught the loose pony, stays with the injured child. Nine times out of ten, the injury consists merely of the wind having been knocked out of the child. In this case it is necessary only to give the victim time to catch his breath and get his wits about him, when he can be remounted and taken along on the lead rein. If a child loses consciousness, even for a short period, it indicates a brain concussion. The victim should lie perfectly still until all dizziness has disappeared. If a car is available he had better return to the stable in that, but if the accident occurs far out on the trail, he can be remounted and taken back at a walk. Doctors differ in the methods of treating minor concussions. Some prefer to keep the patient absolutely quiet for several days; others prefer to have him go about his normal activities. If the child has been unconscious for more than a few seconds, the parents will probably want to have his head X-rayed for other possible injuries. Delayed symptoms of a concussion are severe headache and vomiting. Usually the patient cannot remember the events just preceding the accident or the accident itself.

Skull fractures are characterized by bleeding of the ears or mouth, uneven dilation of the pupils, and prolonged loss of consciousness. The victim must be kept perfectly still until he can be moved on a litter.

If a rider falls and breaks a bone in his arm or his collar bone, a sling should be improvised. If his leg is broken, one leg can be bandaged to the other to make it more comfortable. In both cases, help will have to be sent for to transport the victim. Let me reiterate that falls as serious as these are very, very rare, but they do occur occasionally. All riding instructors should take a course in First Aid so that they may know the best way to handle emergencies. Bandages and disinfectants should be kept in the tack room for minor wounds and scratches. All children who ride regularly should be immunized for tetanus with periodic booster shots.

Runaways

The second class of emergencies liable to occur on the trail is the runaway or "bolting party." If the instructor and assistant always ride so that they can block off a refractory mount, these emergencies will not occur, but once in a while a situation arises which is not preventable.

If one or more horses break out of line and start on ahead, the whole line must stop at once. The leader or assistant should block the other riders, and the instructor, while helping to do this, should call out instructions to the child or children who are in trouble. He should keep his voice calm and make his instructions clear, telling the rider or riders to hold onto the pommel of the saddle with one hand and pull the horse's head around with the other. There is no more helpless feeling than to see unskillful riders departing in the distance out of control. Luckily, however, even though they may fall off, they rarely get hurt, as they will be thrown completely over, landing on their backs. The child who falls off while the pony is standing or walking usually puts his hand out to protect himself and may end up with a broken wrist, arm, or collar bone. Usually riders who have had a lot of practice at vaulting off a moving animal will come down on their feet first, particularly if they remember to hold on to the saddle or to the pony's neck.

EXERCISES IN THE USE OF THE FIXED HAND

This is the most difficult to understand and to apply of any of the uses of the hand, even for riders with years of experience. In teaching the use of the fixed hand, the method of demonstration by holding up a belt buckle illustrated in Figure 104, page 237, is best.

The instructor first explains that the horse's head is never entirely still when he is moving; furthermore, that by using the back and the legs, the rider can push him into the bit. By fixing his hands in one position, the rider can, in effect, erect a barrier (the bit) against which the horse will exert his force. On feeling this immovable barrier, he will stop. Since the reins lose their tension when the horse stops, the horse will automatically receive the reward which he must have if he is to remain responsive to the aids.

Using the belt, the instructor should show the difference between what happens when the horse draws in his head and halts, the rider maintaining a fixed hand, and what happens if the rider pulls. It is assumed that the riders have already been taught the flexibility of the back and the use of the back, both bilaterally and unilaterally (see pages 213 to 214). They can then practice stopping on the "home spots" (page 287).

When riders first practice using the fixed hand, the instructor will have to watch each one very closely to be sure that the hands do not move. In rating a horse at the faster gaits by using the fixed hand, particularly a horse that tries to evade the bit by boring or tossing his head, the rider will know that he is applying the fixed hand correctly if the rein alternately tightens and flaps in response to the movement of the animal's head. If the reins remain taut and there is constant pressure on the bit, the rider is using a pulling hand, and is only inciting his horse to pull harder.

THE HALT AND THE HALF-HALT ON THE FIXED HAND

Halting on the fixed hand has been explained. The riders should now be capable of practicing this with more tactful use of the aids. They can be given "home spots" as before and asked to halt the horse without any visible use of the legs, back, and fixed hand. When they are able to feel the exact amount of exertion necessary to get the horse to stop on the exact spot, on the bit, the riders can begin work on the half-halt.

As explained in Part I, Chapter 7, page 93, the half-halt is an interruption of the gait without slowing the horse or changing the gait. It is a sort of "bringing to attention" that the rider employs before beginning a new movement. It is also used in schooling a horse that is heavy on the forehand to get him to weight his quarters. In first demanding the movement, the rider uses an active hand, the little fingers turning up toward the chin as shown in Figure 42, page 94. Later he should demand the same movement with a momentarily fixed hand plus a bracing (pushing) of the back. Finally the rider should ask the horse to half-halt with no visible use of the aids.

CANTERING IN THE SADDLE

The most discouraging stage of learning to ride, from the point of view of both the pupil and the instructor, is that intermediate stage where the rider can ride well at a walk and trot and can canter bareback on an easy horse but cannot adjust his balance to the canter in the saddle. This is the period when riders are most apt to fall. If they have been taught to vault off quickly they will come to no harm, but they may become so discouraged that they want to stop riding.

Learning to sit the canter is like learning to balance on a bicycle, float in the water, or do a change of edge on ice skates. The instructor can explain the principle and demonstrate in detail what the rider has to do to stay with his horse, but until he gets the "knack," the rider will continue to bounce. Unfortunately, few horses will long endure the discomfort of a hundred or more pounds bouncing up and down on their backs. They will either slow down, go faster, buck, or make trouble with the other horses. The rider will have no control, since he will have all he can do to keep from being precipitated into the air. He must practice and practice before he will be able to canter safely and without abusing his horse.

The first factor that the instructor must consider is the safety of horse and rider. The horse must not be put in such a position that he can get going too fast. There are several methods which can be used to prevent this. The instructor can put the horse on a longe and so control him. He can voice-train him and have him follow behind a good rider. He can have the riders ride from front to rear, following the track individually, or he can use a track or chute.

The horses used for beginners' cantering should have gaits as slow and comfortable as possible. In teaching, the instructor has the riders take the track at the walk. He draws attention to their position and makes sure that it is upright, the hands following, the legs not clinched, the back supple and following the movement of the horse. "This," he tells the class, "is how you must also try to sit in cantering." He then demonstrates the canter, pointing out that because of the flexibility of his spine, he remains "glued" to the saddle. He then shows how, if he stiffens his spine, he will immediately begin to bounce. He also shows the class that if he puts too much weight in his stirrups and tightens his thigh muscles, he will bounce. He draws attention to the similarity of movement of the spine in sitting the canter and in pumping a swing. He has the riders imitate this motion as the horses stand and as they move at a walk, exaggerating it somewhat. He must be certain that each rider is actually pushing down as he supples his back, not just rocking back and forth on his thighs.

The riders should let their stirrups out at least two holes longer than they normally carry them, as this will help to prevent them from putting too much weight on the stirrups. They should be allowed to hold the pommel of the saddle with one hand or to hold on to a neck strap. If possible, the instruction in cantering in the saddle should immediately follow a practice period when the riders have been cantering bareback. Each rider should practice in turn in one of the several ways suggested above, and the instructor should have the remainder of the class watch closely to decide whether the rider on the track or on the longe is using his back correctly. As explained earlier in this chapter, learning to canter up a grassy hill on the trail is easier than learning to canter in a ring, but it is best to have at least one ring lesson first so that the riders understand what they are expected to do. When they have learned to sit the canter bareback, they can practice cantering with a glove or a hat or a leaf under them to see how long they can keep it there. Sometimes having them sit on one hand and push against their own palm will help.

When the pupils have learned to use the back well and to sit the canter, the instructor can begin to work to refine the use of the back so that it is not apparent to the observer, but this should not be stressed too soon.

JUMPING

Bareback jumping over a low bar has been discussed in the previous chapter. Intermediate riders can jump a bar set a little higher. If a jumping chute is available where a row of jumps can be set, they will profit by working in this with their reins tied and their hands on their waists. The purpose of bareback jumping is not so much to teach the rider to jump as to teach him to have a close seat. If a rider can learn to stick to his horse over jumps up to two feet six inches without the use of his hands or stirrups, he is unlikely to lose his balance if the horse shies suddenly or kicks up his heels. Instructors should explain this point to parents who are leery of having their children taught to jump.

Beginners' Jumping in the Saddle

As soon as the riders can maintain their forward positions at the canter, they may start jumping in the saddle. A good method of introducing this is to place a jump standard halfway down the long wall with the bar running from it to the long wall. Two posts are also placed as shown in Figure 146. At first the jump bar is resting on the ground; then one end can be rested on the standard, the other on the ground; and finally, both ends can be raised. The riders are put on the track in a column of troopers, numbered off by fours, and told to ride inside the posts and jumps. On command, as they reach point *A,* all the odd-numbered riders ride out to the wall and take the jump, falling back into place as they reach point *B.* The even-numbered riders meanwhile continue on the original track. As point *A* is reached a second time, the even-numbered riders keep to the wall and jump while the odd-numbered ones continue straight ahead.

The instructor should stand beside the jump and instruct the riders to balance on their stirrups from the time they are in line with the jump until they have gone three strides beyond it, and to

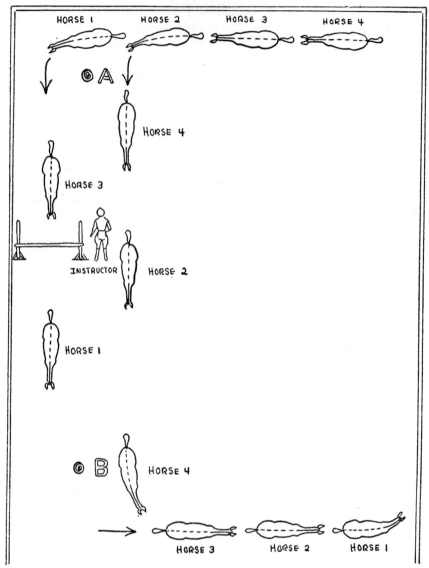

FIG. 146.   Method of teaching jumping which enables all riders to participate.

keep their eyes raised and fixed on a high spot on the wall in front of them. Neck straps should be provided, and all riders made to hold them until they have learned to absorb the motion of the horse in jumping. The neck straps should be halfway between the withers and the poll. The riders should place their hands on the neck straps about halfway between the horse's mane and his gullet. This will give the rider the habit of reaching toward the bit and keeping a straight line from elbow to bit rather than reaching toward the ears and breaking the line upwards. The riders should use only the forefinger on the neck strap. Later they can be taught to spread their fingers and rest them lightly on the horse's neck at that point, but they should not be permitted to try to maintain contact with the horse's mouth until somewhat later in their riding careers.

When the riders have learned to jump in formation as high as eighteen inches, they may be introduced to the jumping lane with a series of jumps. The jumps should again be laid on the ground and raised very gradually. They may be spaced twenty-four feet apart. Riders should keep balanced in their stirrups from the start of the course to the finish, using the neck straps as before. As soon as the riders show that they can jump up to two feet without getting "left behind," the jumps may be arranged in the center of the ring as shown in Figure 125 for the first lessons in bareback jumping. The hardest thing to teach the pupil is to maintain a correct position of the head and eyes. The instructor can hold up his fingers just as the rider jumps and ask him to count the number or he can hold up numbers such as are used to identify riders in shows, but whatever method he uses, he should continue to correct and to watch closely until the rider has established the habit of keeping his eyes up and looking ahead as he jumps. When the rider takes a series of jumps he can be instructed to look at the next jump ahead while jumping the previous one.

Complicated courses requiring turns and changes in direction should not be introduced until the riders have formed good habits of position. The jumps should be at such a height that the horse will take them willingly and the rider can keep his position. The rider should also learn to take jumps from the walk as well as from the trot and canter. Circling the horse is a good exercise for both rider and horse. Negotiating low jumps in the field and on the trail is good for the intermediate rider, but high jumping and jumping at a fast rate of speed should be left until a little later.

THE DIAGONALS

It is important that all riders learn to distinguish between posting on the left and on the right diagonal. They must also know the reason why they should change diagonals at intervals. Most instructions to riders tell them that if they are down in the saddle when a given front foot strikes the ground, they are posting on that diagonal. I have found that this explanation is very confusing to riders. In the first place, they are not in a position to see when the foot strikes the ground, and secondly, to them, posting is rising in the saddle, and is therefore associated with being out of the saddle, not down in it.

I find it better to tell the rider to watch the horse's shoulder blades; if he will rise in his saddle, as a given shoulder blade moves away from him (moves forward), he will be posting on that diagonal. I also have the riders watch another horse being ridden on the track and point out to them that, as the horse moves the forefoot next to the wall forward, more of the animal's chest is visible to the spectator standing in the ring, and that it is at this point that the rider should be rising to the trot. I demonstrate it slowly with my own arms and shoulders, then I have the riders watch their horse's shoulder blades at a walk before trying to follow the movement at a trot. A rider then takes the track at the trot and posts. Each of the other riders is asked on which diagonal he thinks the rider on the track is posting. The rider on the track is also asked which diagonal he himself thinks he is on.

The instructor explains that if you always post on one diagonal, the horse will overdevelop the muscles on one side of his body, and will therefore tire more easily on long rides. For this reason, in trail riding, the rider should take care not to always post on the same diagonal. In ring riding, the rider should post on the outside diagonal. When the horse is on a track with the center of the ring on his left, the rider should post on his outside, or right, diagonal, rising in the saddle as the right shoulder blade moves away from him, sitting in the saddle as the right shoulder blade comes toward him. The reason for this rule is that the outside lateral of the horse travels farther than the inside lateral. If the rider is up in the saddle when the horse's inside foreleg and the outside hind leg are in the air, and down in the saddle when they are on the ground, the horse will not tire as easily.

The rider can change diagonals in one of two ways: he can sit and bounce an extra step, or he can stand for a step. When the riders have learned to distinguish between the diagonals easily by watching the horse's shoulder blades and have learned to change diagonals on command, they should be taught to distinguish between the diagonals by feel alone. To do this, the rider should close his eyes and take up a trot, then say which diagonal he is on with his eyes shut. When he can do this easily, he can be asked to sit the trot for several steps and, without opening his eyes, to take up a designated diagonal.

Training the Rider

There is nothing like mounted drill to teach the intermediate rider control, and to train him to use his aids automatically. He must learn to place his horse in an exact position in relation to the other horses. He must learn to maintain a given gait. He must learn to increase and decrease his gaits smoothly and exactly, and at the same time, to listen to the commands being given by the leader.

Figures 147 to 156 show the execution of the close-order drill. Detailed explanations of these movements can be found in the Cavalry manuals issued for the Army at Fort Riley, Kansas, and in the section "Mounted Troop Work" in the book *Fun on Horseback.** A few elementary rules for conducting mounted drill, which apply to all movements, are given below. The most valuable movements for intermediate riders are forming columns of twos and fours from troopers formation, or single file; returning to troopers from twos and fours; executing squads column left and right about, line, fours left and right, fours left and right about, line of squad columns, and assemble.

Definition of Terms

Army terminology is simple and exact. The following are the most commonly used terms:

About. Any command containing the word *about* means that when the movement is completed, the riders will be moving in the opposite direction from which they started.

Column. A file of riders, one behind the other.

Column of troopers. A single file.

Column of twos or fours. A file of riders, riding in pairs or four abreast.

Distance. The space between riders going from front to rear. The normal distance is four feet from one horse's tail to the nose of the horse behind him.

File-closers. One or two riders not assigned to a regular squad who ride last in the column. In the Army these are usually sergeants. For teaching purposes, less-experienced riders can ride as file-closers while they are learning the drill.

Decrease the front. Reducing the number of riders abreast.

Increase the front. When the riders are maneuvered so that

---

* Margaret Cabell Self, *Fun on Horseback,* Copyright A. S. Barnes & Co., Inc., 1945.

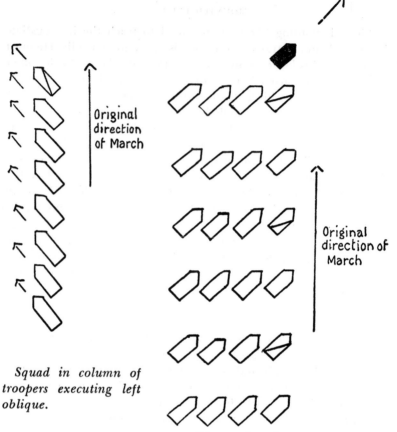

Original
direction
of March

Original
direction of
March

Squad in column of troopers executing left oblique.

Platoon in column of fours executing right oblique.

Fig. 147.   The obliques.

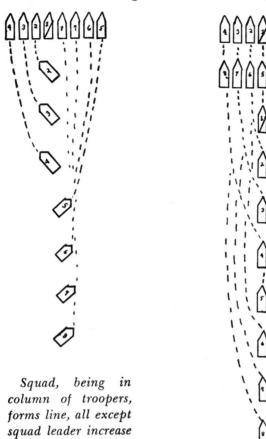

Squad, being in column of troopers, forms line, all except squad leader increase the gait one degree.

Squad, being in column of troopers, forms fours, all except squad leader increase the gait one degree. In both cases if a command to decrease the gait has been given only the squad leader slows down, the others continue at the original gait until the new formation is completed when they take up the new gait.

FIG. 148.

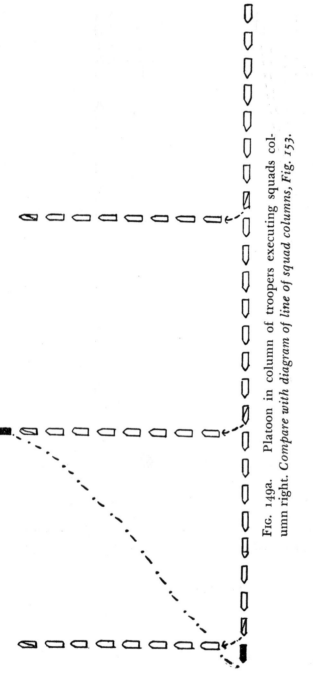

FIG. 149a.   Platoon in column of troopers executing squads column right. *Compare with diagram of line of squad columns, Fig. 153.*

FIG. 149b.   Platoon in column of troopers executing squads column left about and continuing the march.

1st. Squad   2d. Squad   3d. Squad

Direction of march

Original direction of march

1st. Squad   2d. Squad   3d. Squad

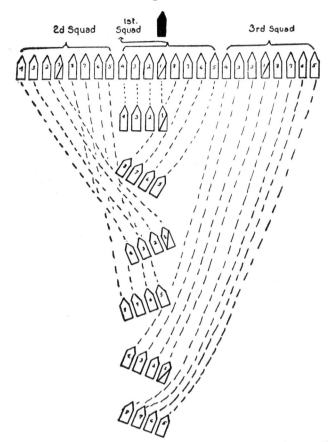

FIG. 150.   Platoon executing line from column of fours. *The first four of the first squad continues at the original gait in the original direction of the march, following the platoon leader. All others increase the gait one degree. The second four of the first squad and both fours of the third squad execute fours half right and follow the tracks indicated. The third squad forms line three paces behind the first squad and decreases to the original gait in time to come up beside and to the right of the first squad which is already in line, the second squad executes fours half left, forms line three paces behind the first squad and comes up beside them to the left. Alinement is to the centre.*

If, at the same time the command LINE *is given a command to decrease the gait is also given, only the platoon leader and the first four of the first squad slow down one degree, the rest continue at the original gait but do not increase the gait until the line is formed when they conform to the gait of the platoon leader and the first squad.*

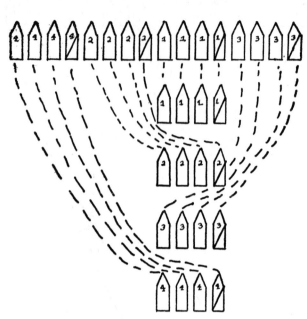

FIG. 151. Small unit drilling in half squads. *Forming line from column of fours. Each four acts as a complete squad. Compare the positions with those of the normal squads on page 194. It will be noticed that whereas the second four of a normal squad always goes to the right of the four in front when coming into line, in half squads the second squad goes to the left and the corporal is therefore always on the right of his squad both in column and in line.*

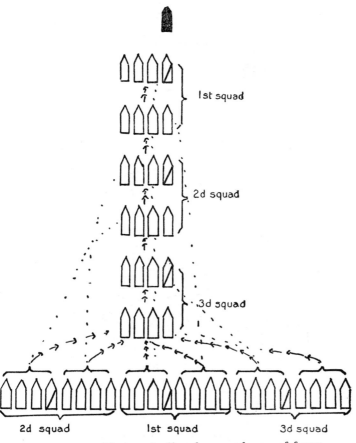

FIG. 152.   Platoon in line forms column of fours.

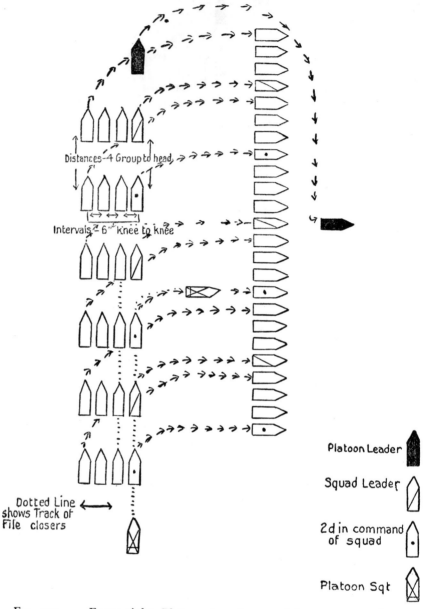

Distances-4 Group to head

Intervals 6" knee to knee

Dotted Line
shows Track of
File closers

Platoon Leader

Squad Leader

2d in command
of squad

Platoon Sgt

Fig. 153.   Fours right. Platoon in columns of fours executes fours
right and continues the march.

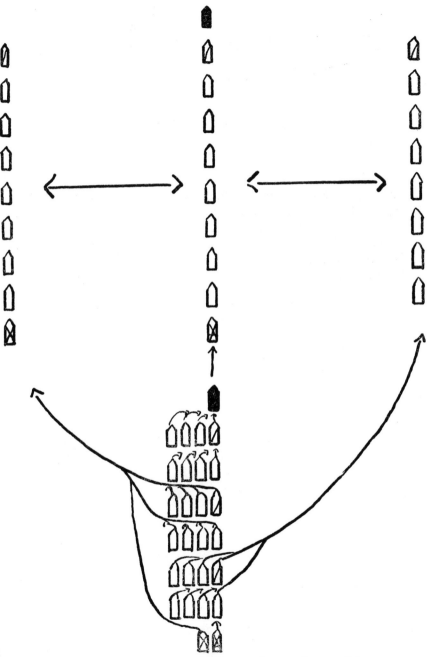

FIG. 154.   Line of squad columns from column of fours.

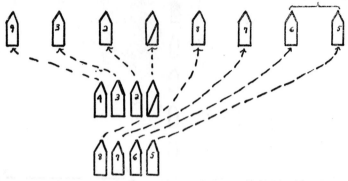

FIG. 155.   Foragers from column of four formed by squad. *Line
is formed in the same way except that, whereas in foragers the intervals are five yards unless otherwise stated, in line all intervals are
normal, namely, six inches from knee to knee. In both instances all
except the squad leader increase gait one degree until the new positions are reached.*

FIG. 156.   Arm signals used in mounted drill.

the number of riders riding abreast has been increased. *Example*: moving from a column of troopers into a column of twos or fours.

Interval. The space between riders going from flank to flank. The normal interval between riders riding side by side is three inches from toe to toe, six inches from knee to knee. Both intervals and distances may be increased on command of the leader.

Move to the flank. To move at right angles to the line of march. Thus, if the riders are in a column of troopers and the command, "By the right flank . . . *ho-o-o*" is given, all riders turn to the right and continue in line across the hall to the opposite side.

Platoon. A platoon consists of three or more squads.

Squad. A normal squad is eight riders. The squad leader is number one of that squad. For groups of riders of sixteen or less, it it is better to ride in half-squads, in which case the squad consists of four riders.

General Rules

All commands are given in two parts: the command of preparation, which tells the riders what to do; and the command of execution, which tells them to do it. The command of execution may be the word *now* or the word *ho-o-o*. For example, "Trot . . . *now*," or, "Column of Twos . . . *ho-o-o*."

All commands are given either by the platoon leader or by the instructor. All commands of preparation are repeated by the squad leaders. If commands are being given by the instructor, the platoon leader repeats the commands of preparation only. If the instructor does not give the command, the platoon leader gives both the command of preparation and that of execution. The platoon may be commanded by arm signals (Figure 156), in which case the squad leaders repeat both the preparatory command and the command of execution.

In increasing the front, all riders except the leaders increase the gait at the same time and take up the original gait on reaching their position. Thus, if the platoon is in a column of troopers at a walk, and the command, "Column of twos . . . *now*" is given, the platoon leader and the leader of the first squad maintain a walk, and the remainder of the riders take up the trot simultaneously, returning to the walk when they are in position. No rider waits for any other rider, so the first pair will be first in place and the last pair in the line will form last.

In decreasing the front, all riders except the leaders decrease the gait one degree and remain in position until they can move out in the new position at the original gait. Thus, if the riders are in a column of fours at the trot, and the command "Column of troopers . . . *now*" is given, all riders except the leader and the leader of the first squad come down to a walk and remain in fours. The leader and the first squad leader continue at the trot, the other riders falling in behind them at a trot in troopers as each one's turn comes. If the column is at a walk, all except the two leaders halt in place.

In drilling green troops in decreasing the front, it makes for a smoother drill if an increase of gait is given. When the riders are at a walk in twos, the command can be "Column of troopers, trot . . . *ho-o-o*." The riders maintain a walk in twos, except for the leaders, who move out on a trot. In the same way, it is easier for inexperienced riders if, when an increase of front is given, a decrease of gait is given. When the riders are at a trot in troopers, the command can be "Column of fours, walk . . . *ho-o-o*." The leaders take up the walk immediately and the other riders continue the trot without increasing the speed of the gait until they are in place.

Riders number off by fours if riding in half-squads, by eights if riding in full squads. To increase to column of twos when riding in a parade ground, all odd numbers continue straight ahead, and all even numbers come up to their left. When riding in a hall on the left track, the odd numbers will be against the rail, the even numbers to the center. In teaching inexperienced riders, it is best to have the column on the left track when increasing the front until the pupils have learned the movement thoroughly. Riding on the right track in a hall or ring, the odd men will have to move to the right to make room for the even numbers who come up on their left alongside the rail.

Beginners profit most by executing the following movements: increasing and decreasing the gaits, increasing and decreasing the fronts, forming lines, and executing squads left and right about.

The instructor or platoon leader must give the commands clearly. Commands of preparation are given with a sustained tone —the voice should not drop at the end of the command. If the command of execution is to decrease the gait, it should be given in a lower tone of voice than other commands. It will require a little practice on the part of the leader or instructor to learn to give the commands in such a manner that the command of execution can be given when the riders are in the best position to execute the movement. Arm signals may be used as shown in Figure 156. The command of preparation is always preceeded by a short blast on a whistle to bring the riders to attention. The leader then gives the desired arm signal (column of twos, trot, for example) the squad leaders repeat it orally and the leader gives the arm signal for *now* (ho-o-).

Riders can be introduced to elementary mounted drill (the movements mentioned above) as soon as they can rate and control their horses at the walk and trot. They should spend from twenty minutes to a half-hour on this each time they ride. The instructor should review the aids used to keep the horses in alignment with each other and should make sure that, in riding in a column of twos or fours, the riders next to the rail maintain the gait and that those toward the center of the ring slow the gait slightly in turning corners. If anything, the horse on the rail should be a little ahead of the horse on the inside on the turns.

THE LAST TWO REIN EFFECTS

The riders by now will understand the use of the leading or opening rein, the use of the indirect rein, and the use of the direct rein of opposition. They must next learn to use the indirect rein of opposition in front of the withers (Figure 97, page 225). After the instructor has explained and demonstrated this rein effect, the riders can practice stopping on the "home spots," using this rein. They should also use it in mounted drill when riding in twos or fours. The horse on the rail will use the inside indirect rein without opposition in making turns at the corners; the horse to the inside will use the indirect rein of opposition in front of the withers to keep close to his partner and to slow up his gait slightly. When this use of the rein is clearly understood, the rider can progress to executing broken lines and serpentines using this rein effect. These movements with the appropriate aids are described in Part I, Chapter VII.

SCHOOLING FIGURES

At this point in their training, the riders are ready to learn the following schooling figures: the pivot on the forehand, backing, leg-yielding, the gallop depart with lateral aids, and jumping in the saddle.

Pivot on the Forehand

In teaching the pivot on the forehand (see page 100), the instructor demonstrates the movement, describing the active and corrective aids used. He then has the class stop at the "home spots" and practice the pivot, moving only three steps away from the wall, and returning to it. He goes from one rider to another, correcting errors, and trying to make the rider aware of what his horse is doing without looking down. Not until the rider can execute the first three steps smoothly should he attempt to complete the half-pivot. When this has been learned successfully, the riders can take positions away from the wall and work on the complete pivots.

Backing

In teaching the rider to back the horse, the instructor should emphasize the importance of the bending of the poll and relaxation of the horse's jaw. The rider must learn to correct with the leg and hand aids the direction and impulsion of movement. Riders may practice parallel to the wall first; later they can back from the wall toward the center; then, from a straight line in the center. Six steps backward is enough. The horse should then move immediately forward.

Leg-yielding

This exercise (described on page 77) is valuable in teaching the rider to use his leg aids independently. Having explained and demonstrated the movement, the instructor has the class take the track at normal or increased distances. As the leader crosses the short wall and enters the long wall, he places the horse in the correct position and moves him along the length of the long wall. On reaching the next short wall, he straightens out the horse and follows the track. At the next long wall the exercise is repeated. Each rider in turn executes the movement as he reaches the points designated. The riders should change direction by crossing the hall on a change of hands at frequent intervals so that the horse can be made to leg-yield both ways.

Gallop Depart with Lateral Aids

The riders should now be secure at the canter and able to use their aids independently. They should be taught the gallop depart from the walk, using the lateral aids. At the same time the teacher can give instruction in and clarify the mechanics of the leads. The riders should first work individually on the gallop depart as they did on the diagonals, with the riders who are awaiting their turns watching the leads to be sure they understand them. Riders taking the gallop depart should not be allowed to look down under the horse. At first they may be allowed to glance at the shoulder for an instant to check their lead; later they should be asked to take the lead with their eyes closed or while looking up at the sky, determining by the feel alone which lead they are on. Emphasis must be put on straightening the horse out and not allowing him to continue with his head to the wall once he has taken the canter.

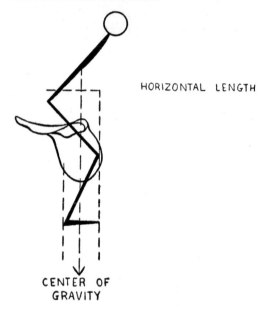

HORIZONTAL LENGTH

CENTER OF
GRAVITY

POSITION AT TROT and GALLOP

FIG. 157.   The principle behind the balanced and forward seats. *This position is easiest on the horse and in jumping the rider will never be thrown off balance by a sudden movement of the horse. For hacking and dressage the leg position remains the same in relation to the upper body but the rider lengthens his stirrups and sits deeper in the saddle enabling him to feel and influence the horse more easily.*

Forward Position at the Gallop (Figures 157, 158).

When the rider has learned to balance in his stirrups at the walk, slow trot, and trot and can remain close to the saddle at the canter, he may be taught to take the galloping position. However, the horse should not be permitted to gallop on; rather he should be put into a slow gallop (canter). The instructor demonstrates the position with emphasis on the angles of the hip, knee, and ankle, the position of the head and eyes; and the hollowing of the loin. The riders should practice while riding on straight lines and on turns and circles. At first they may be allowed to rest their fingers on the horses' necks, maintaining a straight line from elbow to bit, but as soon as possible they should be taught to ride with the hands pushed forward and away from the neck, rein stretched and not pulling or flapping. When riders are secure, they may be allowed to gallop on.

FIG. 158.   Balancing in the stirrups. *This is the most important exercise which the rider of any age can practice. It automatically corrects his position and puts him in balance with his horse. It should be practiced frequently at all gaits during every riding period.*

INTERMEDIATE EXERCISES FOR CONTROL

As riders at this stage of training will want to do more extensive trail riding and to ride at faster gaits on the trail, some time should be spent in ensuring that they have good control over their horses. If a field is available, the following exercises are useful for this purpose.

Exercise 1

The riders line up at one end of the field; the instructor stands at the other. Each rider in turn leaves the line of riders and gallops toward the instructor, using the forward position. When the instructor blows a whistle, the rider circles and halts as rapidly and smoothly as possible, then takes up a slow trot from the point where he has halted to where the instructor is standing.

Exercise 2

All riders trot or canter in a column-of-fours formation, or in a group in any order. On command, one rider halts his horse and stands still while the other riders ride away from him. When they have gone a few hundred yards, the riders are halted and the rider that was left behind has to catch up to them at a walk or a slow trot.

Exercise 3: Equitation

Riders take the track without regard to distance and execute the equitation exercises described on pages 107 to 111 at the trot and at the canter. All should move simultaneously on command.

Exercise 4: Musical Rides

A memorized musical ride, or one in which one group acts as leader and the remaining riders simply follow or execute figures on command, is excellent to develop control in intermediate riders. As many figures as possible should be executed on the slow canter. In turns, the riders should make square corners, and in riding in columns, they must ride exactly in the trace of the rider in front. If lance sockets and lances are available, the ride will be more colorful. Since the riders must ride with the reins in one hand, the aids will have to be used with greater precision.

Exercise 5: Riding on Straight Lines

Few ordinary riders have ever learned to ride a straight line. If working in an indoor hall, markers can be put up about twelve or fourteen feet in from the walls, and the riders can use these to guide on. The horse should turn the corner squarely without going off the track, either before or after he makes his turn. Riding on straight lines may be practiced at the walk and trot for beginners and intermediates, at the canter for advanced riders (Figure 159).

EXTENSION AND COLLECTION OF GAITS

When the instructor has explained and demonstrated the three degrees of the gaits, he can put the riders on the track at the slow trot. They are to count the number of strides the horse takes in going once around the hall or ring. Then they are to take up the ordinary trot, counting strides as before, and finally the extended trot. Each rider reports the results of his counting. There should be fewer strides with the extension of each gait. In teaching this to little children, the instructor should show the difference between the distance covered in short and long strides by himself walking first with "baby" and then with "giant" steps.

The riders should now be far enough along with their riding so that they can ride with the horse on the bit at all times except when resting and can begin to demand a little light collection. The instructor must first explain collection carefully, illustrating the principle by bending a switch at both ends, then freeing it so that it springs straight (see Figure 40). Emphasis should be put on the use of the legs in demanding collection. The riders should not be allowed to think that collection means simply pulling the horse's head in to his chest.

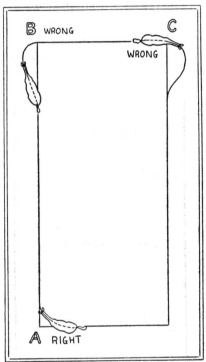

RIDING on STRAIGHT LINES

FIG. 159.   This is an exercise for control that will benefit both the rider and the horse.

INTERMEDIATE GAMES AND CONTESTS

Trotting races and walking races are excellent contests for intermediates. In the former, only two horses should trot at once. Races at the canter, in which the last rider to complete the course without breaking the canter is the winner, are also good contests. Riders may compete in such a slow cantering contest the length of the ring, then have a walking race back. Saddling and bridling up races, or races to see who can put a bridle together the fastest, are useful. Bandaging races in which the contestants see who can put on the best bandage of a designated type in the shortest time will encourage them to practice this.

The following games are most enjoyed by intermediates:

Red Rover

All riders except one line up at one end of the arena. When the one in the center says, "Red Rover, Red Rover, come over, come over," the riders try to get to the other end of the arena without being tagged by "It." As each rider is tagged, he joins the rider in the center and helps to catch the others. The last rider caught wins and is "It" for the next game.

Fig. 160.   Playing field for game of prisoner's base.

Prisoners' Base

This is the best team game for intermediate or advanced riders. Those who are just beginning to ride bareback will gain a great deal

342

of confidence, relaxation, and ability to control their mounts. The field is marked out as shown in Figure 160. Riders from Team A, in order to make a goal, have to ride over and touch B's goal, and vice versa. Each goal counts one point. Any B rider tagged behind A's base line must remain behind that line until a member of his own team tags him. Freeing one rider who is a prisoner frees all the others on that team who are also being held prisoner. If an A rider is riding in the free territory and a B rider comes out from his base line *after* the A rider has left his base line, the B rider can tag the A rider. Any rider making a goal or freeing a prisoner is allowed a free trip home.

If a rider is dismounted for any reason, time is called until he is remounted. He returns to his own base line before continuing to play. The game is played in chukkers of ten or fifteen minutes with a five-minute rest in between. The teams change goals after each chukker.

In an area fifty or sixty feet by a hundred feet, the teams should consist of five riders to a side, one player on each side guarding the goal. In a larger area, more players can participate.

Chapter 16

PROGRESSIVE STEPS IN
TRAINING: ADVANCED

*T*he movements described in this chapter are suitable for riders of more experience and aptitude. These advanced riders should, of course, be able to execute all figures and exercises described in the preceding two chapters.

TURNS ON THE HAUNCHES

The method for teaching the turns on the haunches should follow that described in Chapter XIV, pages 336 to 337, for pivoting on the forehand. The movements are illustrated in Figures 46 and 49, and their correct execution, together with the aids to be employed, are described.

When the riders have learned the half-pivot in place, they can also practice the broken lines and the serpentines and circles holding the haunches. When they have learned the full pivot, they can practice the circles with the haunches held in.

COLLECTION

As the rider becomes more tactful in the use of the aids and is able to feel and to interpret what his horse is doing under him, he can begin to use more collection. It should be emphasized to him continually that there should be no loss of impulsion when the horse is collected but that the impulsion should be transferred from *extension* to *elevation* of the strides. The cadenced walk and the collected trot as differentiated from the slow walk and trot should be practiced. Cantering races in which the winner is the rider who finishes last without breaking the canter will make the riders more aware of

Training the Rider

the feel of the collected canter than any other method. They should then practice the school figures at the collected canter, always bearing in mind that only a few minutes at a collected gait should be permitted before the horse is allowed to extend. At this stage of riding, there should be a great deal of work done on repeated extension and collection of all the gaits as described in Part I, Chapter 6 and Part II, Chapter 14. Horses used for intermediate riders will retain their schooling if ridden in this manner by advanced riders.

GALLOP DEPART ON DIAGONAL AIDS

The gallop depart on the diagonal aids can be taught as soon as the rider is sure of his leads and can maintain impulsion, still keeping good control at the slow canter. Methods of teaching this to the horse are described in Part I, Chapter 7, pages 123 to 125. These methods are explained to the rider, who then practices them.

FIGURE-EIGHTS AT THE CANTER

When the rider has learned to execute the gallop depart on diagonal aids, he may progress to figure-eights at the canter. This will impress upon him the advantage of training the horse to the diagonal aids. He should practice the figure-eights as described in Part I, Chapter VI, taking a few trotting steps between each change of lead. He should sit these steps, giving the signal to change on the "hard" beat of the canter.

CLOSE AND EXTENDED MOUNTED DRILL

When the riders have learned the simpler movements of close-order mounted drill in an exclosed area, they will profit by being taken to a large area—several acres if possible—where the ground is not too rough, and practicing the more difficult figures at faster gaits.

In riding in this manner, it is best to use the arm signals. The platoon leader always blows his whistle before giving the preparatory command, which is repeated aloud by the squad leaders. They also repeat the *"ho-o-o"* when he gives the command of execution.

It requires good control to come into line at a canter, keep the alignment and intervals, and break out again into twos or fours without changing the gait. There is no prettier sight than a well-executed mounted drill.

ADVANCED JUMPING

Advanced jumping should include practice in Olympic type jumps, both up-and-down and spread jumps. The courses can be made gradually more difficult as the skill of the rider improves. Jumps should always be placed so that there is a multiple of twelve feet between them, and so that turns can be made smoothly without interruption of gait. Mental-hazard jumping, in which the horse jumps objects such as rattling pails, a water hose, a Christmas tree, or a bed, will do much to improve the boldness both of the horse and of the rider.

Competitions such as a maze-jumping contest are valuable in improving skill and confidence. The rider does not see the course until he enters the ring. Each jump has a red flag on one side or the other. The rider must take every jump with the red flag on his right. He decides himself in what order the jumps are to be taken. He is timed from the moment he enters the ring, and every knockdown adds a second to his time. The rider to complete the course in the shortest time wins.

TEAM JUMPING

Riders should practice team jumping over Olympic type courses. The riders jump individually and the lowest aggregate score wins. Riders should also practice team jumping as hunt teams with hunting type jumps, the riders to follow one another at a safe hunting distance and to be judged on manners, performance, and way of going. These contests can be held either in the ring or over the outside course. When riders have become proficient over the outside course, they are ready for cross-country work and hunting.

Bloodhound hunting (see pages 153 and 402) is a good solution for schools where there is no fox hunting available.

TRAIL-RIDING COMPETITION

Long rides are held in certain parts of the country to determine the stamina of the various breeds of horses and the riders' knowledge of horsemastership. The most famous of these is the Vermont Trail Ride. Details of this contest are given in the Appendix, pages 393 to 398. Preparing and entering a horse for such a contest is very valuable experience for the advanced rider who is interested in broadening his knowledge.

DRESSAGE MOVEMENTS

The rider is now ready to undertake some of the more difficult ressage movements. He should by now have developed a good feel and the ability to use his aids independently and tactfully. He should have a clear understanding of the fundamentals of good horsemanship. He can begin work on the following figures: the shoulder-in, the travers, the two-track, the counter-change of hands on the two-track, the false canter on the elongated serpentine, the gallop depart on circles from a halt, the gallop depart on a straight line, and the flying change. All of these movements are described and illustrated in Part I, Chapter 7, pages 112 to 126. In teaching them, the instructor should use charts to show the position of the horse's body, and should demonstrate each movement, asking the pupils to suggest what aids might be used to execute the movement. The class should practice at will with the instructor going from one to the other to give help and criticism. As soon as the class can execute several figures successfully, the instructor should plan little courses which combine these figures. For ordinary practice, the rider can be told which figure is coming next and where he is to execute it.

Later, competitions can be arranged, with each rider being given a certain amount of time to prepare himself and his horse for the contest. The course must be memorized and each rider enters the ring alone to execute it. He is judged and graded on the correctness of the movement as performed by the horse, on the horse's calmness and obedience, on the correctness and tact of the rider's use of the aids, and on the artistic merit of the whole performance. Several such courses of varying degrees of difficulty, together with a judging sheet, will be found in the Appendix, pages 398 to 402. Riders should be marked mathematically and given a place in the group of riders: the one with the highest score is number one, the second highest is number two, etc. After several months, the same riders should compete again so as to see whether they are making average, better than average, or less than average progress.

LEARNING TO TRAIN A COLT

The advanced rider can gain a great deal of knowledge if he gets a colt of his own and spends a few years training it under supervision. Unfortunately, most children and young people are inclined to be impatient, and even those who have had excellent preparation often will spoil a young horse by rushing his training, particularly in jumping. The instructor or parent who is supervising should check at frequent intervals to see that the colt is not being rushed. He should have the pupil make out a work sheet, using the earlier chapters of this book as his model, and should reiterate constantly the importance of careful, slow work in developing a first-class horse.

Chapter 17

STABLE MANAGEMENT

*T*he Pony Clubs in England put great emphasis on the importance of instruction and practice in the general care of the horse and in ordinary stable routine. This branch of horsemanship is all too often completely neglected in American establishments. Yet no person can be called a horseman who does not know how to feed and care for his horse in sickness and in health.

In giving such instruction, the teacher should stress feeding, grooming, care of tack and equipment, general repairs, First Aid, and preventive measures for ordinary illnesses and injuries of the horse. The instructor can discuss common ailments such as thrush, heaves, and founder, making the children familiar with their causes, and the proper methods of treatment and prevention. He can point out the areas on the horse most sensitive to injury and bring the class's attention to any wind puffs or splints. The children will learn best and fastest if they are allowed to help in the care and treatment of an animal which is ill or injured. They can learn to bandage, to take temperatures, respiration, and pulse. They must know how to hold a restless horse and keep him calm while the veterinarian works on him. They must learn to tell when an injury or illness is serious and the veterinarian must be called, and when it is something superficial which can be treated without professional help.

The more time that the child can give to actually working with his horse, grooming him, checking him for injuries, caring for his tack, the better horseman he will become. Each horse reacts differently. Some have an aversion to being groomed under the belly or around the head. Some will not pick up their feet readily. It is only

348

by working with different animals that the child really becomes proficient in handling his mount.

It is sometimes difficult to assign time for this work. In most schools the children come only for the riding hour and then leave. It is the policy in the New Canaan Mounted Troop to encourage the children who have passed the early beginner stages of riding and can handle their horses on foot to come early or stay after their riding period. These children help to get the horses ready, help beginners to mount, and help to put away the horses after the lesson. In summer, especially, it is possible to give them a great deal of practice in working in the stalls with the animals. Even quite young children can come to be proficient in handling any average horse or pony carefully and successfully with sufficient practice.

At camps and schools where other activities interfere with a program such as I have described, rainy days can be utilized for instruction in grooming and care of the horses and their tack. Few camps have indoor riding halls, and waterfront counsellors are delighted to have the children sent down to the stable to be instructed and entertained when it is not possible to use the ordinary camp facilities. In planning such a program, the following subjects should be covered.

FEEDING

The horse needs grain to give him energy and to build up his muscles, hay for his main nourishment, and salt. Grain can be whole oats, crushed oats, oats and bran, commercial horse feed, or corn. A mixture of oats and bran is better than oats alone. In winter the mixture is one part bran to two parts oats; in summer, one part bran to three parts oats. Some trainers prefer to give the oats plain and supply a bran mash once a week before a day when the horse is to be rested. Commercial horse feed contains corn, alfalfa, oats, bran, molasses, and minerals. It is usually very fattening, and animals kept on horse feed are sometimes not in as hard condition for work such as hunting as are other horses. In those parts of the country where field corn is grown, horses and mules are fed on this grain. However, horses not accustomed to corn will often develop bad skin conditions.

The average horse weighing from eight hundred to eleven hundred pounds and doing from two to four hours a day of ordinary work will need nine to twelve pounds of grain daily. This should be divided into three portions and fed to the horse after he has been offered water and after the hay has been put into his rack. The instructor should explain that if a greedy horse is given grain first, he will often gulp it down without chewing it, and that if, not having had water for some time, he is then offered water, he may drink so much of it so fast that some of the unchewed and undigested grains may be washed into the intestines, where they will set up an inflammation and cause colic. If the horse is not working, his grain ration should be cut in half, unless he is in poor condition, in which case he may continue on full ration but should have access to a paddock or pasture. If the horse has not been on grain previously he should start with three pounds a day and increase the amount gradually.

The average horse needs from fifteen to twenty pounds of hay a day. Half of this should be fed to him at night. The remainder can be divided into three parts, two-thirds of it fed to him in the morning and the remaining third at noon. Some trainers prefer to give the day's hay supply in only two feedings. In this case, give two-thirds at night and the other third in the morning. Hay should be timothy and clover, or a mixture of timothy, clover, and alfalfa. It should have a good green color with no rust or mold, and it should be crisp with a good smell. Hay that is cut too late has little nutriment in it and is characterized by lack of odor and a dead yellow color.

The horse should always have salt in front of him. Old-fashioned rock salt can be kept in the manger or brick salt in a container can be put in the stall.

WATER

Most authorities agree that the horse should have access to water at all times. The only exception to this is when he is brought in very hot. However, if the trainer follows the procedure, as he should, of never putting a horse into a stall and allowing him to stand while hot but walks him slowly until cool and then rubs him down, it is safe to keep fresh water in his stall. Some stables provide a rack in the corner on which the water pail is set. Others have automatic water fountains such as are used in cow barns. Whatever method is used to supply the horse with water, it must be checked daily for cleanliness.

GROOMING

Every horse should be groomed every day, regardless of whether or not he is ridden. Grooming stimulates the circulation and so helps the horse to get the best out of his feed. It gives the groom a chance to notice any little cuts, blemishes, swellings, or unusual heat. Horses that are sick or in bad condition should be groomed thoroughly twice a day.

The following grooming tools are necessary: rubber curry comb, body brush, course brush (dandy brush), hoof pick, mane and tail comb, cleaning cloth.

Starting with the neck on the near side, the groom works with the curry comb in one hand and the body brush in the other. He keeps his arm straight and uses a circular motion with the curry comb to get the dandruff out, cleaning the curry comb every few strokes by knocking it against his heel. He uses sweeping strokes with the brush, following the direction in which the hair grows. He uses the curry comb to clean the brush every few strokes. The brush alone is used on the legs below the knees and hocks and on the face. When he has finished with the near side, the groom begins at the neck on the off-side. When the horse's body, legs, and face are finished, the groom may do the mane and tail. In England and in parts of this country, the comb is not used on the tail, since it breaks the hairs and makes it difficult to braid. In most hacking stables, however, the comb is used as it saves time. In combing or brushing a badly matted tail, the groom should hold the tail up and take the hairs in little sections as they fall, beginning near the root of the tail and at the ends of the hairs, working backwards gradually.

The horse's mane should be trained to stay on one side. After combing the mane, the groom dips the dandy brush in water and uses it to smooth the hair down. If the hair persists in separating, the mane should be braided and left this way for several days or a week to train it.

The care of the feet is of the utmost importance. The old slogan, "no foot, no horse," is all too true. The feet must be cleaned out carefully each day and thoroughly examined for the presence of small stones or grit which might irritate the horse and for signs of thrush. In using the hoof pick, the groom cups the horse's foot in his hand and works from the frog toward the toe. In attending to both the front and the hind feet, he should face the horse's tail. He must be careful in putting down the foot not to drop it with a bang but to replace it gently. The cracks on either side of the frog, called the "commissures," must be picked carefully as this is where thrush usually starts. Thrush can be identified by a foul odor and a discharge which makes the frog appear to be mushy. Often a crack appears at the center of the frog and the thrush is found to be imbedded deeply in this area. Sometimes it will be necessary to trim the hoof out and clean out hidden pockets in which the thrush develops. Blue stone packed into the crevices will cure thrush, as will a number of other remedies, some of which are given in the list of First Aid materials at the end of this chapter. When the horse is brought in from the ride, his foot may be examined again for stones, but if it is packed with good moist dirt or mud, it is a good idea to leave it so, as this will help to keep the sole soft.

When the feet and mane and tail are finished, the groom takes the rub rag and polishes the horse with this, finishing by running his hand over every inch of the animal to be sure that all is smooth and that there are no bruises, swellings, lumps, or heat which would indicate injuries.

Young children will need careful supervision and constant inspections to check the thoroughness and correctness of their grooming. They are prone to use the curry comb on the hairless parts of the body and on the head and legs. This will make the horse restless about his grooming and may injure him. They neglect the difficult places such as behind the ears, the brisket, the hocks, and the fetlock joints and pasterns. They do not pick out the feet carefully. They almost always leave the grooming tools around. If possible, the instructor should set up a grading system whereby the pupils are given demerits for improper grooming, careless adjustment of tack such as failure to fasten keepers, and failure to replace the grooming tools. At the end of a given period, children with the highest points on grooming for that period can be given a prize. This will do more to stimulate attention and care in grooming than will any amount of scolding.

CARE OF TACK

All tack should be cleaned each time it is used. Different people have different preferences as to the type of soap or other cleaner which they use. The important thing is to be sure that all mud and sweat marks are taken off, and that whatever is used is rubbed well into the leather. Glycerine soap comes in bars and does as good a job as any of the ordinary saddle soaps which come in cans. Some people like a more liquid soap such as the English Crown soap, which is in the form of a jelly. Not much water should be used with this jellylike soap; a little oil can be added if desired. There are many other preparations which are good for cleaning tack, such as Lexol, which contains oil; various harness creams; and a new product containing a detergent, oil, and soap, called Neatsope. These preparations soften and feed dried leather. If soap alone is used, all bridles, saddles, martingales, and other equipment should be taken apart once a month and oiled thoroughly with Neatsfoot Oil Compound.

Special attention must be paid to the care of the bit. As soon as the bridle is taken out of the horse's mouth, the bit should be washed and dried. The bridle can then be hung up until it can be cleaned. From the first lesson, the beginner should be taught to wash and dry his bit before he hangs up his bridle. Cleaning the bridle is never difficult if this practice is followed, and no horse will get a sore mouth from caked dirt, grass, and saliva. If this is neglected, the bit will have to be soaked for fifteen or twenty minutes and then scoured with steel wool to get it clean again.

Saddle pads should be brushed and dried after using. Those of good quality can be run through a washing machine at intervals to get off the dried sweat. Since the billet straps are most apt to wear out unless they are kept supple and soft with oil, these as well as the stirrup leathers should be well soaked in oil at frequent intervals.

Even though a pad is used, the lining of the saddle needs daily attention. If any dirt accumulates which cannot be wiped off, a bristle brush such as a nail brush should be used with plenty of water and soap, and the panel scrubbed. If the water and soap are left on for a few minutes, it will be easy to wipe off the dirt. A saddle and bridle properly cared for from the time they are first put into use will last many, many years.

In a stable where tack belonging to different people is kept, it is wise to get a stamping outfit and stamp the articles with their owner's initials. This is also a good practice if horses are being shown, since there is then no question of ownership, should the tack be mixed with that of another stable.

Either bags or baskets must be provided for storing grooming tools. If each tool is marked with a number and the container marked with the same number, it will be easy to keep the equipment in order.

THE TACK ROOM

The tack room should be as convenient as possible to the stable so that there is not too much carrying back and forth of equipment. It should have running water, and, if possible, some way of heating water. Each saddle and bridle should have its own rack with the name of the horse over it. There should be cleaning racks where saddles can be put as well as bridle hooks from which the lighter equipment can be hung for cleaning. The cleaning equipment should be either in a drawer or on a shelf. Another drawer or shelf can be given over to spare parts of bridles for repair work. Extra stirrup leathers, girths, halter shanks, and pads should be hung together. The medicine cabinet can also be in the tack room, as well as a bulletin board on which can be listed the schedule for the day.

CARE OF THE STABLE

The instructor must set a high standard of cleanliness and neatness in the stable. Prospective clients coming to inquire about riding for their children will not want to register them if the stable is dirty and smelly, the tack room untidy, and the horses unkempt. Droppings should be picked up as often as it is practical. Box stalls must be cleaned out regularly and plenty of bedding used. Stable tools *must* be kept hung on a rack, and this rack should be one which will hold them firmly. Nothing frightens a nervous horse more than to brush across a shovel, broom, or rake and have it fall down on him. A rake or pitchfork left lying on the ground can be a lethal menace, since a horse or a child stepping on it can get a severe puncture wound which, if uncared for, may result in death from tetanus.

REPAIRS

The horse's great strength makes it necessary to inspect the premises constantly, and the owner will find that every day little repairs or bigger ones will have to be attended to. Unless the instructor or owner of the stable sets up a high standard of maintenance, the whole establishment will deteriorate gradually until what was once a first-class plant becomes a poor third-class one. Children must be made to pick up papers, even when they did not throw them down, and to replace any pieces of equipment found lying around. Painting of fences, trim, or the whole building will be necessary every so often. Asbestos shingles are very practical for stables since they lessen the fire hazard, add insulation, and do not require painting, but the trim must still be painted. Electric fences need no painting but must be inspected regularly for breaks or for objects which may short-circuit them and cut off the current. Outdoor rings need to have the stones removed every few months. These stones work up from underneath as the surface is worn down.

For many years I was troubled with the problem of dust in both the indoor and outdoor rings. The indoor ring could be watered by hand, which took several hours a week, but this was not feasible for the outdoor ring. A few years ago I discovered a perfect and very inexpensive solution. Oil which has been drained from automobile crankcases can be secured at no charge from most garages. Sprinkled lightly over the ring, it becomes thoroughly worked into the surface and completely eliminates the dust. It is necessary to apply the oil only two or three times a year. An adequate oiler can be made from a fifty-gallon drum, a length of pipe, pipe fittings including a cut-off, and a compressor which works off the spark plug of a car. The tank is mounted on the back of a jeep or truck. The pipe is drilled with holes and hung horizontally below the tank. The flow of oil can be checked at will by the cut-off. The compressor runs to the spark plug of the car. One man can drive around the ring, moving so that the whole surface is covered with little lines of oil. After the field has been used for a few minutes by a group of horses, these lines disappear, and the surface simply becomes a slightly darker color. The dust will now rise only a few inches, even after a long period of trotting or cantering by a group of riders.

SHOEING

Proper shoeing of a horse is a craft which requires long practice. Unfortunately, all too many blacksmiths, although they may have been in the profession all their lives, do not know how to shoe correctly. If your horses consistently overreach or grab their heels, if they develop frequent cases of thrush, if they stumble or go lame for no apparent reason, look to your blacksmith. For horses with normal feet, the blacksmith seeks to fit a shoe to the foot so that it gives a maximum of support but does not extend so far back or is so pulled in at the heels that the horse develops contracted heels. The outside wall should not be rasped away to fit the foot. The horse should be shod so that his frog can touch the ground and act as the shock absorber nature intended it to be. This is not always possible with the back feet, since, in jumping horses, low heels are usually used to prevent slipping, but it can be done with the front feet. Some horses need therapeutic shoeing to correct faults in the way they travel, such as toeing in or out, knuckling over, or forging.

Children should be taught how a properly fitted shoe looks on a horse, and what to have the blacksmith do if the horse does not travel straight. Instructors should get the blacksmith to show them how to remove a shoe that has become twisted and that, if left on, will injure the horse. Many ignorant horse owners think that if the shoes do not come off of themselves, the horse can continue to wear them, or that if a horse is to be turned out for eight months, his feet will need no attention. One has only to go to an auction or sales stable where such unfortunate creatures are brought in with feet so misshapen that they can hardly move about, to refute this fallacy. A horse must have his shoes checked at least once a month, and if he has outgrown them, even though the shoe may still be good, it must be removed, the horse's feet trimmed, and the shoe reset.

HANDLING THE STABLE HELP

One of the instructor's or stable manager's main problems is getting and keeping good help. Experienced men who are responsible and trustworthy are very hard to find. Some stables both here and in England have given up using men and are hiring woman grooms and stable hands since they are less apt to drink, are more patient with the horses, and are more willing to follow instructions. A new man coming into the stable should have his references thoroughly checked. For the first few days, the instructor or stable manager should try to be in the stable as much as possible, both to show the newcomer the ropes and to observe how he handles the horses. Any sign of undue roughness should set the manager looking for a replacement. Once a man has proved himself efficient and responsible, he should be left alone to run the horses his own way. A schedule should be set up for him, giving the hours of feeding, the amount each horse is to get, and the times the horses will be used; then he should be allowed to follow this schedule himself, using his own methods. Some men like to get out very early and do the feeding and cleaning up before they have breakfasted themselves. Others prefer to get their own breakfast and then start in with the stable work. As long as the work is done at the time set by the trainer or manager, the man should be allowed to work in the way in which he is accustomed.

The regular schedule should not be interrupted unless it is absolutely necessary to do so. If the horses are normally fed at five-thirty or six o'clock, they should not be kept away from the stable until later, even though the riders may want to do so. If possible, one day a week should be a day of rest for the horses. On this day the trainer can go over the tack and discuss repairs and other matters pertaining to the care of horses, tack, and stable with the men. Each man should have one full day a week off. If this is not possible, he should at least have the time between the morning and the night feeding.

No man will remain happy and contented with his work if he is not housed and fed properly. The stable manager must see that there are proper accommodations for the stable personnel. Generally, a married man will be a better workman and will remain in a position longer than a single man. This requires that a suitable house or apartment be provided, and that the man's wife and children are made welcome and comfortable. If the establishment is a large one, it may be found wise to rent or build a sizable house in which the head groom and his wife can live and in which single men or stable boys can be boarded.

Training the Rider

In handling the men under him, the trainer should remember that no person is perfect. He must weigh each man's good qualities against the bad and decide whether the good traits make up for the undesirable ones. Having made up his mind, he should accept the man as he is and not expect perfection. The children should be taught to be polite to the men and not to cause them any unnecessary trouble but to help as much as possible.

It is unwise to allow undue familiarity between the children and the stablemen, but the relationship should be a pleasant one. Some men get along well with children; others cannot stand having them underfoot. If a man does not like children, he may work out well in a training stable, but he will never be happy in a riding school.

THE SELECTION AND JUDGING OF HORSES

In connection with stable management, children should be taught the selection and judging of horses. The instructor should bring out horses of different conformations and point out the beauties and the blemishes in each. He should explain why it is important that the horse be deep through the heart, why his legs must be set in a certain way, what makes for strength in the quarters, how to tell good cannons and tendons from poor ones, what are the marks of a finely bred horse, and why the way a horse's head is set onto his neck affects his manner of going.

DIAGNOSIS AND TREATMENT OF AILMENTS

Along with this goes the discussion of ordinary ailments and injuries. The care of simple wounds, sprains, coughs, shipping fever, thrush, and scratches should be explained. Preventive care is as important as First Aid after there has been an injury or when a diseased condition has developed. Children should understand why a horse develops laminitis (founder), scratches, or ring bones. They should know how a horse may be protected against tetanus, and what to do in traveling around to shows to prevent him from contracting shipping fever. They should know that a horse's normal temperature is about 100° or 101°, how to take it, what his normal pulse and normal breathing are. A dull coat may be a symptom of worms, a bad intestinal condition requiring a purgative, or inadequate food. The instructor should include discussions of this in his talks during the rest periods of the class. Every horse must have his teeth examined every six months and, if necessary, they should be floated. The children should be taught why this is necessary and how the teeth affect the general condition of the animal.

When a horse shows signs of lameness or discomfort, he should be taken out of the class immediately and examined to determine what is causing the lameness. Children should be taught that on no account must they continue to ride any animal if their doing so causes him physical distress. Only too often, horses with bad saddle or girth galls, loose shoes, or quarter cuts are hired out. Since the first maxim of the good horseman is to think of his horse at all times, no injury, however trivial, should be overlooked.

Children should be trained to start looking for causes of lameness by first examining the foot. A pebble may be lodged in the frog or a larger stone jammed against the sole. A horse often picks up a nail which runs into the foot for its full length and is therefore difficult to see. Even a sharp little stick can sometimes penetrate the sole or frog. In such a case, either the blacksmith or the veterinarian will have to cut around the wound after the object has been removed, the wound will have to be treated with a disinfectant, and the animal given a preventive tetanus shot. Stone bruises and corns are common causes of lameness in horses, as are contracted heels, bad shoeing, and hard soles. The blacksmith will have to remedy the first two conditions. Packing the hoof with white rock, a clay used for this purpose, or soaking the foot in water for several hours, and applying a good hoof dressing will soften the sole.

Thrush is one of the most common causes of sudden lameness. Fortunately, it is usually easy to cure, especially if it is treated before it gets very deep. Several remedies are suggested in the list of medicines and applications on page 363. Cuts on the coronet band and on the bulbous heels caused by overreaching or brushing are very painful and should be treated as wounds. The horse should not be used until they are healed. The shoeing should be checked, and if overreaching is the cause of the injury, the front shoes should be set a little back and the horse's toes shortened, and the back shoes set forward with the toes left a little long. This will cause the horse to pick up his front feet sooner to get them out of the way of the back feet.

In any case of lameness, the wall of the foot should be felt for heat, which indicates navicular disease and laminitis (founder). Soaking the feet in cold water or packing them with white rock and medication sometimes will help founder, but nothing can be done in severe cases. A veterinarian should be consulted.

Scratches is a condition similar to chapped hands, in which the back of the pastern becomes scabby and raw. The area should be soaked in a disinfectant solution, carefully dried, and a heavy ointment applied.

Ring bones and side bones are injuries of the coronet band. A hard enlargement is formed and the horse is usually very lame, although sometimes the horse can have a bad ring bone or side bone and not be troubled by it at all.

Wind puffs around the fetlock joints are seldom serious and need no treatment. They are characterized by a rubbery feeling.

Sprains and strains, diagnosed by swelling in the joints or tendons, heat, and severe lameness, should have a veterinarian's attention. They can be treated with hot or cold epsom salts compresses or with liniments and hand rubbing. In severe cases, a blister must be applied.

Capped elbow or shoe boil is a boil which forms on the elbow due to pressure of the shoe when the horse is lying down. This will have to be opened and syringed out daily with an antiseptic solution. The area should be painted with Churchill's iodine or rubbed with iodex.

Shoulder ailments are hard to diagnose and to cure. Sometimes there is a strain behind the shoulder blades, and the horse is lame only intermittently or when he is jumped or ridden hard. Usually a strong blister is required. Sometimes, after having been lame for some time, a horse will continue to "go short," even when there is no longer any real soreness. This can come from a shortening of the muscles or tendons from lack of use. The horse should be used lightly but steadily in this case.

Bowed tendons are a form of strain affecting the tendons, particularly of the front legs.

Splints are bony enlargements on the splint bone which nature develops in an effort to reinforce the bone when it is subjected to hard blows or unusual work. They are common in young horses and often go away after a period of years. They do not generally cause lameness after the first few days or weeks. Horses with large splints will sometimes hit themselves with the opposite foot and go lame for a few steps.

The hocks are subject to several types of injury. Bog spavins are soft enlargements on the lower inside of the hock in which fluid forms between the covering ligament and the bone. A strong blister or pin firing is recommended. Curby hocks and thoroughpins are also common. Thoroughpins are puffy enlargements in the hollows of the hocks, and are not serious. Curby hocks form at the back below the point of the hock, and can be serious.

Some horses consistently have trouble with the stifle joint. A severe blister will tighten up the ligament.

Abrasions, cuts, and wounds must be treated according to their type, severity, and location. Generally speaking, wounds on the body are not serious and heal quickly, leaving little if anything in the way of scars. Wounds on the legs, because of the poor circulation, absence of fleshy tissue, and the constant movement, are difficult to heal and are very apt to leave scars. The same care should be given to the horse that would be given to a human. Every effort should be made to keep the wound clean and to prevent infection. Wounds which do become infected and develop "proud flesh" will need a veterinarian's attention. He may want to cut away the proud flesh or to burn it off with a caustic pencil. Home treatment for proud flesh is an application of powdered alum; this cannot do any harm and will often do away with the rough areas which will not heal.

Occasionally a horse receives a wound which cuts an artery. Unless pressure is applied at once and the bleeding checked, the animal will quickly bleed to death. Wounds which require stitching are common. If the wound is not over a joint, such as a shoulder or stifle joint, the stitches will hold and the wound will heal without leaving a bad scar. Even though the stitches do not hold, if a wound on the horse's body is cared for so that it does not become infected, it will heal well.

The horse's eyes are subject to several diseases, the most common of which is periodic ophthalmia. There is a variety of opinion as to the cause and prevention of this disease. There is no known cure, although some authorities claim that the addition of riboflavin in the diet will check it. Attacks occur at intervals. The horse's eye becomes swollen and puffy, and the eyeball turns misty and yellow or green. Eventually, after a series of attacks, the horse will go blind. This disease is supposedly not transferable nor is it inherited. Some horses get attacks of what looks like ophthalmia at certain seasons of the year, especially when there is much pollen and hay or flower seed in the air. In these cases the eyes seem to water but the attack is not as serious as in the periodic ophthalmia proper. There is also a type of contagious ophthalmia evidently caused by a virus.

Another type of eye ailment is one in which the retina becomes more or less paralyzed and so does not enlarge or contract properly. There is no known cure or treatment for this condition, and it often goes unnoticed, as to the casual observer, the eye appears normal.

The horse's respiratory system is subject to the disease known as heaves. Heaves can be brought on by eating dusty or bad hay, by overwork, and by neglect. Some horses develop heaves as an after-effect of shipping fever or of sinus infection. Some develop it for no discernible cause. There is no real cure, although many people claim to have cured it. Certainly wetting all the feed and hay, giving the horse regular and light use with plenty of fresh air, and administering a mild kidney stimulant such as saltpeter or one of the heaves remedies will help to keep the disease under control.

Equine coughs are common in horses. If not accompanied by fever or symptoms of heaves, they are not serious. Shipping fever is often very serious, as it can go into a condition called strangles or into pneumonia. It is characterized by a cough, loss of appetite, heavy discharge from the nose, fever, dullness of coat, and swelling in the glands around the head and neck. A veterinarian should be called at once and the animal kept isolated. Sinus infections seem to be becoming more and more common. The horse has a heavy discharge from the nostrils, especially when the head is lowered, and often has great difficulty in breathing. The weather seems to affect the condition. It is possible to operate and drain the sinuses, but this is a serious operation, and should be undertaken only after all other remedies have failed.

THE MEDICINE CABINET

Every well-run stable, private or commercial, should have a supply of medications on hand to treat at least the most common ailments of the horse. Some of the recommended items are listed below.

For Abrasions, Cuts, or Wounds

Gentian Violet or Methyl Blue (Blue Gall Remedy). A liquid wound dressing with a drying effect. For minor cuts and abrasions.

Red Wound Dressing. A liquid wound dressing in an oil base, non-drying. For wounds, cuts, and abrasions.

Penicillin Topical Ointment or Penicillin Calcium Topical Ointment. Prevents infection, is non-toxic. Must be kept refrigerated, preferably in a dark place. Loses strength after period of time.

Furacin Ointment. For deep wounds that are hard to heal. Aids regrowth of hair.

Alphamel Ointment (Canadian). An ointment containing cod-liver oil and vitamins. Promotes healing and toughens skin.

Sulphathiazole Ointment (20 to 24 per cent) or *Sulphadiazene.* Prevents proud flesh. Strong anti-bacteria agent. Good for deep body wounds and leg wounds.

Sulphathiazole or *Sulphadiazene Powder.* Dust into wounds.

Balsam of Peru. Very healing, but liquid disinfectant should also be applied.

Isotonic Salve. Especially recommended for puncture wounds. Can be used before cleaning wound or after syringing it with saline solution or other disinfectant.

Churchill's Iodine. Use on puncture wounds in sole, also as mild blister. In this case, paint area once a day for 3 days, then wait for 3 days and repeat.

Lysol Solution. Use as directed on bottle for good disinfectant wash for all wounds before applying other medication.

B.F.I. Powder. Excellent healing powder. Dust on wounds that do not need to heal from inside.

For Proud Flesh Resulting from Wounds

Powdered Alum. Apply frequently and heavily to area. If necessary, keep area bandaged.

Copper Sulphate (Blue Stone). Rub on wound to cauterize.

Caustic Pencil. Apply as above.

White Lotion. (25 gr. Zinc Sulphate and 30 gr. Lead Acetate in 1 pt. sterile water). Can be used as astringent to check proud flesh, also as cold wet pack for sprains. Shake before using.

For Infections Resulting from Wounds

Epsom Salts (1 cupful in ½ pail hot water). Bathe area with towel for 20 minutes. Water must be kept hot. If wound is on lower leg or foot, use a deep utensil and soak. Bandage heavily. Keep wet for 24 hours.

Antiphlogistene. Use as directed on jar for poultice.

Neosilvol. Can be squirted directly into deep puncture wounds from tube, which has ophthalmic cap. Has deep penetrating qualities.

For Eye Infections and Irritations

For mild irritations caused by injury or dust, use boric acid solution, saline solution, or Argyrol.

Penicillin Ophthalmic Ointment. Use on inside of lower lid, then close lid and massage gently. Loses strength after period of time.

Neosilvol. Use as above.

Furacin Ointment for Eyes. Non-toxic, can be used freely.

For Sprains, Strains, External Swellings, Bowed Tendons

Tuttle's Leg and Body Wash. For use as a body wash or muscle bracer on legs, mix Liquid Analgesic (S. Pfieffer Mfg. Co., St. Louis, Mo.) with 2 qts. alcohol and 2 qts. witch hazel.

Slim Jim Horse Liniment.

½ oz. Aqua Ammonia
1 oz. Oil of Sassafras
1 oz. Tr. Aconite Root
½ oz. Oil of Hemlock
½ oz. Oil of Cedar
½ oz. Oil of Origanum
½ oz. Tr. Camphor
½ oz. Tr. Myrrh
½ oz. Spirits of Turpentine
½ oz. Chloroform

Add enough rubbing alcohol to the above items to make 2 pints of liniment. Use daily to relieve sprains and strains or to relieve stiffness. Rub in well. Do not bandage or cover.

Churchill's Iodine. Apply daily for 3 days, omit for 3 days, and repeat. If area is not mildly blistered, repeat.

Red Blister. 1 part Biniodide of Mercury to 8 parts lard. Rub in well but do not bandage. Keep horse's head tied up so that he cannot lie down or reach area with his mouth. When soreness is gone and area is blistered, wash blister off. Horse can then be turned out. Area will remain hot and swollen for some time. Horse may not be sound until new hair has grown in again.

Black Blister. 1 part Cantharides with 7 parts lard. Boil lard and add Cantharides. Produces a stronger blister than the Red Blister. Apply as above.

Iodex or Stainless Iodide Ointment (Gilman Bros., Inc., Boston, Mass.). Use for mild sprains and to reduce swelling. Rub in until color disappears. Does not blister.

For Thrush

Calomel Powder, Powdered Alum, or Powdered Blue Stone. Clean out area thoroughly. Pack with any of above powders. Pack cotton in to keep powder in place. Repeat daily until sprain has cleared up.

For Scratches

Wash area with mild soap and pick off scabs. Cover with any of the following: Furacin Ointment, Resinol Ointment (very good as it prevents scab from reforming), Chloresium Ointment. Keep area well covered with ointment, and bandage if possible.

For Shipping Fever, Coughs, Respiratory Ailments

Horses to be shipped can be inoculated 2 weeks before shipping. This inoculation is not always effective, but at least serves to lighten the attack.

Sulmet Powder (Lederle Co.). First dose, 12 tbsps. in feed which has been dampened. Next 3 days, one dose of 6 tsps. daily. Also give equal amount of baking soda.

Sulphanilamide. Administer same as Sulmet Powder but do not exceed 240 grams per dose. If tablets are used, multiply human dosage by 9.

Oil of Tar and Aconite. 1 tsp. on horse's tongue will help relieve coughs. In any respiratory infection, the feed and hay should be kept damp as dust irritates the affected membranes.

For Minor Skin Eruptions

Capsicum Methyl Salicylate. Add to saline water solution and bathe affected areas. If cause is hives, give hot bran mash and add 1 tbsp. mineral oil or linseed oil per quart grain in daily feed until condition clears up.

Minraltone (Near's Food Co., Inc., Binghamton, N.Y.). Improves skin, bones, and appetite by supplementing mineral deficiency indicated by rough coat, scaly hoofs, or lack of stamina.

Mineralized Salt. Minerals can be added to the horse's diet by using mineralized block salt instead of ordinary salt.

For Lice or Mites

Horses that are not used regularly or hard enough to cause sweating, especially if they are in poor condition, will often be attacked by lice. The animal should be clipped and bathed with an ordinary solution of Lysol. Repeat in 3 days. These lice will not get on human beings and are easily eliminated.

Tools, General Remedies

The medicine chest should be equipped with the following utensils and articles:

sterile absorbent cotton
rolls of 3-inch gauze
wooden tongue depressors (for the application of ointments)
heavy turkish towels (for applying cold or hot compresses)
clean sponge
water bucket kept for medical purposes only
leg bandages
clean muslin which can be torn up to make special types
    of bandages
surgical scissors
penknife and blacksmith's knife
twitch (for controlling restless horses)
rectal thermometer
enema pail
large and small syringes
2 veterinarian guns (one for administering capsules and one for
    liquids)

In addition to the foregoing list, the medicine cabinet should contain, for human use, peroxide or hexylresorcinol (ST 37), band-aids, gauze squares and adhesive tape, and sulpha ointment.

Of the remedies listed on pages 363 and 364, every stable should have at least the peroxide, one of the liquid wound dressings, one of the ointments for use on wounds, veterinary vaseline to use around infected areas and to promote the growth of hair, epsom salts, boric acid powder, B.F.I. powder, a good liniment and a thrush remedy. Call the veterinarian as soon as possible if the injury or ailment is more than superficial.

Chapter 18

GETTING STARTED AS AN INSTRUCTOR

*B*efore deciding where or how he is to begin his career as a teacher, the prospective riding instructor should consider his own personality and ability. If he has had little or no training as a teacher, he should plan to get such training at a regular school which offers training for riding instructors. If this is not possible, he should look for a school or camp with a well-run program and an experienced instructor and apply for a position as assistant. He will not make much if any money, but he will gain a great deal of experience. This is not as good a method as taking regular training since he will learn only what is being taught, and he will not learn much about program planning and many other subjects, but it is better than nothing.

The instructor who has had training and is qualified has the choice of taking a position in a school or camp where he will receive a salary plus his board, or of taking a position in a club or stable where he will probably be paid according to the number of pupils he has, or of starting his own stable.

POSITIONS AT SCHOOLS AND CAMPS

If he decides to work at a school or camp, the instructor can give his name to one of the bureaus which supply sports instructors. He will be asked to fill out a form giving his age, experience, training, and several references. There are always many more positions than there are trained instructors. The applicant should not jump at the first offer but should compare one with another, going to see the camp or school so that he can get a good idea of the equipment and of the standards of the establishment.

Some schools and camps leave the riding program entirely up to the instructor. Others require modifications. For example, some will not permit any jumping since they feel it to be dangerous. Usually the well-qualified instructor will be happiest where he is allowed a free hand. In going for his interview, he should be prepared to tell the head of the school or camp exactly how he plans to teach, how he plans to organize his classes, and what he considers a well-organized program. He should make out a list of questions before going to the interview pertaining to the equipment, the type and number of horses, the stable help, the daily program, the hours or days off, and the living conditions. Many camp directors have only vague ideas of efficient riding programs. Some will want to organize the riding as they do the waterfront activities, sending forty or fifty children down to the ring at a time when there may be only ten horses. The riding instructor must be prepared to explain tactfully but convincingly why this is not feasible. Usually mentioning the danger of allowing unattended children around horses is sufficient to convince the director that riding cannot be run like baseball or swimming.

The riding instructor considering a position in a school or camp should try to find out how congenial the other members of the staff will be. Some camps have only one or two mature instructors; the rest will be sixteen- and seventeen-year-old junior counsellors. If possible, the applicant should talk also with the heads of the other departments in order to learn something about the standards of the camp or school. This is particularly important in applying to camps. Some camps aim only at giving the children a good time; others really try to send them home not only happy but with more knowledge and skill than they had when they came.

The choice of horses is extremely important. If the camp or school owns its own horses, the prospective instructor should see these animals and should try them out before accepting the position. If they get a new string each season, the prospective instructor should have a contract which allows him to discard horses that are either unsuitable or unsound. If possible, he should arrange to pick out his own horses. In doing this, he should have a contract with the owner of the horses and should specify in detail, both by description and by name, the horses that he chooses. The owner of the horses must have them examined for soundness by a veterinarian and must provide a certificate guaranteeing them. The instructor should make sure that the camp or school will agree to having them examined by a veterinarian before returning them. A contract for rental should include all necessary information, to protect the camp. If the school or camp owns its own tack, the prospective instructor must check it with an eye to suitability, condition, and amount. If he needs more neck straps, halter shanks, or other equipment, he should specify this before he signs the contract. Some schools and camps are very stingy with equipment and the instructor can find himself badly handicapped by the lack of ordinary necessities.

In deciding on a specific camp or school, the instructor should look to the future. Will he like this position well enough to continue with it year after year and so build a reputation for himself? If the instructor is a success and the school or camp gets children back a second year because of his well-organized program, it will be willing to pay him a higher salary than it would to a new instructor. Some people like to teach young children; others prefer older ones. Some like a well-organized and conventional type of school; others like a freer program. Whatever he chooses, the instructor should consider his own suitability and whether he will like not just the first year but the future years as well.

POSITIONS AT CLUBS AND HACKING STABLES

A position in a club or hacking stable presents somewhat different problems than working at a school or camp. An instructor taking such a position must be able to get along with and teach all ages of people. He must be well grounded in stable management and able to handle the workers under him without friction. Before taking such a position, he should check on the condition of horses and tack and the type of clientele. If he is to teach entirely on a commission basis, he should try to find out how many riders rode the previous season, what the potentialities are as to new riders, and so forth. A person with varied interests will do better in this type of work than one who is interested in riding only. However, the instructor who is working for a club or hacking stable rarely has the freedom of one who teaches at a school or camp or who has his own establishment. He may have to share the use of the facilities, such as rings, jumps, and mounts, with members who are not his pupils. It is extremely difficult to teach beginners in a ring when experienced riders are galloping around or taking jumps.

STARTING A STABLE AND RIDING SCHOOL

The instructor who is planning to start his own stable has the most difficult problem of all. He can rarely count on making any profit at all the first year or so. Before doing anything he should study the situation very carefully, talking to the heads of schools in the vicinity, finding out about the prices of grain and hay, making contacts with as many different people as possible If he has plenty of capital he can buy what he needs, but he should be careful of over-expansion until he is sure of his future pupils.

Many times riding schools can be started in a very small way and developed slowly. For example, a person who has one or two horses and a barn can add a few more, put up a simple ring, and start with just a few pupils, gradually building up the group and using the profits to increase the facilities. This takes a great deal of hard work and it will be years before there can be any very large monetary reward. On the other hand, there is little risk. Before starting even a simple program, a careful estimation of the costs involved should be made, including the necessary equipment and horses and the monthly upkeep. Then the community should be approached through the schools and clubs, and if possible, the pupils should be signed up before the outlay is made. Knowing how much the running of the plant will cost, the instructor can estimate how many pupils he will need and how much an hour he will have to charge them in order to make his costs and put by a certain sum to cover deprecia-tion and improvements.

He will find that group lessons for children are the most satis-factory. He may be able to arrange to provide riding for nearby private schools, organizing his program to suit theirs. An advertise-ment in the local paper may bring him enough replies to show that there is sufficient individual interest to justify his efforts. Talks with Y.M.C.A. and Y.W.C.A. groups, Girl and Boy Scouts, etc., will tell him whether or not he is wise in going ahead with his project. He should be prepared to present his program attractively and in a businesslike fashion. He will probably have to start with very low prices, planning to raise them as time goes on. These prices can vary with the number of riders in the group. Under no circumstances should he agree to have children ride by the lesson. They should ride by the month or season. If he has no indoor riding hall, he will have to make up lessons cancelled due to bad weather and should be sure to allow time for this. Children who miss lessons because of ill-ness should be allowed to make them up by riding with another group, but those who miss them because they prefer to go to some other engagement should forfeit their lesson.

Whether he teaches in a school, camp, club, or hacking stable, or whether he has his own establishment, the riding instructor should plan his program carefully. The more carefully organized his pro-gram, the smoother it will run, the better impression he will make, and the fewer will be the problems which are bound to present them-selves.

Obtaining Community Support

A well-organized and thought-out program is particularly important for the instructor who is in the process of starting up a school of his own or of taking over one that has already been started and may not have been too popular. In going to interview parents, heads of schools, or organized groups, the instructor should be prepared to tell in detail what he proposes to teach and what his goals are. He should stress the value of riding as a sport, its relation to health and character training. He should direct his discussion to the particular audience. A group of cub scouts will be interested in learning about the horses and ponies, how they will be taught to take care of them, how they will learn to play games on them and go on trail rides. Older boys and girls will be interested in a discussion of more advanced riding, competitions, showing, and overnight rides. Parents will want to know about the safety factor, the cost, and required equipment, as well as the ways their children will benefit by learning to ride. In their case, the instructor might read a prepared lesson plan and discuss the danger of allowing children to go to hacking stables and take out horses on their own before being properly taught.

The impression the riding instructor makes at these interviews is all-important, and it is up to the instructor to present himself in as good a light as possible. Once the school has started or the instructor has begun his duties at the club or camp, he must make every effort to make this first season a successful one. It is at this time that he sets his standards and it is by this first season's work that he will be judged.

Needed Mounts and Equipment

For the instructor starting a new school, certain minimum equipment is necessary. First, he must of course have suitable mounts. Bearing in mind the number of pupils he will have and the number he must be able to mount at a time, he starts looking for his horses or ponies. Auction sales and private sales are advertised in the horse papers and the sports sections of the Sunday newspapers. Inquiring of veterinarians will sometimes provide a good lead. As soon as it is known that he is in the market for horses, the instructor will be besieged by people who have horses to sell. He should have every animal he buys checked by a veterinarian, and if possible, he should arrange to have all animals on trial for at least a few days. If this is not possible, he should take an experienced child along when he goes to try out a horse to be sure that it will be manageable. The buyer should look first for gentleness, good stable manners, and above all, willingness, letting looks come last. Animals that are suited to the size of the children to be taught should be purchased. A young animal in bad condition can sometimes be bought cheaply and brought back into condition fairly quickly, but there is no use buying a horse over fourteen years old that is too run down. Getting him into shape will take too long a time. Good mouths are important as well as willingness to respond to the leg aids. Animals that are too heavy on the forehand or those that will not take a flat-footed walk and a quiet trot should be by passed. No horse is perfect, but certain undesirable traits are easier to cope with than others.

Some sort of stable is necessary. In warm climates, a three-sided shed with stall partitions can be used. In cold climates, a good tight building is necessary. If any remodeling is to be done, the placing of the various units such as watering trough, tack room, and feed should be planned carefully to save steps. Stable tools will be needed as well as grooming tools.

Every horse should have his own saddle and bridle. Army bridles, though not pretty, are perfectly satisfactory and very inexpensive. Second-hand saddles are good, but the instructor should be careful in selecting them to see that those chosen will fit the horse and put the rider in a good position.

A paddock into which a sick horse or one which has not had enough exercise can be turned is very important. If pastures are available, they must be well fenced. Some sort of ring is most important. A very satisfactory type is one with an area about ninety by two hundred feet. A second fence built to form a track around the one which encloses the ring, and about thirty feet from it, will be very valuable, but it is not absolutely necessary. European instructors prefer a ring with square corners so that pupils can learn to ride out the corners, but most American rings have curved corners.

An indoor riding hall will more than triple the income of a school, and if sufficient funds are available, it should certainly be constructed. It should not be narrower than sixty feet—seventy is better. Its length should be a multiple of its width. It should have plenty of light, a gallery for visitors, and both an in and an out gate.

As time goes on, the instructor can add improvements to his plant in the way of jumping and hunt courses, dressing rooms, etc. Everything should be built with an eye to the future, and with the thought that a plant that is well constructed of good materials will pay in the long run.

Appendix A

Mounting and Dismounting

Position

Head up and not bent to side.

Eyes straight ahead or, in jumping courses and those requiring sharp turns, the rider should look where he plans to go.

Shoulders erect but relaxed, not slouching or stiff.

Chest raised.

Loin supple, relaxed but elevated.

Arms bent at elbows, elbows in front of hips, arms close to body but not pressed on body, straight line from elbow to bit seen both from the side and from above. In correcting horse or executing certain movements line may be broken upwards but never downwards.

Hands held at about 30 degrees inside the vertical, six to ten inches apart. Fingers hold reins lightly and only close tightly when used actively to rate or turn the horse.

Upper body angled very slightly forward from hips at halt, jog trot, and slow canter, considerably more at posting trot, gallop, and jump.

Arms, shoulders, elbows, wrists, and fingers always relaxed and following movement of horse except when purposely resisting.

Rider sits on forward part of pelvic bones, not on fleshy part of buttocks, in center or lowest part of saddle.

Knee is pushed down toward point of horse's shoulder.

Lower leg is so angled that point of knee and toe are in a line.

Stirrup tread is on ball of foot. Foot is against inside of stirrup, any extra stirrup being to outside of foot.

Ankle is relaxed and broken inward so that stirrup tread is angled and a person standing on ground can see bottom of tread.

Heel is below toe but is held in this position by weight of rider, not by having feet braced down.

Rider's ear, hip and ankle bone should be in a vertical line. Inside knee bone should always remain in contact with saddle but it should be held there not by grip but by correct position of knee and rotation of thighs.

Inside calf from knee to halfway down boot is normally in light contact but is only squeezed to urge horse forward or to maintain seat in emergency.

Feet are angled according to natural build of rider, should be from twenty to forty degree angle from perpendicular axis of horse's body. Turning toes out too far puts back of rider's calf against horse and pushes knees away from saddle. Turning toes in pushes knees out and pushes heels out. Position of lower legs and feet is governed by rotation of thigh at hip.

Relaxation in all parts of the body but without slumping is most important element to be considered as it allows rider to feel what horse is doing under him and to use his aids lightly.

The rider's balance must adjust itself to the movements of the horse so that he is with his horse at all times.

Feel

Through his own body the rider learns to feel what the horse is doing and what he is about to do.

Interpretation

From experience and instruction the rider learns to interpret what he feels.

Influence (control)

From his experience he learns to control and influence his horse. There are many types of control needed and some of them are listed below in the order in which they are usually taught.

Put the horse into motion.

Stop the horse.

Turn the horse.

Rate the horse (change his rate of speed within the gait) and go from one gait to another.

Back the horse.

Schooling movements in order given in this book.

Control the horse in company so that the rider can maintain his distances and ride in formation.

Ride toward or away from a group at a designated rate and gait.

Control the horse in a group of riders to the extent that the rider of the individual horse decides on the direction, gait and rate that his horse takes regardless of what the other riders are doing.

School a green horse and reschool a badly trained horse.

Control the horse on the approach, flight, and landing in jumping.

On-the-Ground Control

This must include leading and general handling, may include longeing, and long-rein driving.

Stable Management

Grooming
Feeding and watering
General stable routine
Stable and shipping bandages
Treatment of minor illnesses and injuries
Knowledge of how a shoe should be fitted
Care of tack and stable equipment

General Knowledge

Colors of horses
Terminology of tack and points of horse
Tests for soundness
Selection of horses
Types and breeds and their purposes

In addition to the above fundamentals, riders may be taught hunting procedure and etiquette, showing, and other principles.

Appendix B

SAMPLE LESSON PLANS

LESSON PLAN FOR BASIC CLASSES

This is a lesson plan for Basic Classes, children eight to ten. It is the first lesson. The instructor is on foot; one assistant is on foot,

Appendix

one mounted. Grooms are present to help with adjusting stirrups and mounting if possible. Barred-off area is to be used. Baskets serve as markers on the side. Mounted demonstrations are to be given by assistant, instructor explaining and pointing out what she is doing.

Subject	Explanation and Steps with Demonstration	Time
Leading horse	Position of rider	1½ minutes
	Left side of horse, right hand six inches from bit, holding all reins, eyes front. Demonstrate how horse stops when leader turns to look or halts himself. Instructor to demonstrate this. Four foot distance important and why.	
	Practice by students, halting and leading forward again on command. Four foot distance must be continually checked. Horses halted at end and turned to face center.	4 minutes
Mounting	Explanation and steps with assistant demonstrating.	3 minutes
	Pull down left stirrup, walk around head, pull down right stirrup. Walk back around head, face shoulder. Let down left stirrup leather so rider can reach stirrup. (Many will need help to open buckle.) Take buckle of rein in right hand, slide left hand on two reins down to withers. Let go right hand. Face rear, left hip on horse's left shoulder. Hold stirrup with right hand. Put foot in stirrup, grasp pommel, spring up on stirrup, carry right foot over, and settle quietly.	

Mounting	Practice for riders	4 minutes if done only once

Repeat explanation as riders go through process step by step together. Wait until all have completed each step before going to next. Give commands such as, "Let down left stirrup, *now*. Walk around head and let down right stirrup *now*," etc. Assistants should help with lengthening buckles and give a boost if necessary, but do not give hand up without rider's toe in stirrup. If class is agile and most can mount without help or if there are enough helpers, riders can be taught to dismount at once and can remount again. This will give confidence and make riders agile but if class is too full of small ones, do not spend time on this now but give instruction in dismounting at end of lesson.

Dismounting	Explanation, demonstration.	1 minute

Assistant to demonstrate steps.

Commands

Prepare to dismount, reins in left hand, right hand on pommel, left hand on mane, right foot out of stirrup.

Dismount . . . One

Right foot over, stand in stirrup.

Two . . .

Left foot out of stirrup, arms and knees straight, click heels.

Three . . .

Push away from saddle and drop to ground.

Practice by pupils with commands.	½ minute

	Remount with commands.	1½ minutes
Adjustment of Stirrups	Demonstration and explanation. Assistant to demonstrate.	1½ minutes

Measure stirrups first, feet out.
Feet back in. Little weight on stir-
rups.
Position of hand on leather.
Eyes up.

(If enough helpers, omit this lesson but have assistants and groom
adjust stirrups for riders. This instruction to be given next lesson.)

5 minutes

Position of Rider in Saddle	Steps and Demonstration.	1½ minutes

Eyes.
Back.
Place of buttocks on saddle.
Hands and reins (include adjust-
ing length of reins).
Legs.
Feet.

	Practice and exercises by pupils.	2 minutes

Raise hands over head to
straighten back.
Reach for stirrups, eyes up.
Say "I have them."
Stand in stirrups, eyes up, knuckles
on pommel.
Sit down. Repeat from beginning
once.

Walking	Steps and Demonstration	1½ minutes

Moving horse forward.
Body inclination.
Squeeze legs.
Follow with hands.

Halting horse.
Raise hands slightly.
Open and close fingers.
Shoulders back.

Turning horse on track, active leading hand.

Practice by pupils.   3 minutes
Mounted assistant to be in lead.
Other assistant on foot, opposite
end of ring from instructor, helps
to keep riders out. Make corrections of position only if horse is
not moving out or going too fast.
Horses to halt each time column
completes circuit of ring and
move out again. Give directions
for halting as riders halt and for
moving out as riders move out.
After three minutes riders halt,
face center, drop stirrups and
stretch legs and hands.

Exercises at walk   3 minutes

Commands, 1st Exercise

Drop stirrups now.
Look up at ceiling.
Look down on ground.
Say hello behind you.
Look up at ceiling.
Catch stirrups, say, "I have them."

(Repeat three times)

Commands, 2nd exercise

Drop reins . . now reach both
hands up, high as possible, look
up. Bring arms down relaxed.
Pick up reins and adjust.

(Repeat three times)

Commands, 3rd Exercise   3 minutes

Reins in one hand . . . now. Extend other hand in front and look
at it. Over head and look at it.
Wave, smile, and say hello to per-

378

son behind. (Instructor to do movements with riders.)

Repeat three times. Change direction and repeat three times, use change of hands for change of direction.

Trotting Explanation and Demonstration 3½ minutes

Class halted and facing center.

Instructor shows posting exercise on ground. Riders try it while horse is standing.

Assistant demonstrates posting on horse, first posting, then sitting, then posting. Riders copy movements, instructor calling, "up . . . down" in rhythm. Riders to hold saddle, manes, or neck straps.

Practice 10 minutes

Riders take track at walk following assistant. Practice standing in saddle for three steps at time. Then practice posting at walk, instructor calling rhythm and making individual corrections. If unsuccessful with most of class, have them stand at walk for longer periods.

When all can post at walk, instructor says, "Prepare to trot," and cautions, "Take hold of saddle." "Trot . . . now . . . up . . . down . . . up . . . down."

Class should trot halfway around ring, then walk on command, pat horses, relax, and rest.

Repeat, length of trot without resting will depend on ability of class. Make continual individual corrections of those who have not got rhythm as each passes you. Rest and walk at frequent intervals. If class finds this too difficult you will have to go back to walk and practice posting at that gait.

Last ten minutes of period	*Riders at walk.* Review of use of leading, active hand to steer, change hands twice by way of practice. Drop stirrups and relax legs. Emphasis on following, relaxed reins. If class is not relaxed but seems tense still, begin discussion of colors of horse and name those in ring. Get riders to point out horses of same color and tell what *color* horse they are riding. Review halting.	5 minutes
	Riders at halt. Face center. Review or give instruction in dismounting. Riders dismount on commands. Put up stirrups (give demonstration and instruction). Lead horses once around, check four foot distance. Emphasis on not looking at horse while walking. End with "See you next time."	5 minutes

LESSON PLAN FOR INTERMEDIATE CLASSES

This is a lesson plan for an Intermediate Class. The instructor is on foot. The assistants are on foot until the riders are mounted.

Movements	*Steps and Explanations*	*Time*
Horses led into ring, halted, and faced to center.	Corrections on leading four foot distance emphasized.	3 minutes
Mounting	Riders told to mount in unison on command.	5 minutes

Appendix

Commands

Pull stirrups down (caution not to let
go rein and to move around head of
horse) *Prepare to mount* . . .

> Let left stirrup leather down if
> necessary. Face shoulder, pick up,
> and adjust reins. Hold stirrup with
> right hand, put toe in.
> *Mount. . . . One*
> > spring up on ball of foot, arms
> > straight.
>
> *Two* Carry right leg across well
> above rump.
>
> *Three* Sink gently into saddle.
>
> *Adjust stirrups.*

Notes

Assistants and grooms to give a boost
if necessary and to help younger
ones with stiff buckles but no more
help given than absolutely essential.
Check length of stirrups. If some
pupils are very slow, they can finish
adjustment of stirrups in center of
ring while class walks around them,
but try and get all moving out together.

Walking

Commands and explanations   5 minutes

Take track at walk, four foot distance.

> Drop stirrups and reins.
> Stretch up as high as you can.
> Bring arms down relaxed.
> Pick up reins and adjust.
> Look up at ceiling, down at
> ground, say hello to person behind
> you, looking over left shoulder,
> over right shoulder.

*Look up at ceiling.
Catch stirrups while looking up, say, "I have them."
Repeat* twice.
Resting fingers or knuckles on withers, stand in stirrups at walk and balance.
Give explanation while riders practice this of how stirrups should hang.
Check body and leg position.
Sit down, drop stirrups, let reins be stretched out and rest. Pat your horse. While pupils are riding at ease, give explanation of army commands. (Command of preparation such as "trot" tells you what to do and to get ready for it, command of execution, "now" or "ho" tells when.)

Trotting

Commands and Explanations   3 minutes
Preparation, questions while riders are walking.

What do all riders do first in preparing to trot? (Shorten reins)
Why? (Horses hold heads higher)
What does rider do to make horse trot? (Inclines body slightly forward from hips, squeezes legs, follows with hands, eyes up.)
Reminder . . . When I say, "trot" shorten your reins, when I say, "ho," take up the trot.

Trot . . . (Check to see if reins   7 minutes
are all shortened, riders and horses alert) If any start before "ho" get them walking before giving the command.

Ho . . . If class can all post, they can all continue several times around the ring while instructor makes individual position or hand corrections.

After 3½ minutes (length of phonograph record) command is *Walk . . .* ho.

Change hands

Trot (Caution riders to get ready to trot but not to start until the word "ho.") *Ho.*

Riders trot 3½ minutes in this direction. If any cannot post at all they should be pulled into the center of the ring during first trotting period. When riders change hands those who need help may be sent out with an assistant to work on posting at a halt and walk as given in basic lesson. If basic lesson has not been given, assistant should be briefed on this before advanced lesson begins. Do not separate class unless absolutely necessary.

Halt

Exercises and Explanations to Teach Active and Following Hands.   5 minutes

Riders brought to halt on command after second trotting period as described above. Told to rest and relax, drop stirrups, pat horses, allow them to go on floating rein as reward. While riders are walking at ease, give explanation of following and active hand, using belt or strap to demonstrate. Ask when each is used. What to do with weight and legs as these hands are used? When does use of active hand cease? (As soon as horse *begins* to obey.) Draw attention to movement of horse's head at a walk. Have riders pick up reins and adjust length, watching movement of head and trying to follow it with hands. Have riders halt on command, using active hand, horses to be halted at four foot distance, bodies on track. Repeat three times.

Jog trot

Commands

5 minutes with frequent walking periods.

Drop stirrups. Rest ends of little fingers on withers.
jog trot. . . . *ho.*
Trot once around only. Then walk and explain why relaxation is necessary. If class is very stiff, borrow horse and demonstrate how stiffening thigh muscles and loin causes rider to bounce and makes horse uncomfortable so that he goes too fast. Use example of hard and soft balls to make picture clear. Ask questions if possible. Repeat jog trot and watch for improvement. Make individual corrections. Draw attention to any rider who is doing particularly well. Stop jog as soon as any rider looks very uncomfortable or horses get out of hand. End by saying (while class is at a walk), look up at ceiling, catch stirrups and say, "I have them."

Walking

Relaxation of elbows at trot to improve hands.

3 minutes

Commands and Explanations with demonstration.
This is given while class is walking. Instructor takes position on

Appendix

ground as though riding. Posts and
show how hands go up and down.
Then demonstrates straightening
elbows. Class touches little fingers
to withers and practices at walk.
Ask questions as much as possible.

Trotting

Practice at trot, fingers touching
ing withers. Remind riders to use
active hand when coming down
to walk. End with command,
"Walk and Rest."

3 minutes
in each di-
rection with
change of
hands at
walk.

*Explanation and demonstration of
leading rein effect.*

Explanation, having assistant ride
circle using leading rein, and
drawing attention to horse's head
and neck, outside leg to be applied, hand to be carried forward,
to the side, and used actively.

3 minutes

Trotting

Riders practice at a trot, riding
on large circle following each
other at four foot distance. Make
position corrections as well as rein
effect corrections. Return to walk
and walk at ease ½ minute.

*Trotting with
hands on waist*

Commands

Take reins very long in outside
hand, leader to keep reins in normal position. All except leader
put both hands on waist. Trot
. . . *ho.* Use only your outside
hand to control horse if he cuts in,
do not take your inside hand off
your waist.

3½ minutes

Walking

Walk last five minutes. Explain
why one always walks the first and
last five minutes of each period.
Make mental or written notes of

385

outstanding riders or those not up to this group. Check with assistant on assignment of horses for next time with these riders in mind.

Appendix C

NATIONAL HORSE SHOWS ASSOCIATION
RULES AND SCORING

TABLE OF PENALTIES, OPEN JUMPERS

Touch with any part of the horse's body behind the stifle....½ fault
Touch with any part of horse's body in front of stifle........1 fault
Touch of standard or wing in jumping obstacle without
    touching obstacle ....1 fault
Knockdown with any part of horse's body behind stifle......2 faults
Knockdown with any part of horse's body in front of stifle....4 faults
Landing in water or ditch jump, knocking down obstacle
    placed before, over, or beyond water or ditch with hind
    foot ....2 faults
Same as above with forefoot...........................4 faults
Placing any foot in a Liverpool.......................4 faults
First disobedience (run-out, refusal, circle)...............3 faults
Second disobedience ....6 faults
Third disobedience ....Elimination

Note

Disobediences are cumulative throughout the course except in children's equitation classes when the judges may allow two refusals at each obstacle before elimination. Same is true in Maiden, Novice and Limit Classes. The third refusal at any one obstacle means elimination.

Fall of horse and/or rider..........................Elimination
Jumping obstacle before it is reset..................Elimination
Showing horse any obstacle after entering ring or after a
    refusal ....Disobedience
Starting before starting signal......................Elimination

GENERAL RULES

After entering ring, competitor may make one circle at any gait. After that any such circle, unless necessary after a runout or refusal to get back on course, is a disobedience.

Appendix

Horse must maintain forward movement at walk, trot, or canter. Failure to do so constitutes a disobedience.

Elimination trials.

Where entries warrant, elimination trials may be held. The scores of the horses selected by these trials are kept and added to their final scores to determine the winner.

Jumper Class Specifications

MAIDEN JUMPERS, open to horses who have not won a
blue in this division in an open show............Jumps 3'6"
NOVICE JUMPERS, open to horses not having won 3
blues ....Jumps 3'6" or 3'9"
LIMIT JUMPERS, open to horses not having won 6 blues..Jumps 4'
OPEN JUMPERS...........................Jumps at 4' or 4'6"
JUMPERS RIDDEN BY AMATEURS........Jumps at 3'9" or 4'
KNOCK-DOWN-AND-OUT ....Jumps at 4' or 3'6"
TOUCH-AND-OUT ....Jumps at 4' or 4'6"
HANDY JUMPERS......Jumps at 3'6" or 4' or 4'6", horse to be
judged on handiness within a specified time limit. All seconds
over time limit to be added to jumping faults.
SCURRY JUMPERS......Jumps at 3'6", 4', or 4'6". Judged on
time plus jumping faults.
FIVE FOOT CLASS...............................Jumps at 5'
HIGH JUMP......Jumps start at 4'6". Only one jump is set up
and a horse is allowed three tries at each new height. The third
refusal eliminates.
TRIPLE BAR......Three bars at 3', 4', and 4'6" spread to start
at 6'. Each horse allowed three tries at each spread, third refusal
or shy-out eliminates.
BAREBACK CLASS......Jumps at 3'6" or 4'. Performance 100%
or performance 50%, horsemanship 50%.

For general definitions, see F. E. I. Rules.

EQUITATION CLASSES

Equitation classes are in three divisions, Saddle Horse seat, Hunting Seat or Stock Saddle Seat. The entry blank must show which seat is called for. Sometimes a Military Seat is asked for.

The National Horse Shows Association rule book gives a general definition of the seats but it is not specific enough to eliminate what we know to be incorrect position. Until the 1950 rule book came out, no distinction was made between the hunter and the saddle seats although the two seats were mentioned. The 1951 rule book states that in the "hunter" seat the stirrups are shorter. It can be seen from this that no really correct analysis of the seats has been incorporated into this book. Until such a careful analysis is made, the riders will continue to be judged on the preference of the judges.

Appendix D

F. E. I. RULES

TABLE OF PENALTIES USED IN JUMPING COMPETITIONS

First disobedience (refusal, shy-out, circle) ....3 faults
Second disobedience ....6 faults
Third disobedience ....Elimination

Note

Faults are cumulative, rider is eliminated on third disobedience anywhere in round.
Knockdown, front or hind feet or body of horse............4 faults
Landing on marking tape in water jump or one foot or one
    or more feet in water between obstacle and tape........4 faults
Fall of horse or rider or both..........................8 faults
Any horse resisting for more than sixty seconds anywhere on
    course (rearing, refusing to go forward, balking, etc.) Any
    horse taking more than sixty seconds to take any jump.
    Any horse taking more than sixty seconds to pass starting
    line ....Elimination
Knocking over boundary flag ....4 faults
Jumping obstacle that has been knocked over before it is reset
    and not waiting for starting signal...............Elimination
Horse leaving ring mounted or loose..................Elimination
Showing any obstacle to the horse before the start or after
    a refusal, starting before signal, jumping one or more ob-
    stacles before start, jumping obstacle out of proper se-
    quence, jumping obstacle before rectifying error in
    course, jumping obstacle not forming part of course Elimination
Exceeding time allowed for course............¼ fault start of each
                                            overtime second

Note

Courses are timed and above penalty is exacted up to end of time limit.
Exceeding time limit......... ....Elimination

Appendix

Note

Time limit is double time allowed.
Failing to retake all jumps in doubles, triples, or multiples
after refusal, run-out, or fall at any element of these
.... Elimination
Failure to jump each element of a multiple jump separately
.... Elimination

TABLE OF PENALTIES FOR HUNTING COMPETITIONS

In hunting competitions (cross country against time) the penalties are translated into seconds as follows:
Obstacle knocked over ....10 seconds
First and second disobediences, and falls are penalized automatically by the elapsing of time.
Third disobedience ....Elimination
All Elimination penalties concerning correctness of courses, etc. in above table for open jumping hold for hunting courses done on time.

In certain cross-country competitions, riders may choose their own courses and must only pass between marking flags placed ten yards on the near side and fifteen yards on the far side of each obstacle that must be taken. Disobediences of any kind not within the areas of these flags are not penalized except automatically by the lapse of time.

For certain events, specified rates of speed must be maintained. These are as follows:

Puissance ....300 metres per minute

Note

A "puissance" competition is one in which all the straight jumps in the course except the first are a minimum of four feet seven inches. The course usually consists of 6 to 8 fences, one of them a double which counts as one obstacle. In event of a tie for first place only, there is a jump-off over a reduced number of obstacles which have been raised or increased in width. Penalty table is as for open jumping competitions and time except where competitor exceeds time limit is not counted.

Hunting competitions....................350 metres per minute
Jumping competitions ....350 metres per minute
Cross country..........................450 metres per minute
Steeplechases ....600 metres per minute

Over roads and tracks . . . . as designated
Prix des Nations and Grand Prix at Olympic Games
. . . . 400 metres per minute

For all F. E. I. events, the time for the course is estimated on the above table and posted with the course. In jumping and cross-country competitions, double the time allowed is the time limit. Any horse taking longer than this is eliminated. In some F. E. I. competitions, the horse completing the course in the shortest time with *the fewest faults* is the winner. A horse with no faults beats a horse with a shorter time but with faults. Sometimes no credit is given for a shorter time except in a jump-off.

Only ties for first place have jump-offs. In ties for lower places, the competitors tying are both awarded the place.

OUTSIDE ASSISTANCE

Any rider in either a class in the arena or a cross-country or outside course class receiving outside assistance intended to help him is *eliminated*. This includes advice, physical assistance, information as to time elapsed, etc. Outside assistance does *not* include catching a runaway horse after a fall and assisting the rider to mount.

DEFINITIONS

Knockdowns. An obstacle is considered knocked down when any part or the whole of it falls, thus lowering its height. This includes one end of a bar falling, or a bar falling and being caught on another before touching the ground. It also includes the knocking down of any part of the supporting structure. Displacements and touches which do not change the height of the jump or of its structure are not counted. When more than one bar or element of either a straight jump or a spread jump consisting of several elements, all of which must be taken at one jump, are displaced and fall, only one penalty (four faults) is given.

Falls. A rider is considered to have fallen when he is separated from his horse which has not fallen and must remount.

A horse is considered to have fallen when the shoulder and quarters on the same side have touched either the ground or the obstacle and the ground.

In the event of a fall of horse or rider in refusing or in knocking down an obstacle, the penalty for the fall (8 faults) is added to the penalty of the knockdown or refusal.

If a competitor is eliminated, he has the privilege of taking *two*

Appendix

more jumps before leaving the ring provided he does not spend more than 60 seconds on each. If he takes more than two jumps after being blown out, he is liable to a fine of $10, American money.

Appendix E

THE OLYMPIC GAMES

The value of athletic competition, which in turn stimulated the development of the sound and beautiful body, was considered as important by the Greeks of early times as the development of the mind. Contests in which Spartan youths took part became very popular and were held at various places. These contests had a religious significance and were always held in honor of specific Gods.

The greatest of these games were the Olympic Games, held at Olympia every fourth year at the time of the first full moon after the summer solstice. The first Olympic Games on record were held about 884 B.C. and continued without interruption until 393 A.D., a period of 1,277 years! In 395 A.D. they were abolished by the Roman emperor Theodosius.

Representatives from many cities competed in these games which, beginning with only a few competitions in foot races, gradually increased to a number and variety of contests which included types of chariot competitions, and racing on horseback was among them. For a month a sacred truce was declared at Olympia and no armed person was permitted to enter. Also the different cities competing had short truce periods to enable their contestants to go safely to and from Olympia. It can thus be seen that the Olympic Games stood for peace in addition to providing an opportunity for peoples of different cities, often at war with each other, to meet on a friendly basis.

Only Greeks by birth were permitted to compete in the games. Women were not allowed to compete and were not even permitted to view the events. The winner received an olive wreath, a palm branch, and the right to erect a statue in the Altis. But although he did not receive any pecuniary award, he was a hero for life and often received special privileges reserved for such heroes.

Chariot racing was introduced in the twenty-fifth Olympiad (680 B.C.). Four full grown horses to a chariot were used. The length of the course was 1,325 feet with a sharp turn at each end. This course had to be run through from one to twelve times, depending on the regulations. Twelve times was the equivalent of three miles.

Racing on horseback was introduced in 648 B.C. at the thirty-

391

third Olympiad. A combination foot race and horse race called the Kalpe, in which mares only were used is described in which on the last lap of the race the rider had to dismount and lead in past the winning post.

The revival of the Olympic Games is largely due to the efforts of Baron Pierre de Coubertin. He founded the International Olympic Committee in 1894 and the first modern Olympic Games were held in Athens two years later.

Baron de Coubertin felt that by means of these games it would be possible to stimulate and encourage in youth a desire for physical fitness, so that they would set high standards of courage and endurance; also that nations of the world would benefit by a spreading of good will. Baron de Coubertin was interested above all in the development of the sporting spirit as opposed to the "cup-hunting" spirit. He said, "The important thing in the Olympic Games is not winning but taking part, for the essential thing in life is not so much conquering as fighting well."

The first games did not include equestrian events but these were introduced in 1912. There was still a great deal of lack of uniformity among nations in definitions of dressage movements, scoring of dressage and jumping competitions, etc., and these differences led to a great deal of dissatisfaction. In 1921 the Fédération Equestre Internationale (F.E.I.) was founded and this board has since formed international rules which have done away with the former disagreements.

The booklet of statutes and General Regulations pertaining to the Olympic Games put out by the F.E.I. comprises some 144 pages. It is naturally not possible to include here all of these regulations but the following will be of interest. In another chapter of the appendix, the scoring tables are given for jumping competitions.

In most equitation competitions amateurs only are eligible. This is true of all the competitions in the Olympic Games but contests in which professionals may compete under F.E.I. rules are part of nearly all other international competitions.

To date (1951) ladies may compete only in the Grand Prix (Dressage) competition.

All riders in international competitions, whether amateur or professional, are issued licenses by the F.E.I. These licenses may be withdrawn without explanation at any time.

Horses may not be more than fifteen years of age. A horse is considered to be in his first year from the date of his birth until December 31st of that year. On the first of January he becomes a two-year-old.

Thus a horse born in May 1950 is a two-year-old, technically speaking, on January 1st 1951.

Equestrian events in the Olympic Games include the individual dressage competitions, the individual and team jumping competitions, and the Three-day Event. The Prix des Nations is an individual and team competition over jumps. Each nation enters four riders and four horses. The course comprises thirteen to fourteen obstacles necessitating between sixteen and twenty jumps. The height can vary between one metre 30 and one metre 60. The course must include a water jump at least four metres wide.

The teams are classified by taking the scores in jumping faults and time faults of the three best horses of each team and totaling them.

The individual is classified by totaling the time and jumping faults of each horse.

Appendix F

THE VERMONT TRAIL RIDE

The Green Mountain Horse Association sponsors a splendid event known as the Vermont Hundred Mile Ride. It is held each year during the first week of September. A route of a hundred miles is laid out, through the winding, hilly trails of the Vermont countryside. Sixty riders are accepted. Forty miles must be ridden the first day, forty the second, and twenty the third. Horses of any type, size, or breed are eligible. Winners are placed according to performance and condition of the animal at the end of the ride. Trophies are also given for horsemanship.

A fifty mile, "pleasure" ride is held for those who do not wish to take the longer ride.

The purposes of this ride are: to demonstrate the value of type and soundness and the proper selection of horses for a long ride; to learn and demonstrate the proper method of training and conditioning for such a ride; to encourage horsemanship in long distance riding and to train and demonstrate the best methods of caring for the horse during and after the ride.

The conditions of the ride are as follows:

Eligibility

Open to mares, stallions or geldings, any breed. Entries to be made on blanks provided and must be filed with the Green Mountain Horse Association, Rutland, Vermont, not later than August 10th. At only sixty horses can be accepted it is wise to get the entries in as early as possible. All horses must be at the Woodstock Inn by 2 p.m. the day preceding the ride and will be stabled there for the ride.

An entry fee of twenty-five dollars will be charged for each horse and will be returned if the horse is withdrawn before August 10th.

The entry fee covers the cost of the feed and stabling of the horses during the ride, the day preceding and the day following the ride, the rider's lunches on Thursday and Friday, the breakfast lunches at the lunch stops, a banquet on Wednesday, a dance on Friday night, and the big farewell supper on Saturday night.

Officials

The officials, selected by the Board of Trustees of the Green Mountain Horse Association, will consist of two or more judges, one of whom shall be a veterinarian, a recorder, route master, farrier, watchman, and weigher.

The Recorder records officially the findings of the judges, weigher, and veterinarian during the ride and files them with the Board of Sponsors after the ride.

The Weigher superintends the taking of all official weighing and measuring during the ride and shall do so in front of at least one judge.

The Veterinarian examines the horses prior to the official examination by the judges and makes a record of any blemishes or defects, which he reports to the judges at their examination. He may also recommend that any horse which in his opinion is not fit for the ride or which, during the ride, shows lack of ability to finish, be withdrawn. Such a recommendation disqualifies the horse.

The Farrier sets or replaces shoes at feeding stations and along the road as far as possible. No charge is made for his services. Bar or three quarter shoes are permitted, no limitation being put on weight, toe or heel clips or number of nails used, but no type of pad is permitted. Contestants may do their own shoeing or hire an outside farrier if they wish.

A Watchman is on duty at night and no contestant is permitted in the stable between the hours of 9 p.m. and 5 a.m.

The Course

The Course is laid out by the route master. The Ride will take place regardless of weather. The course is plainly marked and all contestants must follow it.

Appendix

Judging

Preliminary judging begins at 2 p.m. on the day preceding the ride. Actual judging begins at 6 a.m. the day of the ride and ends when the prizes are awarded by the judges. Awards and placings are made 60% for condition and 40% for time.

Condition

Horses will be examined and measured at the beginning of the judging. All faults, blemishes, and unsoundnesses noted by the judges and the veterinarian or claimed by the contestant and allowed by the judges shall be recorded. Horses considered unfit for the ride can be disqualified at this time. Final judgment will be based on observation throughout the ride but especially at the end of the ride. Each horse is given a credit of 60 points at the beginning and no horse may leave the judging ring at the finish of the ride until the awards are made, except as directed by the judges.

Speed

Contestants start between 6:30 and 7:30 a.m. each morning of the ride unless the judges feel that the weather is such that an earlier start is better. Time on the road is reckoned from "Check out" in the morning to "Check in" at the finish of each day's ride. The minimum time permitted in any day is seven hours, the maximum is eight. Horses may be held up on the road for observation by the judges at any time but the time elapsed during such observation will be recorded and credited to the time of that horse. Horses going over the time limit will be disqualified. The maximum score in points for time for the seventeen hours is 40 points. For every three minutes consumed over the minimum time the horse will be penalized one "time" point. Those finishing not more than ten minutes less than the minimum time will be allowed to dismount and stable their horses without penalty.

Rider

No substitution of riders is allowed except in cases of sickness or accident when a written request must be made to the judges. If a substitute rider is permitted, the original rider may not re-enter the ring. Riders must remain in the saddle when the horse is moving forward but may dismount and rest at any time so long as the horse does not advance.

Care of Mounts

Each rider may have the help of one groom to care for his horse at the night station and is responsible for the conduct of the groom. Each rider must look after his own horse during the ride and may receive only slight assistance such as saddling or holding. The use of halters, clothes, saddle pads and ordinary grooming tools is permitted but no bandages or boots (horse). The use of hand rubbing and water at normal temperature is permitted but no liniments, salves, salt or any medication. In case of injuries the condition is reported to the judges and the veterinarian who treats the injury, the judges deducting from the score of the horse if they deem it proper.

Horses will not be allowed out of the stable before the start nor is it permissible to walk them up and down in the aisle to warm them up. They may be cooled out in a paddock behind the barn at the end of each day's ride but may not leave this area without permission from the judges.

Divisions

The horses will be divided into three divisions, lightweight, heavyweight and junior. The lightweight division comprises those horses which carry a minimum weight (rider and all tack) of 155 pounds and a maximum of 188 pounds. If rider and tack do not weigh 155 pounds the weight must be made up with dead weight. The heavyweight division is for horses carrying a total weight of 180 pounds or more. The junior division is for riders of from twelve to sixteen years of age inclusive. There is no weight restriction for them but they observe all the other rules of the ride.

Awards

Horsemanship awards are presented to the man and the woman considered to have shown the best horsemanship. Each junior completing the ride is presented a certificate grading him *A, B,* or *C.* An award for horsemanship is also presented to the junior showing the best knowledge of how to care for his horse.

The Pleasure Ride or Class B ride is not a competition. It is a fifty mile ride with horsemanship certificates presented to juniors completing it. One hundred entries will be accepted. A gymkhana is held the day after the ride and many types of events are enjoyed.

HINTS TO CONTESTANTS

Careful condition of both horse and rider is all-important. When one realizes that riders to hounds often cover as much as forty miles in a day with a long hack home afterwards, one understands that the Vermont Trail Ride is not a gruelling grind but a perfectly fair test of the condition to be expected from any rider and horse. Hard riding one or two days a week and then nothing for the rest of the week will not condition either the horse or the rider. Two hours a day of a well-balanced program including much work at the walk up and down hills, much work at the ordinary trot and at least fifteen minutes at the gallop—this fifteen minutes can be divided into two periods—is what is needed.

Careful and thorough grooming each day for several weeks before the ride and during the ride will do almost as much to condition the horse as the exercise recommended. Grooming stimulates the muscles and increases the circulation, thus relieving fatigue and enabling the horse to benefit from his rations as well as toughening his skin.

Sensible feeding including feeding at regular hours and a proper division of the feed ensures good digestion and good health.

Plenty of water at the right time is important. *Not* when the horse is overheated or blowing, not immediately after a heavy feed of grain, but all he wants at other times. Do not keep water away from your horse all night and then let him fill himself up the next morning, just before he starts the ride. Let him have all he wants to drink some time after the last feed, then refill the pail and leave it with him for the night.

Plenty of salt, either in block form or mixed with the feed.

On the trail walk the first mile out to warm the horse up slowly. Walk on the hills. Trot wherever able, but do not canter any more than necessary. In the trot change the diagonals frequently. In cantering change the lead. In resting a horse on a hill, stand him across the grade, not up and down it.

Watch your horse's feet! Pick them out carefully before leaving and inspect and pick them out at all rest stations.

Watch your tack to see that it is perfectly clean, especially any part of it that touches the horse. The girth should be smooth, clean, flexible, and comfortably loose. A good rider does not need a tight girth to balance. In mounting, hold the pommel of the saddle and the withers, neck, or mane so that the saddle is not pulled out of place. If you cannot mount without a tight girth, lean down and loosen it a hole or two after you are up. Your horse cannot breathe properly with a tight girth and he may develop girth sores. The girth must be so adjusted that it uses the same hole on each side of the billets. Don't have it way up on one side and down on the other. The bridle must

397

be correctly fitted with especial attention to the curb chain if one is worn. The throat lash should be loose. If the horse has flat ribs by all means wear a breast plate.

Your horse is probably not accustomed to bearing the weight of a rider for seven or eight successive hours for three days. He will be far less apt to develop tenderness, swellings or abrasions under the saddle if the following precautions are taken:

Do not ride more than ten minutes at any one gait.

At least once an hour dismount, loosen the girth, and lift the saddle for a few seconds to allow the air to get under it. Be sure the hair is lying flat both under the saddle and under the girth.

At the end of the ride loosen the girth and walk the horse with the saddle in place. This allows the circulation to come back slowly. After removing the saddle give the animal a thorough hand rubbing.

When you groom your horse at the end of the ride, pay particular attention to the following parts:

The base of the ears (use only your hand or a cloth).
Under the brisket, under the girth, all the saddle area.
Behind the pasterns. Be sure all mud is removed and that the area is rubbed dry.
The soles, frogs, clefts, etc. of the feet.
Under the tail and around the dock.
Inside the flanks.

To be sure that your horse is well groomed run your bare hand over every inch of him. This will also enable you to notice any minor injuries or heat.

Appendix G

DRESSAGE TESTS

As has been stated, the purpose of dressage training is to make the horse agreeable to ride. Being a foreign term, the word dressage has been a handicap in promoting interest since many people have misconceptions regarding its definition and its purpose. A horse is not trained in dressage movements solely in order that he may pass tests, but the tests are also useful in measuring his progress and in stimulating an interest in training the horse through competition.

The British Horse Society and the British Pony Club have instituted a series of competitions in horse shows under the title, "Best Trained Horse Tests" and "Best Trained Pony Tests." These tests are carefully graded and, like the Horsemastership Meets described in another part of this book, are so designed that the rider is encouraged

Appendix

to start with the simpler tests and bring his mount back time after time to show the progress in his schooling. The same tests can be used for both competitions (Best Trained Pony and Horsemastership Meets).

Below is a list of requirements for horses and ponies of different degrees of training.

Standard specifications for an arena with the standard markings is shown in Figure 161. It is not necessary that the arena be this exact size but for the advanced tests the length should be three times the width and for less advanced tests it should be twice the width.

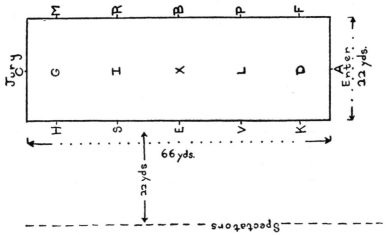

FIG. 161.   Arena marked for dressage competitions.

An enclosed arena is not necessary for dressage training and tests though it is a convenience. A level space with good footing is necessary. The side letters can be made of boxes or of blocks and either fastened to the posts or to stakes driven in the ground. The central letters can be marked on the ground with whitewash. In an enclosed arena the central letters can be overhead.

GENERAL RULES FOR DRESSAGE TESTS

Conformation does not count.

Lameness disqualifies.

Any weight rider is allowed.

Use a plain English saddle, either double bridle or snaffle bridle, if the latter is specified.

No boots, martingales, or whips allowed.

Competitors must memorize tests.

Every second or part of second over specified time limit is penalized ....½ point
Errors on course are penalized as follows:

> First time ....2 points
> Second time ....5 points
> Third time ....Elimination

In the event of a tie, judges may ask to have any movement repeated. For methods of judging dressage, see page 414.

Movements required in Novice Equitation are suitable for children or adults. This class is called Class N in the British tests, Class A in the Continental tests, Class C in the Horsemasterhip Meets. The tests are made up from the following movements in any order desired but usually starting with the slower and less difficult movements.

> Mount and dismount.
> Walk—ordinary and free walk on long rein.
> Trot—ordinary and slow (not collected).
> Canter—ordinary and strong.
> Transitions from a walk into a trot.
> "   "   "   " into a halt.
> "   "   a trot into a walk or canter.
> "   "   a canter into a trot.
> "   "   a halt into a walk.
> "   "   "   " into a rein-back.
> Rein back a given distance. (1, 2, or 3 yards. It can also be given in number of steps desired.)
> Half-circles and circles at all three paces.
> Change of rein (change hands) at all three paces.
> Turns on forehand.
> Jumping, from two to four fences, 2′ 6″ high or four feet wide may also be included.

Note. The novice horse is expected to be able to vary his speed under proper control at the trot and at the canter. At the trot, he should take an ordinary trot and one slightly slower but should not be asked to show true collection. The canter should include the ordinary canter and one slightly faster but need not show true extension.

In Elementary Equitation, snaffle bridle or double bridle is specified and all movements are performed with reins in both hands. Movements required in Elementary Equitation, known as Class E in the British tests, Class L in the Continental tests, and Class B or Light Dressage in the Horsemastership Meets, are, in addition to movements required for novices as follows:

Trot—slow, ordinary, strong.

Canter—slow, ordinary, strong, simple changes of leg (change of lead), counter-lead (false canter).

Transitions—from any pace to any other pace. From any pace into a halt and from a halt into any pace. From any pace into a rein-back and vice versa.

Circles, half-circles, change of lead (rein) on circles at all paces, serpentines.

Turns on haunches from the halt and from the walk.

Jumping may be included if desired, jump from two to four fences three feet high or six feet wide.

Note The elementary horse is expected to be able to vary his speed under proper control but not to show full collection or full extension.

Additional movements required for Medium Equitation, known as Class M, British; Class M, Continental; Class B or Intermediate Dressage, Horsemastership, are the following:

Walk—collected; extended; on two-tracks.

Trot—collected; extended; on two-tracks.

Canter—collected; extended; repeated changes of leg; counter-change on the circle.

Jumping—from two to four fences 3' 6" high or 8 feet wide

DRESSAGE TEST FOR YOUNG HORSES AND RIDERS

Enter at ordinary trot on the middle line

Full stop at center and salute

R. H. Ride on in ordinary walk on the right hand (halfway around the ring)

Middle of the next short side, trot on, ordinary trot (once around)

Cross the ring

L. H. Continue ordinary trot (halfway around)

Next two short sides, ordinary trot; two long sides, extended trot)

In the middle of the short side, full stop

Trot on, ordinary trot, on the circle and develop ordinary canter (twice around the circle)

Ordinary trot (on the circle)

Change out the circle

R. H. On the circle and develop ordinary canter (twice around the circle)

Ordinary trot, then straight ahead

Posting trot, (once around)

Sitting trot, and change direction through the middle line

L. H. Continue sitting trot (halfway around); down the middle line

Full stop in the center of the ring and salute

R. H. Free extended walk without reins (halfway around)

One jump three feet high, taken in both directions

Note. Rider should sit to the trot except where otherwise directed.

For definitions of movements, consult the glossary of this book. For descriptions of movements and methods of training the horse and the rider, consult the index for page references.

Appendix H

BLOODHOUND HUNTING

Bloodhound hunting is not a substitute for fox hunting, but it can be used to teach children proper hunting etiquette and procedure and it can substitute, in areas where fox hunting is not feasible, for such activities as paper chases. Bloodhound hunting requires no great outlay of capital. One or two bloodhounds are all that are necessary. Bloodhounds, unlike foxhounds, are not dependent on the pack to keep to the line. Each hound hunts his own line and seldom loses it, so more than two hounds are unnecessary. If two hounds are used, they must have about the same natural rate of speed. For this reason two from the same litter are apt to work out best. If more hounds are available, they should be run in couples, one couple following the line until the first "fox" is found and then a fresh couple starting.

The hounds are very easily trained. If there is a trained hound available, it will only be necessary to run the green hounds once or twice with the old hound and they will immediately get the idea. If no old hound is available, the following is the procedure: Starting not younger than the age of three months, the hounds should be taught to come at a certain signal. It can be a hunting horn or, if no horn is available, a specific call or a whistle. Each time the pups are fed this call is given until they associate the call or horn with food. Next have one person hold the hounds while a second, first showing them the food, runs out of sight with it and then calls. The hounds

Appendix

are released and encouraged by the holder to pick up the scent and track. This they will do. It is only necessary now to increase the distance of the "line" until the hounds will track for five or ten minutes. The "fox" can now take to a horse. Again someone holds the hounds while the other person rides away calling or blowing the horn. The puppies will soon learn to follow his scent while he is mounted as readily as they did when he was on foot. When they are able to track for from fifteen minutes to a half-hour they can be taken hunting. The procedure is the same. The "fox" or "foxes" ride away, the hounds being restrained or taught to stay. After five or ten minutes of grace, they are released and put on the line by the huntsman. The huntsman should follow some little distance behind so as not to frighten them but beware of letting them get out of sight as bloodhounds can be as fast or faster than foxhounds and it is easy to lose them. While running, bloodhounds run with their heads up as the scent to them is breast high. They only drop their heads occasionally to check the line or if they are puzzled. They often run from fifty to a hundred yards off the actual line, picking up the scent through the air. They are not disturbed by water, hard roads, other animals, or attempts by the fox to fool them by circling. They will often take sudden short cuts through territory that is impassable to horses, so bloodhound hunting, contrary to ordinary opinion, is often very fast.

Bloodhounds are the gentlest of all breeds. On reaching the quarry they lick him delightedly and accept the worry in a most gentlemanly manner. In fact they are often so interested in the hunting that they don't bother to eat the worry!

Don't think you have to kennel your hounds. They can have the run of the place and still be keen to hunt.

Since it is rare that bloodhounds lose the scent, the only way of having a check is for the "fox" to stop. The bloodhounds then "run him to ground" and receive their worry. After a short run a new fox is chosen and the hunt is on again.

This sport is particularly recommended in territories where riding is restricted to certain trails and fields. People of every age participate and the various runs are adjusted to their capabilities and the capabilities of their mounts.

Appendix I

METHODS OF JUDGING EQUITATION AND
HORSEMANSHIP JUMPING CLASSES

One of the most unsatisfactory situations in the horse show world today is the generally accepted method of judging equitation and horsemanship jumping classes. Faced with a large class, most judges make notes on their sheets of the numbers of the contestants who seem to be outstanding. After a few minutes on the rail at the walk, trot, and canter these riders are lined up and the rest excused. Generally not more than ten riders out of a class of thirty or more are kept in, often no more than seven. The seven are then looked at with care; the judges may or may not make legible comments on their sheets. Sometimes the riders are asked to change mounts. Eventually the winners are placed. I do not wish to imply that the best riders are not usually the ones picked, but to point out that from a large class of young riders who have entered the ring to do their best and possibly to learn something, two-thirds are turned away, having learned nothing and with no possible way of knowing what they did or did not do that displeased the judges. Surely every child competing in an equitation class should have the opportunity of finding out what the judge thought of his riding. There can be no reason for such classes unless the education of the rider, the horse, or both is advanced.

Yet one is faced with the problem of very large classes and of the spectators' points of view. Equitation classes are dull and to judge as many as thirty riders fairly takes a good hour—which means devoting only two minutes to each child. There are two possible solutions. Have eliminations and reduce the riders to ten or twelve or, if the ring is large and there are several judges, divide the group up, give each judge a half or a third, and have them pick three or four riders each. These will all then ride against each other. This latter method still is far from ideal as one group may contain most of the best riders and by eliminating half of them, one may place poorer riders in the finals. If the show is held outside, it may be possible to run other events, such as jumping or hunting classes, at the same time and so give the spectators not interested in equitation something to watch.

Unfortunately the requirements of American equitation competitions make the position of the rider almost the sole standard of judging. Equally unfortunately it is usually the rider mounted on the smooth gaited, attractive, easily controlled horse that comes off with the ribbons. Until we get away from the same old walk, trot, and canter, reverse, and canter with possibly a figure of eight or a gallop depart on a straight line, this is bound to be so. Since position seems to be the most important feature to be judged then at least let us judge the position of each rider at the different gaits in detail and then post the judges' sheets where all the riders can look at them and get some ideas as to how they may improve their riding.

For the last four years I have been using the judging sheets (Figures 162, 163). In every show that I have judged, both in the United States and in Canada, parents, children, and instructors have come up to me later and told me how much they liked this method of judging since it showed clearly what I had seen in the ring and gave the contestants something to work on. It takes practice to use the sheets successfully and few judges will attempt them, but they are really quite simple. It will depend on the size of the class whether every column can be filled out but enough can be shown to prove that the judge had reasons behind his or her choice.

The most successful method of using these sheets is to have each judge provided with a "secretary" who follows him around, makes the necessary checks or crosses in the appropriate columns and writes in the comments. The secretary starts by filling in the numbers of the riders. The class then being at the walk, the judge, without taking his eyes off the rider, can comment as follows: "Head and eyes poor, looking around, hands poor, flat, too close together, legs good, feet poor, pushed forward, seat (general position) fair, etc." This will take only about twenty seconds and the judge will be ready for the next rider. He can then look at all of them on a trot and mark each thing or, if the position at the trot is much the same with the exception of one or two riders, he can mark those. It usually saves time in the first judging to have the riders canter from front to rear individually so that the judge can get a good look at each. The whole class having gone through at the three gaits, the secretaries then add the scores, with each cross eliminating a check, and the "fairs" not scored. Thus if a rider had six checks, four crosses and a fair, his score would be plus two. The judges can then pick the seven or ten riders with the highest scores and excuse the rest. Now he should pay attention to the control of the individual riders, of their ability to push their horses into the bit and to rate them, of details such as diagonals. He can ask them to exchange horses or to execute special figures such as gallop departs from backing, etc. It is true that the best riders will thus receive a more detailed criticism than the rest but all will have

JUDGE'S CARD

EQUITATION

CLASS NO. ________ SIGNED ________________

NO.	HEAD	HANDS			LEGS			FEET			SEAT			DIAGON	LEADS	JOG TROT	BACKING	POSITION WHILE STANDING	CONTROL	REMARKS
		WALK	TROT	CANTER	WALK	TROT	CANTER	WALK	TROT	CANTER	WALK	TROT	CANTER							

SYMBOLS
V✓—GOOD
X—BAD
F—FAIR

FIRST PLACE ________ FOURTH PLACE ________
SECOND PLACE ________ FIFTH PLACE ________
THIRD PLACE ________ SIXTH PLACE ________

JUDGE'S CARD

HORSEMANSHIP JUMPING

CLASS NO. ________ SIGNED ________________

NO.	HEAD	HANDS	LEGS	FEET	SEAT	CONTROL	PACE	REMARKS

SYMBOLS
V—GOOD
X—BAD
F—FAIR

1ST PLACE ________ 4TH PLACE ________
2ND PLACE ________ 5TH PLACE ________
3RD PLACE ________ 6TH PLACE ________

FIG. 162.

learned something from the judge's sheet and no one will feel that he just wasn't looked at at all.

In judging horsemanship over jumps the same method of judging position is used. Since it is hard to see all the details at a glance, some judges prefer to concentrate on one thing at each fence, the eyes at the first, the hands at the second, the legs and feet at the third, marking any outstanding faults such as a rider getting left behind, coming back too soon, or leaving the saddle too much.

If a judge is not willing to make out a detailed sheet such as this, then he should meet with the riders after the class and discuss with them their mistakes. Some children are hesitant about asking for criticism but at least it should be made possible for them in one way or another to find out just what the judges thought of their performances.

Appendix J

ORGANIZING HORSESHOWS AND GYMKHANAS

Organizing a horse show or a gymkhana is not an easy job. It requires hours of thought and paper work, of collecting materials to be used, of making up and drawing up the jumping courses, etc. The more carefully organized the show, the more successful it will be both from the contestant's and from the spectator's point of view.

There are a number of different types of shows, gymkhanas, and exhibitions from which one may choose and in deciding to organize and give a show, one must first of all decide upon the type. The open show is one which will be open to outsiders. This type of show may be given to raise money for some charity or for the stable giving it. In preparing the program for such a show, one must first think of the ages, interests, abilities, and mounts of the possible entries. Is there a big interest in riding for young children? Then be sure to have plenty of classes for them and their mounts. These would include classes for children that are divided according to age, classes divided according to experience, and others arranged on the basis of previous winnings. It should also include classes for children's mounts, which are divided as to size or previous winnings.

Is the principal interest in jumping? Then there should be many different types of jumping classes. Those for novice and maiden horses, those for horses under or over certain heights, scurries, F. E. I. classes, etc., all will serve to provide variety. Is the show to be given in a hunting country? Then classes for young hunters, for conformation and working hunters, for models of different ages, for handy hunters, handy hunter hacks, etc., can be emphasized. Shows held in parts of the country where there are saddlehorses, parade horses, driving or combinations horses, etc. will all necessitate different types of programs.

Perhaps this is to be a purely local show. If so, it should be so stated in the prize list and classes should be made up accordingly. Perhaps this is not to be an open show but a "school" show or a "camp" show. Since most of the classes will be equitation classes, a few gymkhana events should be introduced to lend variety and prevent spectators and horses from becoming too bored.

An all-junior show is always good but if the juniors who are organizing it have not had a great deal of experience, some older person should help with advice.

Exhibition shows given for charity should consider spectator interest as being of the most importance. No two classes can be alike and all should be carefully planned and practiced.

Straight gymkhanas are usually informal but they too need a great deal of thought and planning. Each contestant should be given a rule sheet for the various games and told to inquire ahead of time if he does not understand the rules. For the benefit of the spectators a short explanation of each event should be given over the public address system as the ring is being prepared for that event.

Having determined the type of show and the kind of classes, it will now be necessary to figure out about how many classes may be run off in the time appointed. More and more shows are making the mistake of not allowing enough time for the events with the result that classes sometimes run three or four hours late. This is particularly bad where children are involved and does not make the contestants want to enter another year. The following is a fair time schedule:

Equitation classes, not more than ten riders............
....................................thirty minutes
Equitation classes, ten to fifteen riders.................
...............................forty-five minutes
Equitation classes, fifteen to twenty riders........one hour
(If more than twenty riders are expected, eliminations should be held.)
Horsemanship jumping classes, not more than ten riders
...............................twenty minutes
Horsemanship jumping classes, ten to twenty riders......
· ....forty minutes

Appendix

Open jumping classes, fifteen riders or under............
.............................twenty minutes
Open jumping classes, fifteen to thirty riders...........
.............................forty-five minutes

F. E. I. rules classes do not require quite as much time since they are judged on time and there will not be so many jump-offs. Knock-down-and-out or touch-and-out, allow about a minute per rider. Time for hunter classes, will depend on the outside course. Clock the length of time it takes to make the course, add a half a minute to allow for judges' notations, multiply by the number of entries anticipated, and add five minutes for assembling, placing of judges and jump crew, etc.

Handy hunter classes, depending on the course, should take about two and a half to three minutes per rider. Bridlepath hack, not more than twelve riders, thirty minutes; fifteen to twenty riders, forty-five minutes. For Model classes, allow one and one half minutes for each entry, and for saddle horse classes, about two minutes per entry.

Do not overload your schedule. It is better to have fewer classes and have time for each to be run off fairly than to try and have too many. It is true that the more classes the more entry fees, but the reputation of the show should be considered also.

If the show is to be held outdoors and enough judges are available, double features can be run off, combining equitation and bridlepath hack classes with outside jumping courses, hunters shown in hand, etc. A good deal of thought must be given to the planning of such a show since contestants will complain if the classes conflict. However it is fair to assume, for example, that children under eight will not be competing in open jumping classes, etc.

The next thing to do is to make up the prize list and send copies to all competitors. The requirements of each class must be clearly stated. The order of classes may be given with an approximate time sheet but this is not required. The prize list may be printed or mimeographed. The entry blank must be enclosed.

Every effort should be made to contact as many potential contestants as possible. Local hunt and riding clubs and schools which include riding in the program should be asked for a list of their members. The blacksmith, the feed stores, and the veterinarians will have suggestions as to possible competitors. If there have been previous shows nearby by all means get hold of a program and send prize lists to all competitors.

It is sometimes very difficult to find judges. The National Horse Shows Association Rule Book contains a list of all recognized judges with their addresses. When asking a judge to officiate, be sure to explain the type of show and the kinds of classes which you plan. Sometimes a judge who is unable to oblige will give you the name of another whom he knows to be interested in the type of show you are putting on.

As the entries come in, they should be analyzed and each one entered in the class indicated. A ledger or book of some sort is best for this and all entries must be kept in case of argument later as to whether a horse was or was not entered in a specific class.

Deciding on the prizes and trophies and purchasing same or having them donated must be done beforehand. Open classes usually have money prizes in the big shows, but in shows devoted principally to local and children's classes trophies are better. Interested residents may be asked to donate either a trophy or the money toward one, and local stores will often contribute. If no contributions are given, money may be appropriated from the entries. One or two people on the committee must be assigned to procuring prizes and each should be marked or tagged with the number and description of the class.

Ribbons are an expensive item, costing from twenty-five to fifty cents or more. They must be ordered at least two weeks in advance. They usually have the name of the show and the year printed in gold on them. It is wise to order at least one extra set in case of ties. The ribbons should be arranged in layers in a box, each layer marked for a certain class. Order six ribbons for equitation classes, four for other classes.

Numbers to be used by the contestants must be provided. These may be purchased where the ribbons are made. If a set is left from former years, it should be checked through and any missing ones replaced. If possible, a different number should be provided for each horse and equitation entry. The horse or child then wears the same number throughout the show. This does away with much confusion. Since contestants are often careless about returning numbers, some shows now require a deposit of twenty-five cents which is returned to the rider when he turns in his number.

Jumping courses must be drawn up. Make these with india ink or sheets of poster board large enough to be clearly seen. The poster board can then be covered with cellophane and will not be damaged if a shower comes up, thus saving the courses for future use. A big bulletin board should be provided to hold these courses and the judges' sheets which should be pinned up immediately after each class.

Materials for each jump must be assembled and checked over. One of the biggest mistakes in amateur shows is the failure to have all jump materials together and a good crew of jump boys trained to set them up. Boys who are to take care of jumps should be rehearsed the day before the show. Each jump should have two boys assigned to take care of it. The crew should then practice setting up each course against time and taking it down again. A well-trained crew can set up a complicated course in less than two minutes and take it down in half the time. In many shows as much as fifteen or twenty minutes or longer is often wasted. Boys from ten to fourteen enjoy this work and will have fun seeing which pair can get the jump up the fastest. A free ticket to the show, a word of thanks over the public address system toward the end of the day, and a free ice-cream or cold drink is ample reward. A member of the committee should be put in charge of the jump crew to train it and also to check the height and placing of each jump before the class begins. There is nothing more annoying to judges, spectators and contestants than to have a jump course set up incorrectly with the top rails uneven, the multiple jumps incorrectly spaced, etc.

Some time before the show, the condition of the outside hunt course must be carefully checked. If jumping and hunting classes are to be run simultaneously, a second jump crew will have to be trained. A position must be chosen for the judges which will allow them to see as much of the course as possible. If it is not possible for them to see every jump from this position, stewards will have to be placed at these jumps to report refusals, knockdowns, etc. A farm wagon makes a good platform for the hunter judges.

Arrangements will have to be made for the stabling or picketing of visiting horses. One-day shows often simply assign an area and leave the competitors to devise their own means of tethering or picketing. If horses are to be stabled overnight, arrangements will have to be made for them. No visiting horses should be allowed to use the public water troughs and it would be best to take the stoppers out of them so that they cannot be filled. Usually the fee for stabling includes bedding with the exhibitor paying extra for feed, but this must be stated on the prize list.

It is best to contact the printer who is to do the program some days ahead of time so that he can be prepared to do a rush job. The final date for receiving of entries is usually a week before the show, which leaves about two days for going over the entries, assigning numbers, making the final time sheet based on the actual number of entries, etc. The most satisfactory type of program contains the list of classes with the exhibitors' names, horses' names, numbers, and descriptions, as well as an alphabetical list of all stables and competitors, with their numbers and the classes in which they are competing. Many programs contain only the classes without the supplementary list. If this is done, alphabetical lists should still be made out for certain of the committee and helpers. The person in charge of giving out numbers should have one. The person in charge of post entries (if post entries are permitted), the person at the gate in charge of mounting riders (if this is a school show and the same horse is ridden by a number of different riders), the announcer, and the person giving out the ribbons and keeping track of the winners, all these need alphabetical lists. Much time is saved if this list is made out before the list of classes and the numbers assigned corresponding to the alphabetical order. Thus the announcer, seeing number seven about to come up for a prize, can look at the alphabetical list and immediately know the name of the competitor.

Sometimes the alphabetical list alone with a list of the classes can be used without indicating the competitors in each class, but if this is done there should be extra copies made of each class with its competitors and their numbers for the starter and the person in charge of numbers.

Programs are one of the more expensive items in giving a show. Printed ones look best and if there is someone willing to undertake the printing, advertising space, sold to local merchants, will pay for it. Programs can also be mimeographed but these are much more bulky and awkward.

A public address system is almost a necessity for a show of any size. It can be rented from electricians for a reasonable sum. In some towns a permit is necessary if it is to be used out of doors.

By the night before the show, all equipment should have been checked and placed where needed. The numbers should be strung up in order on clothesline. The bulletin board with the jumping courses should be up. People should be assigned to the following jobs and told to be on hand a half-hour before the opening of the show:

A starter for the in-gate to get horses in quickly and relay their numbers to the announcer. If two classes are to be run at the same time, one over the outside course and one inside the ring, two starters will be needed.

Appendix

Two people in charge of numbers, three if deposits are to be taken. One gets out the numbers and hands them to the exhibitors, one collects the numbers, and the third takes and refunds deposits.

A ringmaster to stay in the ring. He should have a hunting horn or a whistle. He repeats the judges' orders and blows out horses in jumping classes that fail to complete the course. He may also be in charge of checking the jumping courses in the ring.

A jump crew with a leader. These people should stay with the jumps and be ready to come out immediately when they are told.

An announcer. He calls the classes, warns the next classes to get ready, and announces the winners. In jumping classes he announces the name and number of each competitor as he enters the ring and, for open jumping or F.E.I. classes, gives the score of each competitor as he leaves.

A person in charge of ribbons and prizes. This person designates someone to present the trophy in each class and himself gives the ribbons. He may also keep track of all winners for publicity purposes.

A timekeeper with a stop watch if F.E.I. classes are being run.

A person in charge of post entries. This person should sit near the numbers.

For school and camp shows where there are many equitation classes being run off, with the same horses being used, there should be at least six older children or adults assigned to help mount the younger children and help adjust their stirrups. Two or three people should also be assigned to stable duty to help children get their horses out. Children become careless and excited at times like these and are apt to put their mounts away incorrectly or take them out in a hurry without checking their equipment.

If there are games requiring special props such as potatoes, balloons, etc., one person should be put in charge of these.

If this is an all-day show, an entertainment committee must be on hand to take care of the judges at the luncheon recess, and to handle their transportation to and from the station if they are not in their own cars.

Someone must be assigned to cover the publicity for the local papers immediately afterwards and there should also be a clean-up crew that will come the following day and put everything back in order. If the show is organized as suggested, everything should run smoothly and quickly and the reputation of the stable or school giving the show will be enhanced.

413

Appendix K

HORSEMASTERSHIP MEETS

The purpose of Horsemastership Meets is to improve the education of the horse and of the rider. These meets should be held at regular intervals announced annually. Two types of classes are held, dressage and jumping. The dressage classes should be divided in to *light* (very simple movements comprising turns and circles, halts, half-halts, riding on straight lines and pivoting on the forehand), *intermediate* (this can include decreasing and extension of gaits, pivoting the forehand around the hindquarters, two-tracking and shoulder-in at the walk and slow trot, serpentines, circles with the haunches ranged in or out, gallop departs from the walk, and simple changes of lead), and *heavy dressage* (can include counter change of hands on the two-track, flying changes of lead, gallop departs from the halt after backing on a straight line, etc.).

The dressage courses should be mimeographed and sent out at the beginning of the year with a letter explaining the purpose of these meets. The competitors should be told that no more than ten will be allowed to compete in any event; that if more than this number apply, eliminations will be held; that there will be no entry fees and no prizes or ribbons but that each competitor will be carefully marked and graded by a competent judge. The competitor with the highest score will be marked 1, the second highest 2, etc. Thus each can see where he stands in relation to the rest of the class. The next time he comes to a meet he will ride the same horse and, by competing in the same division, can show how he has progressed with his horse's training. Only those who place within four positions from the top should be permitted to compete in the next higher division at the next meet.

The judging of these classes is done as follows: The number of movements in the course are counted and numbered. The judge, with a secretary, watches closely and as each competitor completes a movement, he dictates two scores to the secretary. Each score may be either from one to five or from one to ten. The latter system is used in judging the Olympic Games. One score denotes the performance of the horse, taking his calmness, obedience and execution of the movements into consideration. The other score denotes the performance of the rider, taking his position, artistic aspect, harmony with his horse and correctness of his use of aids into consideration. If the riders are scored from one to ten, ten would be perfect; nine, excellent; (almost perfect) eight, very good; seven, good; six, fairly good; five, sufficient; four, moderate; three, passable (poor); two, bad; one, very bad; zero, failure.

In marking from one to five the scoring is as follows: five, perfect; four, excellent; three, good; two, poor; one, bad; zero, failure.

The judges' cards should be posted after the class so that the competitors can know what to work on. If the judges, in addition to scoring, can make any general comments either in writing or to the group, so much the better. The scores for all movements are added and competitors placed accordingly.

The jumping classes should be designed to show the obedience and calmness of the horse and the progress of his training as well as the ability of the rider. Each jump should be scored in two parts, as was done for the dressage test. Sometimes the regular horsemanship jumping sheet shown on page 406 can be used. The former method is better as it gives the judge a chance to score both the performance of the horse and of the rider. Sometimes two judges can work together, one scoring the horse and the other the rider, again the calmness and obedience of the horse and the artistic aspect and harmony of the rider being considered as well as the actual faults.

As a final event of the year, a Three-day Event competition can be held. The first day should be given over to dressage competition, the second to a cross-country ride of not less than ten miles, some of it over natural obstacles, and the third to jumping. The same horse and rider compete in all three. The competitors may be divided and classified with lower jumps and easier dressage tests for the younger, less experienced riders.

The dressage and jumping days are run off as described above. For the cross-country ride special preparations will be necessary. A map must be made so that the competitors can know the course. Each fork or crossroads must be marked with arrows. Each jump must have four flags, the red on the right and the white on the left of the approaching rider, between which he must pass. Two are placed on the near side 10 yds. before the jump, 2 on the far side 15 yds. from jump.

A veterinarian should check the horses as they leave and should examine each horse as he returns.

The riders are started at ten minute intervals. The course may be divided into phases classified as follows: *along roads and trails*, horse to be ridden at a walk or slow gait, a maximum time of completion allowed, no premium for bettering this time; *cross-country*, rider to choose his own gait, a maximum time for completion allowed.

no bonus or premium for bettering this time; a *steeplechase section*, maximum time given, bonus of points added for completion in less time.

Usually the phases are in the following sequence: first phase, along roads and trails; second phase, cross-country; third phase, steeplechase; fourth phase, along woods and trails.

Stewards should be placed at different points along the route to check on the horsemastership of each rider, observing how he crosses roads, how he goes down paved hills or over rough places, etc. Stewards will also be needed at the jumps. The riders are judged on their time, the condition of their horses, their horsemastership as noted by road stewards, and their jumping faults.

Appendix L

HOW THE PRESENT SYSTEM OF HORSE SHOWS COULD BE IMPROVED

The present system of horse shows could be improved by standardizing judging and requiring that in all classes judges turn in cards to be posted.

A wider variety of tests and classes in equitation could be provided. These would include "Best-Trained Pony" (light and intermediate dressage) tests and more interesting classes for children's mounts of different sizes.

The following are suggested improvements:

More variety in hunter and jumper classes.

Holding eliminations or limiting the number of entries.

Providing more exhibition features at both large and small shows, such as those given at Madison Square Garden, which would increase the knowledge of the spectators and exhibitors and stimulate their interest in various branches of equitation.

Appendix M

HOW STABLES AND INSTRUCTORS COULD BE RATED

The British Horse Society has developed a means whereby all hacking and public stables are rated and instructors licensed. A board of examiners checks the stable, horses, and equipment and then issues a certificate grading the stable which is posted where clients can see it. Instructors take tests and are graded according to their ability and their experience.

In the United States such an organization is badly needed. Efforts are being made to promote such a control but so far it has not been generally accepted. The National Section of Women's Athletics holds meets at which instructors may be tested and then graded according to their riding ability. So far these testing centers have been held on the East Coast only. The Equestrian Sports Association headed by Major G. de Roaldes is doing the same thing on the West Coast and hopes to broaden his field to include all of the United States. Until we raise our standards of instruction in this way we cannot hope to compete with European countries. And as long as parents are willing to allow their children to ride under not only completely inadequate but often an almost total lack of supervision it will not be possible to do much to raise the standards.

An active society could do as the British Horse Society has done. Boards in all parts of the country could be appointed to observe and check the conditions at the riding schools and stables and to withhold certificates from those which are not properly equipped and run. Through the newspapers and sports periodicals parents could be educated to send their children only to such stables, schools, or camps that had a rating. If this were done, men and women going into the business as instructors would make some attempt to learn their trade properly.

Appendix N

ORGANIZING A JUNIOR MILITARY UNIT

The purpose of Junior Cavalry units is to use riding as a means of developing in young people certain desirable character traits. Among these are the ability to undertake responsibility, the ability to think and act quickly, a sense of the value of sportsmanship, a love of animals, a respect for authority, agility and strength, neatness, and courtesy.

A Junior Cavalry unit may be started by any group of interested parents. They will need a capable leader who understands children, knows not only how to ride but how to teach riding, and is enthusiastic. They will need suitable mounts which can either be owned by the organization, owned by the children themselves, or rented. They will need a suitable place for instruction.

Certain standards of conduct and tests to grade the riders have been set up. These are in the Cadet Manual which may be obtained by writing to the Junior Cavalry of America, New Canaan, Connecticut.

When a unit is formed, the chairman of the parent's committee applies for admission to the central organization. An inspection is then held and if the new unit is found to be one which lives up to the ideals and standards set up by the central organization, it is admitted. A membership fee of twenty-five dollars is charged to each unit as an initiation fee. Each cadet in each unit pays one dollar a year to the organization. This money is used to print the Cadet Manuals and one is given each cadet each year.

All decisions in each individual unit in regard to fees, uniforms, hours of teaching, etc. rest with the parent's committee of that unit but every effort should be made to make the fees as reasonable as possible so that children of all financial backgrounds can take part. No member of a parent's committee can take any money for his services and every unit is a non-profit organization.

Glossary of Terms

AIDS

The aids are the means by which the rider communicates with and controls the horse. The *natural* aids are the rider's hands, legs, back, voice and the way he uses his weight (equilibrium). The *artificial* aids are mechanical means which the rider can use to support the natural aids. These include such things as check reins, martingales, whips and spurs. Of the artificial aids only the spurs may be used in international dressage competitions. Martingales and whips may be used in jumping competitions.

AIDS

To be on the aids. The horse is said to be *on the aids* if, when the natural aids are used either all together or independently, the horse immediately responds in the manner desired by the rider. This includes such responses as increasing or decreasing the gait, changing direction or lead, changing from one gait to another, etc.

BACK

By *Bracing the back,* using the back *unilaterally* and *bilaterally,* the rider uses the back to control the horse. This is discussed and pictured in Part II, Chapter 5, page 213.

BALLAST

This is the use of the rider's weight to balance the horse in making turns etc. is important. The rider should think of a boat which is carrying material to act as ballast and so balance it. The rider should use his weight the same way. This is apart from the use of the weight to give commands to the horse.

BASE OF SUPPORT

The *base of support* is one of the four elements of the seat, the others being the upper body, the lower leg and the equilibrium. The base of support is that part of the rider's body which touches the horse or any part of the saddle. It includes the rider's crotch, inside thighs, inside knees, upper part of the lower leg and foot.

BETWEEN THE RIDER'S HANDS AND LEGS.

This is a term used to describe the principle that the rider controls the forepart of the horse with his hands, the part behind the saddle with his legs and that he unites the horse under him by the use of these aids. The horse is thus held between the hands and legs and is in perfect readiness to execute any movement.

CADENCE

The cadence of the stride is the "beat". A trot has a two beat cadence, an ordinary strong and extended gallop a three beat, a very collected and a racing gallop a four beat cadence. The cadence is determined by the order in which the horse's feet touch the ground. *To cadence* a horse is so to regulate the stride that the beat of the cadence is perfectly regular.

CANTER (GALLOP)

The correct term for the canter is the gallop and until a few years ago only the term gallop was used in international competition. However many people think that a canter is the slow form of a gallop and in the most recent book on the Olympic Games put out by the British Horse Society the term *canter* is used.

The following are the forms of the canter (gallop):

Slow . . . a gait that is not highly collected with little animation or impulsion. The strides are short.

Collected. A highly animated canter with plenty of impulsion but the strides are short, the impulsion and energy of the horse being used for elevation. It is a four beat gait in its most collected form.

Ordinary. The ordinary or average canter is at the rate of twelve miles an hour. The horse is on the bit and in hand but not highly collected nor fully extended.

Strong. The strong canter is a faster gait than the ordinary canter, the horse traveling sixteen miles an hour. It is still a three beat gait.

Extended. This is a gait in which the horse takes longer strides but the cadence is the same as at the strong, ordinary canter. The head and neck are fully extended, the horse reaches well under him with his back legs as well as in front of him with his forelegs. It is a three beat gait as a rule but when pushed into a *racing* gallop it becomes a four beat gait.

CAPRIOLE

See *Off the Ground Airs.*

CHANGE OF HANDS

To change hands is to change direction as illustrated in Figure 94.

CHANGE OF LEAD

A *flying* change of lead is when the horse changes lead in the air in one stride. See page 131. A *simple* change is when the horse is brought down to a trot for not more than four strides and then takes off on the opposite lead.

COLLECT, COLLECTION

The horse is said to be collected when his long axis is shortened by means of flexing the poll, raising the head and neck, dropping the croup and bringing the hind legs under him, see Figure 41 page 92. Each gait has its collected form. There are three degrees of collection, light, medium and heavy. These are described in Part I, Chapter 7.

CONFIRMED

To be confirmed in a movement, on a long or loose rein or to a use of the bit is to be so schooled that, once having been put on the desired gait at the desired speed the horse maintains it without further effort from the rider. A horse confirmed on the loose rein, for example, will canter indefinitely without attempting to go faster or slower, with the reins hanging on his neck.

CORBETTE

See Off the Ground Airs.

COUNTER CHANGE OF HANDS

A counter change of hands is a change of direction repeated a number of times. This movement is usually executed on the two-track or half-pass. For diagram see page 122.

COUNTER (FALSE) LEAD

If the horse in circling to the left travels on the right lead he is said to be galloping false or to be on the counter lead.

In schooling young horses for early work this is discouraged but later it is so taught as a gymnastic exercise to develop balance and is used before teaching the flying change.

DRESSAGE

The term dressage is a French term and means to train. Because this training is a gymnastic training requiring that the horse execute many different movements the term dressage is usually used to denote those movements which are required in the Olympic Games Dressage competitions. They include the following:

Two track (half pass).

Travers.

Renvers.

Counter change of hands.

Collection and Extension of Gaits

Voltes.

Pivots.

Circles ranging the haunches in or out.

Counter Gallop or False Gallop.

Serpentine.

Change of Lead at a designated number of steps.

Pirouette.

Passage.

Piaffe.

These movements are all described and pictured in Part I, Chapters 6, 7 and 8.

EXTENSION OF GAIT

To extend the gait is to lengthen the long axis of the horse by causing him to reach forward with his head and neck and well forward with both his front and his back legs.

EQUILIBRIUM

The rider's equilibrium is one of the four basic elements of the balanced seat. The rider, by placing his weight according to the speed with which the horse is moving and the direction in which he is turning, aids the horse to balance himself. The rider keeps his center of gravity over that of the horse. He also uses his weight or equilibrium to control the horse and communicate with him.

FEEL

Before the rider can be one with his horse he must develop a sense of feeling. This is carefully discussed on page 204.

Glossary of Terms

FLANK MOVEMENTS

Moving to the flank means turning an arc of ninety degrees (a quarter turn) and riding straight forward in the new direction.

FREE-SCHOOLING

To *free-school* a horse is to work him without a rider or a longe. It is described in detail in Part I, Chapter 4.

GALLOP DEPART

or Gallop Departure is the taking up of the gallop or canter by the horse either from a halt, a walk or a trot. Teaching gallop departs to the horse is described in Part I, Chapters 6 and 7, to the rider in Part II, Chapters 15 and 16.

HALF-PASS

A dressage term also meaning "two-track". It is pictured and described on pages 119 and 120.

HALTER SHANK

This is the rope which is attached to the halter for the purpose of leading or tying the horse. Military teams wear specially tied white halter shanks for exhibition purposes.

HAUNCHES, TO ENGAGE THE

To engage the haunches is to cause the horse to carry his haunches further under him and use them more actively. TO RANGE. To range the haunches is to cause them to be carried off the track to one side or the other.

HAUNCHES IN (OUT)

This is a dressage term. It means to carry the haunches towards the center of the curve of the horse's spine in "haunches in", towards the outside in "haunches out." *Haunches-in* is also called the *travers, haunches out* the *renvers.* See Figures 60 and 61.

INFLUENCE

Having felt and interpreted what the horse is doing or is about to do under him the rider uses his aids to *influence* the animal into doing what he wants him to do.

INSIDE LEG

The inside leg of the rider or of the horse is the leg towards the center of the curve when the horse is working in a circle or when he is doing a movement which requires that his body be bent. To bend the horse around the rider's inside leg is to so use the aids that the spine of the horse bends on the rider's inside leg. The outside leg and the hands push the haunches and head in. Notice how the horse's body curves in the pictures in this book showing the shoulder-in and the voltes. Pages 107 and 114.

INTERPRET

After the rider has felt, through his body and his aids what the horse is doing under him he must learn to interpret what he feels, see page 205.

JUMPS, SPREAD, UPRIGHT

A *spread* jump is one consisting of two or more elements which are not placed directly above one another, and which must be taken at one leap. Such jumps are excellent for teaching the horse to extend himself, to jump big and not to refuse. The elements need not all be the same type but can be combinations of rails, chicken-coops, brush etc. An *upright* jump is one consisting of one or more elements which, if multiple are placed exactly over each other.

LEG, ACTIVE, ASSISTING, HOLDING

The *active* leg is the one which is being used to command the horse. The *assisting* leg keeps ready to assist the active leg, to correct a too strong reaction on the part of the horse. The *holding* leg is also an assisting leg and it is held against the horse to prevent him from moving his haunches in that direction.

LEVADE

See Off the Ground Airs page 425.

LOWER LEG

The lower leg is one of the basic elements of the balanced seat. It is that part of the rider's leg which is not in contact with the horse but which can be moved freely into one of the three leg positions (see page 241) and then can be used either actively or as an assisting or holding leg. The lower leg includes the heels or spurs of the rider. The impulsion of the horse comes from his hindquarters. This impulsion is stimulated and directed by the lower leg.

Glossary of Terms

MECHANICS OF A GAIT (OR JUMP)

The mechanics of a gait are the movements that the horse employs in executing that gait or jump. The mechanics of the jump are carefully pictured on page 138.

NEAR SIDE

The left side of the horse.

OFF THE GROUND AIRS

These are difficult movements which were originally used in warfare but which are now taught in only a few places, the best known of which is the Spanish Riding school of Vienna. They include the following:

The Levade, a movement in which the horse sinks back onto his haunches and balances on his hind legs, his front legs being off the ground. The horse then maintains this position immobile.

The Croupade. The horse springs from the levade, carrying his feet under him.

The Ballotade, a movement similar to the croupade but more difficult. The horse as he draws his feet up under him prepares to kick out so that the bystander sees the soles of his back feet.

The Capriole. A still more difficult movement developed from the ballotade in which the horse, being high in the air, kicks straight out behind him. A most useful movement to get rid of one's enemies but one difficult of execution both for the horse and for the rider!

The Corbette, a series of little jumps or hops executed from the levade without allowing the forelegs to touch the ground.

OFF SIDE

The right side of the horse.

OVER REACH

Over reach can mean an injury caused by the horse stepping on his own front heel with his back feet. It is also used to mean how far the track of the back feet passes the track of the front feet at the various gaits. A long over reach indicates an active, strong horse with powerful quarters.

PASSAGE

This is a High School Movement described on pages 135 and 136 and pictured in Plate XXII.

PIAFFE

This is a High School Movement described on pages 132 to 134 and pictured in Plates XV and XXI.

POSITION

Teaching *position* includes teaching all the elements of the seat.

RATE

To rate a horse is to cause him to increase or decrease his gait and to maintain that rate.

REACH FOR THE GROUND

An expression used by European trainers to describe the action of a horse that has been ridden correctly on the bit and, when the reins are lengthened, reaches his head downward to feel the bit.

REIN, LONG, LOOSE, NORMAL

A *long* or *stretched* rein is one in which the rider makes no attempt to maintain any degree of collection but does maintain contact with his horse's mouth. A *normal rein* is one in which the rider not only maintains contact with the horse's mouth but so places his hands that he will not have to change their position to drive the horse further into the bit and so ask for more collection. A *loose* or *floating* rein is one in which the rider does not attempt to maintain contact with the horse through the bit.

REIN-BACK

To cause the horse to move backwards. For correct execution see page 95.

RENVERS

This is a schooling or dressage movement which is also called *haunches-out*. It is pictured on page 118.

SCHOOLING MOVEMENTS

These are movements, steps and figures used to teach the horse to be supple and obedient. They include the dressage movements but not the off the ground airs. All these movements are described in Part I, Chapters 6, 7 and 8.

SEAT

This has come to mean a definite method of riding. The three seats used today are the classical, the balanced and the forward. For descriptions and pictures see Part II, Chapter 1.

Glossary of Terms

SHOULDER-IN

This is a schooling movement, but not a dressage movement. It is described and pictured on pages 113 to 117.

STRAIGHT LINE

When the horseman speaks of the "straight line" which must be maintained by the rider he is referring to the line from the rider's elbow to the bit. In the balanced and forward seats this line must be straight when seen both from the side and from above. In the classical seat the hands are held closer together and the line, as seen from above is broken inwards. In using the hands actively to correct a green or badly schooled horse the straight line as seen from the side may be momentarily broken upwards but under no circumstances should it be broken downwards by having the rider drop his wrists or hands.

STRAIGHT LINES

To ride on straight lines is to cause the horse to so move that his hind quarters exactly track his forehand. As this is unnatural to the horse it requires practice on his part and great skill on the part of the rider.

STRIDE

The stride of the horse is his movement from the time a given leg leaves the ground until it is returned to the ground. A stride may consist of four steps (in the walk or rack) two steps (trot, pace, rein-back) three steps at the canter.

TACT

The tact of the rider is his ability to judge exactly how strongly to use his aids.

TACTILE SENSITIVITY

This is ability of the rider to sense through his body what his horse is about to do or is doing.

TRAVERS

This is a dressage movement described and pictured on page 117.

TRAVELING CRABWISE

All horses by nature are one sided and tend to travel with the hind quarters not in line with the forehand. A horse that exaggerates this as a vice to get away from the rider's aids is said to "travel crabwise".

TROT

This is a two beat gait in which the diagonal legs move together. The trot has five forms. *Slow,* in which the horse takes short steps with little animation or impulsion, *collected* in which the horse takes short steps with much animation and elevation, *ordinary* a trot of from eight to nine miles an hour with average impulsion and animation, *strong* a gait with more extension and impulsion than an ordinary trot but not as much as an extended trot. *Extended* in which the horse reaches well forward with his forelegs and well under him with his hind legs. The cadence is not increased but since the horse is taking longer strides he moves much faster than at the other trots.

TURN

A *turn* is a circle by the horse of 360 degrees. He therefore ends up going in the same direction that he was when he started. A *half-turn* is a half circle, 180 degrees. A *quarter turn* is a flank movement, 90 degrees. For executions of turns and half turns see pages 110 and 111.

TWO-TRACK

This is a dressage movement described and pictured on pages 119 and 120. It is also called a *half-pass.*

UPPER BODY

The upper body is one of the four elements of the balanced seat. It comprises all of the rider's body including the hands, that is above his hip line.

WALK

This is a four beat gait of the horse. The slow walk is a gait with short strides and not much impulsion or animation. A collected walk is one with short strides but with great animation and impulsion. An ordinary walk is a free moving walk between the collected and the extended. The extended walk is a very difficult gymnastic exercise for the horse as it requires that he use immense energy and great control. In all its forms the walk should be evenly cadenced and flat footed.

BIBLIOGRAPHY

American Horse Shows Association, *Rule Book,* New York, 1951.

Anderson & Collier, *Riding and Driving,* Macmillan, New York.

Barrett, Maj. J. L. M., *Practical Jumping,* Country Life Ltd., London, 1930.

Beach, Belle, *Riding and Driving for Women,* Charles Scribner's Sons, New York, 1912.

Beudant, E., *Horse Training, Outdoor and High School,* Charles Scribner's Sons, New York, 1931.

Brooke, Maj. Gen. Geoffrey, *Horse Sense and Horsemanship,* Charles Scribner's Sons, New York, 1934.

——— *Way of a Man with a Horse,* Scribner's, New York, 1924. Lippincott, Philadelphia.

Chamberlin, Lt. Col. Harry D., *Training Hunters and Jumpers and Hacks,* Derrydale Press, New York, 1937.

——— *Riding and Schooling Horses,* Derrydale Press, New York, 1937.

de Bañuelos, Luis, *Libro de "La Gineta."*

de la Guérinière, M., *École de Cavalerie.*

de Pluvinel, Antoine, *L'Instruction du Roy en L'Exercice de Monter à Cheval.*

de Sousa, Baron, *Principles of Equitation,* E. P. Dutton and Co., New York, 1922.

——— *Advanced Equitation,* E. P. Dutton and Co., New York.

Fawsett, William, *Thoroughbred and Hunter,* Charles Scribner's Sons, New York, 1934.

F. E. I., *Statutes,* Federation Equestre International, 1950.

Fillis, James, *Breaking and Riding,* Hurst and Blackett, London.

Grisone, Federico, *Ordini di Cavalcare.*

Hance, Capt. J. E., *School for Horse and Rider,* Charles Scribner's Sons, New York, 1932.

Hayes, Capt., *Veterinary Notes for Horse Owners,* Hurst and Brockett, London, 1924.

Horsemanship and Horsemastership, Cavalry School, Fort Riley, Kansas, 1950.

Bibliography

Hrozný, Bedřick, *L'Entraînement des Chevaux chez les Anciens Indo-Européens d'après un Texte Mîtannien-Hittite Provenant du 14° Siècle avant Jésus-Christ.*

"Jorrocks," *The Private Stable*, Little, Brown and Co., Boston, 1899.

Lewis, Benjamin, *Riding*, Garden City Publishing Co., New York, 1939.

Littauer, Capt. V. S., *Jumping the Horse, Riding Forward, More About Riding Forward*, all privately printed in New York, no dates given.

Lyon, W. E., *First Aid Hints for the Horse Owner*, Charles Scribner's Sons, New York, 1934.

Müseler, W., *Riding Logic*, Methuen Co. Ltd., London, 1949.

Podhajsky, Alois, *Die Spanische Hofreitschule*, Verlag Rudolph Hans Hammer, Vienna, 1948.

Santini, Piero, *The Forward Impulse*, Huntingdon Press, New York, 1936.

Schmit-Jensen, E., *Equestrian Olympic Games*, Welbecson Press Ltd., London, 1948.

Self, Margaret Cabell, *Teaching the Young to Ride*, Harper Bros., 1935.

Taylor, W. G. Langworthy, *The Saddle Horse*, Henry Holt and Co., New York, 1925.

Widmer, Jack, *Practical Horse Breeding and Training*, Charles Scribner's Sons, New York, 1942.

Wright, Gordon, *Learning to Ride, Hunt and Show*, Secor Farms Riding Club, White Plains, N. Y., 1950.

Xenophon, *Treatise on Horsemanship.*

INDEX

(See also the Glossary, page 419.)

Index

Confidence,
of horse, as characteristic ability, 17
as training requisite, 15
of pupil, in horse, 196-197
in teacher, 192-196
Concussion, first aid for, 315
Conformation hunter, 152
Consideration of pupil, for horse, 196-198
for other riders, 198
Corners, cutting, remedy for, 82
Counter-change of hands, 121-123, 347
Counter lead, 129-130
Crabwise movement, remedy for, 82
Crowding in stall, cure for, 31-33

Defenses and vices of second stage of training horses, 78-82
Diagonal aids, 124-126
Diagonals, posting on, 321-322
Direct rein of opposition, 223, 224-225
Diseases (see Ailments of horses)
Dismounting, by numbers, 265-268
teaching young children, 259-260
Dodge, Colonel Richard I., *Riders of Many Lands*, 215
Dress, standards of, at riding school, 182-183
Dressage, 87-90
heavy, 128-129
(See also Haute école)
Dressage movements (see Haute école; Schooling movements)
Dressage tests, 88, 398-402
Dust in rings, control of, 354-355

Egyptians, seat of, 161
Elementary training for pupils, 277-309
active, following, and pulling hand, 285-287
active hand, exercises in using, 287
bareback riding, 290-293
in correct use of equilibrium, 285
games, 293-296
in good position, of base of support, 283-284
of head and eyes, 285
of lower leg, ankle, and foot, 284-285
of upper body, 277-278
indirect rein, use of, 290
leg aids, using, 288
monkey drill, 294-309
rating horse and changing gaits, 289-290
in relaxation and confidence, 279-283

Elementary training for pupils (Cont.)
vocabulary, teaching, 288-289
weight, use of, in starting, stopping, and turning, 287-288
Emergencies on trail, 314-316
falls, 314-315
runaways, 316
English Grand National, 72-73
English hunting seat, 167, 168, 170
Equestrian Sports Association, 417
Equilibrium, 243-245
exercises in correct use of, 285
Equitation classes, Nat'l Horse Shows Ass'n, 387-388
Estradiota school of horsemanship, 162-163
Excitability as basic characteristic of horse, 17
Exercises,
bitting and flexing, for horse, 57-60
for correct use of equilibrium, 285
for elementary jumping, 293
for good position, of base of support, 283-284
of head and eyes, 285
of lower leg, ankle, and foot, 284-285
of upper body, 277-278
intermediate, for control, 339-340
monkey drill, 294-309
in rating horse and changing gaits, 289-290
for relaxation and confidence of pupil, 279-283
suppling, for pupil, 212-214, 270, 271
using active hand for stopping and turning, 287
using indirect rein, 290
Extension, adequate work in, 132
of gaits, 340-341
Eyes, of horse, construction and position of, 20-21
diseases of, 360
of rider, exercise for good position of, 285

Fear,
as basic characteristic of horse, 17
of failure, by pupil, 188
of horse, by pupil, 189
of unknown, by pupil, 185-188
Feeding horse, 349-350
Feel, as basic principle of horsemanship, 204-205, 373
Feet, grooming, 41, 351-352
F.E.I. rules, 156, 388-391

433

Index

435

Index

Index